The Future of Multilateralism and Globalization in the Age of the U.S.–China Rivalry

Despite the growing consensus that the rise of China is transforming international relations, policy makers and scholars have not sufficiently addressed the geopolitical and geoeconomic implications of a new paradigm, especially since the Covid-19 pandemic and the Russo-Ukrainian war. This book fills this gap.

This is an original and innovative book that investigates how a new modus vivendi between China and the United States in a post-globalized world requires more economic independence because of the distrust between G20 economies, but heightened international cooperation, in order to avert a shift to nationalism and protectionism and to fight financial and climate crises.

The book is divided into four parts. Part I investigates the specific features of Chinese and U.S. capitalisms; Part II argues that several flaws observed in the multilateral architecture since the early 2000s have caused global imbalances and increased misunderstanding and mistrust between the two superpowers; Part III analyzes how the China–U.S. rivalry has manifested in Asia, Latin America, and in terms of global development finance; and finally, Part IV provides a blueprint for a successful and revamped international order. The book provides an ambitious interdisciplinary analysis of the future of multilateralism and globalization with contributions from economists, lawyers, and political scientists.

Due to its multidisciplinary approach, the book will attract the interest of scholars and postgraduate students from wide-ranging fields, as well as practitioners working in international organizations, policy makers, and more generally educated lay readers interested in the topic.

Norbert Gaillard is an economist and independent consultant (www.norbertgaillard.com).

Fumihito Gotoh is a lecturer in East Asian Studies at the University of Sheffield.

Rick Michalek is a New York-based independent legal and financial consultant.

"*The Future of Multilateralism and Globalisation in the Age of the US-China Rivalry* is a fascinating and timely volume of the highest quality. The volume brings together a group of leading scholars with policy expertise to examine the political economy of China's challenge to the liberal order and the response of the US and other powers in the cases of manufacturing, finance, trade, institutions, standards, development assistance, supply chains, climate change and regional political and security cooperation. There is no other volume with this range of coverage and expertise that tackles these pressing contemporary issues with such insight and critique. The volume is required reading for academics, policy analysts and advanced students."

Christopher W. Hughes, *Professor of International Politics & Japanese Studies, Department of Politics and International Studies, University of Warwick*

"A serious book from expert scholars and financial practitioners, exploring how the most pivotal relationship in the world, the US-China rivalry, is reshaping the world economy and the international order. It provides new insight into how US-China economic interdependence has turned into tension and rivalry – for instance how a convergence of US and China's capitalisms has given rise to the US-China tensions, not their purported differences. A valuable resource on how reckless financialization of the US economy, China's unconventional role in the WTO, Chinese development lending and debt restructuring practices, and US-China competition and cooperation in global standard setting are recasting the global economy. This comprehensive study draws attention to the major dilemmas posed by geopolitics, pandemics, and climate change, and it invites us to reflect on how the US, China and others *should* respond."

Gregory T. Chin, *Associate Professor, Department of Politics, York University & Mayling Birney Global Scholar (2022-23), The London School of Economics and Political Science*

"This volume provides a clear account of the challenges the liberal international order has to face in a context of a rising US-China rivalry. More importantly it also offers recommendations as to how to shift to a "post-globalized" world. A must read for people interested in understanding the present international economic system and where it is heading."

Françoise Nicolas, *Center for Asian Studies, Ifri, Paris*

Routledge Studies in the Modern World Economy

208. The Future of Economic Development in the Gulf Cooperation Council States
Evidence-Based Policy Analysis
Weshah Razzak

209. Economic and Political Democracy in Complex Times
History, Analysis and Policy
Andres Solimano

210. Free Trade and the US-China Trade War
A Network Perspective
Yoon Heo

211. The Evolution of China's Political Economy
Rich Marino

212. Foreign Direct Investments in Selected Emerging Asian Economies
An Evaluation of Pandemic and Policy Shocks
Edited by Paul Cheung, Ammu George and Xuyao Zhang

213. Linkage Power Europe
The EU's Trade Negotiations with China (1975-2019)
Zhang Xiaotong

214. Economic Development Parables
From Siam to Thailand
Winai Wongsurawat

215. The ASEAN Digital Economy
Towards an Integrated Regional Framework
Edited by Paul Cheung and Xie Taojun

For more information about this series, please visit: www.routledge.com/Routledge-Studies-in-the-Modern-World-Economy/book-series/SE0432

The Future of Multilateralism and Globalization in the Age of the U.S.–China Rivalry

Edited by Norbert Gaillard, Fumihito Gotoh, and Rick Michalek

Routledge
Taylor & Francis Group
LONDON AND NEW YORK

First published 2024
by Routledge
4 Park Square, Milton Park, Abingdon, Oxon OX14 4RN

and by Routledge
605 Third Avenue, New York, NY 10158

Routledge is an imprint of the Taylor & Francis Group, an informa business

British Library Cataloguing-in-Publication Data
A catalogue record for this book is available from the British Library

ISBN: 978-1-032-37489-5 (hbk)
ISBN: 978-1-032-37490-1 (pbk)
ISBN: 978-1-003-34043-0 (ebk)

DOI: 10.4324/9781003340430

Typeset in Sabon
by SPi Technologies India Pvt Ltd (Straive)

Contents

Illustrations

Figures

Tables

About the editors

Norbert Gaillard is an economist and independent consultant (www.norbertgaillard.com). A Fulbright Fellow, he studied at Sciences Po Paris and Princeton University. He was a Euromoney Country Risk expert for more than 10 years. He has taught at the Ecole Supérieure de Commerce de Paris, the University of Geneva, and the Graduate Institute. He has served as consultant to the International Finance Corporation, the World Bank, the State of Sonora (Mexico), the OECD, the European Parliament, and various financial institutions. His main areas of expertise are public debt and sovereign risk, local government debt and subnational risk, credit rating agencies, and country risk. He has authored more than 80 press articles. He has published more than 30 research articles/book chapters and 6 books since 2009.

Fumihito Gotoh is a lecturer in East Asian Studies at the University of Sheffield. Previously, he was a teaching and research fellow in the Department of Politics and International Studies at the University of Warwick, where he also obtained his PhD. His research interests include East Asian politics, International Political Economy, comparative capitalisms (particularly between Anglo-American countries, Japan, and China), globalization and resistance, and politics of finance and technology. His monograph, *Japanese Resistance to American Financial Hegemony*, was published in the Routledge RIPE Series in Global Political Economy in 2019. His articles have appeared in *Review of International Political Economy*, *The Pacific Review*, and *Contemporary Politics*. He used to be a senior credit analyst at the Industrial Bank of Japan, Merrill Lynch, and UBS Investment Bank.

Rick Michalek is a New York-based independent legal and financial consultant. He graduated from Columbia University with both a JD and an MBA. Rick is a former senior credit officer at the rating agency Moody's Investors Service in the structured derivatives group. He worked abroad as a securitization consultant to the New Zealand law firm Chapman Tripp and as an associate attorney in the New York office of Skadden Arps. He has consulted on a number of complex structured derivative litigation matters and continues to consult hedge funds and private equity investors on matters relating to the rating agencies and their processes. Rick has also assisted various U.S. governmental agencies responsible for reforming the laws and regulations governing financial services.

Contributors

Ronaldo Au-Yeung is an MA candidate in the Department of Political Science at Simon Fraser University. His primary research interest focuses on theory of international politics and alliance behaviors.

Kim Emmanuel is an associate professor at Jindal Global University. Her research areas include China's emergence in the developing world as well as U.S.–China relations.

Robert Gmeiner is an assistant professor of Financial Economics at Methodist University. He is the author of *How Trade with China Threatens Western Institutions* (Palgrave Macmillan, 2021).

Andy Hira is professor and chair of the Department of Political Science at Simon Fraser University (SFU). He is the director of the Minor in Public Policy at SFU and of the Clean Energy Research Group.

Yu-Wai Vic Li is an associate professor at the Education University of Hong Kong (Department of Social Sciences). His primary research is the political economy of finance and regulation in East Asia.

Tai Wei Lim is a professor at Soka University of Japan (SUJ). He is an area studies specialist and historian focusing on East Asia.

Elisabetta Montanaro was formerly full professor of Bank Management at the University of Siena. Her research focuses on banking crises and prudential regulation of financial intermediaries.

John Seaman is a research fellow at the Center for Asian Studies of the French Institute of International Relations (Ifri). He studies the geopolitical implications of China's economic transformation and U.S.–China–Europe triangular relations.

David Skidmore is a professor of Political Science at Drake University. His recent research deals with international political economy, China's Belt and Road Initiative and U.S. foreign policy.

Michael Waibel is a professor of international law at the University of Vienna. His teaching and writing focus on international law, international economic law, sovereign debt, and international dispute settlement.

1 Globalization and the liberal international order threatened by the U.S.–China rivalry

Norbert Gaillard, Fumihito Gotoh, and Rick Michalek

The "Open Door Policy" implemented by Chinese authorities from the late 1970s paved the way to globalization. With its large and cheap workforce, China attracted foreign manufacturers and specialized in the production and export of labor-intensive goods. This evolution led to a deindustrialization process in the United States and a high degree of interdependence between developed and developing economies. The recurrent financial crises in Western countries and the rapid ascent of Chinese firms in global value chains have transformed China into a super competitor of the United States. Considering that its growing power was insufficiently embedded in the U.S.-led liberal international order, China has managed to free ride on World Trade Organization rules, challenged the multilateral financial architecture, and privileged Sino-centered strategies, such as the Belt and Road Initiative. Since the 2010s, the U.S.–China rivalry has spread from the economic to diplomatic and security spheres. These tensions stem primarily from the competition over hegemony in the Indo-Pacific and advanced technology. The lack of trust between the two superpowers will inevitably involve a shift to a post-globalized world. For example, the Western dependence on China over strategic products and commodities will have to be phased out.

1.1 The rise of China and the triumph of globalization

After nearly three decades of autarky, Maoist China – primarily under the auspices of Deng Xiaoping – shifted its economic model in 1978 and opened to Western investors and exporters. One of the most symbolic and decisive measures of this nascent era was the promulgation of the Joint Venture Law in July 1979. This legislation stipulates:

> With a view to expanding international economic cooperation and technical exchange, the People's Republic of China [PRC] permits foreign companies, enterprises, other economic organizations or individuals to join with Chinese companies, enterprises or other organizations in establishing joint ventures in the PRC in accordance with the

DOI: 10.4324/9781003340430-1

> principle of equality and mutual benefit and subject to approval by the Chinese government.
>
> (Richdale and Liu, 1991, p. 125)

In fact, this "Open Door Policy" was a major paradigm change in the history of world capitalism. Starting in the 1980s and consistent with the Heckscher–Ohlin theory (Samuelson, 1971), international trade and foreign direct investment (FDI) flows reorganized in a more efficient manner. Taking advantage of a large and cheap workforce, China managed to attract many foreign manufacturers and increased dramatically its exports of labor-intensive products (e.g., toys, clothes, medical devices, consumer-electronic products, automotive components, etc.). Between 1982 and 2021, the share of China in world exports of goods soared from 1.1% to 14.6%.[1] In the meantime, as demonstrated by Gaillard and Michalek in Chapter 3 of this book, U.S. capitalist system specialized in financial services, which led to a significant deindustrialization process. The concomitant transformation of China's collectivist economy and U.S. traditional liberal capitalism into state-led and financial capitalist systems, respectively, was a pillar of "economic globalization." This notion, which can be defined as "the increasing integration of economies around the world, particularly through the movement of goods, services, and capital across borders" (International Monetary Fund, 2008) was the dominant economic and financial paradigm until the 2010s.[2]

Following the end of the Cold War, globalization coincided with a unipolar geopolitical era where the United States was the sole superpower. The U.S. hegemony partly relied on key multilateral institutions established at the end of World War II, namely the International Monetary Fund (IMF), the World Bank, and the General Agreement on Tariffs and Trade, which was superseded by the World Trade Organization (WTO) in 1995. By the end of the 20th century, the so-called liberal international order (LIO) – i.e., the order "organised around open markets, multilateral institutions, cooperative security, alliance partnership, democratic solidarity and United States hegemonic leadership" (Ikenberry, 2010, p. 512) – seemed robust and undisputable. This view turned out to be illusory.

1.2 China as a "super competitor" and multilateralism called into question

While the Asian financial crisis of 1997 engulfed South Korea and many neighboring countries, the Chinese government accelerated the restructuring of state-owned enterprises and reformed the financial system to make integration with foreign capital and domestic socio-economic stability compatible (Gruin, 2019). This move boosted China's competitiveness spectacularly. Furthermore, China's accession to the WTO in 2001 and the substantial undervaluation of the renminbi (Garton and Chang, 2005; Bergsten and Gagnon, 2012) contributed to the rapid growth of the Chinese economy.

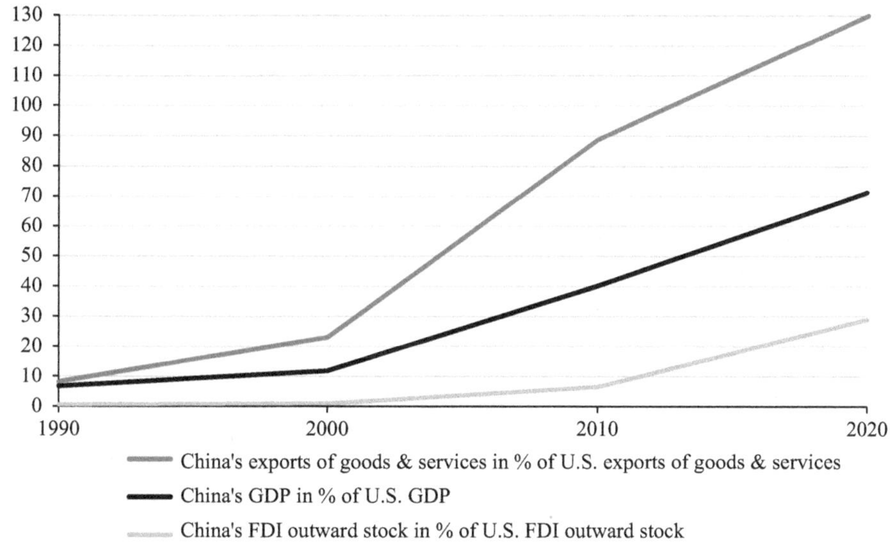

Figure 1.1 China's economic catch-up

Sources: United Nations Conference on Trade and Development and World Bank data.

As Figure 1.1 shows, its capacity to catch up with the U.S. economy has been impressive so far, although Beijing has surpassed Washington only in terms of exports of goods and services.

With China's economic success and the recurrent financial crises in the United States and Western Europe, various critics (e.g., Ramo, 2004; Xinbo, 2010; Bell, 2015) described the nature of the Chinese political economy as contrasting with the Anglo-American model and the "Washington Consensus"[3] by using terms such as the "Beijing Consensus" and "China model." Doshi (2021) claims that the global financial crisis made Chinese leaders view American power as declining and take a more aggressive stance. The mixed results of the micro- and macroprudential rules established by Western powers and institutions to stabilize the world economy – studied by Montanaro's Chapter 6 – tend to support Doshi's arguments as well as Chinese ambitions.

China has obtained significant economic benefits from the LIO but has not accepted American unilateralism and liberal universalism, which can be considered aggressive from a Chinese perspective. Political legitimacy in China (performance legitimacy) differs from that in the West (legal-rational legitimacy). The most important interest of the Chinese government is the Chinese Communist Party's legitimacy, which includes its autonomous domestic governance and China's "rightful place in the world."

Since the early 2010s, the PRC has succeeded in gaining influence in terms of international standardization (see Seaman's Chapter 7 in this book).

More worryingly, Chinese authorities have challenged the international financial architecture (IFA) through disruptive sovereign lending and debt restructuring practices (see Gaillard and Waibel's Chapter 5 in this book). On top of that, we can observe that the Xi Jinping administration has promoted nationalistic rhetoric to defend China's state-led development policy, while the Trump administration instigated strong nationalist appeals to justify its massive protectionist measures against major U.S. trade partners, including China (Helleiner, 2021, p. 230). This tit-for-tat game is very likely to undermine multilateralism in the medium to long term.

The U.S.–China trade conflict has intensified since 2018. Gmeiner, in Chapter 4 of this book, shows how China has managed to free ride on WTO rules. Other U.S. policy makers and academics denounce the Chinese economic system as incompatible with the U.S. system (e.g., Meltzer and Shenai, 2019; Teece, 2020). However, China has better adapted to American-led neoliberal globalization than a U.S. ally, Japan, which was reintegrated into the global economy under "embedded liberalism" (a combination of open international trade and restricted international capital mobility) in the 1950s, entrenching the interests of Japanese anti-market liberal elites. This is because a country is fundamentally influenced by the hegemonic power's institutions when integrated into the global economy (Whittaker et al., 2020). Gotoh and Li's in Chapter 2 of this book argue that the power of both political (re)centralization and economic decentralization has been at work since 1978, shaping the characteristics of Chinese capitalism, namely, the co-existence of state-led developmentalism and neoliberalism.

Paradoxically, the United States and China share remarkable similarities: i.e., policies that enhance wealth and power, exceptionalism (the "American way of life" and Sino-centrism), and growing economic inequality. They have both the mixed characteristics of developmental and neoliberal states and are not necessarily incompatible. U.S.–China tensions stem from the competition over hegemony in East Asia and advanced technology rather than the different economic models (Kim, 2019). This analysis is supported by U.S. actions against Huawei (the world's largest telecommunications equipment maker) and the CHIPS and Science Act of 2022, which is aimed at countering China and securing supply chains of semiconductors.

1.3 From U.S.–China competition to U.S.–China systemic rivalry

Since the 2010s, the U.S.–China rivalry has spread from the economic to diplomatic and security spheres. The Belt and Road Initiative (BRI), an international infrastructure development strategy launched by China in 2013, is its most important economic diplomatic initiative targeting many developing countries (Ekman et al., 2019; Skidmore, 2021, International Institute for Strategic Studies, 2023).[4] China also proposed the establishment of the Asian Infrastructure Investment Bank (AIIB) in 2013 and has its largest voting shares. In 2022, around one-third of AIIB loans financed BRI projects.[5]

The BRI and AIIB may be regarded as challenges to the American-led LIO. The West was increasingly critical of these Chinese initiatives attracting developing countries: it rolled out the Build Back Better World program for alternative infrastructure development in emerging economies, but competing with China in this field will likely be an uphill task (Crabtree, 2021). Skidmore's Chapter 8 in this book provides excellent accounts of Chinese development financing, including the AIIB and the Western responses.

Yet, the diplomatic and military tensions in the Indo-Pacific have become a major source of concern. In addition to the long-lasting tensions in the Taiwan Strait, with China's rapid expansion of economic and military power, the territorial disputes in the East and South China Seas between China and its neighbors (including Japan, the Philippines, Vietnam, Malaysia, and Indonesia) have intensified since 2012. Furthermore, North Korea has developed inter-continental ballistic missiles and nuclear weapons, thus threatening South Korea, Japan, and the United States. In Chapter 9 of this book, Lim points out Taiwan and North Korea as potential flashpoints of the U.S.–China rivalry. The escalation of the Russo-Ukrainian war has also enhanced the tensions in East Asia. Under such circumstances, the Kishida administration decided to double Japan's defense budget from 1% of GDP in 2022 to around 2% in 2027. Hughes (2022) argues that Japan is transforming from a minimalist role within the U.S.–Japan security alliance to a more muscular military power to strengthen the alliance and proactively contribute to the Indo-Pacific strategy.

In contrast to the intensified traditional military security relations between the two superpowers, non-traditional security domains (e.g., pandemic, natural disasters, climate change, human and drug trafficking, and transnational crime) have more room for cooperation between the United States and China. Emmanuel's Chapter 10 in this book examines how Latin America and the Caribbean fought the COVID-19 pandemic with the support of China, the United States, and international financial institutions (IFIs). Hira and Au-Yeung in Chapter 11 discuss how we could shift from separate national climate governance systems to global coordination in carbon emissions reduction. These two chapters suggest that the LIO is certainly the most suitable environment to deal with non-traditional security issues as common threats to many countries.

Unfortunately, the resurgence of economic nationalism and political realism in the 21st century has undermined multilateralism and globalization, increasing the risk of a high-intensity conflict between the United States and China. We contend that the international liberal economic order (ILEO) under the Bretton Woods-GATT system (embedded liberalism) and what we call post-globalization share a strong sense of pragmatism. Embedded liberalism, which restricted international capital mobility (i.e., capitalist power) and tolerated government intervention to maintain domestic social stability, did not cover the global political economy but was based on the U.S.-led coalition with Western Europe and Japan. Subsequently, with the transition from embedded liberalism to neoliberal globalization in the 1980s, the ILEO was expanded and accommodated countries with norms and values different from the West, resulting in international conflict (Ikenberry, 2018). Gaillard's Chapter 12 proposes that policy makers in the West, particularly the United States, should shift from the current international economic system to post-globalization, which entails phasing out the Western dependence on China over strategic products and commodities. As the West's radical decoupling from China is dangerous, post-globalization will be a pragmatic solution to maintain the ILEO and the LIO.

1.4 Outline of the book

This book is divided into four parts. Part I investigates the specific features of Chinese and U.S. capitalisms. Part II examines the flaws in the multilateral system, driven by the emergence of China as major economic power and the limits of the U.S.-led international financial system. Part III studies three cases of competition and rivalry between China and the United States. Part IV analyzes how the LIO may be revamped in the medium to long term, focusing on global climate change governance and post-globalization.

In Chapter 2, Gotoh and Li compare the characteristics of Chinese capitalism with the American and Japanese models and examine a case study of China's vehicle electrification. They argue that the powers of both political (re)centralization and economic decentralization have shaped the characteristics of Chinese capitalism (i.e., the co-existence of developmentalism and neoliberalism) and that China's political power is more concentrated than that of Japan and the United States. This co-existence is nothing new in China, and this resembles the relations between the emperor and scholar-bureaucrats in imperial China. For Gotoh and Li, China has been better adapted to neoliberal globalization than Japan since the 1980s due to political power concentration, economic rationalism, and the timing of its integration into the global economy. However, the strength of Chinese capitalism is often exaggerated, and as the automobile electrification case illustrates, excess capacity is a serious side-effect of pervasive government intervention. Despite the growing American criticism that Chinese capitalism is irreconcilable with American capitalism, both capitalist models share the combination of developmentalism and neoliberalism (albeit with different mixture proportions) and are not necessarily incompatible. The U.S.–China rivalry stems from the competition over hegemony in East Asia and advanced technology rather than the different economic models.

Gaillard and Michalek in Chapter 3 argue that, starting in the 1980s, U.S. traditional liberal capitalism has transformed into an unstable financial capitalism. This evolution, largely driven by neoliberal ideas and massive deregulation, has led to the emergence of so-called too-big-to-fail banks, encouraged moral hazard and rent-seeking, distorted regulatory rules, exacerbated regulatory capture and arbitrage, intensified financial sophistication, shortened investment horizons, altered corporate governance and risk management, widened inequalities, and increased systemic risk in the United States and all around the world. Not only did credit rating agencies and the Federal Reserve (two long-time financial gatekeepers) fail to assess credit risk adequately as well as dangerously ease access to credit, but they also seemingly ignored the growing proportion of firms and banks engaged in "speculative and Ponzi financing." The recurrent financial crises and the subsequent costly bailouts observed for several decades suggest that Eugene Fama's efficient market hypothesis has shown its limits while Hyman Minsky's financial instability hypothesis has gained ground. Lastly, the supposed complementarity of U.S. and Chinese economies, once advocated by some policy makers, hid the fundamental weaknesses of U.S. financial capitalism and accelerated the deindustrialization of the U.S. economy.

In Chapter 4, Gmeiner asserts that, since acceding to the WTO in 2001, China's trade with the world has increased dramatically, but so have complaints about its unfair trading practices. These allegations include differential treatment for domestic and foreign firms, dumping, intellectual property theft, environmental pollution, and unfair labor practices. These concerns have the common denominator that China is trading on terms designed for developed, market economies that respect human rights and the rule of law while simultaneously not following these norms. "Free riding" can describe this behavior of taking a benefit but not contributing to its production. China's trading partners complain, but seldom take substantive action. Despite this free riding, the mutual gains from trade do exist, leading to a situation in which unfair trade practices persist as China's trading partners willingly continue to trade. Gmeiner explains the terms of China's accession to the WTO, the guiding principles of the WTO, and the complaints against China's trading practices. From there, he describes the nature of this free riding dynamic and explains the ways in which China does and does not free ride on the surplus generated by international trade.

Chapter 5 investigates how and why the present IFA has been weakening since the early 2010s. Gaillard and Waibel identify several factors that have hindered the reorganization of the current IFA, accelerated the bipolarization of international financial relations, and reshaped the balance of power between sovereign debtors and creditors as well as between creditors themselves. The post-Bretton Woods IFA has been centered around the United States. The U.S. dollar has remained the world's most important reserve currency. The Federal Reserve and the U.S. Treasury have acted as the only reliable international lenders of last resort since 2008. Further, the United States has a veto at the IMF. China has launched regional initiatives that threaten to fragment the IFA. It has signed central bank swap agreements to prevent cross-border spillovers and to internationalize the renminbi. The AIIB is a key institution to support the BRI whereas the New Development Bank is another innovative and independent institution. Gaillard and Waibel contend that China is reshaping the IFA primarily through its sovereign lending and debt restructuring practices. Chinese contracts are built on harder terms than Western contracts, showing that China wants its creditors to obtain preferential treatment in the event of a default.

Following Minsky's insights, Chapter 6 analyzes the main strengths and weaknesses of the micro- and macroprudential approaches that have ruled the banking sector since the early 2000s. Despite the impressive succession of reforms, Montanaro finds that the ultimate objective of international financial regulation (i.e., safeguarding financial stability while fostering economic growth) has been missed. The reforms did not actually result in the radical changes needed to prevent the build-up of leverage and maturity mismatch within the global financial system. The more stringent capital requirements have increased neither the long-term solvency of Western and Chinese banks, especially those more based on traditional business models, nor their ability to support the real economy. The fragility of their profitability, arising from the pressure exercised by shadow banking and the innovative intermediation circuits, demonstrates the flaws of the current regulatory framework. The new macroprudential paradigm has consisted of merely enhancing micro-prudential tools and establishing new standards for large banks. More importantly, the absence of any formal enforcement mechanism or a rescue framework capable of shrinking the systemic footprint of global financial actors and reducing the expectation that governments will ultimately bail out too-big-to-fail institutions has exacerbated moral hazard.

In Chapter 7, Seaman analyzes the growing role of China in technical standardization. As the global economy sits at a crossroad between connectivity-driven globalization and strategic decoupling, technical standardization provides a valuable measure of where we are headed. Long thought of as a benign, apolitical defining of baseline processes, products, and services, standardization has ballooned into a field of geopolitical competition, particularly as the United States, China, Europe, and others wrestle over technological leadership in the industries of the future. Driven largely by private enterprise initiatives, the West has long held the high ground in setting technical standards. While China is a newcomer to the field, it has grand ambitions of becoming a premier purveyor of global standards and has laid the groundwork for building out a more China-centered ecosystem through efforts such as the BRI. In this context, the "twin transitions" toward a low-carbon and digital future, where many standards remain to be set, offer an opportunity for Beijing. Ultimately, whether China chooses a collaborative path with the West on standards development, how the latter respond to China's initiatives, and whether multistakeholder, consensus-based standardization processes can resist the push and pull of geopolitics will go a long way to determining the degree of cohesion and fragmentation in the global economy for decades to come.

Skidmore's Chapter 8 argues that the global development finance regime has been transformed by China's emergence as the largest and most consequential source of development funding. At the multilateral level, China's impact has been incremental and largely consistent with existing norms.

Regarding bilateral development finance, China has operated outside of the Western-dominated regime of Official Development Assistance as represented by the Development Assistance Committee. Instead, the BRI serves to export China's own post-2008 model of infrastructure-led development. Western responses to Chinese development finance have denounced China's norm-breaking behavior while seeking to compete on the ground of infrastructure development, which remains attractive to recipient countries. Beijing, in turn, has gradually adapted some of its policies in response to both Western and recipient country criticism. As a result, a process of competitive convergence points toward an evolving development finance regime that reaffirms many of the procedural and institutional norms of the past while broadening the substantive vision of development beyond neoliberalism to encompass a stronger state role resembling the embedded liberal norms of the early Bretton Woods order.

Chapter 9 focuses on the U.S.–China rivalry in the Indo-Pacific. Lim recalls that the American-led Indo-Pacific order consists of preserving a status quo based on free trade, freedom of navigation, international law, and a series of regional arrangements and alliances. The Quadrilateral Security Dialogue (involving Australia, India, Japan, and the United States) was reinvigorated in 2017 to manage China militarily and diplomatically. Since 2021, the United States, the United Kingdom, and Australia have engaged in an emerging Anglo-centered military alliance (AUKUS), featuring nuclear-powered submarines. President Biden's objectives are to affirm America's return to multilateralism, the staying power of its military strength, and the reversal of former President Trump's unilateralism. China's regional order building is boosted by its perception that the United States is declining in the region. In contrast, China appears as a rising economic, military, diplomatic, and political power with a greater influence on multilateral international organizations. A centerpiece of Chinese economic power is the BRI. Its focus on infrastructure construction and connectivity has appealed to many developing economies which are less concerned about geopolitical issues unless their national interests are threatened in a direct manner.

In Chapter 10, Emmanuel argues that the COVID-19 pandemic raised fundamental questions over the resilience of the LIO. At first glance, the early part of the crisis seemed to have substantiated the Realist proposition that, faced with a risk of anarchy, states pursue their national interests to ensure their survival. This vision involves that competitive and even antagonistic dynamics between states may exacerbate and jeopardize the LIO. The pandemic restricted interstate interactions but, more dramatically, the relations between the United States and China became increasingly contentious. However, nationalistic stances reached their limits within a few months. Once severely affected by the COVID-19 pandemic, Latin American and Caribbean developing states advocated and followed a well-tested approach to overcome the crisis: they actively cooperated with the two superpowers and IFIs. During this process, China, the United States, and the IFIs played a pivotal role and shaped regional responses to the pandemic. Despite obvious tensions within the LIO, this evolution has highlighted the strength and resilience of liberal principles.

Chapter 11 focuses on climate change and assumes that the current voluntary agreements have failed to stem temperature increases. As a result, the central challenge for global climate change governance is to overcome negative externalities and create collective action. Hira and Au-Yeung examine how China, the United States, and the European Union – the largest greenhouse gas (GHG) emitters – have fought global warming. The European Union is the undisputed leader of GHG emissions reduction owing to a strong domestic support and the development of green jobs. In the United States, the lobbying power of the fossil fuel industry has stymied policy progress at the national level. In fact, climate change policies have flourished within U.S. states. China presents the clearest path for emissions reduction by responding to the enormous domestic costs of climate change through centralized as well as decentralized planning. However, this approach has been complicated by China's economic development. Hira and Au-Yeung find lessons for a more effective global governance. These include transparency on climate change costs and GHG emissions reductions, the value of policy experimentation, the payoff of integrating energy markets, the business opportunities created by the green transition, and the need to subsidize the losers of this transition.

Finally, in Chapter 12, Gaillard contends that the resurgence of nationalism and neo-mercantilism has undermined the LIO and globalization, threatened critical mineral supply chains (CMSCs) and global value chains (GVCs), and increased the risk of a high-intensity conflict between the United States and China. He argues that policy makers in advanced economies (especially in the United States) need to soothe diplomatic relations with China over Taiwan. Next, they should rethink the present international economic system and shift to a "post-globalized" world. Post-globalization entails a world economy governed by "a logic of high interdependence in economic, commercial, migratory and technological fields between States (and their companies) whose strategic and geopolitical interests are convergent, or at least compatible." Several criteria can be used to classify countries according to their reliability in CMSCs and GVCs: they include a country's respect of property rights and rule of law, its "geopolitical compatibility" with the investing or importing nation, and its resilience to climate change. These criteria must be kept updated and further refined to fit the needs and the interests of Western governments and multinational companies. In any case, the Western dependence on China over key products and commodities should be phased out.

Notes

1 Authors' computations based on https://data.worldbank.org.

2 For Gaillard (2020), the golden age of globalization began with the collapse of the Soviet Union in 1991 and ended with Brexit and the election of Donald Trump in 2016.
3 The term "Washington Consensus" was coined by economist John Williamson (1990). This Consensus, which served as a macroeconomic roadmap for many countries, spurred free trade, liberalization of inward FDI, privatization, and deregulation. Ironically, it also recommended the achievement of a competitive exchange rate.
4 The BRI is designed to promote the "China model" of development and support Chinese investments abroad. These investments include infrastructure projects (e.g., roads, railways, ports, airports, electric grids, dams, power plants, pipelines, etc.) worldwide, especially in Asian, African, and European countries.
5 Z. Jordan and S. Deliwala, "Why Washington Should Care about India's Support for the AIIB," *Council on Foreign Relations*, 24 May 2022, available at https://www.cfr.org/blog/why-washington-should-care-about-indias-support-aiib.

References

Bell, D. A. (2015) *The China Model: Political Meritocracy and the Limits of Democracy*. Princeton: Princeton University Press.
Bergsten, C. F. and Gagnon, J. E. (2012) "Currency Manipulation, the US Economy, and the Global Economic Order," *Peterson Institute for International Economics, No. PB12-25*, December.
Crabtree, J. (2021) "Competing with the BRI: The West's Uphill Task," *Survival*, Vol. 63, No. 4, pp. 81–88.
Doshi, R. (2021) *The Long Game: China's Grand Strategy to Displace American Order*. Oxford: Oxford University Press.
Ekman, A. (Ed), Nicolas, F., Pajon, C., Seaman, J., Saint-Mézard, I., Boisseau du Rocher, S., Kastouéva-Jean, T. (2019) "China's Belt & Road and the World: Competing Forms of Globalization," *Etudes de l'Ifri, French Institute of International Relations*, April, available at https://www.ifri.org/sites/default/files/atoms/files/ekman_china_belt_road_world_2019.pdf.
Gaillard, N. (2020) *Country Risk: The Bane of Foreign Investors*. Cham: Springer.
Garton, P. and Chang, J. (2005) "The Chinese Currency: How Undervalued and How Much Does It Matter?," *Economic Roundup, Spring* 2005, pp. 83–109.
Gruin, J. (2019) *Communists Constructing Capitalism – State, Market, and the Party in China's Financial Reform*. Manchester: Manchester University Press.
Helleiner, E. (2021) "The Diversity of Economic Nationalism," *New Political Economy*, Vol. 26, No. 2, pp. 229–238.
Hughes, C. W. (2022) *Japan as a Global Military Power*. Cambridge: Cambridge University Press.
Ikenberry, G. J. (2010) "The Liberal International Order and Its Discontents," *Millennium*, Vol. 38, No. 3, pp. 509–521.
Ikenberry, G. J. (2018) "The End of Liberal International Order?," *International Affairs*, Vol. 94, No. 1, pp. 7–23.
International Institute for Strategic Studies (2023) *China's Belt and Road Initiative – A Geopolitical and Geo-economic Assessment*. London: Routledge.
International Monetary Fund (2008) "Globalization: A Brief Overview," available at https://www.imf.org/external/np/exr/ib/2008/053008.htm.

Kim, M. H. (2019) "A Real Driver of US–China Trade Conflict: The Sino–US Competition for Global Hegemony and its Implications for the Future," *International Trade, Politics and Development*, Vol. 3, No. 1, pp. 30–40.

Meltzer, J. P. and Shenai, N. (2019) "The US–China Economic Relationship – A Comprehensive Approach," *Global Economy and Development at Brookings and American Enterprise Institute*, available at https://www.aei.org/wp-content/uploads/2019/02/US-China-Economic-Relationship_final.pdf.

Ramo, J. C. (2004) *The Beijing Consensus*. London: Foreign Policy Centre.

Richdale, K. G. and Liu, W. H. (1991) "The Politics of 'Glasnost' in China, 1978–1990," *Journal of East Asian Affairs*, Vol. 5, No. 1, pp. 104–143.

Samuelson, P. A. (1971) "Ohlin Was Right," *The Swedish Journal of Economics*, Vol. 73, No. 4, pp. 365–384.

Skidmore, D. (2021) "Searching for a 'China Model' along the Belt and Road," *Asian Politics & Policy*, Vol. 13, No. 3, pp. 326–348.

Teece, D. J. (2020) "Fundamental Issues in Strategy: Time to Reassess?," *Strategic Management Review*, Vol. 1, No. 1, pp. 103–144.

Whittaker, D. H., Sturgeon, T., Okita, T. and Zhu, T. (2020) *Compressed Development – Time and Timing in Economic and Social Development*. Oxford: Oxford University Press.

Williamson, J. (1990) "What Washington Means by Policy Reform," in Williamson, J. (Ed) *Latin American Adjustment: How Much Has Happened?* Washington, DC: Institute for International Economics.

Xinbo, W. (2010) "Understanding the Geopolitical Implications of the Global Financial Crisis," *The Washington Quarterly*, Vol. 33, No. 4, pp. 155–163.

Part I

Chinese and U.S. capitalisms

2 Is Chinese capitalism developmental or neoliberal?

Comparison with the Japanese and American models

Fumihito Gotoh and Yu-Wai Vic Li

This chapter compares the characteristics of Chinese capitalism with the American and Japanese models and examines a case study of China's vehicle electrification. We argue that the powers of both political (re)centralization and economic decentralization have been at work since 1978, shaping the characteristics of Chinese capitalism, i.e., the co-existence of developmentalism and neoliberalism, and that China's political power is more concentrated than that of Japan and the United States. This co-existence is nothing new in China, and this resembles the relations between the emperor and scholar-bureaucrats in imperial China. China has been better adapted to neoliberal globalization than Japan since the 1980s due to political power concentration, economic rationalism, and the timing of its integration into the global economy. However, the strength of Chinese capitalism is often exaggerated, and as the automobile electrification case illustrates, excess capacity is a serious side-effect of excessive government intervention. Despite the growing American criticism that Chinese capitalism is irreconcilable with American capitalism, both capitalist models share the combination of developmentalism and neoliberalism (albeit with different mixture proportions) and are not necessarily incompatible. The U.S.–China rivalry stems from the competition over hegemony in East Asia and advanced technology rather than the different economic models.

2.1 Introduction

Branko Milanovic (2019) contrasts the liberal meritocratic capitalism developed in the West with the state-led political (authoritarian) capitalism and argues: "the economic rebalancing of the world is not only geographical; it is also political. China's economic success undermines the West's claim that there is a necessary link between capitalism and liberal democracy." This kind of perspective has been common recently, but Chinese capitalism has been characterized by divergent labels, including "state-led," "developmental," "illiberal," "hybrid," and even "neoliberal." The specific aspects of the Chinese political economy (e.g., central planning and industrial policy, state

DOI: 10.4324/9781003340430-3

capitalist dominance of strategic industries, private sector development, and business competition between provinces) inform each characterization focused on by the researcher.

This chapter compares the characteristics of the Chinese capitalist model with the American and Japanese models and examines a case study of China's vehicle electrification. During the U.S.–Japan trade conflict from the 1980s to the early 1990s, some American elites heavily criticized Japan's economic system and business customs as different from Western norms and unfair (e.g., Prestowitz, 1988; Fallows, 1989). Since 2018, the United States has intensified the trade conflict with China, and an increasing number of Americans have denounced the Chinese economic system as incompatible with the U.S. system (e.g., Meltzer and Shenai, 2019; Teece, 2020). Our research question is to what extent the Chinese capitalist model is similar to and different from the Japanese and American models. Some scholars view the "China model" of development and governance as different or unique (e.g., Ramo, 2004; Bell, 2015), while others regard it as a new variant of the developmental state (e.g., Breslin, 2011 and 2021; Knight, 2014; Tsai and Naughton, 2015; Whittaker et al., 2020). There are no agreed definitions of the "model" or the developmental state. One common position is the identification of alternatives to the Anglo-American neoliberal model. However, some scholars have identified neoliberal traits in Chinese capitalism (Harvey, 2005; Weber, 2018). We contend that the diverse definitions and perspectives of both the developmental state and neoliberalism contribute to the divergent views of Chinese capitalism. We demonstrate that developmentalism and neoliberalism are not necessarily as dichotomous as many may think.

We argue that developmental-state and neoliberal characteristics have co-existed in the Chinese political economy since the 1990s. Here, we adopt Leftwich's (1995, p. 401) definition of developmental states, i.e.,

> states whose politics have concentrated sufficient power, autonomy and capacity at the center to shape, pursue and encourage the achievement of explicit developmental objectives, whether by establishing and promoting the conditions and direction of economic growth, or by organizing it directly, or a varying combination of both.

Among various definitions of neoliberalism, we agree with Harvey (2005) that neoliberalism advocates free capital mobility between sectors, regions, and countries, which suggests capitalist dominance restored from the Bretton Woods system that constrained capital mobility. In this respect, neoliberalism is not necessarily the opposite of developmentalism. Moreover, it could be claimed that today's Chinese party-state has mobilized more developmental-state power than post-WWII Japan, given the higher political power concentration in Beijing, which holds substantial leverage over key industry development. This contrasts with the Japanese state between the 1950s and 1980s, which primarily coordinated numerous vested interests. We contend that the features of the Chinese and Japanese capitalist models result from the global hegemonic norms (e.g., "embedded liberalism" and neoliberalism) when they were integrated into the global economy, the different stages of their economic development, and their divergent domestic social norms (informal rules about how to behave in a group or society), such as power concentration or dispersion and attachments to intermediary organizations, which are intertwined with the mobility of labor and capital (Whittaker et al., 2020; Gotoh, 2021).

Whether or not Chinese capitalism is neoliberal is contentious and depends on focusing either on government intervention or on capitalist dominance in its domestic political economy. Although the Chinese economy experiences significant intervention from the central and regional governments, China also has a more substantial degree of capitalist dominance than Japan, where an alliance between management and regular employees against shareholders seeking short-term financial profits can still be witnessed. However, in contrast to its political power concentration in the central government, fiscal and economic decentralization in China has promoted economic dynamism through intense competition between businesses in different provinces, towns, and villages, local experimentation, and acquisition of foreign direct investment (FDI) and technology from foreign capital (including that of the Chinese diaspora). But the decentralization has also caused local protectionism. Japan's proportion of inward FDI in stock to GDP (gross domestic product) is much smaller than China's. Also, state-owned enterprises (SOEs) have experienced neoliberal restructuring since the 1990s. Chinese capitalism appears to have both liberal and illiberal elements. Furthermore, even the United States is not a purely free-market economy. Consider, for example, the significant contribution of its enormous state spending and investment (including defense spending) to the development of advanced technology such as computers, semiconductors, the internet, and artificial intelligence (Block, 2008; Mazzucato, 2013).

The automobile industry in China is closely linked with the above points of industrial policy, local business competition and protectionism between jurisdictions, and inward FDI (Meier, 2009; Chin, 2010). China has successfully enticed foreign automakers to transfer new technologies by taking advantage of the extraordinary domestic market scale – a condition that was simply absent in other East Asian economies. The large amounts of automobile-related FDI inflows and cut-throat competition between automakers located in different Chinese provinces may lead to the impression that China is market-oriented. However, the central government has heavily influenced the automobile industry through industrial policy and finance. Relations between the central and regional governments in contemporary China resemble those between the emperor and scholar-bureaucrats in imperial China. Furthermore, economic rationalism (belief in the efficiency of market economies) has been deeply embedded in society since late imperial China, when the emperor liberalized the economic and social system by substantially eliminating fixed intermediary organizations that had provided social protection (Jing and Luo, 1978; Miyakawa, 1955; Gruin, 2019). In this sense, today's Chinese capitalism has incorporated both aspects of autocracy and economic rationalism. Nevertheless, inter-provincial business competition in China shares some similarities with that between corporate groups in Japan, causing excess production capacity and debt in key industries for both countries.

We begin by examining the characteristics of the Chinese capitalist model and subsequently compare it with the Japanese and American models to identify both similarities and differences, focusing on the concepts of the developmental state and neoliberalism as well as global hegemonic norms and domestic social norms. We then shed light on the features of Chinese capitalism by using automobile electrification as an example and describe its strengths and weaknesses. Finally, we illustrate its excess production capacity as a major side-effect of government intervention.

2.2 Characteristics of the Chinese capitalist model

The Chinese economic system has transformed dramatically since Deng Xiaoping announced the reform and opening up in 1978. China today is very different from the command economy during the pre-reform period and also from the "Wild West Capitalism" from 1979 until the late 1990s (Naughton, 2017). Since 1978, China has achieved an unprecedented average annual GDP growth of almost 10%. This has made many Western elites and scholars interested in the distinctiveness of China's economic reform and capitalist model.

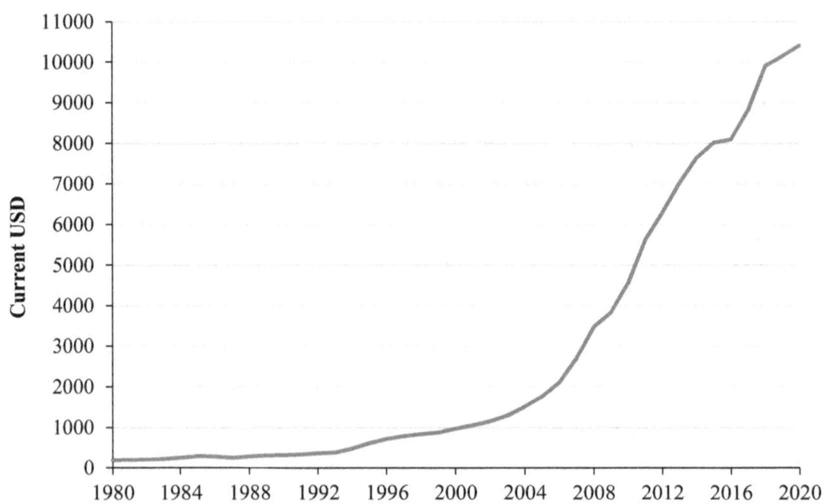

Figure 2.1 China's GDP per capita, 1980–2020

Source: World Bank's World Development Indicators.

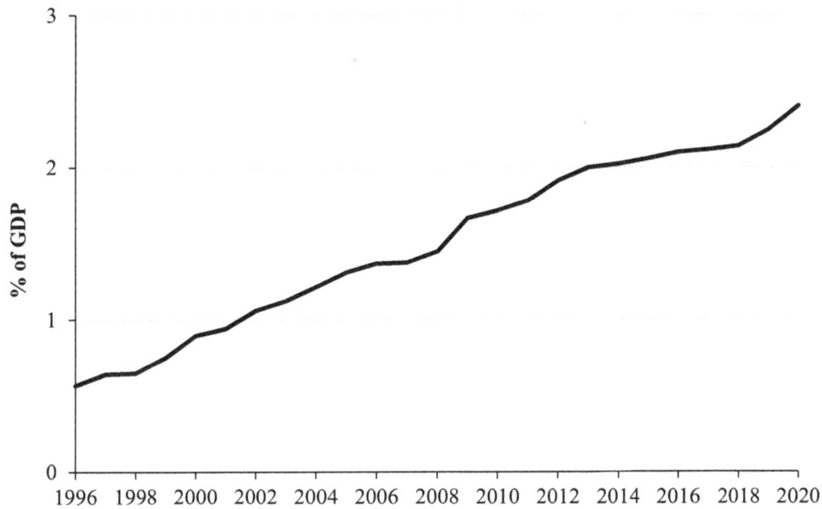

Figure 2.2 China's R&D expenditure (in % of GDP), 1996–2020

Source: World Bank's World Development Indicators.

The concepts of the Beijing Consensus and the China model have given Westerners an exaggerated impression that Chinese capitalism is in stark contrast to theirs. Ramo (2004) coined the Beijing Consensus as an alternative development path to the Washington Consensus, a set of liberal economic policies recommended for developing countries. The global financial crisis, which heavily damaged North America and Western Europe, has promoted attention to the Beijing Consensus and the China model as an alternative to the neoliberal development model. Although Ramo's (2004) Beijing Consensus consists of innovation-led productivity growth, sustainable and equitable development, and China's self-determined and unique development strategy that apparently is appealing to other developing countries and challenging the United States, Kennedy (2010, p. 462) contends that the consensus "is a misguided and inaccurate summary of China's actual reform experience" by pointing out that the growth was not based on its own technological innovation and that the reform adopted not only many prescriptions of the Washington Consensus (including fiscal discipline, liberalization of trade, interest rates, and inward FDI, and a competitive exchange rate) but also some state-intervention policies of East Asian neighbors (Kennedy, 2010, pp. 468–471). "China model" is sometimes used interchangeably with "Beijing Consensus." Bell (2015, pp. 179–180) claims that, although the China model is often described as a combination of free-market capitalism and one-party state authoritarianism prioritizing political stability, his concept of the model refers to political governance – authoritarian meritocracy at the top, experimentation in the middle, and democracy at the bottom – rather than an approach to economic reform. He also maintains that the

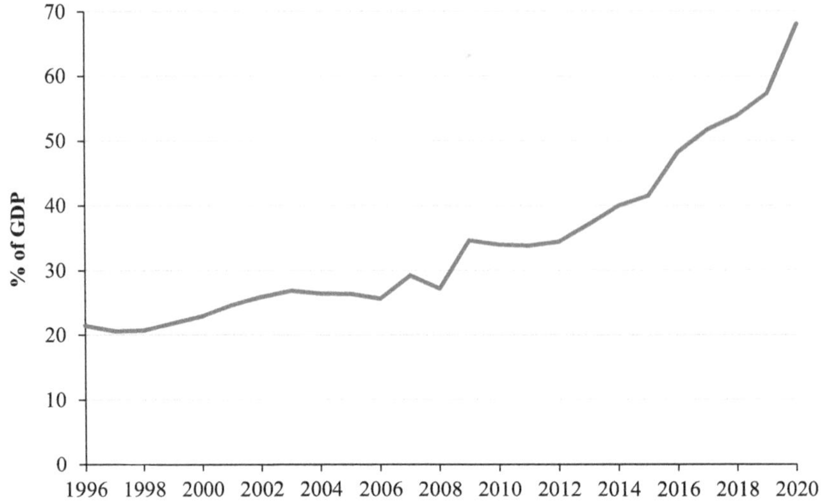

Figure 2.3 China's general government gross debt (in % of GDP), 1996–2020

Source: https://fred.stlouisfed.org/series/GGGDTACNA188N.

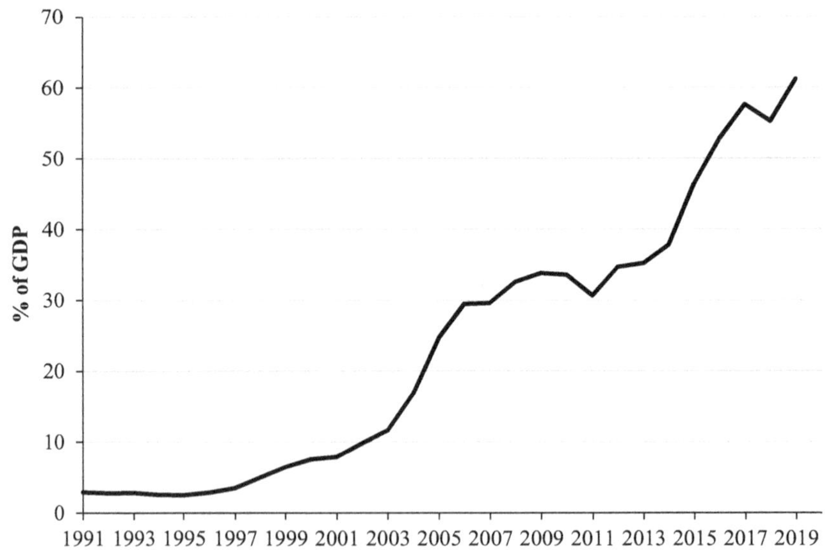

Figure 2.4 China's outstanding domestic private debt securities (in % of GDP), 1991–2019

Sources: https://www.gurufocus.com/economic_indicators/2067/outstanding-domestic-private-debt-securities-to-gdp-for-china (1991–1999) and https://fred.stlouisfed.org/series/DDDM03CNA156NWDB (2000–2019).

Chinese state still has a firm grip over SOEs and core strategic industries, while China's three-tiered enterprise systems consist of central SOEs, hybrid local and foreign large firms, and small-scale capitalists, which appears to be in accordance with the political governance (Bell, 2015, pp. 179–180). Skidmore's and Lim's chapters in this book maintain that, through the Belt and Road Initiative (BRI), China promotes its model as an example for developing countries.

Despite radical economic reform, China is still a long way from free-market capitalism. China's private sector has grown rapidly since the 1990s, while the government restructured SOEs from the early 1990s until the 2000s. Although it is challenging to measure SOEs' contribution to the economy accurately as Chinese economic data do not clearly distinguish the state sector from the private sector (Zhang, 2019), the respective proportions of SOEs in China's GDP and employment were estimated to be 23–28% and 5–16%. At the end of August 2022, major private companies such as Tencent (internet-based platformer), Alibaba (e-commerce and internet company), CATL (battery manufacturer), Meituan (delivery platformer), and BYD (automaker) were included in the 20 largest Chinese companies by market capitalization. However, the power of the state sector is more significant than these proportions suggest as:

i SOEs cover the "commanding heights" of the economy, such as energy, basic heavy industries, production of heavy machinery, infrastructure engineering, transportation, telecommunications, automobiles, and military equipment;
ii SOEs possess a much larger share of key resources (the ratio of SOEs' combined assets to GDP was around 205% in 2015) – including finance, land, and energy – than their contribution to economic output;
iii SOEs are an integral part of the Chinese Communist Party's (CCP) political power structure; and
iv much of the private sector depends on investments or patronage by senior government officials (Kroeber, 2020).

Regarding the second point, the party-state still maintains substantial ownership of the economy, while urban land is one of the most critical resources for local governments to pursue economic development in their domains (Naughton, 2017).

Fiscal decentralization and competition between SOEs and private companies in different local governments' jurisdictions have contributed to the rapid growth and adaptability of the Chinese economy. The central government directly manages major SOEs in key strategic industries such as energy, transportation, telecommunications, automobiles, military equipment, and banking, while smaller SOEs in industries with few strategic concerns are less prominent in state ownership and are likely to be owned by local governments. However, no SOEs, apart from a handful of exceptions, are in monopoly positions, as the state has maintained competition between multiple enterprises (Kroeber, 2020). In contrast to centralized political control, which means that local governments are agents of the central government, the bulk of economic management is decentralized to local governments, incentivized by performance rankings of local government officials in the personnel system and the decentralization of fiscal responsibility and power (Knight, 2014). The central government has the dominant ability to foster top-down initiatives, for instance, by implementing industrial policies for strategic industries, while local governments compete for economic performance with each other, invite FDI into their jurisdictions, back local companies in their domains, and influence the evolution of policymaking. Local governments first adopted many of China's most successful policies, which initially violated the policy of the central government, before the local policies were subsequently approved centrally (Kennedy, 2010, p. 472).

In addition to SOEs and local private companies, foreign capital has played a significant role in China's rapid growth during the 1990s and early 2000s. The average rate of China's inward FDI flows to GDP between 1985 and 2005 reached 3%. Three reasons can be identified: China's strategy for swift technology catch-up; China's willingness to access to international markets in exchange for multinational corporations' (MNCs) market access to China; and MNCs' exploitation of cheap labor in China (Kroeber, 2020). China's central government sought inward FDI to boost the productivity and competitiveness of domestic industries based on technology spillover and knowledge transfer, particularly through joint ventures between foreign and local firms (Meier, 2009). For instance, without enormous inward FDI, the Chinese automobile industry could not have developed rapidly. China's vast domestic market has enabled the central government to force MNCs headquartered in the United States, Europe, and Japan to set up such joint ventures, while the Chinese diaspora has also made a sizable investment in China (Yeung, 2004). Such inward FDI has significantly contributed to China's exports through global value chains. Notably, almost half of inward FDI has been via Hong Kong, whose legal system is based on common law (used widely in English-speaking countries), offering better protection for investors than civil law.

Quoting Yao's perspective (2015, p. 162) that China's political system has become more flexible to accommodate the increasing decentralization of economic decisions and the diverse regional development, Breslin (2021, p. 78) argues that "no clear consensus exists over where the balance of authority lies in China's political economy: in the hands of private actors and market forces, or in the hands of the state." Jones and Hameiri (2021, pp. 12–13) question the assumption of the Chinese state as a monolithic, unitary actor and contend that the fragmentation, decentralization, and internationalization of party-state apparatuses since 1978 have transformed China into a Chinese-style regulatory state in which the central leaders mainly use mechanisms to guide other actors (including local governments and private companies) in favored directions. We agree with Breslin (2021) and Jones and

Hameiri (2021) that the Chinese political economy has been decentralized over the last four decades, but the question remains: to what extent has China's state power fractured *vis-à-vis* other countries such as Japan and the United States?

We argue that the powers of both political (re)centralization and economic decentralization have been at work since 1978, shaping the characteristics of the Chinese political economy, and that, as will be discussed in Section 2.3, China's political power is more concentrated than that of Japan and the United States. The co-existence of economic decentralization and political centralization is nothing new in China, and this resembles the relations between the emperor and scholar-bureaucrats in imperial China. By the 2000s, the Chinese party-state decided to incorporate established private entrepreneurs into the political sphere, but the CCP aimed not only to foster rapid capital accumulation by private interests and use a part of accumulated capital for its statist purposes but also to retain Leninist discretionary political power and carefully examine the trustworthiness and reliability of those entrepreneurs (McNally, 2011). Furthermore, although fragmented authority was witnessed in the decision-making and administration of the Chinese automobile industry in the 1980s, the shift to a greater degree of centralized political and regulatory coordination took place from the early 1990s onward (Chin, 2010). Breslin (2021, p. 82) also maintains that "the market isn't trusted to do everything that the state wants to happen in the economy and to achieve the state's grander overarching objectives."

2.3 Comparison with the Japanese and American models

This section will compare the Chinese capitalist model with the Japanese and American models by focusing on developmentalism and neoliberalism, as well as the American-led international economic order, domestic social norms, and the causes of U.S.–China rivalry. To what extent are these models similar and different? When this comparative analysis is conducted, how the concepts of the developmental state and neoliberalism are defined is crucial. The term "developmental state" was coined by Chalmers Johnson (1982) in his work on Japan's economic development and industrial policy. Subsequently, this concept was applied to other East Asian countries, including South Korea, Taiwan, and Singapore, and emerging countries in other regions (e.g., Amsden, 1989; Wade, 1990; Leftwich, 1995). Although developmental states have various definitions, we adopt Leftwich's (1995) definition as mentioned above.

There are contrasting views on the developmental state: whether it has been demised or transformed under neoliberal globalization (Wade, 2018; Whittaker et al., 2020). In the "demise view" camp, Carroll (2017) views the developmental state as being historically contingent and having been replaced by the "variegated market state" while Pirie (2018) claims that South Korea and Taiwan have moved from developmental states, whose primary objective is capital mobilization in pursuit of industrial policy, closer to neoliberal states governed by the market. By contrast, in the "transformation view" camp, O'Riain (2004) maintains that the "developmental bureaucratic state," in which state bureaucracy is closely coupled with big domestic businesses, has been transformed into the "developmental network state," connecting domestic actors with global actors within global investment flows. For Thurbon (2016), the "developmental mindset" (aiming for national techno-industrial catch-up and export competitiveness through state economic intervention to enhance national power in a hostile world) remains in the Korean political economy. We agree with the transformation view regarding China as the elements of the developmental network state and the developmental mindset have been observed in the Chinese political economy under neoliberal globalization, but it is difficult to apply this view to Japan, which has resisted neoliberal globalization (Gotoh, 2021). Keep in mind that developmentalism is seminal in the works of Friedrich List (1789–1846) – a German-American economist – and Alexander Hamilton (1757–1804) – a founding father of the United States – reflecting the economic policies of Germany and the United States, which were at catch-up stages in the mid-19th century (Breslin, 2011). The developmental mindset is not confined to East Asia or the non-Western world.

There are no countries that fully adhere to neoliberalism, and developmental and neoliberal voices compete in many countries (Thurbon, 2016). Although the United States and the United Kingdom are often regarded as neoliberal states, they are not purely free-market economies. In this respect, Vogel (2018) indicates the following crucial points regarding government–market relations: free markets do not exist; governments play the central role in creating markets by building institutions (e.g., laws, regulations, practices, and social networks and norms) rather than destroying them; and the government-versus-market dichotomy is misleading. In our view, neoliberalism is linked to enhanced capital mobility or capitalist dominance rather than the retreat of governments. The "market liberalization" during the 1980s and 1990s was not caused by the withdrawal of governments but was driven by both governments and private actors, mainly in the West.

Japan from the 1950s to the 1970s and China since the 1990s can be viewed as a developmental bureaucratic state and a developmental network state, respectively. On the one hand, Japan from the 1950s to the 1970s and China since the 1990s share many similar characteristics, including the central bureaucracy's strong commitment to economic development, industrial policies promoting targeted industries, state intervention in industrial credit allocation through the bank-centered financial system, close government–big business relations, very high rates of investment to GDP, and export-oriented industrialization (Meier, 2009; Stubbs, 2018; Wade, 2018). In this sense, Japan and China, during their respective high growth periods, could be regarded broadly as developmental states. However, on the other hand, they also indicate striking differences in various areas, such as: (i) international environment (characteristics of the U.S.-led international economic order), (ii) social relations and norms, (iii) country size and central–local government relations, and (iv) relations with foreign capital (Meier, 2009; Tsai and Naughton, 2015; Whittaker et al., 2020). These differences will be examined more closely here.

Firstly, one weakness of Johnson's (1982) seminal work on the Japanese developmental state was that it paid insufficient attention to the international economic order. The period of a country's integration into the global economy is critical because it is influenced by the institutions of the hegemonic power of the time (Whittaker et al., 2020). When Japan was integrated into the global economy in the 1950s, it was influenced by the U.S.-embedded liberalism (a combination of open international trade and restricted international capital mobility under the Bretton Woods system for giving governments greater autonomy to manage domestic economic stability while maintaining international economic openness), which entrenched the interests of anti-free market elites. However, since the global economic order shifted from embedded liberalism to neoliberalism in the 1980s, these elites' interests have conflicted with changes in Japan's industrial structure. By contrast, China was integrated into the global economy during the 1990s, when U.S. neoliberalism and its institutions were dominant and influenced China's institutional formation. The CCP reduced the SOE role in providing social security from the mid-1980s until the 1990s and has restructured SOEs through drastic job cuts, bankruptcy, consolidation, and privatization since the 1990s. However, China's market liberalization boosted its economy dramatically. The two different international economic orders, embedded liberalism and neoliberalism, contributed to the respective two countries' rapid growth.

Secondly, although Chinese civilization influenced Japan, the two societies have notable differences in social relations and norms. Among the three broad paths to sociability based on (i) family and kinship, (ii) intermediary organizations outside kinship, and (iii) the state, the Japanese rely heavily on the second path, while the Chinese depend on the first and third paths (Fukuyama, 1995). Furthermore, according to Hofstede (2015), Chinese society's power distance (degree of less powerful people's accepting unequal power distribution) is higher, but its uncertainty avoidance is lower than Japanese society, which means the former tolerates higher levels of power concentration and risk than the latter. The divergent social relations and norms in Japan and China have contributed to their different social protection systems. According to Miura's (2012, pp. 12–14) typology of work and welfare, Japan is categorized into a system of "work through welfare" in which "employment maintenance policies functionally substitute for income maintenance policies" whereas Anglo-American countries are classified into "workfare" (a combination of low income maintenance and low employment maintenance). Contemporary China is also categorized into workfare (Chan and Ngok, 2016). Notably, Japanese social norms, including strong attachments to intermediary organizations (e.g., village and company), "industrious norms" (respect for labor and a negative view of financial profit), and "systemic support" (ruling elites' support and protection of subordinates in exchange for the latter's obedience and loyalty), conflict with the mobility of capital, labor, and technology (Gotoh, 2021). Power in Japanese society and organizations is dispersed, while class compromise (or inter-class cooperation such as management–labor cooperation) is a norm in Japanese intermediary organizations. Also, further to the historical power dispersion and status quo orientation of numerous interest groups, the central bureaucracy's power has been weakened by strong U.S. criticism against government intervention and the prolonged economic stagnation since the bubble burst in the early 1990s. These factors have not only prevented Japan's transition to the developmental network state but also significantly weakened Japan's developmental bureaucratic state features. In contrast, the high concentration of power among elites and economic rationalism have been embedded in Chinese society since the late imperial period, when the autocratic emperor and his scholar-bureaucrats promoted liberalization (e.g., the development of the monetary economy, the diffusion of markets) of the economic system (Gruin, 2019; Jing and Luo, 1978). Such power concentration and economic rationalism have facilitated contemporary China's state-led development under neoliberal globalization.

Thirdly, there is an enormous difference in geographical size between China and Japan. Due to the geographical vastness, the Chinese central government had already decentralized decision-making to local governments during the Mao period, and fiscal and economic decentralization has been promoted since the opening up (Meier, 2009; Tsai and Naughton, 2015). As the automobile electrification case illustrates in Section 2.4, economic decentralization in China has not only enhanced economic dynamism through inter-jurisdictional business competition but also caused local protectionism and excess production capacity. Many local governments adopt inter-jurisdictional trade barriers against one another because local officials' performance is evaluated mainly by their jurisdictions' economic output, business growth, and improvement of living standards (Meier, 2009, pp. 126–128). Furthermore, incentives from local governments have created excess production capacity in the automobile industry.[1]

Lastly, in connection with the first difference, China's and Japan's relations with foreign capital contrast. This is because anti-free market elites entrenched their power in Japan under embedded liberalism, which restricted international capital mobility and tolerated government intervention, while China has achieved rapid economic growth under neoliberal globalization, which has enhanced international capital mobility. Since 1990, China's proportion of inward FDI stock to GDP has been much higher than Japan's.[2] China's openness to FDI has contributed to access to foreign technology, while Japan has regarded inward FDI as a threat (Tsai and Naughton, 2015).

Let us now move on to the comparison of the U.S. and Chinese economic models (for an analysis of U.S. capitalism, see Gaillard and Michalek's chapter in this book). The two countries' rivalry has intensified since the election of Donald Trump as the U.S. president in 2016. The statement by the U.S. Ambassador, Dennis Shea, at the World Trade Organization General Council in 2018 exemplified American criticism of the Chinese economic model,[3] including (i) the Chinese party-state intervention in the market and control over the allocation of resources including land, energy, and capital; (ii) SOEs' outsized role in the economy; (iii) state economic planning and market-distorting industrial policies that create excess capacity; and (iv) unreasonable policies and practices that harm U.S. intellectual property rights, innovation, and technology development. Such critics of China tend to view the country as state capitalism (e.g., Blanchette, 2020). Although there are significant differences between the American and Chinese economic models, such as the significance of the state sector, the financial system (capital market development), the size of manufacturing, and trade balance, neither China is purely state capitalism nor the United States is a free-market economy.

Although the United States has few government-owned companies, unlike China, the U.S. economic success is attributed partly to state spending and investment (including military expenditures) in innovation and advanced technology, such as computers, semiconductors, the internet, the iPhone, artificial intelligence, biotechnology, and nanotechnology, rather than laissez-faire policy (Block, 2008; Mazzucato, 2013; Wade, 2014). Block (2008) contends that the federal government dramatically expanded its financial support to accelerate technological development from 1980 to 1992 while keeping the U.S. developmental state hidden due mainly to the dominance of market fundamentalist ideas. Wade (2014) demonstrates that despite the dominance of the market fundamentalist narrative in American public policy discourse, the United States has adopted much more industrial policy (including network-building industrial policy) than this narrative implies, outlining a history of the U.S. developmental state, such as Alexander Hamilton's strategy for promoting American manufacturing to catch up with Britain and strengthen its military, Abraham Lincoln's building of the transcontinental railway, Franklin Roosevelt's New Deal (e.g., the Tennessee Valley Authority's provision of electricity generation and fertilizer manufacturing) and the strengthening of the government–military–industrial complex from the 1940s onward. Also, Mazzucato (2013, p. 77) views the United States as an "entrepreneurial state" which is the primary risk-taker in massive investment in radical new areas to spur innovation. She argues that "if the rest of the world wants to emulate the US model, they should do as the US actually did, not as they say they did: more State not less" (Mazzucato, 2013, p. 1).

The divergent American and Chinese economic models are not necessarily incompatible. Rather, American unilateralism and concern over hegemonic decline, Chinese nationalism and desire for China's rightful place in the world that are vital for the CCP's legitimacy and the competition over advanced technology critical for both economic prosperity and military security can be regarded as sources of the intensified rivalry. Meanwhile, the United States and China share stunning similarities, namely, policies that enhance wealth and military power (国富兵强), exceptionalism (American and Sino-centrism), and growing economic inequality in both societies, despite their GDP per capita gap. The U.S.-led international liberal economic order has enabled China's remarkable economic ascent, but China cannot accept Western-centric liberal universalism (e.g., liberal democracy and individualist human rights) and American liberal interventionism into authoritarian regimes. Breslin (2021, p. 25) claims that China is not committed to a liberal international order (LIO) but to an order built on the sovereignty, plurality, diversity, and equality principles underpinning the United Nations Charter.

These factors affecting the U.S.–China rivalry are closely linked to the crisis of the American-led LIO. It used to be a community of Western liberal democracies in which member states were physically safe and economically secure, but the end of the Cold War and the globalization of the liberal order (accommodating numerous non-Western states, including China) have undermined American hegemony, the sense of security community, and the characteristics of embedded liberalism, making the international order neoliberal (Ikenberry, 2018). Neoliberalism has not only divided American society but also facilitated the drastic restructuring of SOEs and the streamlining of social protection in China, expanding economic inequality in both countries (Duckett, 2020). Unsurprisingly, American and Chinese leaders have promoted economic nationalism and distracted public attention away from domestic problems to international affairs.

Regarding the U.S.–China rivalry, Mearsheimer (2010, pp. 388–390) contends that the United States has not historically allowed another state to become a regional hegemon and that regional hegemons try to prevent the rise of would-be hegemons in other regions because of their fear that great powers in other regions would cause trouble in their backyard. However, this assumption that other great powers behave like the United States may be misleading and even dangerous. One measure for mitigating the U.S.–China rivalry and maintaining the LIO is to reintroduce some elements of embedded liberalism into the order to provide governments with the capacity to pursue economic and social security, stable employment, and higher living standards while accommodating diverse political economic systems (Ikenberry, 2018).

2.4 Automobile electrification as an industry example

The co-existence of developmentalist and liberal elements in today's China is best exemplified in the takeoff of the car electrification policy initiatives, of which the China's central authorities have adopted a typical approach of other East Asian developmental states. Beijing has assumed leading roles in initiating the policy framework that creates and defines the overall market structure, providing incentives to industry market players and local governments to support the attainments of national policy goals. Notwithstanding, following the industry's exponential growth, Beijing has induced market competition, albeit in selective fashion, within the industry to promote consolidation among firms and foster their competitiveness vis-à-vis foreign counterparts.

To begin with, the growing demand for automobiles since the 1990s has generated alarming concerns among Beijing's decision-makers about the environmental implications (notably air pollution) of the country's increasingly congested road traffic, and competitiveness of the domestic industry as consumers have gradually turned to foreign vehicles with better cost-performance. Motivated by these concerns, Beijing debuted a new energy vehicle (NEV) technology roadmap during the 10th National Five-Year Plan (FYP) period for 2001–2005. In what is known as the "Three-by-Three Research and Development Strategy" that continues to shape the country's approach of car electrification, the government would prioritize NEVs development powered by fuel cell, hybrid generation and electricity and support indigenous technological innovation of powertrain control systems, driving motors, and batteries – the critical component technologies for NEVs (Jin et al., 2021).

The 11th FYP, released in 2006, outlined in more details how Beijing would leverage its four-way partnerships to kickstart industry growth. Central government ministries, the automobile industry, universities, and research institutions would join in formulating and executing the nation's NEV strategy. A high-level advisory committee was created as a multipartite platform providing inputs from industry players and experts to Beijing. A year later, the National Development and Reform Commission (NDRC), a powerful coordinating body within the State Council vested with encompassing authorities in steering the country's development, released a market entry guidance that defined the technical requirements for domestic manufactures to commercialize their NEV prototypes (Jin et al., 2021).

These paved the basis for the "Ten Cities, Thousand Vehicles" program, launched in 2009, with a goal to add a thousand NEVs for public transportation in ten pilot cities every year over a three-year period. The program, however, did not proceed as smoothly as expected. Among the 25 cities involved, only 40% met the public fleet NEV goals; in 2012, only seven cities met their annual new NEV target (Gong et al., 2013). To galvanize local and industry supports, the central government refined its policy focus, leaving out the conventional hybrid vehicles in subsequent policy frameworks. Beijing's *Plan on Development of Energy-Saving and New Energy Auto Industry (2012–2020)* aimed at promoting the mass popular use of particular types of NEV, including battery electric vehicles (BEV), plug-in hybrids (PHEV), and fuel-cell vehicles (FCV) (State Council, 2012).

Rounds of new research and development fundings were injected in the NEV industry to develop better core technologies; and mandates were enforced on local authorities to prioritize the growth of NEV fleets in connection with the local environment protection and energy conservation plans, the successful implementation of which would be linked to the performance reviews of local cadres. By 2020, cumulative sales of five million NEVs and industry production capacity of up to two million vehicles were expected. This combination of central fiscal support and incentive system imposed on local authorities spurred considerable interest nationwide to promote NEV uses. Pilot cities involved in the NEV pilot grew from 25 to 88 in 2015; many had become the enthusiasts with "creative" policy innovation promoting car electrification, including road access privileges and purchase subsidies for NEVs (Jin et al., 2021). In two years' time, China's NEV fleet jumped from 18,000 to over 330,000 vehicles, making it the largest market worldwide in 2015.

As Xi Jinping became China's top leader, his administration elevated car electrification into a national agenda associated with the country's strong power ambition. In 2014, Xi declared that NEV development was the only way that would turn China from "a big automobile country to an automobile power."[4] The rather nationalist agenda was codified in the *Made in China (MIC) 2025* blueprint released in 2015, which affirmed that China's car electrification would become an integral part of the nation's strategic industrial policies to promote homegrown research and innovation in NEV industries, and their global competitiveness (State Council, 2015). The MIC 2025 also became the basis for the many endeavors of various central ministries to back NEV research and deployments. The finance ministry, for instance, provided tax waiver and infrastructure subsidies for charging facilities, NEV purchase subsidies would be extended nationwide for five years from 2015 (Ministry of Finance, 2015). In 2016 alone, RMB9.57 billion was allocated for switching 72,000 government vehicles into NEVs made by 92 domestic firms (Ministry of Industry and Information Technology (MIIT), 2019).

Vested with autonomy in policy design and implementation in order to meet the national guidance and specific targets, more than 300 cities – close to half of China's total – laid out local guidance not just to increase local NEV use but also to get involved in the production chain in concert with automobile and component companies. Leading cities like Beijing created three industrial campuses for NEV firms. Similarly, Shenzhen authorities capitalized their local industrial base in battery production and electricity storage system to jumpstart their share in domestic production. The NEV market grew exponentially as a result (Zhang and Bai, 2017; Li et al., 2018). Although the central authorities would take stock of and evaluate the local initiatives, the decentralized implementation that offered considerable flexibility to local governments has given rise to local protectionism, of which some local authorities favored local industries' interests by way of preferential subsidy schemes to firms and consumers within the area, leading to barriers for market expansion of NEV producers without an existing national sales network and, over the longer term, raising concerns about excess production.

Accordingly, despite the multiple policy supports from Beijing for car electrification, the central authorities also decided to phase out the national-level subsidy that would increase the requirements for domestic NEV makers to obtain government supports and subject the firms to market competition, both within and outside China. In 2017, Beijing planned to wind down all subsidies by 2020 and replaced them with a "dual credit scheme" that would expect individual automakers to make a minimum number of NEVs to earn extra credits from the government (failing to attain the minimum, on the other hand, would invite penalties). These happened at the same time more ambitious goals of car electrification were announced by Beijing. By 2020, an annual production of two million NEVs was expected, and they were to account for 20% of all new car production by 2025 (MIIT, 2017).

To ease market entry of foreign automakers, foreign ownership limits on local automakers and restrictions on NEV joint ventures were abolished in mid-2018 (Ministry of Commerce, 2018). In a drastic break from previous practice, foreign NEV firms were allowed to start manufacturing without first creating a joint venture with domestic firms. These policy changes prompted a surge in joint venture production between domestic makers and foreign counterparts as a result of the more competitive market landscape at home."[5] Shortly after the policy easing was announced, Tesla began its first production line in Shanghai's free trade zone.[6] Global automobile giants also established their footprint in NEV productions in China. BMW partnered with Great Wall Motors in making an electric version specific to China's market; Toyota also worked with BYD, now a leading non-state-owned domestic NEV firm, battery makers, and other domestic high-tech component firms. In only a few years' time, $137 billion investment capital in NEV headed to China, accounting for one-third of the global total with half coming from European automakers (Jin et al., 2021).

The presence of foreign automakers has intensified competition within China's NEV market and galvanized market segmentation in response to market demands and consumer affordability. Notably, foreign firms often partnered with non-state-owned domestic counterparts, breaking the monopoly of state-owned firms in the automobile industry.[7] China's internet giants like Alibaba, Baidu, and Tencent also formed industry coalitions with NEV and component firms in order to promote their smart mobility platforms.[8]

Beijing has viewed these market trends as conducive to promoting industry consolidation. In the words of the top MIIT official: "Some (NEV firms) will fall, some will survive, not all will thrive... That will be left to the market to decide."[9] In fact, despite the earlier plan to cut back government's subsidies, the plan was put on hold in response to the slowing economy and the Covid-19 pandemic. Domestic automakers continued to benefit from the various fiscal support measures from central and local authorities at least until the end of 2023. The continuing state intervention has resulted in the predominance of domestic firms. In 2021, around 80% of NEVs sold in China were locally made due not just to the price advantages of homegrown firms but also to the government's supports and incentives (Wakabayashi and Fu, 2022).

These coincided with the more aggressive push of Xi's government to promote car electrification. The 2020 NEV development plan by China's State Council (2020) expected the mainstreaming of non-hybrid NEVs on China's roads and that all public vehicles would be powered by electric platforms. The 14th FYP for 2021–2025 further specified that half of the vehicles on road would be electric or fuel-cell powered by 2035. This would contribute to China's attainment of peaking its carbon emissions by 2030 at the latest and, perhaps more importantly, accelerate China's industry upgrading across the various industries involved in NEV production, even while bolstering the local firms' global competitiveness vis-à-vis foreign counterparts.

The trajectory of China's car electrification echoes the observations of China specialists about the very nature of the country's political economy. While there has been notable decentralization of decision-making authorities and surge of market power over the past few decades, the central government has maintained its commanding role over the economy, engaging in macro-level management and steering, as well as micro-tinkering, if not direct intervention, of policy particulars that would shape the preference and policies of industrial and local government players. These contrast with the Japanese experience in which the Tokyo government lacked the comparable and necessary leverages over the domestic leading players (Toyota, Nissan, and Honda) to coordinate their different R&D focuses and strategies, to ramp up their EV productions and to partner with local authorities that would ultimately accelerate the switch to electric cars among everyday road users.

2.5 Strengths and weaknesses of Chinese capitalism

The major strengths of Chinese capitalism include adaptability stemming from the dual social-cohesive forces of the state and kinship, economic rationalism deeply embedded in society, and a Chinese-style developmental network state (in which networks between the central government, local governments, SOEs, local private businesses, and foreign capital are built). These traits have enabled China to be more adaptive to enhanced mobility of capital, labor, and technology than Japan under globalization.

Firstly, the heavy power concentration in the party-state enables the Chinese economy to respond promptly to international and domestic changes, while kinship offers people social protection. These dual forces for social cohesion provide high economic adaptability for China. In contrast, the Japanese tend to depend on intermediary organizations (e.g., companies, ministries, and local communities) whose vested interests often hamper adaptation to changes. Furthermore, China's top priority is the legitimacy and survival of the CCP, which makes its policies pragmatic. During the 1980s and early 1990s, the CCP favored cautious change, which was pragmatic and oriented around concrete material realities, meaning that the planned-economy ideal should not be replaced by the perfect market–economy ideal (Weber, 2018, p. 225).

Secondly, economic rationalism deeply entrenched in Chinese society has facilitated the mobility of capital and labor to be enhanced by reducing social protection provided by intermediary organizations (SOEs and communes) since 1978. Chinese economic rationalism is more compatible with neoliberalism and financialization, which started in Anglo-American countries, than the Japanese social norms centered on systemic support and industrious norms, which have constrained capital and labor mobility.

Lastly, associated with the first and second points, the Chinese-style developmental network state has accelerated economic growth through inter-jurisdictional business competition, enormous inward FDI, and foreign technology transfer. The central government's industrial policy often improves gradually, considering the outcomes of local experiments. Local governments have competed to attract business, including foreign capital, to publicly owned land and associated infrastructure in their jurisdictions for extra-budgetary revenue rather than protect already existing local companies since these governments were transformed into "tax collectors" from "asset owners" (of town and village enterprises and SOEs) in the early 1990s (Whittaker et al., 2020). Furthermore, McNally (2011, pp. 2–3) defines *guanxi* as "long-term reciprocal relationships that can create enduring trust" and claims that "to enhance firm success, private entrepreneurs use political *guanxi* networks to embed themselves in party-state institutions, carving out over time increasingly powerful positions *vis-à-vis* the state mediated by the application of *guanxi*."

However, the flip sides of these strengths are their weaknesses, which derive from excessive central and local government intervention, the insufficient rule of law, and the state's prioritization of economic development over social security and development. These weaknesses include side-effects of excess government intervention (e.g., excess production capacity, local protectionism, and public and corporate debt), inadequate business transparency and compliance (as well as corruption), growing economic inequality, and weak social protection.

Although industrial policy and government incentives encourage businesses to take greater risk and may achieve higher growth in target industries, excessive intervention sometimes causes severe side-effects. Public spending and monetary easing in China during the global financial crisis have brought about enormous investment in infrastructure, properties, and production facilities, leading to huge debt. Also, government intervention has contributed to excess production capacity in the steel and automobile industries. The glut of steel in China led to a flood of exports to the United States and Europe and caused trade friction. Local governments introduced protectionist measures to defend local automakers and their tax revenue from the fierce inter-jurisdictional competition, for instance, by raising market entry barriers against outside automakers and giving direct subsidies or tax incentives for buying local brands (Meier, 2009; Barwick et al., 2017).

Next, insufficient business transparency and compliance (e.g., opaque corporate ownership and government–business relations and violations of intellectual property rights) have invited Sino-skepticism among Western political and business leaders (see Gmeiner's chapter in this book), while prevalent corruption has had a negative impact on the CCP's legitimacy. According to the World Justice Project, on the rule of law, China was ranked 98th out of 139 and placed 12th out of 15 in the East Asia and Pacific region.[10] Furthermore, there is a clear difference between *guanxi* (based on trust) and corruption, which pertains to illegal, short-term transactional reciprocity (Luo, 2007). In addition, power concentration, little transparency, and few checks and balances make corruption a significant problem (Naughton, 2017). The Xi Jinping administration has conducted far-reaching anti-corruption campaigns although Skidmore contends that these campaigns have been politically motivated.[11]

Lastly, growing economic inequality and weak social security threaten social stability. Over the last two decades, social policies have done little to reduce disparities between large coastal cities and rural areas, rural-urban migrants and urban residents, and between men and women (Duckett, 2020). Responding to these disparities, the Chinese government has shifted its policy objective from a single-minded focus on economic growth to a diverse set of goals, including redistribution and social security (Naughton, 2017, p. 17).

2.6 Excess capacity

Despite the phenomenal growth of China's NEV market, the intense market competition-cum-government's proactive involvement in directing the car electrification pathway has resulted in excess capacity in China's NEV industry, especially since the late 2010s. Following the NEV boom in the mid-2010s, the proliferation of NEV makers and firms involved in the associated manufacturing activities for components has gradually become an acute problem. In response to Beijing's policy initiatives, local governments aggressively foster local industrial production irrespectively of the financial viability of the firms. Immediately after the "Ten Cities, Thousand Vehicles" project was announced in 2009, Shandong provincial government supported a little-known automobile firm to produce low-speed and light weight vehicles as part of its plan to galvanize local industry upgrading (Pearson, 2019). Even in the absence of Beijing's subsidies, the firm had produced 30,000 low-speed NEVs. Many other cities have taken a similar approach and justified their supports to low-end NEV productions, including three-wheeled vehicles and mini-electric vehicles popular among China's consumers (Chen et al., 2018). Although these models demonstrated far poorer road performance than regular-size ones, these products have quickly captured the market share and took up to 60% of all new electric car sales in 2015.

In fact, despite Beijing's safety concerns (due to their light weight) and likelihood that mini-NEVs might disrupt regular traffic, the central authorities have softened their opposition to low-end NEVs, making them eligible for EV subsidies. Together with the higher-end and premium NEV segments, China's NEV market has become very competitive. In 2019, there were well over 600 NEV firms, most of them homegrown, in the domestic market. The scale of excess production capacity that resulted, though unsurprising to analysts, have pointed to the very cut-throat nature of the industry. An MIIT estimate revealed that the gross industry production capacity was about 26.7 million new EVs, but annual NEV sale in 2019 was less than 10% of all automobile outputs. By the end of 2021, only 80 companies appeared to be making new cars and the rest had ceased production despite Beijing's support to car electrification.[12]

The very multi-tiered market structure and decentralized competition between local governments and firms they backed have complicated the matter. Some have turned to NEV production as a short-cut to attract quick investment from automakers in order to maintain local economic momentum during the pandemic. Wuhan government, for instance, fast-tracked its review of factory expansion plan of Dongfeng Motor, a leading state-owned firm that would produce 100,000 new EVs every year. Despite the postponing of the subsidy phase-out, regulatory changes have exerted negative pressure on the NEV industry growth (Wu et al., 2021).

A more recent assessment by China's automaker association has warned of the coming crisis of excess NEV production in China and called for industrial consolidation and "soft landing" of the uncompetitive manufacturers and noted that the provision of government subsidies until 2023 would only help keep some NEV firms afloat. The association forecast that, by 2025, less than 50% of the then-existing firms would be able to make profits, and production capacity would remain at least double the sales volume even in the most optimistic scenario.[13]

Notwithstanding these trends, the central authorities' emphasis on expanding China's NEV market scale (and power) and the industry's global competitiveness has remained little changed. As an integral part of China's environmental policy (NEV to cut carbon footprint) and industrial roadmap (NEV being an important element of homegrown technologies), Beijing appears to be willing to accept the market costs of excessive capacity and the failure of the uncompetitive firms. The authorities, after all, are ready to clean up the market landscape through consolidation and other policy instruments at their disposal.

2.7 Conclusion

China has better adapted to neoliberal globalization than Japan and achieved an unprecedented economic growth since the 1980s due to political power concentration, economic rationalism, and the timing of its integration into the global economy. Despite the growing American criticism that Chinese capitalism is irreconcilable with American capitalism, both capitalist models share the combination of developmentalism and neoliberalism (albeit with different mixture proportions) and are not necessarily incompatible. The U.S.–China rivalry stems from the competition over hegemony in East Asia and advanced technology rather than the different economic models (Kim, 2019). Better understanding of each other's true intentions and the tolerance for divergent political economic systems in the LIO are needed to mitigate the rivalry.

The strength and effectiveness of the Chinese capitalist model are often exaggerated. As the automobile electrification case exemplifies, it has both strengths and weaknesses, and serious excess capacity can be seen as a serious side-effect of excessive government intervention. Charles Lindblom (1977) once argued that the state, which is all thumbs and no fingers, is a powerful but clumsy instrument.

Notes

1 W. Shih, "Excess Capacity in China's Auto Industry Is Not Likely to have a Happy Ending," *Forbes*, 23 January 2019, available at https://www.forbes.com/sites/willyshih/2019/01/23/excess-capacity-in-chinas-auto-industry-is-not-likely-to-have-a-happy-ending/?sh=37899dbc27d5.
2 See https://unctadstat.unctad.org/EN/Index.html.
3 See https://geneva.usmission.gov/2018/07/27/55299.
4 D. Wakabayashi and C. Fu, "For China's Auto Market, Electric Isn't the Future. It's the Present," *New York Times*, 26 September 2022.
5 Y. Liu, "Renewed Policy Incentives to Keep Chinese EV Carmakers Afloat," *South China Morning Post*, 12 October 2017.
6 T. Ding, "Tesla Breaks Ground on Gigafactory in Shanghai," *Xinhua News*, 7 January 2019, available at http://www.xinhuanet.com/english/2019-01/07/c_137726534_10.htm.
7 D. Ren, "China's 'Dual-Credit' Policy that Spurred the EV Sector Will Be Revised in Bid to Ensure High Quality Growth," *South China Morning Post*, 28 November 2021.
8 D. Ren, "China's Electric Car Start-ups – NIO, Xpeng and WM Motor – Each Have a Big Tech Backer. What Is Riding on Their Success?" *South China Morning Post*, 29 December 2020.
9 J. Yang, "工信部部长苗圩:特斯拉带来竞争压力是好事" ["MIIT's Miao Wei: Good for Competition Coming from Tesla"], *China Securities Net*, 12 March 2019, available at https://www.cs.com.cn/xwzx/hg/201903/t20190312_5930204.html.
10 See https://worldjusticeproject.org/sites/default/files/documents/China_2021%20WJP%20Rule%20of%20Law%20Index%20Country%20Press%20Release_1.pdf.
11 D. Skidmore, "Understanding Chinese President Xi's Anti-Corruption Campaign," *The Conversation*, 27 October 2017, available at https://theconversation.com/understanding-chinese-president-xis-anti-corruption-campaign-86396.
12 B. Liu, "近 200 家车企大混战" ["Nearly 200 Car Companies Compete in the Electric Car – Knockout Race to Accelerate"], *Sina*, 17 March 2021, available at https://finance.sina.com.cn/tech/2021-03-17/doc-ikknscsi6524922.shtml.

13 S. Tabeta, "中国EV出现产能过剩隐忧，开工率或破 50%" ["Concern about Chinese EV's Oversupply, Utilization Rate May Fall Below 50%"], *Nikkei Chinese*, 17 May 2022, available at https://cn.nikkei.com/china/ccompany/48533-2022-05-17-05-00-55.html.

References

Amsden, A. (1989) *Asia's Next Giant: South Korea and Late Industrialization*. New York City: Oxford University Press.

Barwick, P. J., Cao, S. and Li, S. (2017) "Local Protectionism, Market Structure, and Social Welfare: China's Automobile Market," *National Bureau of Economic Research, Working Paper No. 23678*.

Bell, D. A. (2015) *The China Model: Political Meritocracy and the Limits of Democracy*. Princeton: Princeton University Press.

Blanchette, J. (2020) "From 'China Inc.' to 'CCP Inc.': A New Paradigm for Chinese State Capitalism," *China Leadership Monitor*, Vol. 66, pp. 1–13.

Block, F. (2008) "Swimming against the Current: The Rise of a Hidden Developmental State in the United States," *Politics & Society*, Vol. 36, No. 2, pp. 169–206.

Breslin, S. (2011) "The 'China Model' and the Global Crisis: From Friedrich List to a Chinese Mode of Governance?," *International Affairs*, Vol. 87, No. 6, pp. 1323–1343.

Breslin, S. (2021) *China Risen?: Studying Chinese Global Power*. Bristol: Bristol University Press.

Carroll, T. (2017) "Late Capitalism and the Shift from the Developmental State to the Variegated Market State," in Carroll, T. and Jarvis, D. (Eds) *Asia after the Developmental State – Disembedding Autonomy*. Cambridge: Cambridge University Press.

Chan, C. K. and Ngok, K. (2016) "Workfare in the Undemocratic States: The Case of China," *International Social Work*, Vol. 59, No. 4, pp. 479–493.

Chen, B., Midler, C. and Ruet, J. (2018) "The Development of Electric Vehicles in China: Market Facts and Regulatory Trends," *Gérer & Comprendre, English Language Online Selection*, No. 4, pp. 1–10, available at: https://annales.org/gc/GC-english-language-online-selection/2018/1ChenEtAl.pdf.

Chin, G. T. (2010) *China's Automotive Modernization – The Party-State and Multinational Corporations*. New York City: Palgrave Macmillan.

Duckett, J. (2020) "Neoliberalism, Authoritarian Politics and Social Policy in China," *Development and Change*, Vol. 51, No. 2, pp. 523–539.

Fallows, J. (1989) "Containing Japan," *The Atlantic Monthly*, May, pp. 40–54.

Fukuyama, F. (1995) *Trust, the Social Virtues and the Creation of Prosperity*. New York City: The Free Press.

Gong, H., Wang, M. and Wang, H. (2013) "New Energy Vehicles in China: Policies, Demonstration, and Progress," *Mitigation and Adaptation Strategies for Global Change*, Vol. 18, No. 2, pp. 207–228.

Gotoh, F. (2021) "Social Norms and (De-)Financialization: Japan's and China's Divergent Paths in Consumer Credit," *Contemporary Politics*, Vol. 27, No. 4, pp. 397–418.

Gruin, J. (2019) *Communists Constructing Capitalism – State, Market, and the Party in China's Financial Reform*. Manchester: Manchester University Press.

Harvey, D. (2005) *A Brief History of Neoliberalism*. Oxford: Oxford University Press.

Hofstede, G. (2015) "National Differences in Communication Styles," in Brzozowska, D. and Chlopicki, W. (Eds) *Culture's Software – Communication Styles*. Newcastle upon Tyne: Cambridge Scholars Publishing.
Ikenberry, G. J. (2018) "The End of Liberal International Order?," *International Affairs*, Vol. 94, No. 1, pp. 7–23.
Jin, L., He, H., Cui, H., Lutsey, N., Wu, C., Chu, Y., Zhu, J., Xiong, Y. and Liu, X. (2021) *Driving a Green Future: a Retrospective Review of China's Electric Vehicle Development and Outlook for the Future*. The International Council on Clean Transportation, available at https://theicct.org/publications/china-green-future-ev-jan2021.
Jing, S. and Luo, L. (1978) *Landlord and Labor in Late Imperial China: Case Studies from Shandong*. Cambridge (MA): Harvard University Press.
Johnson, C. (1982) *MITI and the Japanese Miracle: The Growth of Industrial Policy, 1925–1975*. Stanford: Stanford University Press.
Jones, L. and Hameiri, S. (2021) *Fractured China – How State Transformation Is Shaping China's Rise*. Cambridge: Cambridge University Press.
Kennedy, S. (2010) "The Myth of the Beijing Consensus," *Journal of Contemporary China*, Vol. 19, No. 65, pp. 461–477.
Kim, M-H. (2019) "A Real Driver of US–China Trade Conflict: The Sino–US Competition for Global Hegemony and Its Implications for the Future," *International Trade, Politics and Development*, Vol. 3, No. 1, pp. 30–40.
Knight, J. B. (2014) "China as a Developmental State," *World Economy*, Vol. 37, No. 10, pp. 1335–1347.
Kroeber, A. R. (2020) *China's Economy – What Everyone Needs to Know* (Second Edition). Oxford: Oxford University Press.
Leftwich, A. (1995) "Bringing Politics Back in – Towards a Model of the Developmental State," *Journal of Development Studies*, Vol. 31, No. 3, pp. 400–427.
Li, W., Yang, M. and Sandu, S. (2018) "Electric Vehicles in China: A Review of Current Policies," *Energy & Environment*, Vol. 29, No. 8, pp. 1512–1524.
Lindblom, C. E. (1977) *Politics and Markets: The World's Political-Economic Systems*. New York City: Basic Books.
Luo, Y. (2007) *Guanxi and Business* (Second Edition). Singapore: World Scientific Publishing.
Mazzucato, M. (2013) *The Entrepreneurial State: Debunking Public vs Private Sector Myths*. London: Anthem Press.
McNally, C. A. (2011) "China's Changing *Guanxi* Capitalism: Private Entrepreneurs between Leninist Control and Relentless Accumulation," *Business and Politics*, Vol. 13, No. 2, pp. 1–29.
Mearsheimer, J. J. (2010) "The Gathering Storm: China's Challenge to US Power in Asia," *The Chinese Journal of International Politics*, Vol. 3, No. 4, pp. 381–396.
Meier, N. (2009) *China – The New Developmental State? – An Empirical Analysis of the Automotive Industry*. Frankfurt am Main: Peter Lang.
Meltzer, J. P. and Shenai, N. (2019) "The US–China Economic Relationship – A Comprehensive Approach," *Global Economy and Development at Brookings and American Enterprise Institute*, available at https://ssrn.com/abstract=3357900.
Milanovic, B. (2019) *Capitalism, Alone: The Future of the System That Rules the World*. Cambridge (MA): Harvard University Press.
Ministry of Commerce (2018) "外商投资准入特别管理措施 (负面清单)(2018年版)" ["Special Administrative Measures on Access to Foreign Investment

(Negative List) (2018 Version)"], available at: http://images.mofcom.gov.cn/wzs/201806/20180628222647715.pdf.

Ministry of Finance (2015) "关于 2016–2020 年新能源汽车推广应用财政支持政策的通知" ["Notice on Financial Policies for New Energy Vehicle Promotion during 2016–2020"], available at http://www.gov.cn/xinwen/2015-04/29/content_2855040.htm.

Ministry of Industry and Information Technology (2017) "汽车产业中长期发展规划" ["Medium- and Long-Term Development Plan for the Automotive Industry"], available at https://www.most.gov.cn/xxgk/xinxifenlei/fdzdgknr/fgzc/gfxwj/gfxwj2017/201705/t20170517_132856.html.

Ministry of Industry and Information Technology (2019) "关于2016及以前年度新能源汽车推广应用补助资金初步审核情况的公示" ["Public Announcement on the Preliminary Review of Subsidies for the Promotion and Application of New Energy Vehicles in 2016 and Previous Years"], available at https://www.miit.gov.cn/gzcy/yjzj/art/2020/art_9d9989f446684639bf222bce8dc82f23.html.

Miura, M. (2012) *Welfare through Work – Conservative Ideas, Partisan Dynamics, and Social Protection in Japan*. Ithaca (NY): Cornell University Press.

Miyakawa, H. (1955) "An Outline of the Naito Hypothesis and its Effects on Japanese Studies of China," *Far Eastern Quarterly*, Vol. 14, No. 4, pp. 533–552.

Naughton, B. (2017) "Is China Socialist?," *Journal of Economic Perspectives*, Vol. 31, No. 1, pp. 3–24.

O'Riain, S. (2004) *The Politics of High Tech Growth – Developmental Network States in the Global Economy*. Cambridge: Cambridge University Press.

Pearson, M. M. (2019) "Local Government and Firm Innovation in China's Clean Energy Sector," in Brandt, L. and Rawski, T. G. (Eds) *Policy, Regulation, and Innovation in China's Electricity and Telecom Industries*. Cambridge: Cambridge University Press.

Pirie, I. (2018) "Korea and Taiwan: The Crisis of Investment-led Growth and the End of the Developmental State," *Journal of Contemporary Asia*, Vol. 48, No. 1, pp. 133–158.

Prestowitz, C. V. (1988) *Trading Places: How We Allowed Japan to Take the Lead*. New York City: Basic Books.

Ramo, J. C. (2004) *The Beijing Consensus*. London: Foreign Policy Centre.

State Council (2012) "节能与新能源汽车产业发展规划 (2012–2020 年)" ["Plan on Development of Energy-Saving and New Energy Auto Industry (2012–2020)"], available at http://www.gov.cn/zwgk/2012-07/09/content_2179032.htm.

State Council (2015) "中国制造 2025" ["Made in China 2025"], available at http://www.gov.cn/zhengce/content/2015-05/19/content_9784.htm.

State Council (2020) "新能源汽车产业发展规划 (2021–2035 年)" ["Plan on Development of New Energy Auto Industry (2021–2035)"], available at: http://www.gov.cn/zhengce/content/2020-11/02/content_5556716.htm.

Stubbs, R. (2018) *Rethinking Asia's Economic Miracle* (Second Edition). Basingstoke: Palgrave Macmillan.

Teece, D. J. (2020) "Fundamental Issues in Strategy: Time to Reassess," *Strategic Management Review*, Vol. 1, No. 1, pp. 103–144.

Thurbon, E. (2016) *Developmental Mindset: The Revival of Financial Activism in South Korea*. Ithaca (NY): Cornell University Press.

Tsai, K. S. and Naughton, B. (2015) "Introduction – State Capitalism and the Chinese Economic Miracle," in Naughton, B. and Tsai, K. S. (Eds) *State Capitalism,*

Institutional Adaptation, and the Chinese Miracle. Cambridge: Cambridge University Press.

Vogel, S. K. (2018) *Marketcraft: How Governments Make Markets Work*. Oxford: Oxford University Press.

Wade, R. (1990) *Governing the Market: Economic Theory and the Role of Government in East Asian Industrialization*. Princeton: Princeton University Press.

Wade, R. (2014) "The Paradox of US Industrial Policy: The Developmental State in Disguise," in José, M., Salazar-Xirinachs, J. M., Nübler, I. and Kozul-Wright, R. (Eds) *Transforming Economies – Making Industrial Policy Work for Growth, Jobs and Development*. Geneva: International Labour Office.

Wade, R. (2018) "The Developmental State: Dead or Alive?," *Development and Change*, Vol. 49, No. 2, pp. 518–546.

Weber, I. M. (2018) "China and Neoliberalism: Moving Beyond the China Is/Is not Neoliberal Dichotomy," in Cahill, D., Cooper, M., Konings, M. and Primrose, D. (Eds) *The SAGE Handbook of Neoliberalism*. London: SAGE Publications.

Whittaker, D. H., Sturgeon, T., Okita, T. and Zhu, T. (2020) *Compressed Development – Time and Timing in Economic and Social Development*. Oxford: Oxford University Press.

Wu, Y. A., Ng, A. W., Yu, Z., Huang, J., Meng, K., and Dong, Z. Y. (2021) "A Review of Evolutionary Policy Incentives for Sustainable Development of Electric Vehicles in China: Strategic Implications," *Energy Policy*, Vol. 148, Part B, 111983.

Yao, Y. (2015) "China's Approach to Economic Diplomacy," in Ikenberry, J., Jisi, W. and Feng, Z. (Eds) *America, China, and the Struggle for World Order – Ideas, Transitions, Historical Legacies, and Global Visions*. New York City: Palgrave Macmillan.

Yeung, H. W. C. (2004) *Chinese Capitalism in a Global Era: Towards a Hybrid Capitalism*. Abingdon: Routledge.

Zhang, C. (2019) "How Much Do State-Owned Enterprises Contribute to China's GDP and Employment?," *World Bank Working Paper*, available at https://openknowledge.worldbank.org/handle/10986/32306.

Zhang, X. and Bai, X. (2017) "Incentive Policies from 2006 to 2016 and New Energy Vehicle Adoption in 2010–2020 in China," *Renewable and Sustainable Energy Reviews*, Vol. 70, pp. 24–43.

3 Features of U.S. financial capitalism

Norbert Gaillard and Rick Michalek

We argue that, starting in the 1980s, U.S. traditional liberal capitalism has transformed into unstable financial capitalism. This evolution, largely driven by neoliberal ideas and massive deregulation, has led to the emergence of so-called too-big-to-fail banks, encouraged moral hazard and rent-seeking, distorted regulatory rules, exacerbated regulatory capture and arbitrage, intensified financial sophistication, shortened investment horizons, altered corporate governance and risk management, widened inequalities, and increased systemic risk in the United States and all around the world. Not only did credit rating agencies and the Federal Reserve (two long-time financial gatekeepers) fail to assess credit risk adequately and dangerously ease access to credit, but they also seemingly ignored the increasing proportion of firms and banks engaged in "speculative and Ponzi financing." The recurrent financial crises and the subsequent costly bailouts observed for several decades suggest that Eugene Fama's efficient market hypothesis has shown its limits while Hyman Minsky's financial instability hypothesis has gained ground. Lastly, the supposed complementarity of U.S. and Chinese economies, once advocated by some policy makers, hid the fundamental weaknesses of U.S. financial capitalism and accelerated the deindustrialization of the U.S. economy.

To Frank Capra's George Bailey

3.1 Introduction

U.S. traditional liberal capitalism has been transformed since the 1980s into an unstable financial capitalism. This evolution, largely driven by neoliberal ideas – especially the "Chicago School" ideology – has allowed, if not directly encouraged, moral hazard, itself spearheaded by the emergence of and culture within the so-called "too-big-to-fail" (TBTF) banks.

The key factors that have accelerated the financialization of the U.S. economy and the exportation of U.S. financial capitalism are as follows: the deregulation of the finance industry, the increased acceptance and even reliance on bailouts in response to individual corporate and industry failures, the

DOI: 10.4324/9781003340430-4

combined development of financial sophistication (e.g., complex structured finance and increasing exposure to compounded leverage via derivative products) and the concomitant bias toward ever shorter investment horizons, the technological advancements resulting in the commodification of investment products and the simultaneous development of consumers as assets, and finally, the consequent adaptation toward leniency by the regulatory community and the Federal Reserve (insofar as its monetary policy has tilted toward greater accommodation).

The United States acknowledges the impossibility of eliminating an apparently permanent budget deficit (with an ever increasing "debt ceiling") and instead focuses on the challenge of servicing the debt and managing the *comparative* value of the U.S. dollar. When, at the federal level, solvency only means having sufficient income to service periodic obligations, it is difficult to avoid a common culture that shares a similar perspective. And that culture accepts the increasing occurrence and presence of moral hazard even as it encourages rent-seeking, rather than value-adding, behavior.

Following the advent of globalization in the 1980s, the growth of the Chinese economy was long considered a unique opportunity for U.S. multinational companies (MNCs) to offshore a growing share of their business segments and increase their profitability so long as part of Chinese savings was funneled to purchase T-bonds and T-bills.[1] In fact, the supposed complementarity of U.S. and Chinese economies was a decoy that hid the fundamental weaknesses of U.S. financial capitalism. Counteracting this drift toward apparent optimality (wherein U.S. industrialization is offshored to lower cost labor and is supplanted by Western financial engineering) ultimately requires both political will and regulatory enforcement.

The remainder of this chapter is organized as follows. Section 3.2 examines the neoliberal roots of U.S. financial capitalism. Section 3.3 analyzes the dramatic changes in Wall Street culture. Section 3.4 focuses on the triumph of the finance industry. Section 3.5 shows that, in an increasingly cyclical economic and financial environment, the capital markets' gatekeepers have been unable to "stabilize an unstable economy." Section 3.6 argues that U.S. deindustrialization is a real phenomenon, but it is mitigated by the high profitability of large U.S. manufacturing firms. Section 3.7 concludes.

3.2 The neoliberal roots of U.S. financial capitalism

This section focuses on the most influential neoliberal publications that flourished in the 1970s and paved the way to U.S. financial capitalism from the 1980s. Five key issues and seven charismatic intellectuals are identified here.

3.2.1 Milton Friedman and the "social responsibility" of business

In 1970, the *New York Times* published Milton Friedman's seminal essay entitled "The Social Responsibility of Business to Increase Profits." This essay, which crystallized the principal theme of his 1962 book *Capitalism and Freedom* and has been cited favorably in numerous articles, can be seen as the inevitable reaction to the social and economic events of the period. Severe social upheavals in the late 1960s, including racial unrest and the growing demonstrations and turmoil in reaction to the Vietnam War, were bringing the corporate establishment into the crosshairs of popular culture even as policy makers were increasingly attempting to address each crisis with government intervention. The most striking sentences contained in Friedman's article may be the following ones:

> The businessmen believe that they are defending free enterprise when they declaim that business is not concerned "merely" with profit but also with promoting desirable "social" ends; that business has a "social conscience" and takes seriously its responsibilities for providing employment, eliminating discrimination, avoiding pollution and whatever else may be the catchwords of the contemporary crop of reformers. In fact they are – or would be if they or anyone else took them seriously – preaching pure and unadulterated socialism.

At the end of his essay, Friedman concludes that the only social responsibility of business is to "use its resources and engage in activities designed to increase its profits so long as it stays within the rules of the game, which is to say, engages in open and free competition without deception or fraud." One may assume that this last point was undoubtedly a key element in Friedman's thought, but Sections 3.4 and 3.5 suggest that it was dramatically overlooked by some U.S. firms.

3.2.2 George Stigler and the "regulation" problem

Like his friend Milton Friedman, George Stigler was an original attendee of the Mont Pelerin Society,[2] a member of the Chicago School, and a Nobel Prize winner. His work advocating for less governmental regulation is summarized in his 1975 book *The Citizen and the State: Essays on Regulation*. He developed the regulatory capture theory and, more controversially, stated that "regulation and competition are rhetorical friends and deadly enemies" (Stigler, 1975, p. 183).

Stigler also created an edited version of Adam Smith's *Wealth of Nations*, which removed substantially all of the tempering elements of Smith's analysis, including his recommendations for bank regulation, living wages for workers and the use of taxes for public works (Oreskes and Conway, 2023, p. 7). This edited version illustrates how neoliberal thinkers have managed to monopolize and distort seminal liberalism.

3.2.3 Aaron Director, Robert Bork, and the new "antitrust" approach

Another significant member of the Chicago School whose influence can still be felt was Aaron Director, a professor of law at the University of Chicago.

Considered a founder of the field of Law and Economics, he helped develop the "Antitrust Project," intending to rationalize U.S. antitrust law, arguing that monopolies are simply the survivors of competition and natural selection. One of Director's students was Robert Bork, whose 1978 book *The Antitrust Paradox* may have been the most significant work of that time. Bork (1978, p. 405) contends:

> The only goal that should guide interpretation of the antitrust laws is the welfare of consumers. Departures from that standard destroy the consistency and predictability of the law; run counter to the legislative intent, as that intent is conventionally derived; and damage the integrity of the judicial process by involving the courts in grossly political choices for which neither the statutes nor any other acceptable source provide any guidance.

Bork's doctrine involves that mergers should not be prevented and concentration in any industry should not be attacked provided consumer welfare is improved, especially through more efficient production processes. After teaching at Yale Law School, Bork served as judge on the U.S. Court of Appeals for the D.C. Circuit from 1982 to 1988. He used his antitrust arguments against U.S. Department of Justice prosecutions; his arguments continue to be referenced.[3]

3.2.4 Eugene Fama and the "efficient market hypothesis"

Eugene Fama – still another University of Chicago professor and Nobel laureate – is widely considered the "father of modern finance" for his promotion of the "efficient market hypothesis." Fama (1970) insists that capital markets are perfectly efficient as long as prices "fully reflect" available information. Fama's arguments have several shortcomings. First, he tends to underestimate the number of cases where investors or experts have monopolistic, oligopolistic, or privileged access to any information relevant for price formation. Put differently and as Grossman and Stiglitz (1980, p. 405) demonstrate, "because information is costly, prices cannot perfectly reflect the information which is available, since if it did, those who spent resources to obtain it would receive no compensation." Besides, under certain circumstances, the price mechanism may be "overwhelmed," which leads to price bubbles, price busts, herding, or contrarian behaviors (Avery and Zemsky, 1998).

3.2.5 The "Black–Scholes model"

In 1973, Fischer Black and Myron Scholes published their seminal paper on the valuation of derivatives, presenting their model for option pricing (Black and Scholes, 1973). The so-called "Black–Scholes model" introduced a new approach to analyzing securities: finance began to disaggregate corporate obligations and capital structures into respective separate "bundles of rights" and risk preferences that could be individually priced.[4]

A fundamental weakness of the Black–Scholes model lies in the assumption that the price of the risky asset follows a geometric Brownian motion. This assumption involves the persistent underestimation of infrequent but very risky events ("fat tails"), thus increasing the probability of financial crisis. The most remarkable criticism of the Black–Scholes model came from mathematician Benoit Mandelbrot (see Mandelbrot and Hudson, 2004).

Between Friedman's advocation for a more disciplined pursuit of profits, Stigler's anti-regulation stance, Bork's new antitrust approach, Fama's argument that stock prices reflect most if not all necessary information, and the Black–Scholes model, the Chicago School and its allies successfully infiltrated business school curriculums and helped to shape the future Wall Street culture (e.g., the maximization of shareholder value, the steady foreshortening of investment horizons, the overreliance on quantitative models, and the triumph of "money manager capitalism").

3.3 Wall Street culture

3.3.1 Maximizing shareholder value and the dominance of price over value

Maximizing shareholder value became the dominant focus, and in the 1980s, mergers and acquisitions, leveraged buyouts and hostile takeovers, with the goal of removing "inefficient management" became popular (Holmstrom and Kaplan, 2001). Investment banks catered to "corporate raiders," and premier law firms established "Mergers and Acquisitions" specialists to represent either the acquirer's pursuit or the target company's defense. Structured finance, and the early beginnings of "securitization," wherein new debt, supported by pools of purchased debt obligations, issued in different tranches (with each tranche entitled to different elements of the cashflow generated by the underlying pool) also began in the decade. This financial activity and sophistication created a significant demand for talent, and compensation at the finance houses and law firms accelerated well beyond prior growth rates (Greenwood and Scharfstein, 2013).

Corporate managers began to realize they could exploit an element of agency theory (i.e., a firm's success is optimized by ensuring that the interests of the managers are well aligned with those of the shareholders). By awarding themselves with additional compensation in the form of convertible options whose value was determined by the share price of the firm, the managers had a natural incentive to maximize the firm's share price. Bonus compensation became linked to annual and even quarterly results. Near-term performance outweighed long-term results. Managers also realized that by repurchasing shares of the corporation, they could increase the apparent quality of their financial reporting (e.g., earnings per share), which would accelerate share price improvement. Company boards began to link CEO compensation to price performance as well (Rappaport, 2005).

The cost, however, was the diversion of capital away from longer term projects and research and development (J.P. Morgan, 2014).[5] The manifestation of shorter investment horizons was not only seen in managerial behavior. Investors, too, have forgone long-term investments with share turnover steadily increasing. For example, average holding time for equity investors fell from 4 years in 1945 to less than 9 months in 2000. With high-frequency trading, the average holding time for an individual share dropped to 22 seconds in 2011 (Patterson, 2012).

The shift to shorter investment horizons has generated a vicious cycle: increased diversion of investment capital decreases the future returns from capital investment. This pressures management to seek new and additional short-term results. Share price becomes the cause, rather than the effect of manager behavior. At the individual and institutional investor level, the decreased holding time is logically correlated with a loss in the discipline expected from owner supervision. Consistent with Fama's arguments, price becomes the supervising agent. With price ascending to the key component of corporate management and institutional and individual investment, the dominance of immediate quantitative analysis, to the exclusion of longer-term considerations, fundamentally altered corporate governance and risk management.

3.3.2 Overreliance on quantitative models

The contribution of technology to the shift from qualitative to quantitative analysis deserves examination. While mainframe computers have been in use from the 1950s, electronic communication and decentralized computing did not penetrate Wall Street until the 1970s. Nasdaq, the original acronym for "National Association of Securities Dealers Automated Quotations," was a subsidiary of the National Association of Securities Dealers and launched the first electronic trading system in 1971.[6] Bond and equity traders traditionally operated with handheld calculators and paper and pencil analysis. The first spreadsheet program for microcomputers, Visicalc, written for the Apple and DOS operating systems, was not available until 1979 (Fridson, 2022). With the introduction of personal computers in the 1980s, the ability to assemble and manipulate an ever-larger amount of *data* shifted the financial analysts' pursuit away from the intangible and elusive concepts of *value* and toward the more easily attainable: prices and price history.

From 1980 to the dot-com bust in 2000, finance on Wall Street became dominated by the "quants." Math and engineering PhDs were recruited into the large investment banks and charged with implementing new financial models for the creation of innovative products to be sold to the yield and return-hungry investors seeking the highest possible "IRR."[7] The greatest concentration of the recruited quantitative modelers was found in structured finance – especially in the development of complex derivative debt instruments.

The seminal event on Wall Street that epitomized the culture shift toward quantification, and the intrinsic interlinking between markets and exchanges, was the October 19th, 1987 stock market crash that saw the Dow Jones Industrial Average drop 22.6% in a single day.[8] Not only did the 1987 crash reveal critical flaw in reliance on the Black–Scholes pricing model (due to its inherent assumption of lognormal price distribution), but it also demonstrated the law of unintended consequences. Concretely, market regulations required 1-day settlement for option trades, but 3-day settlement for stock trades. Market participants with theoretically hedged stock positions faced cash shortfalls for the settlement mismatch. An injection of liquidity in the afternoon of October 20th by the Federal Reserve helped to resolve the impasse (Bernhardt and Eckblad, 2013).[9]

The modeling of price histories and the use of quantitative models for predictive purposes became commonplace in the 1990s. While debt markets were expanding their offerings with new structured products and increasingly complex securitization offerings, "fundamental analysis" and value assessment based on traditional metrics of earnings and sales were being sidelined. Given the novelty of the emerging internet and the lack of any previous price histories, capital for the initial public offerings (IPO) of the startup technology companies was raised on the basis of the projections generated by the investment bankers, who were very happy to compare their projections to the oversubscribed and stratospheric projections of the latest IPO. Immediately prior to the collapse in March 2000, the price to earnings ratio of the Nasdaq Composite stock index reached 200 (the index itself had risen 400% over the preceding 5 years). In comparison, the Japanese Nikkei 225 index had peaked at 80 during the real estate asset price bubble of 1991 (Teeter and Sandberg, 2017).

The most glaring failure of quantitative risk modeling underlies the great financial crisis of 2008–2009. The topic has been exhaustively discussed in the literature (e.g., Rajan et al., 2015). In addition, overreliance on the (legally protected from negligence) opinions of the rating agencies combined (to everyone's disadvantage) with intentional dislocation of the responsibility for risk. The result of which was to ultimately require the taxpayers to pay for sustaining the financial system and endure, in many cases, permanent reductions in living standards (Gaillard and Michalek, 2019).

3.3.3 The "banking problem" and "money manager capitalism"

The financialization of the U.S. economy manifests also in the modern measurements of economic growth and reported profits. From the early 1980s, as regulations began to loosen (see Section 3.4.1), the reported profits of U.S. private sector financial institutions as a share of total corporate profits more than doubled to over 20%. At the same time, wages in the finance sector relative to total average wages in non-finance sector rose from 1:1 to approximately 1.7:1 (Mazzucato, 2018, p.139). With the finance sector representing an increasingly large proportion of total economic activity, there remains a question of accounting; a question of whether "banking & finance" truly is adding value – and thereby worthy of being counted as a product in gross domestic product (GDP) or whether it is simply extracting rents. This "banking problem" has long bothered economists. However, in 1993, the System of National Accounts (SNA), the internationally agreed set of recommendations on how to measure economic activity, was revised to count as value added the banking sector's financial intermediation services (i.e., maturity transformation, provision of liquidity, and credit assessment). The change was formally presented at the 2002 International Association of Official Statistics conference with most national accounting systems soon after recognizing financial intermediation as a contributor to domestic GDP (Fioramonti, 2013, p. 111).

With the formal acknowledgment of financial intermediation as a value adding activity, the way was clear for "asset management" to become a significant contributor to GDP, notwithstanding that only 15% of funds generated go to businesses in non-financial industries (Foroohar, 2016, p. 7). The activity of asset management is but one example of the steady transformation of *ownership* into fees, rents, and subscriptions. The investor is paying the asset manager a fee to manage property; in this case, the investor's purchased interest in a portfolio of financial assets. The aggregated change in the *price* of the assets in the portfolio, less the fees paid to the asset manager, will be returned to the investor upon disposition of that portfolio. The proceeds of that disposition will very likely never be delivered as cash, but instead will appear as a credit in the investor's bank, brokerage, or other financial institution account. That financial institution may collect fees for further transactions using those proceeds. And while nothing may actually be produced from this activity, the collected fees will count toward the nation's GDP.[10]

We turn now to the legislations, regulations, and policies that have consecrated the Wall Street culture and the finance industry since the 1980s. They have allowed and, in many ways, encouraged the emergence, and ultimately, the dominance of the too-big-to-fail and systemically important financial institutions. We also investigate the sources of growing systemic risk and instability inherent to U.S. financial capitalism.

3.4 The finance industry at its climax

3.4.1 Financial deregulation since the 1980s

Starting in the 1980s, influenced by neoliberal ideas and frequently working in a bipartisan manner, the U.S. Congress passed several laws that accelerated the transformation of the finance industry. Two major sets of legislations are briefly examined here.

The first series of laws are those designed to restore the profitability of financial institutions and avert their failure. The Depository Institutions Deregulation and Monetary Control Act of 1980 phased out interest rate ceilings on deposits to boost savings and increased the deposit insurance coverage offered by the Federal Deposit Insurance Corporation (FDIC). The Garn–St Germain Depository Institutions Act of 1982 allowed banks to provide adjustable-rate mortgage loans in order to revitalize the housing industry. The International Lending Supervision Act of 1983 required federal banking agencies to establish capital requirements.[11] The Financial Institutions Reform, Recovery, and Enforcement Act of 1989 enhanced the status of the FDIC as top supervisory authority over savings and loan associations (S&Ls).[12] The Emergency Economic Stabilization Act of 2008 authorized the Treasury to spend up to $700 billion to purchase non-performing assets from banks and supply them with cash, which was akin to a global bailout of the financial system. Lastly, the Dodd-Frank Wall Street Reform and Consumer Protection Act of 2010, among many other provisions, was intended to reinforce the oversight and supervision of TBTF banks and impose more stringent regulatory capital requirements.

The second set of laws involves the "decompartmentalization" process of banks' activities. The Riegle-Neal Interstate Banking and Branching Efficiency Act of 1994 permitted adequately capitalized and managed banks to acquire competitors in any state. The Gramm-Leach-Bliley Act of 1999 repealed the Glass Steagall Act of 1933, thus allowing investment banks, commercial banks, securities firms, and insurance companies to consolidate beyond their traditional core business.[13] It is interesting that Congressmen invoked economic efficiency and consumer welfare – two of Bork's arguments – when they passed the Gramm-Leach-Bliley Act (Kress, 2022, pp. 550–551).

3.4.2 *The finance industry is only moderately concentrated*

All this legislation reshaped the landscape of the finance industry. During 1980–2019, a total of 2939 banks and thrifts failed (12 times as many as during the previous four decades) and more than 16,000 bank mergers were registered.[14] The higher concentration of the sector can be illustrated in several manners.

The most common measurement is banks' assets. The top 10 banks accounted for 60% of total industry assets in 2021, compared to 27% 30 years earlier (Federal Reserve Bank of New York, 2022, pp. 37–38). Although the expansion of the 10 largest institutions was spectacular during 1991–2009, that cohort continued to acquire competitors in recent years. For example, PNC Financial Services (ninth largest U.S. bank) purchased RBC Bank (USA) and BBVA USA in 2012 and 2021, respectively. Leader JPMorgan

Chase (2022, p. 61) has rather prioritized the acquisition of financial technology companies.

A second measurement involves examining the underwriting business of financial firms' debt. This activity is crucial as financial institutions issued around 32% of total U.S. public firm debt during 1979–2014. Becher et al. (2015) find that the share of debt underwritten by top 10 banks increased from 53% during 1979–1999 to 74% during 2000–2014. In addition, the likelihood for a bank to underwrite the debt issued by another bank plummeted dramatically during the post-Gramm-Leach-Bliley Act years. In the early 1980s, more than 80% of issues were underwritten by a rival of the debt issuer. In the early 2010s, around 90% of deals were underwritten by the issuer itself, typically an institution ranked in the top 10.[15]

These two criteria tend to support the view that the finance industry is highly concentrated. This is untrue: this sector does *not* pose antitrust problems. An important tool on which the U.S. Justice Department relies to predict whether a merger may substantially lessen competition is the Herfindahl–Hirschman Index (HHI).[16] This index may range from zero to 10,000. A market is "moderately concentrated" if the HHI is between 1,500 and 2,500 points and "highly concentrated" if it exceeds 2,500 points.[17] The HHI in the financial sector is 824 or 719, whether we consider the market share of U.S. banks by assets or financial firms' debt underwritten. These scores reflect a competitive market and are by far lower than the HHI observed in the automobile industry at any point in the past six decades.[18]

3.4.3 "TBTF" is the fundamental problem

We argue that the main challenge presented by the finance industry is not its degree of concentration but rather the characteristics of big banks, especially their overall size, their complexity, and their interconnectedness with other financial institutions. Because of the critical functions performed by banks in the economy, these idiosyncrasies have encouraged risk taking and moral hazard and generated systemic risk.

The privileged status of the finance industry emerged at the dawn of the international debt crisis of 1982. In order to save those U.S. banks heavily exposed to Latin American debt, the Reagan administration prompted coordinated efforts by the International Monetary Fund (IMF), debtor countries, official creditors, and financial institutions. The sovereign debt restructurings and the granting of new loans averted systemic risk (Cline, 1984). 2 years later, the costly rescue of Continental Illinois, a major commercial and industrial lender, led the Comptroller of the Currency to admit that some banks were "too big to fail" due to the impact that their failure would have on the whole financial system. This announcement fostered moral hazard and institutionalized bailouts (Gaillard and Michalek, 2022). From then on, the top objective of U.S. banks was to take advantage of this new "moral hazard" paradigm by starting a *race to bigness* to become TBTF (Wilmarth Jr., 2002).

This *race*, expedited by the wave of deregulation and financial sophistication observed since the 1980s, has resulted in several evolutions.

The first changes involve the heightened scale and scope of the banking sector. The total amount of assets held by all commercial banks increased tenfold between 1984 and 2021 while the U.S. GDP jumped by a factor of 6. Next, the complexity of the largest banks has reached inconceivable proportions. For example, the number of domestic and foreign subsidiaries of JPMorgan Chase rose from 51 in 1986 to 3,391 in 2011.[19] Interconnectedness has intensified dramatically, being either direct – through interbank loans, syndicated loans or bonds to the same corporate or sovereign debt issuers, securities holdings,[20] derivative contracts, etc. – or indirect – through the exposure to the same class of assets, as illustrated by the subprime crisis of 2007–2008.

The "race to be TBTF" has also caused a significant and durable degradation of *ethical standards* that the Dodd-Frank Act and public debates have not reversed. Intentional misconducts, fraudulent and abusive practices are rife, but the Justice Department shows reluctance to push for prosecution, thus suggesting that TBTF banks and their top executives enjoy some form of immunity (Wilmarth Jr., 2020, pp. 299–334).

These different factors coalesced to render systemic banks "too big to supervise" (Menand, 2018). In fact, the supervision of TBTF entities has suffered from four significant shortcomings. First, regulators struggle to adequately oversee banks. They lag behind the innovations and endeavors of the institutions which manage to expand their off-balance-sheet operations, manipulate derivatives transactions or foreign exchange markets, rig their leverage and risk-weighted capital requirements, etc. Second, regulators are sometimes subject to cognitive or cultural capture. The case of Alan Greenspan is very telling (see Cohn, 2019) but other illustrations can be found among those who served as U.S. Securities and Exchange Commission (SEC) Commissioners in the 2000s and 2010s. Third, the micro-prudential and macroprudential frameworks implemented decade after decade have not addressed the build-up of procyclical leverage (see Montanaro's chapter in this book). Fourth, the inexorable growth of the financial sector has meant that further materialization of systemic risk is likely to have increasingly devastating effects. This fear has led financial gatekeepers to sweeten their decisions and follow lenient policies to financial institutions and the investor community. These points are tackled now.

3.5 The illusory stabilization of an unstable economy

The systemic risk inherent to U.S. financial capitalism has deeply distorted the role, objectives, and practices of the two key U.S. financial gatekeepers, namely the Federal Reserve and credit rating agencies (CRAs).[21] Since the 1990s, those two have vainly attempted to stabilize an "unstable capitalist system" by making their decisions even more predictable and lenient to major investors.

3.5.1 Credit rating agencies

Since the advent of financial globalization, the credit rating industry has made significant efforts to enhance its communication and the transparency of its methodologies. The two major CRAs – Moody's and Standard & Poor's (S&P) – have progressively given up on assigning unsolicited ratings, which, in its heyday, contributed to improve information exchange with debt issuers.[22] They have also developed new tools to guide investors during the likely trajectory of credit ratings in the short and medium terms. In the aftermath of Penn Central's default in 1970, they launched short-term ratings. A decade later, Moody's and S&P started issuing rating reviews and outlooks.[23] These opinions are designed to enhance the consistency of credit ratings and help the investor community anticipate their direction.

Next, CRAs have made their rating process more formal than it was prior to the 1990s, involving meetings with key individuals at the debt issuer, extensive exchange of data and information, the establishment of a rating committee, and the possibility for the debt issuer to appeal the rating assigned. The transparency of rating methodologies has also become much more quantitative and detailed. Moody's and S&P rate "through the cycle" to (i) dampen ratings volatility and (ii) announce downgrades and upgrades only once changes in credit fundamentals are beyond doubt. This approach has been praised for ensuring the stability of ratings. Over the period 1999–2008, Moody's (2009) finds that just 4% of its corporate ratings experienced more-than-two-notch rating changes. In comparison, 49% of bond-yield implied ratings showed a greater than two-notch change during the same period. Similarly, rating reversals (i.e., an upgrade followed by a downgrade or vice versa within 12 months) affected only 1% of Moody's corporate issuers, vs. 82% for bond-yield implied ratings. In fact, the "through-the-cycle" methodologies sound like a reluctance to bear bad news or fear of triggering systemic risk despite the market's prior apparent awareness.

More worryingly, several initiatives launched by CRAs were designed to satisfy major debt issuers and investors. Consider the development of requests for comments and the CRAs offering ancillary business, especially in the structured finance (SF) segment. Requests for comments have enabled investors and bond issuers to influence, sweeten, and even oppose the methodology updates advanced by CRAs. A recent illustration hit the headlines in May 2022: S&P withdrew several proposals for new criteria regarding the rating of insurance and reinsurance companies after receiving negative feedback from the industry.[24] Pressures to shape CRAs' methodologies have been frequent since the 2000s.[25] Requests for comments have undoubtedly reflected the persistent leniency of CRAs vis-à-vis powerful lobbies and TBTF firms, and the inherent competition between the CRAs for market share.

Ancillary business has had even more dramatic consequences. Starting in the 1990s, CRAs collected high fees by advising financial intermediaries on how to securitize residential and commercial mortgages, auto loans, etc. and obtain a specific rating for the subsequent mortgage-backed securities, asset-backed securities, etc. These ancillary services generated conflicts of interest that were soon identified (see International Organization of Securities Commissions, 2004), but regulators failed to address the issue. As TBTF banks were simultaneously top lenders, originators, underwriters, sellers, and buyers, CRAs had no alternative except to inflate SF ratings in order to keep these "super" clients.[26] The abusive and dishonest practices by CRAs were made public after the subprime crisis broke out in July 2007. Senate and SEC investigations found that CRAs had used inaccurate rating models, succumbed to competitive pressures, deliberately underestimated credit risks due to mortgage fraud and lax underwriting standards, refrained from lowering thousands of SF ratings until mass downgrades became unavoidable and shocked financial markets (see U.S. Senate, 2011, pp. 243–317).

Despite the Dodd-Frank Act provisions imposing a stricter regulation of CRAs, inflated ratings have remained a major concern. For example, Gaillard and Harrington (2016) stress that SF ratings are still flawed because SF methodologies ignore the credit risk from bank counterparties to derivative contracts. The case of financial institutions' ratings is even more disturbing. The pretty high ratings assigned to TBTF financial institutions in the 1990s and 2000s were underpinned by the implicit government support in the event of a major turmoil. Following Lehman's collapse in September 2008, S&P considered that government bailouts were less likely and revised its bank methodology accordingly. Yet, it cut the ratings of JPMorgan Chase, Bank of America, Citigroup, Wells Fargo, Goldman Sachs, and Morgan Stanley by only one notch.[27] By March 2022, these TBTF banks had managed to preserve their ratings whereas the support by the U.S. administration was considered uncertain (S&P, 2022).

3.5.2 The Federal Reserve

The Federal Reserve had been, for the longest time, very reluctant to comment on future interest rates (Nelson, 2021). A significant drift was observed after the massive hikes in the fed funds rate announced in 1994 triggered a bond market debacle. That episode convinced Alan Greenspan, Federal Reserve Chairman during 1987–2006, that market expectations of Federal Open Market Committee's (FOMC) future actions were a key factor in transmitting monetary policy. In the following years, under the influence of Donald Kohn – secretary of the FOMC (1987–2002) and member of the Federal Reserve Board of Governors (2002–2010) – the FOMC espoused a gradual monetary policy by adjusting interest rates incrementally, through small or moderate moves in the same direction.[28]

A milestone was reached in August 2003. After cutting the fed funds rate to 1% but seeking to further stimulate the economy, the Federal Reserve policy makers stated: "in these circumstances, the Committee believes that policy accommodation can be maintained for a considerable period."[29] This announcement paved the way to the so-called "forward guidance," designed to inform and influence investors about the state of the economy in the short and medium terms and the likely future course of monetary policy. This novel communication tool was refined in the subsequent years with more precise dates provided for possible monetary tightening or easing (see Yellen, 2013).

However, one may raise doubt about the true objectives of the forward guidance, especially once the New York Fed's Open Market Trading Desk decided to survey primary dealers on economic, financial, and monetary issues. In these surveys, top investment banks and financial services companies are asked (among other questions) to estimate the most likely outcome for output and inflation and provide (for a series of possible ranges) the percent chance they attach to the federal funds target rate at the 12- and 24-month horizons. The latter question is puzzling as one may assume that Federal Reserve policy makers want to know precise market anticipations (if not preferences) before taking monetary policy decisions, which are expected to influence investors.

This perceptible paradigm shift where leaders become laggards is supported by the examination of primary dealers' forecasts of the fed funds rate target at the 12- and 18-month horizons during 2011–2018.[30] The fed funds rate was systematically in line with the primary dealers' consensus, except in 2015 and 2019 when the monetary policy turned to be *more* accommodative than expected the previous year. The increasingly accommodative stance by the Federal Reserve is mirrored in the constant decline in the average differential between the fed funds rate and the inflation rate, from 4.2 percentage points during 1980–1989, to 1.9 percentage points during 1990–1999, 0.1 percentage point during 2000–2009, and -1.2 percentage points during 2010–2019.[31]

The lenient monetary policy conducted between the mid-1990s and 2021 contributed to magnify the fundamental shortcomings of U.S. financial capitalism. First, it boosted the ratios of U.S. public and private non-financial debts to GDP from 40% and 97%, respectively, in 1980 to 117% and 150% in 2021.[32] Second, it favored consumption to the detriment of savings. Third, it sustained equity prices, which exacerbated inequalities (Domanski et al., 2016). Fourth, it contributed to greater spillover effects in speculative activities in capital markets (Demirer et al., 2021). Fifth, in connection with the previous point, it inevitably nurtured financial sophistication, leading to the development of products and deals likely to offer higher yields: asset- and mortgage-backed securities, and derivatives products since the 1990s, leverage loans since the 2000s, and crypto-assets since the 2010s. It is not surprising that the IMF (2019, pp. 39–50) warned, a few months prior to the outbreak of the COVID-19 pandemic, that the persistently low-interest-rate environment had negative implications for financial stability.

3.5.3 How CRAs and the Federal Reserve weakened the U.S. economy

The conclusion one can draw is that the efforts deployed by the CRAs and the Federal Reserve to stabilize U.S. financial capitalism were illusory and even counterproductive. The "through-the-cycle" methodologies and the ancillary business developed by CRAs as well as the unconventional monetary policy followed by the Federal Reserve had several dramatic consequences.

They show that long-time financial gatekeepers conceded independence and submitted to capital markets' preferences. A key question then arises: why did this evolution happen? The Federal Reserve's and CRAs' policies seem to have converged toward a form of "willful inertia." Their top objective was to postpone the occurrence of a "Minsky moment" that could foreshadow the materialization of systemic risk. In an increasingly financialized environment, the Federal Reserve and CRAs realized that systemic risk would involve increasingly costly bailouts. So, they did their best to (i) avoid antagonizing TBTF banks and other major investors and (ii) postpone market disruptions.

The problem is that their policies actually exacerbated the instability of the U.S. economy.[33] Not only did CRAs and the Federal Reserve fail to assess credit risk adequately and dangerously ease access to credit but they also increased the proportion of firms and banks engaged in what Minsky (1986, pp. 7–8) calls "speculative and Ponzi financing" to the detriment of traditional "hedge financing." On top of that, they encouraged morally hazardous behaviors among TBTF banks, leading to greater risk-taking and more frequent delinquent practices.

The recurrent financial crises and the subsequent increasingly costly bailouts suggest that Fama's efficient market hypothesis has shown its limits while Minsky's financial instability hypothesis has gained ground. In fact, U.S. capitalism seems to be more fragile today than 40 years ago. This evolution was fundamentally driven by the excessive financialization of the economy. This "preference for finance" – largely driven by neoliberal ideas – was also a key factor that transformed manufacturing and accelerated deindustrialization in the United States.

3.6 The mutation of U.S. manufacturing

The advent and progress of both globalization and U.S. financial capitalism have deeply transformed the U.S. manufacturing sector. Its robustness has been a controversial issue among policy makers and economists, thus revealing the complexity of the changes that have occurred so far.

3.6.1 Deindustrialization without manufacturing decline

Several figures support the view that manufacturing has been declining for four decades. First, the U.S. manufacturing trade surplus registered in 1980 (+0.4% of GDP) turned into a large deficit by 2019 (-3.6% of GDP), with China accounting for more than half of this deficit.[34] Second, the share of manufacturing in total U.S. nonfarm employment fell from 22% in 1979 to 8.5% in 2019. More than 6.7 million manufacturing jobs were lost in 40 years (Harris, 2020). This evolution has largely fed so called "Trumpism" since the mid-2010s. Third, General Motors and Ford, standard bearers of U.S. manufacturing, have languished. Their aggregated market share in the United States dropped from two thirds to one third between 1980 and 2019. General Motors defaulted during the great financial crisis of 2008–2009. Although they both benefitted from the government's Troubled Asset Relief Program, their prestige suffered.

This bleak picture of manufacturing must be mitigated. The sector represents 55% of patents and 70% of R&D spending in the United States (Carr et al., 2022), outperforming all job-creating sectors (e.g., trade, transport, utilities, construction, leisure, education and health services, professional, business, and financial services). Next, the biggest industrial firms have thrived dramatically. Table 3.1 presents the 25 most profitable U.S. firms among the Fortune 500 ranking. The proportion of manufacturing MNCs in the top 25 has remained stable since 1980 (almost 50%) but their profile has evolved. Automobile and chemical giants have been supplanted by firms specialized in pharmaceutical products, software, and high-technology services.[35] Besides, profits are now less correlated with revenue than they used to be.

Table 3.1 Most profitable U.S. companies among the Fortune 500 ranking

1980			*2020*		
Most profitable firms	*Profits ($ bil.)*	*Fortune 500 rank by revenue*	*Most profitable firms*	*Profits ($ bil.)*	*Fortune 500 rank by revenue*
1. Exxon	4.295	1	1. Berkshire Hathaway	81.417	6
2. IBM	3.011	8	2. Apple	55.256	4
3. General Motors	2.893	2	3. Microsoft	39.240	21
4. Mobil	2.007	3	4. JPMorgan Chase	36.431	17
5. Standard Oil of Cal.	1.785	6	5. Bank of America	27.430	25
6. Texaco	1.759	5	6. Intel	21.048	45
7. Standard Oil (Ind.)	1.507	10	7. Wells Fargo	19.549	30
8. General Electric	1.409	9	8. Citigroup	19.401	31
9. Gulf Oil	1.322	7	9. Verizon Com.	19.265	20
10. BP America	1.186	32	10. Facebook	18.485	46
11. Ford	1.169	4	11. Pfizer	16.273	64
12. Atlantic Richfield	1.166	12	12. Johnson & Johnson	15.119	35
13. Shell Oil (US)	1.126	13	13. Walmart	14.881	1

(*Continued*)

Table 3.1 (Continued)

1980			*2020*		
Most profitable firms	*Profits ($ bil.)*	*Fortune 500 rank by revenue*	*Most profitable firms*	*Profits ($ bil.)*	*Fortune 500 rank by revenue*
14. Eastman Kodak	1.001	30	14. Exxon Mobil	14.340	3
15. Du Pont de Nemours	0.939	16	15. Fannie Mae	14.160	24
16. Phillips Petroleum	0.891	22	16. AT&T	13.903	9
17. Continental Oil	0.815	15	17. UnitedHealth	13.839	7
18. Dow Chemical	0.784	24	18. Comcast NBCUniv.	13.057	28
19. Sunoco	0.700	20	19. Visa	12.080	137
20. 3M	0.655	51	20. Cisco	11.621	63
21. AT&T	0.636	19	21. Amazon	11.588	2
22. Getty Oil	0.604	62	22. Home Depot	11.242	26
23. Procter & Gamble	0.577	23	23. Oracle	11.083	82
24. Tenneco	0.571	18	24. Walt Disney	11.054	49
25. Xerox	0.563	40	25. Merck	9.843	69

Source: Fortune 500.

3.6.2 *The internationalization of U.S. manufacturing firms and its consequences*

Two series of factors have changed U.S. manufacturing most significantly. The first one encompasses all the technology breakthroughs (from information technology to artificial intelligence) that generated the so-called third and fourth industrial revolutions. These issues have already been addressed by Greenwood (1997) and Schwab (2017). The second one includes the development of free trade, the increasing mobility of capital, the reorganization of value chains, and the evolving nature of the largest firms' international activities. They are analyzed here.

Look first at the phenomenon of offshoring U.S. jobs. The number of manufacturing jobs in foreign affiliates of U.S. parents rose by 21% between 1982 and 2019, climbing from 4.43 million to 5.37 million. This modest increase of less than 1 million falls far short of explaining the 6.7 million jobs lost during this period. It is interesting that Mexico and China – frequently held responsible for the U.S. deindustrialization – respectively accounted for only 15% and 13% of manufacturing jobs in foreign affiliates of U.S. parents in 2019.[36] Rather than simply offshoring domestic jobs, U.S. industrialists have developed automation, enhanced labor productivity, operated in new activities requiring less labor and more capital, adopted ambitious outsourcing strategies, and participated in complex global value chains (Gaillard, 2020, pp. 70–71).[37]

Turn to the nature of U.S. direct investment abroad. If one takes into account the industry of the U.S. parent, the percentage of manufacturing in total direct investment abroad fell slightly from 54.5% in 1982 to 49.3% in 2021 but it stands far ahead of the banking, finance, and insurance sector (19.4%). However, if one examines the industry of affiliates, the share of manufacturing plummets while the category "holding companies" soars, representing nearly 50% of all U.S. direct investment abroad. In 2021, around 71.5% of manufacturing investments abroad involve financial and accounting operations.[38] They may consist of lending, borrowing, managing assets (such as patents, trademarks, and real estate), or underpaying corporate income tax. That more than 83% of investment in holding companies is concentrated in Ireland, Luxembourg, Singapore, Switzerland, the Netherlands, the United Kingdom, Bermuda, and the British Caribbean Islands suggests that tax optimization and possibly tax avoidance are primary objectives.[39] These presumptions are consistent with Wright and Zucman (2018) who find that the effective foreign tax rate paid by non-oil multinationals fell by half between the late 1990s and 2015.

Focus lastly on trade patterns of U.S. manufacturing firms. A key feature is the trade capacity of U.S. affiliates. In 2007, the sales by foreign-based affiliates of U.S. manufacturing MNCs to foreign buyers was more than four times as large as merchandise exports by all U.S.-based manufacturing firms. A complementary feature is the different dynamics between small- and medium-sized enterprises (SMEs) and large firms. In 2007, around 81% of foreign sales by SMEs consisted of traditional exports from within the United States. In contrast, 89% of foreign sales by large firms were registered through their affiliates abroad.[40] This dichotomy has had important implications in the context of volatile exchange rates observed for several decades. The appreciation of the U.S. dollar during recessions has more procyclical and damaging effects for SMEs than MNCs. This sheds new light on the debate on trade deficit and currency manipulation (see Gagnon, 2020). If one assumes that it remains a key issue, cutting the U.S. trade deficit entails (among other measures) a stronger support to SMEs. Next, currency manipulation exists, but this problem should be kept in perspective. The relative "over appreciation" of the dollar in the long run has contributed to decrease the price of foreign assets for U.S. firms. To sum up, the international status of the dollar and the financialization of the U.S. economy have supported the expansion of MNCs but hampered the business of SMEs.

The changes experienced by the U.S. manufacturing sector are impressive. Today, large companies are much more capital-intensive and internationalized than 40 years ago. Their growing financial activities through their affiliates abroad have ensured them a greater profitability. The position of SMEs is radically different: they have little leeway for tax optimization, struggle to borrow at low interest rates (IMF, 2019, p. 32) and those able to export their products remain vulnerable to the dollar appreciation. This two-speed manufacturing echoes what can be observed in the banking sector between TBTF banks and all other financial establishments.

3.7 Conclusion

We have argued the financialization of U.S. capitalism has its roots in the neoliberal influences of the Chicago School and its mission to reduce regulatory and governmental interference with business. Further, we have shown how technological advancements and the elevation of the importance of "price" over that of "value" were well correlated. We also have shown that the drive for maximum share value enabled a shift in corporate governance with management benefitting, and increased mergers and acquisitions flourishing. The development and use of tools in furtherance of those objectives generated Wall Street's demand for quantitative experts. That development, with the disaggregation of capital structures, ushered in securitization and its designed dislocation of originator and intermediary liabilities. We discussed the laggard gatekeepers, the CRAs and the Federal Reserve, and their contributions to enabling, rather than regulating and constraining, excessive risk in the U.S. financial system. Lastly, we exposed, by describing the deindustrialization of the U.S. manufacturing and the asymmetrical impact on SMEs and MNCs, the fallacy within the argument that U.S. offshoring of labor and business segments is justified by the dollar appreciation and China's competition.

Perhaps nothing more effectively demonstrates several of the features and flaws of U.S. capitalism than the recent (as of this writing) failure of Silicon Valley Bank (SVB). A favored lender of the start-up technology community eponymous with Silicon Valley, SVB held the deposits of both Silicon Valley venture capitalists, and the successfully funded corporations they had ushered through IPO. It was reported that, among many others, one company, Roku, Inc. had deposits of $487 million at SVB at the time of its closure. By law, the FDIC guarantees only the first $250,000 of a depositor's funds. While SVB managers erred in failing to monitor duration risk on its unhedged "available for sale" securities during the Fed's unprecedented raising of interest rates (started in March 2022), they correctly predicted that the government would not let SVB default or leave its depositors helpless in the face of a consequential liquidity crisis that would quickly spread throughout the technology industry, a significant pillar to the U.S. economy.[41] After this umpteenth morally hazardous episode, we fear that the next financial crisis – especially if it involved a TBTF bank – may lead to a major systemic turmoil.

More insidiously, U.S. financial capitalism has also distorted the notion of "ownership," which is beginning to disappear from the accounts of the consumer. The percentage of home ownership per age cohort has been declining over the past 20 years, with the most significant declines occurring after the 2008 financial crisis.[42] With the migration trends toward urban areas, and the emergence of car services such as Lyft and Uber, an increasing number of young people are eschewing car ownership altogether.[43] Other examples of the "don't own, pay as you use" approach to consumption can be seen in mobile phones (where consumers see an "amortization" of the purchase price of their chosen device in the monthly bill, but with no upfront outlay), vacation homes, entertainment, healthcare (in the form of an annual fee for "concierge services"), delivery services (ranging from package delivery that is billed annually as part of a subscription to an online shopping application, to food delivery for both prepared meals and groceries, to the delivery of internet access itself). There are online applications for even clothing, where members can rent their wardrobe and exchange clothes every season to access current fashions. The operators of these services extract rents with price increases as consumers transfer wealth (obtained through their labor) to the owners of the service companies and product producers. With the population's increasing involvement with, and convenience from, technology, rent-seeking is becoming the dominant business model in U.S. capitalism. This shift is enlarging the income and equality gap as the owners of capital and assets exercise their rent-seeking abilities as the labor class continues to shift away from asset ownership. We can reasonably raise doubt about the future of this economic and financial system.

Notes

1 Gotoh and Li's chapter in this book analyzes the features of Chinese capitalism.
2 The founding meeting of the Mont Pelerin Society in 1947, organized by Friedrich von Hayek, the Austrian economist then teaching at the London School of Economics, included a veritable "who's who" of the leading figures advocating for a new liberalism. Hayek had attained international recognition with his publication of *The Road to Serfdom* and its republication in a popularized form by Reader's Digest.
3 C. Kang, "Judge Throws Out 2 Antitrust Cases against Facebook," *New York Times*, 28 June 2021.
4 The use of derivative contracts can be traced back thousands of years. However, modern use and the creation of new complex derivatives is largely coincident with the development and use of the computer in the 1970s which enabled processing of complex computations that were previously impractical. Futures contracts on financial instruments were first launched in 1972 by the Chicago Mercantile Exchange, and futures on interest rate contracts were first allowed by the Chicago Board of Trade in 1975 (Kummer and Pauletto, 2012, p. 12).
5 J. P. Morgan (2014) compares weighted average cost of capital for S&P 500 companies to median hurdle rates for new projects and finds that the latter require a 10% premium.
6 See https://www.nasdaq.com/articles/nasdaq%3A-50-years-of-market-innovation-2021-02-11.
7 IRR, or internal rate of return, is the metric used to evaluate the profitability of an investment opportunity. With a very high IRR, an investor can recover his original capital outlay in a relatively short period of time.

8 Portfolio insurance, which involves purchasing or selling index and futures equity and commodity options to hedge against price movements in one's "portfolio" of underlying securities, is considered a key cause of the 1987 crash. Price declines (amplified by the lack of liquidity from settlement mismatch resulting in a lack of "bids") triggered additional sales by portfolio insurers, which in turn caused further price declines (Shiller, 1988, pp. 287–297).
9 On the one hand, with its emergency injection of liquidity, the Federal Reserve has reinforced the market's perception of its role as domestic and later global lender of last resort (Bank for International Settlements, 2014). On the other hand, as analyzed in Section 3.5.2, the accommodative monetary policy followed by the Federal Reserve has sustained equity prices and nurtured spillover effects in speculative activities. These two trends have combined and contributed to a culture favorable for moral hazard.
10 Minsky (1992) describes more fully his term "money manager capitalism." See also Montanaro's chapter in this book.
11 Later, this task was partly devolved to the Basel Committee on Banking Supervision through the enactment of so-called "Basel rules."
12 This legislation was in response to the many S&Ls that were bankrupted by unsound real estate lending.
13 As early as 1998, the Federal Reserve had approved the merger between Travelers Group (a holding company for securities, insurance, and other financial services firms) and Citicorp (a commercial bank).
14 See https://www.bankingstrategist.com.
15 One may assume that the Gramm-Leach-Bliley Act enabled banks to enhance their expertise on a wider array of financial activities, which encouraged self-underwriting.
16 The HHI is calculated by squaring the market share of each firm and then summing the resulting numbers.
17 https://www.justice.gov/atr/herfindahl-hirschman-index.
18 Authors calculations based on Becher et al. (2015), Federal Reserve Bank of New York (2022), and https://www.aei.org/carpe-diem/animated-chart-of-the-day-market-shares-of-us-auto-sales-1961-to-2016.
19 See J. P. Morgan (1987), pp. 76–77 and Avraham et al. (2012), p. 71.
20 JPMorgan Investment Management is among the top 10 owners of Bank of America, Wells Fargo, Morgan Stanley, and PNC Financial Services Group. Cross shareholding is also common (e.g., between JPMorgan Chase, Morgan Stanley, and their respective asset-management subsidiaries). See https://money.cnn.com.
21 Gaillard and Michalek (2019) explore how U.S. financial gatekeepers, called the "sweeteners," encouraged moral hazard in the 1990s and 2000s, which exacerbated the financial crisis of 2007–2009.
22 This evolution meant a shift from the investor-pay to the issuer-pay model.
23 A review indicates that a rating is under consideration for a change in the very short term whereas an outlook is an opinion regarding the probable rating direction over the short to medium term.
24 See *Reinsurance News*, "S&P drops new ratings criteria after industry criticism," 9 May 2022.
25 Based on authors' interviews with former CRAs' analysts.
26 Inflated ratings are dangerously procyclical. During low risk-aversion periods, they reduce risk premia for issuers, lower capital requirements for investors, broaden the marketability of rated debt, encourage risk taking and leverage. When a significant economic downturn materializes, the number and the magnitude of downgrades are inevitably greater.
27 *Reuters*, "S&P cuts ratings on big banks after criteria change," 30 November 2011.

28 Kohn's influence was obvious in 2001 when the Federal Reserve started reducing the fed funds rate; see the transcripts of the FOMC meetings held in March, June, and November 2001.
29 The transcript of the FOMC meeting held in August 2003 shows how carefully this sentence was worded.
30 The forecasts released in 2018 for the year 2020 are not examined due to the advent of the COVID-19 pandemic.
31 Authors' calculations based on Federal Reserve data.
32 https://www.federalreserve.gov/releases/z1/dataviz/z1/nonfinancial_debt/chart
33 Even gradualism – a rather uncontroversial monetary policy tool – tends to support our view. Indeed, Stein and Sunderam (2018) show that markets rationally react *more* to a given change in the monetary policy when Federal Reserve moves are more gradual.
34 Authors' calculations based on Census Bureau data.
35 It is also noticeable that oil companies have moved down and been replaced with financial institutions.
36 All the percentages provided in this paragraph are authors' calculations based on Bureau of Economic Analysis (1985 and 2021).
37 This evolution is partly reflected in the "profit per employee" ratio posted by the most profitable "Fortune 500" manufacturing firm at the dawn of globalization and today. This ratio jumped from $9,000 in 1980 (IBM) to $400,000 in 2020 (Apple).
38 This percentage was only 26% in 1982.
39 All the percentages provided in this paragraph are authors' calculations based on Bureau of Economic Analysis (1985 and 2022).
40 The figures provided in this paragraph are based on U.S. International Trade Commission (2010).
41 E. Helmore, "US Guarantees All Deposits After Silicon Valley Bank Collapse, as Biden Promises Action," *The Guardian*, 12 March 2023.
42 https://ipropertymanagement.com/research/homeownership-rate-by-age
43 M. Timmons, "Car Ownership Statistics in the U.S.," *ValuePenguin*, 17 August 2022, available at https://www.valuepenguin.com/auto-insurance/car-ownership-statistics.

References

Avery, C. and Zemsky, P. (1998) "Multidimensional Uncertainty and Herd Behavior in Financial Markets," *American Economic Review*, Vol. 88, No. 4, pp. 724–748.

Avraham, D., Selvaggi, P. and Vickery, J. (2012) "A Structural View of U.S. Bank Holding Companies," *FRBNY Economic Policy Review*, Vol. 18, No. 2, July, pp. 65–81.

Bank for International Settlements (2014) "Re-Thinking the Lender of Last Resort," *BIS Papers No. 79*.

Becher, D. A., Gordon, R. E. and Juergens, J. L. (2015) "Why Hire Your Rival? The Case of Bank Debt Underwriting," available at https://files.fisher.osu.edu/department-finance/public/why_hire_your_rival._the_case_of_bnk_debt_underwriting.pdf.

Bernhardt, D. and Eckblad, M. (2013) "Stock Market Crash of 1987," available at https://www.federalreservehistory.org/essays/stock-market-crash-of-1987.

Black, F. and Scholes, M. (1973) "The Pricing of Options and Corporate Liabilities," *Journal of Political Economy*, Vol. 81, No. 3, pp. 637–654.

Bork, R. H. (1978) *The Antitrust Paradox*. New York City: Free Press.

Bureau of Economic Analysis (1985) *U.S. Direct Investment Abroad: 1982 Benchmark Survey Data*. U.S. Department of Commerce.
Bureau of Economic Analysis (2021) *Activities of U.S. Multinational Enterprises, 2019*. U.S. Department of Commerce.
Bureau of Economic Analysis (2022) *Direct Investment by Country and Industry, 2021*. U.S. Department of Commerce.
Carr, T., Chewning, E., Doheny, M., Madgavkar, A., Padhi, A. and Tingley, A. (2022) "Delivering the US Manufacturing Renaissance," *McKinsey & Co*, 29 August.
Cline, W. R. (1984) *International Debt: Systemic Risk and Policy Response*. Washington, DC: Institute for International Economics.
Cohn, T. H. (2019) "The Effects of Regulatory Capture on Banking Regulations: A Level-of-Analysis Approach," in Hira, A., Gaillard, N. and Cohn, T. H. (Eds) *The Failure of Financial Regulation – Why A Major Crisis Could Happen Again*. Cham: Palgrave Macmillan.
Demirer, R., Gabauer, D. and Gupta, R. (2021) "Monetary Policy and Speculative Spillovers in Financial Markets," *Research in International Business and Finance*, Vol. 56, April, 101373.
Domanski, D., Scatigna, M. and Zabai, A. (2016) "Wealth Inequality and Monetary Policy," *BIS Quarterly Review*, March, pp. 45–64.
Fama, E. F. (1970) "Efficient Capital Markets: A Review of Theory and Empirical Work," *Journal of Finance*, Vol. 25, No. 2, pp. 383–417.
Federal Reserve Bank of New York (2022) "Quarterly Trends for Consolidated U.S. Banking Organizations – First Quarter 2022," *Research and Statistics Group*.
Fioramonti, L. (2013) *Gross Domestic Problem: The Politics behind the World's Most Powerful Number*. London: Zed Books.
Foroohar, R. (2016) *Makers and Takers: How Wall Street Destroyed Main Street*. New York City: Crown.
Fridson, M. (2022) "When the Tech Revolution Came to Wall Street", *Stories. Finance*, available at https://www.stories.finance/stories/fridson.
Friedman, M. (1962) *Capitalism and Freedom*. Chicago: University of Chicago Press.
Gagnon, J. E. (2020) "Taming the US Trade Deficit: A Dollar Policy for Balanced Growth," *Peterson Institute for International Economics, Policy Brief*, 20–15.
Gaillard, N. (2020) *Country Risk: The Bane of Foreign Investors*. Cham: Springer.
Gaillard, N. and Harrington, W. J. (2016) "Efficient, Commonsense Actions to Foster Accurate Credit Ratings," *Capital Markets Law Journal*, Vol. 11, No. 1, pp. 38–59.
Gaillard, N. and Michalek, R. (2019) "How and Why Moral Hazard Has Distorted Financial Regulation," in Hira, A., Gaillard, N. and Cohn, T. H. (Eds) *The Failure of Financial Regulation – Why A Major Crisis Could Happen Again*. Cham: Palgrave Macmillan.
Gaillard, N. and Michalek, R. (2022) "The Institutionalization of Bailouts, 1970–1984," in Flores Zendejas, J., Gaillard, N. and Michalek, R. (Eds) *Moral Hazard – A Financial, Legal, and Economic Perspective*. Abingdon and New York City: Routledge.
Greenwood, J. (1997) *The Third Industrial Revolution: Technology, Productivity, and Income Inequality*. Washington, DC: American Enterprise Institute Press.
Greenwood, R. and Scharfstein, D. (2013) "The Growth of Finance," *Journal of Economic Perspectives*, Vol. 27, No. 2, pp. 3–28.
Grossman, S. J. and Stiglitz, J. E. (1980) "On the Impossibility of Informationally Efficient Markets," *American Economic Review*, Vol. 70, No. 3, pp. 393–408.

Harris, K. (2020) "Forty Years of Falling Manufacturing Employment," *Beyond the Numbers: Employment & Unemployment*, Vol. 9, No. 16. https://www.bls.gov/opub/btn/volume-9/forty-years-of-falling-manufacturing-employment.htm.

Holmstrom, B. and Kaplan, S. N. (2001) "Corporate Governance and Merger Activity in the United States: Making Sense of the 1980s and 1990s," *Journal of Economic Perspectives*, Vol. 15, No. 2, pp. 121–144.

International Monetary Fund (2019) *Global Financial Stability Report: Lower for Longer*. October. Washington, DC: IMF.

International Organization of Securities Commissions (2004) *A Consultation Report of the Chairmen's Task Force of the Technical Committee of the International Organization of Securities Commissions*.

J. P. Morgan (1987) *Annual Report 1986*.

J. P. Morgan (2014) "Bridging the Gap Between Interest Rates and Investment", *JPM Corporate Finance Advisors*, September.

JPMorgan Chase (2022) *2021 Annual Report*.

Kress, J. C. (2022) "Reviving Bank Antitrust," *Duke Law Journal*, Vol. 72, No. 3, pp. 519–598.

Kummer, S. and Pauletto, C. (2012) "The History of Derivatives: A Few Milestones," *paper presented at the EFTA Seminar on Regulation of Derivatives Markets*, Zurich, 3 May, available at https://www.researchgate.net/publication/349485381_The_History_of_Derivatives_A_Few_Milestones.

Mandelbrot, B. B. and Hudson, R. L. (2004) *The (Mis)Behavior of Markets – A Fractal View of Risk, Ruin, and Reward*. New York City: Basic Books.

Mazzucato, M. (2018) *The Value of Everything – Making and Taking in the Global Economy*. New York City: Public Affairs.

Menand, L. (2018) "Too Big to Supervise: The Rise of Financial Conglomerates and the Decline of Discretionary Oversight in Banking," *Cornell Law Review*, Vol. 103, No. 6, pp. 1527–1588.

Minsky, H. P. (1986) "Global Consequences of Financial Deregulation," *Hyman P. Minsky Archive, Paper 378*.

Minsky, H. P. (1992) "Schumpeter and Finance," *Hyman P. Minsky Archive, Paper 280*.

Moody's Investors Service (2009) *Are Corporate Bond Ratings Procyclical?: An Update*, May.

Nelson, E. (2021) "The Emergence of Forward Guidance as a Monetary Policy Tool," *Finance and Economics Discussion Series 2021-033, Board of Governors of the Federal Reserve System*.

Oreskes, N. and Conway, E. M. (2023) *The Big Myth – How American Business Taught us to Loathe Government and Love the Free Market*. New York City: Bloomsbury Publishing.

Patterson, S. (2012) *Dark Pools: The Rise of AI Trading Machines and the Looming Threat to Wall Street*. New York City: Random House.

Rajan, U., Seru, A. and Vig, V. (2015) "The Failure of Models that Predict Failure: Distance, Incentives, and Defaults," *Journal of Financial Economics*, Vol. 115, No. 2, pp. 237–260.

Rappaport, A. (2005) "The Economics of Short-Term Performance Obsession," *Financial Analysts Journal*, Vol. 61, No. 3, pp. 65–79.

Schwab, K. (2017) *The Fourth Industrial Revolution*. New York City: Currency Books.

Shiller, R. (1988) "Portfolio Insurance and Other Investor Fashions as Factors in the 1987 Stock Market Crash," in Fischer, S. (Ed) *NBER Macroeconomics Annual 1988, Volume 3*. Cambridge (MA) and London: MIT Press.

Standard & Poor's (2022) *Banking Industry Country Risk Assessment Update: March 2022*, 31 March.

Stein, J. C. and Sunderam, A. (2018) "The Fed, the Bond Market, and Gradualism in Monetary Policy," *Journal of Finance*, Vol. 73, No. 3, pp. 1015–1060.

Stigler, G. J. (1975) *The Citizen and the State: Essays on Regulation*. Chicago: University of Chicago Press.

Teeter, P. and Sandberg, J. (2017) "Cracking the Enigma of Asset Bubbles with Narratives," *Strategic Organization*, Vol. 15, No. 1, pp. 91–99.

U.S. International Trade Commission (2010) *Small and Medium-Sized Enterprises: Characteristics and Performance*. Investigation No. 332-510, USITC Publication 4189.

U.S. Senate (2011) *Wall Street and the Financial Crisis: Anatomy of a Financial Collapse*. Permanent Subcommittee on Investigations. 13 April.

Yellen, J. (2013) "Communication in Monetary Policy," *Remarks at Society of American Business Editors and Writers 50th Anniversary Conference, Washington, DC.*

Wilmarth Jr., A. E. (2002) "The Transformation of the U.S. Financial Services Industry, 1975–2000: Competition, Consolidation, and Increased Risks," *University of Illinois Law Review*, Vol. 2002, No. 2, pp. 215–476.

Wilmarth Jr., A. E. (2020) *Taming the Megabanks: Why We Need a New Glass-Steagall Act*. Oxford and New York City: Oxford University Press.

Wright, T. and Zucman, G. (2018) "The Exorbitant Tax Privilege," *NBER Working Paper No. 24983*.

Part II

The flaws in the multilateral system

4 Free riding on the surplus of trade

China, the WTO, and Western acquiescence

Robert Gmeiner

Since acceding to the World Trade Organization (WTO) in 2001, China's trade with the world has increased dramatically, but so have complaints about its unfair trading practices. These allegations include differential treatment for domestic and foreign firms, dumping, intellectual property theft, environmental pollution, and unfair labor practices. These concerns have the common denominator that China is trading on terms designed for developed, market economies that respect human rights and the rule of law while simultaneously not following these norms. "Free riding" can describe this behavior of taking a benefit but not contributing to its production. China's trading partners complain, but seldom take substantive action. Despite this free riding, the mutual gains from trade do exist, leading to a situation in which unfair trade practices persist as China's trading partners willingly continue to trade. This chapter explains the terms of China's accession to the WTO, the guiding principles of the WTO, and the complaints against China's trading practices. From there, it describes the nature of this free riding dynamic and explains the ways in which China does and does not free ride on the surplus generated by international trade.

4.1 Introduction

Prior to China's accession to the World Trade Organization (WTO), leaders of developed Western countries had hoped to integrate China into the liberal international order (LIO). This rapprochement began with Mao Zedong's overtures toward U.S. President Richard Nixon, which culminated in formal American diplomatic recognition of the People's Republic of China (PRC). This came despite Nixon's deep suspicions of Mao's intentions and considerable American opposition to the brutality of the PRC and its avowed socialist ideals, something only allayed by the PRC's own animosity toward the Soviet Union. Western acceptance of China came gradually as Western leaders hoped that economic integration with the world would cause China to liberalize, a view that China's leaders encouraged. This eventual liberalization proved to be more of a charade than reality, and China's accession to the WTO has brought increased Chinese economic power on the global stage,

DOI: 10.4324/9781003340430-6

but liberalization has been lacking. Moreover, many countries have accused China of not playing by the "rules" of the LIO. These accusations and complaints have often been more rhetorical than substantive. Many countries value the pecuniary benefits of a trading relationship with China more than the losses about which they complain. This produces a dynamic China's leaders can exploit – if they can offer enough economic benefit other countries will permit them to continue expanding their economic and geopolitical power. This chapter addresses this dynamic and the extent to which China's behavior is an abuse of, or "free riding" on, the rules of the WTO.

This chapter proceeds by reviewing China's negotiations to join the WTO and the terms of its accession, and then details the rules and principles of the WTO. With these things in mind, this chapter examines China's behavior since WTO accession in the context of WTO rules. To address this free riding dynamic, Section 4.2 explains the practices by which a country can free ride on the surplus generated by a set of institutions and rules governing international trade. These practices depend on the relative economic sizes of trading partners and their own domestic economic institutions, all of which are explained in the context of China and the comparatively laissez-faire in the West. From there, Section 4.3 explains the free riding that China does, showing that it does free ride on WTO rules in some respects, but much of its free riding could take place even if it were not a WTO member. The relevance of the WTO is the requirement that other countries open their borders to trade with China, which makes those countries vulnerable. Without WTO membership, China would have to conclude trade agreements with every trading partner. Further sections of this chapter detail China's free riding practices and explain the incentives surrounding them on both sides of the trading relationship and the ways in which this free riding can be prevented.

4.2 Chinese accession to the World Trade Organization

China has neither a free-market economy nor a centrally planned economy. State planning is detailed and affects many industries with a view toward achieving centrally directed aims. Execution of the plan is very decentralized, however, and firms are often free to follow market incentives after meeting state goals. The influence of the Chinese Communist Party (CCP) pervades both private and state-owned firms. Dubbed "socialism with Chinese characteristics" China's economy is very much state-led, but the state has created incentives that mimic those of the market to encourage efficiency (see Gotoh and Li's chapter in this book).

4.2.1 What was China doing along the way?

The World Bank may be perceived as a pro-free market institution, but its behavior toward China shows otherwise. After a mission to China in the 1980s, the World Bank advocated for a state-led, nonmarket economic model.

The Bank's six recommendations were 1) emphasize exports of manufactured goods; 2) avoid excessive foreign borrowing; 3) encourage foreign investment for new technologies; 4) spread foreign investment throughout the country; 5) permit state-owned enterprises to engage in foreign trade with their own arrangements; and 6) regularly rework the framework of the entire economy. This report even hinted at the wisdom of joint venture requirements, which are now seen as extortive, as a way of acquiring foreign technology. The World Bank's recommendations were for heavy-handed state involvement in the economy, but it was of a fundamentally different nature than the Soviet model, the failures of which China's leaders clearly recognized. The report clearly shows economic reasoning and a reliance on economic incentives, but advocates for manipulating those incentives rather than establishing a free market (Pillsbury, 2016; World Bank, 1985). The World Bank's recommendations were in line with the views of economist Béla Balassa, who was very influential at the Bank (Gaillard, 2020, p. 54). This is the light in which to view China's international trade and its goals in joining the WTO.

China's accession process lasted 15 years, a time exceeded only by the accession processes of Russia and Kazakhstan (China Power Team, 2020; Gao, 2012). During this time, it drew extensive scrutiny from many WTO members. Negotiations to join the WTO began in 1986 while the organization was still known as the General Agreement on Tariffs and Trade (GATT). The Director-General formed a working party of 36 member governments, including the United States and European Communities. Under the pre-revolution Nationalist government, China was a founding member of GATT in 1947, but after the revolution and its retreat to Taiwan, it withdrew in 1949. The PRC never recognized this withdrawal (WTO, 2001a). China initially applied for resumption as a member in 1986 without success. After considerable progress in bilateral talks with the United States aimed at winning American support for accession, the Tiananmen Square massacre poured cold water on any hopes of a deal (Halverson, 2004, p. 324). After negotiations resumed in 1992, many members of the WTO working party voiced concerns about China's nonmarket system, its clear preference for local firms over foreign, and its clear use of state power to direct the economy toward state goals. Chinese representatives assured them that China would follow all WTO obligations. Before negotiations were completed, China participated in the Uruguay Round as an observer and supported its agreements, which included the Trade-Related Aspects of Intellectual Property (TRIPS) Agreement. By spring 2001, China had completed negotiations with all members of the working party and was admitted into the WTO by consensus (WTO, 2001b).

4.2.2 Accession terms

China's accession to the WTO came with some commitments beyond those required of other members, and it did not enjoy some rights typical of WTO membership. These special terms lasted until December 2016. For example, China was required to translate all of its foreign trade laws into a WTO official language and offer national treatment to foreign goods and persons. China also received nonmarket status for its economy at the WTO, which offered a disadvantage in antidumping investigations, and alternative benchmarks in subsidy and countervailing measures investigations. This list is not exhaustive, and some of these disadvantages from nonmarket status are balanced by China's status as a developing country, which grants preferential terms in some of these areas. Many WTO members, including the United States, claim that the accession protocol did not require them to grant China the status of a market economy when other special terms ended. The United States still considers China a nonmarket economy (Morrison, 2019).[1]

4.3 Relevant rules of the World Trade Organization

International trade is pursued by governments and firms, all of which seek their own advantage. The GATT was formed after WWII as many countries realized that their Depression-era attempts to shore up their own economies at the expense of trading partners proved detrimental to all concerned. Insofar as the objective of the GATT was to further mutually beneficial trade, nondiscrimination and equal treatment became its guiding principles, although it would take many successive rounds of negotiation to broadly implement them, and some disagreements remain to this day.

4.3.1 Nondiscrimination and other guiding principles

The WTO is built for voluntary compliance; it has no enforcement mechanism. International law does exist, but sovereign governments ultimately make their own decisions based on perceived costs and benefits. Their choices in complying with WTO rules are approached no differently.

The WTO's general principles are nondiscrimination, meaning that a WTO member may not unilaterally impose trade terms on another WTO member that differ from its treatment of all members. WTO members are free to agree to preferential terms among themselves, but this requires mutual agreement. This practice, required of all WTO members, is known as most favored nation (MFN) status (WTO, 2022b). Treating foreigners and locals equally is another principle, as is binding one's commitments when opening new markets and keeping national trade rules clear and public (WTO, 2022b).

A few exceptions exist, such as granting preferential terms to developing countries, which often involve extended time to fully comply with WTO agreements. This principle is critical in China's case, as it has chosen to present itself as a developing country (Gao, 2012). These preferential terms include provisions requiring all WTO members to safeguard the interests of developing countries. Trading partners of developing countries have some discretion in deciding how to grant preferential terms (WTO, 2022f).

These guiding principles are the heart of WTO members' obligations, but they are not detailed, unlike a typical trade agreement. At the Doha Ministerial Conference, WTO members planned to launch negotiations over specific rules, but the subsequent talks broke down over disagreements between developed and developing countries with no material prospects for reaching agreement. The lack of both an enforcement mechanism and detailed rules creates a situation that is ripe for disagreement and free riding. Although all WTO members accepted China's accession terms, they did not and still do not agree on what those terms mean.

4.3.2 Classifications

China's classification as a developing country permits it some special treatment. The WTO does not have a definition of a developing country; WTO members decide for themselves if they are developing, but these assertions can be challenged by other WTO members (WTO, 2022e). China has chosen to classify itself as a developing country, though many question whether its claim is for political and economic advantage (Hu, 2019). This self-classification is somewhat dubious because it has the world's second largest economy as measured by GDP and third most powerful military, it is the world's largest exporter and is one of the largest destinations for foreign investment, and its government brags about lifting the world's largest national population out of poverty. These boastings, which are not all well founded, are of achievements far beyond what any other developing country has claimed.

4.3.3 Relevant trade agreements

Several trade agreements specify additional commitments of WTO members. These include the Agreement on TRIPS, the Agreement on Agriculture, the General Agreement on Trade in Services (GATS), and the Agreement on the Application of Sanitary and Phytosanitary Measures (SPS).

The TRIPS Agreement, which sets minimum standards for intellectual property (IP) protection, is the most relevant for questions about China's free riding. The TRIPS Agreement specifies numerous technicalities, and it covers copyrights, patents, trademarks, geographical designations, and trade secrets. Concerning free riding on WTO rules and agreement obligations, the trade secrets section in Part II, Section 7, Article 39 is the most relevant, yet it is very short. Other clauses that would govern China's system of extortive joint ventures contain carve-outs for some aspects of national law. As with other WTO rules, bilateral agreements are permitted.

Article 7 of Part I of the TRIPS Agreement reads:

> The protection and enforcement of intellectual property rights should contribute to the promotion of technological innovation and to the transfer and dissemination of technology, to the mutual advantage of

> producers and users of technological knowledge and in a manner conducive to social and economic welfare, and to a balance of rights and obligations.
>
> (WTO, 2022h)

Although only a statement of purpose, this clause has a very loaded meaning that can offer broad justification for not respecting IP, especially given China's desire to "transfer" or obtain foreign technology for itself.

4.3.4 Dispute mechanisms

When a WTO member believes that another member is not acting in accordance with WTO agreements, disputes may be heard and adjudicated pursuant to the Dispute Settlement Understanding (DSU). The first step is the Dispute Settlement Body (DSB), which is the General Council of the WTO and is composed of representatives of all member governments operating under specific rules (WTO, 2022c). The DSB may establish dispute resolution panels and refer matters to arbitration. These panels may be requested by a complaining party, but they may not contain representatives of governments that are parties to the dispute. Countries may serve as third parties in the adjudication process and submit written recommendations to the panel if they claim a substantial interest, and China regularly does so (Shaffer et al., 2016, p. 257). The DSB then reviews the panel's recommendation and may adopt it. If a party to the dispute disagrees with the DSB's decision, it may appeal to the Appellate Body. The Appellate Body has seven judges, three of whom hear any specific case. Judges serve staggered 4-year terms and are appointed by the DSB. Any WTO member can withhold consent for a judge to serve. The DSB is obligated to uphold the Appellate Body's decision unless there is unanimous consensus otherwise (WTO, 2022d). WTO members have agreed to adhere to DSB rulings.

The process of adjudicating disputes is straightforward, but enforcement is ultimately up to individual countries. The process of appointing the Appellate Body, however, is vulnerable to any disgruntled member state and falls apart with the slightest intransigence. In 2018, the United States blocked appointments, with U.S. ambassador Dennis Shea claiming that the Appellate Body was reversing factual findings by arbitration panels and interpreting WTO members' domestic laws, which it lacked authority to do (Hart and Murrill, 2021).[2] Much American displeasure centered on the Body's treatment of China. In 2019, the United States withheld its support for a proposal to permit judges to be confirmed to the Appellate Body.[3] Refusal to permit certain persons to serve as judges began during the Obama administration, although consensus was eventually reached. The Trump administration unequivocally refused to let the vacancies be filled, a position which has continued under the Biden administration (WTO, 2022a). This approach to preventing unfavorable rulings is effectively American free riding on WTO rules.

When the Appellate Body rules that one country is not abiding by its obligations, all it can do is authorize a trading partner to take retaliatory action that would otherwise be prohibited by WTO rules. That trading partner may then decide what to do, and it must keep in mind that curtailing trade will have adverse domestic effects. Moreover, a country that flouts WTO rules may retaliate against the WTO-authorized retaliatory action. Wilson (2007) wrote that WTO members generally followed WTO rulings and authorizations of retaliatory action were rare, although Davey (2009) claimed that compliance was not always timely and that countries looked for roundabout ways to appear compliant. This is one of China's routine tactics.

From 2002 to 2019, China was involved in 65 disputes, but during its first 5 years of membership (2002–2006), it was only involved in five. China was not idling away during this time; it was involved as a third party in 51.8% of all disputes. Expertise and time are required to win a dispute, so few developing countries ever initiate disputes, which again casts doubt on China's ongoing self-proclaimed status as a developing country. At the WTO, China's initial approach was to gain this experience and maintain a long-term view. Winning at the WTO is not as simple for China as vetoing a U.N. Security Council resolution. China still loses many of its disputes, though it seldom complies with rulings (China Power Team, 2020).

4.3.5 Relevant non-WTO issues

Many economic issues exist outside the WTO's purview. In the case of environmental disputes that have trade implications, the WTO only adjudicates if the two countries do not have an environmental agreement. The Paris Agreement, which China has ratified but does not follow, may remove some major international disputes from WTO jurisdiction. Forced labor is increasingly important with the mass internment of the Uighur population, but it is not a WTO issue. It is undoubtedly an economic issue, but the WTO has ceded any authority over it to the International Labor Organization (ILO), a UN agency of which China is a permanent member (WTO, 2022g). Although China's behavior on these issues flouts international norms and confers an advantage that WTO rules aim to prevent, there is no role for the WTO in settling these matters.

4.4 China's ongoing behavior

Shortly before China's accession to the WTO, a meeting of its Ministerial Conference was convened in 1999 in Seattle. This conference would have opened another round of trade negotiations named the Millennium Round. The Clinton administration in the United States hoped to facilitate China's accession at this conference; although there were many objections to China's nonmarket economy and labor practices, and these objections would prove prescient (Scott, 1999). The talk of China's accession was quickly overshadowed by anti-globalization protests, which attracted far more media attention than the conference. The talks collapsed abruptly, and the accompanying chain of events was subsequently dubbed "the Battle of Seattle" in reference to the violent nature of the protests and the forceful government response. Anti-globalization sentiment is hardly unique, but this conference came not long after the GATT's rechristening as the WTO. Many protesters feared that the WTO would develop into a one-world government and would harm developing countries and degrade the environment. Developing countries then walked away from the talks, giving the protesters a symbolic victory.

The fears of a one-world government were misplaced; the WTO's ongoing inability to enforce compliance with its rules and guiding principles demonstrates this. Similarly, the inability of the United States and European Union to forge a deal at the conference in Seattle demonstrated that even major trading blocs lacked the muscle to force acquiescence of the remaining WTO members. China entered the WTO against this backdrop in which it knew that, ultimately, wealthy Western nations could not or would not force their way, although it would take more time and economic growth before China could successfully challenge them.

The Doha Development Round of WTO negotiations, generally called the Doha Round, began in November 2001, coinciding with China's accession. Contrary to the expectations of many commentators, China did not play much of a role in these negotiations. Only late in the round, after several years, did China finally interact in a major way with other major decision-making countries. After many attempts at negotiations, the Doha Round was effectively dead by 2008. After a grueling accession process, China's leaders hoped to avoid making additional concessions along with other recently acceded members, a viewpoint that was not strongly opposed by many longtime members. To accomplish this goal, China's leaders tried not to make excessive demands (Gao, 2012).

China's low profile at the WTO during its early years stems in part from its need to acquire expertise. The "free" trade espoused by the WTO rests on a long list of procedural rules specific to WTO operation and on the details of trading countries' laws and policies. These rules are not readily available in a neatly codified format. Although it took several years, China did become a major player in the ongoing Doha Round (Gao, 2012).

Accession to the WTO meant accepting free market principles and implementing them in its institutional structure, which China has not done. These expectations are laid out in the Marrakesh Declaration issued at the conclusion of the Uruguay Round in 1994. Rather than meeting these expectations, China has broadly persisted with the World Bank's nonmarket recommendations from years earlier. Despite public-facing rhetoric about market reforms and opening up to the world, China's leaders have not disguised their "socialism with Chinese characteristics," and a cursory amount of research turns up extensive evidence of a state industrial and trade policy and state control over much of the economy.

China's government is not transparent, although this is not singular and Western governments have had their own transparency issues. China's lack of transparency is considerably worse than the West's, though, and even a detailed amount of research does not always lead to irrefutable knowledge of the details of China's governance structures and their practical reality concerning international trade and investment. This complicates dispute resolution at the WTO or in bilateral negotiations and makes China's superficial compliance look deeper than it is in practice (Office of the United States Trade Representative, 2022).

4.5 Does China free ride on WTO rules?

This section briefly gives an overview of the concept of international free riding on institutions developed in Gmeiner (2021a and 2021b). This concept is the framework within which I answer the question of whether China free rides on WTO rules.

Free riding is consumption by those who do not pay. Insofar as "rules of the game" lead to economic surplus, free riding on these rules means finding ways to appropriate some of the surplus without following the rules. Voluntary trade is mutually beneficial, but the existence and division of the surplus depend on the rules governing that trade. These rules include WTO rules, specific trade agreements, and domestic laws in each country. Free riding on these rules means exploiting them to procure an asymmetric advantage. In the context of this chapter, asymmetric advantage does not refer to differences in input costs or other comparative advantages. Rather, it refers to "underhanded" actions like structuring domestic laws and enforcement action to create a nonlevel playing field. Whether free riding is possible depends on the nature of the surplus and the ability and willingness of relevant parties to punish free riding. China's trade practices are less circumspect than those of many other developed, trading nations. These other countries have grievances about these practices, yet they persist in trading with China.

To understand the surplus that comes from a set of institutional rules, consider the IP rights that create an incentive for innovation and commercialization of technologically advanced products. Trading partners can enjoy the benefits of these economic advances even if they are not very innovative themselves or if they lack the institutions that led to the innovation. If they can produce what consumers in the more advanced country want to buy, they can acquire the innovative products. This trade is mutually beneficial. When a trading partner misappropriates or infringes the IP rights, it reaps the pecuniary benefits of innovation without incurring the costs to do it or establishing the requisite institutions that facilitate it. Profits earned by the infringer come at the expense of the innovator, which dulls the incentive to trade in IP-intensive goods with countries that do not respect IP. The choice to refuse to trade with such a country is not always simple, because trade with the infringer can still bring many benefits, like cheap consumer goods. Such a country may, because of a useful factor endowment, free ride on the innovative potential of a trading partner. It can do so by profiting from misappropriated IP while deterring the victim country from retaliating, and this is free riding on institutions (Gmeiner, 2021a and 2021b). Free riding on institutions is not limited to IP; any set of rules that incentivizes production and exchange creates surplus, and that surplus will be a target for misappropriation attempts. Whether these attempts succeed depends on the rules governing trading relationships.

In the case of China and the United States, the political structures governing their respective economies compound the problem. China's economy still operates with a large measure of state involvement, whereas the American economy is comparatively laissez-faire. Taking action against China for infringement is up to the victim firm in the United States, and it may face retaliation from China for its actions. It may choose to involve the Office of the United States Trade Representative (USTR), but the structure of this office does not permit the victim firm to escape potential Chinese reprisals when seeking a remedy. The USTR may assist American firms, but it does not unilaterally take over their cases like a prosecutor fighting crime, and certainly not in a class-action manner. Moreover, ceasing to trade with China does not guarantee that an American firm will not lose its innovative advantage. These losses can still occur if an American firm that chooses not to trade with China has an American competitor with similar products and that competitor trades with China. That competitor firm will be the proximate victim of Chinese IP theft, but cheaper Chinese infringing products may still erode the profits of the firm that chooses to forego trading with China. American firms thus face a prisoner's dilemma in choosing to trade with China.

Large firms in China are all closely tied to the Chinese government, and they all have committees of the CCP embedded in their management structures. State-owned enterprises are a large proportion of China's economy but are far from the entirety of it. Nominally private firms have CCP committees, granting it considerable sway over their major decisions. As a result, Chinese firms do not face this prisoner's dilemma that their American counterparts do. To be clear, the CCP does not dictate all day-to-day operations of the firm, but high-level decisions with ramifications for CCP objectives are made in accordance with CCP wishes (Gmeiner, 2021b).[4] Even when responding to market incentives, decisions will be made with CCP approval. The division of the surplus from trade depends on bargaining power, and centralized direction over one side of a trading relationship between two countries confers strategic advantage. American firms may collectively wish to avoid problems that attend their trade with China, but this is not trivial. In large measure, this is because of their greater independence from government, not despite it. The Sino-U.S. trading relationship continues because it is seldom in any single American firm's interest to break it. The free-market system is thus an institution that creates surplus that can be misappropriated through trade with unfree economies. China's behavior is not unconstrained; taking this free riding to an excessive degree will eventually cause some firms to leave and may provoke a substantial response from the United States or other trading partners. Precisely where this line is remains uncertain and probably depends on geopolitical and other factors (see Gaillard's chapter in this book).

Firms in China's state-directed economy can efficiently misappropriate trade secrets and infringe patents with the tacit support of their government. This has deleterious effects on American innovative potential and encourages firms to seek advantage through political means rather than innovative competition (Gmeiner, 2021b). This cronyism can erode free market competition, which is the primary reason why it is harmful for free market institutions to trade with large countries lacking those institutions.

Whether China free rides on WTO rules is a distinct issue that is not dependent on the innovative capacity or institutional structures of fellow WTO members. The surplus created by WTO rules is not the equivalent to the surplus created by a country's own institutional structures. Some WTO members are much wealthier and more innovative than others. China's ability to free ride on free market Western economic institutions stems from its large size and its own unique economic institutions. These differences between China and the West give rise to China's behavior toward WTO rules.

4.5.1 The complicated, bureaucratic nature of international trade

It is an oversimplification to say that international trade is mutually beneficial because of the exposition commonly given in basic textbooks. This exposition rests on a set of assumptions that lurk beneath the surface of simple models. These assumptions include the rule of law, reasonable environmental and labor standards, and absence of externalities. The bureaucratic complexity of modern international trade stems from the need to enumerate these unstated assumptions, and this need arises because different countries often have very different rules. As a result, any modern trade agreement will reflect a model of international trade that differs from the textbook version. Trade agreements are lengthy and detailed. When mutually agreed upon by trading partners, they are presumably mutually beneficial, though even this is not without caveats. These include special interests that may influence trade agreements and asymmetric bargaining power that comes from two countries' differences in economic size and geopolitical influence. The size and division of the surplus from international trade will depend on the particulars of the agreement.

WTO rules offer uniformity among members and a mechanism for resolving disputes. This "uniformity" only means that a WTO member will get the same treatment as other WTO members when trading with a WTO member in the absence of a bilateral agreement. Presumably, WTO members were sincere in admitting a new member and any objections about economic and political structures were mild enough to not prevent admission. When a country joins the WTO, regardless of its internal governance, its products will get the same treatment globally as any other WTO member's. WTO members may make their own trade agreements among themselves, which supersede this uniformity. The door to free riding is opened when a country's trading position is guaranteed by WTO rules even if it flouts its obligations. Recognizing this, the WTO does have a dispute resolution mechanism, but as elaborated above, countries have ways to comply superficially but not substantively. When a country does this, it effectively free rides on its trading partners' institutions while removing one way to retaliate, namely asymmetric trade policy.

It is somewhat tenuous to call this free riding on WTO rules, however, because similar outcomes may result even without the WTO. It is reasonable to refer to it as free riding on foreign institutional structures through international trade. This free riding is largely possible because all WTO members were obligated to trade with China when it acceded to the WTO, thus giving it a foothold in the global system. Once that was done, the free riding began in earnest as China's global trade grew exponentially. Although some of China's free riding is free riding on WTO rules, as explained below, most of it is free riding on trading partners' institutions that is facilitated by WTO membership. Had China not joined the WTO, it would have had to conclude agreements with all trading partners, which presumably would have taken more time but could still produce the same free riding potential.

4.5.2 What is not free riding

Comparative advantage determines a country's balance of imports and exports. Innovation, changing resource costs, and geopolitical circumstances affect comparative advantage either directly or indirectly. This list of factors is not exhaustive. When one country's comparative advantage changes, there may not be free riding. Beginning to trade with a country where labor is cheap harms labor-intensive industries in the higher-cost country, but this is not free riding.

Currency manipulation is not free riding, and it may not contribute to China's balance of trade or that of its partners. It may affect bilateral trade balances, but total trade balances may not be substantially affected. A country's need for net imports and exports reflects patterns of national saving and consumption. Regardless of the effects of currency manipulation, it is not a matter for the WTO and, given that a country's central bank may create that country's currency, there is no clear reason why this could be free riding.

4.5.3 Four examples of China's free riding on WTO rules

China free rides on WTO rules in four ways. First, it presents itself as a developing country to receive special treatment. This is somewhat of a gray area given that China has a nonmarket economy, contrary to developed countries.

Second, China's trade negotiations and policies clearly lack good faith as it induces compliance with its wishes through economic might. Third, the joint venture system, which was established in 1979 and encouraged later by the World Bank, facilitates this free riding in a way that is superficially voluntary. Fourth, China's environmental and labor policies yield an economic advantage that has effects on trade but is not part of any trade agreement, thus putting some unfair trade practices beyond the reach of WTO dispute resolution. "Unfair" competition is an easy grievance to voice when a country's comparative advantage is eroding, and it is not always well founded. Some of China's practices are particularly egregious, and these include serious environmental pollution and the use of slave labor from interned Uighurs.

4.5.3.1 Developing country

Is China a developing country? A case could certainly be made for that, and not without reason, though equally powerful arguments to the contrary also exist. China is a notoriously difficult country to research, and its economic indicators are uncertain and may not reflect the entire country. Its per capita income levels are far below the developed West, and this certainly plays into the CCP's argument that it should have preferential treatment. China does have a miserable history of privation from the first few decades of CCP rule, and it was a poor country even before that. To the author of this chapter, it is bewildering that Western countries have not highlighted the CCP's own role in the mass starvation of its people that kept that country so backward for so long when it seeks preferential treatment.

As enumerated above, China has numerous characteristics that are fundamentally unlike any other developing country. Granting preferential terms to developing countries is presumably to help them achieve a higher level of development. The wisdom of this is debatable given that countries must learn to compete on a level playing field at some point. Despite China's somewhat undeveloped status, its economic output has increased sharply, casting doubt on its need for preferential treatment. Its geopolitical ambitions should also signal to the West that granting preferential treatment to China may be more for the CCP's benefit than that of the Chinese people.

4.5.3.2 Incomplete compliance and induced acquiescence

Shaffer et al. (2016) recognize the potential for free riding by taking advantage of other countries' adherence to WTO rules while simultaneously giving its own industries an advantage. They point to claims of the United States and European Union that China "formally" or "nominally" complies with a ruling, but then implements other policies to nullify the ruling's effect. This is often accompanied by threats to retaliate against U.S. and European firms that do business in China so as to blackmail these governments into acquiescing because of the threat to their countries' firms. Webster (2013) views

China's compliance with international norms, or lack thereof, as nuanced. China does comply with some international norms, including some WTO rules. This creates an illusion of good intent, and when there is compliance on some seeming major issues, it gives room to avoid complying with others, especially when a crafty façade masks the noncompliance. Selective compliance is hardly unique, which China's leaders understand well; Western countries do it too, but on different issues. On trade-related issues, this is easier for China than the United States or European Union because China's economy is closely linked to the state. Western selective compliance with international norms may be easier in other areas, such as strategic ambiguity over Taiwan, democracy promotion in developing countries, and propping up dictators who support Western geopolitical interests.

This noncompliance often results in an uneasy truce. China may not fully comply when losing a dispute with the United States, but it knows the incentives of American firms and the American government. The United States may not press the issue for fear of endangering important trade. China also needs this trade to persist, so its behavior is limited, and this uneasy truce can be explained by game theory and strategic thinking. Because of its size and importance to China, the United States has an easier time disputing with China and inducing some compliance. Taiwan and South Korea are heavily dependent on trade with China to a degree far greater than the United States, but neither country files formal complaints at the WTO against China (China Power Team, 2020). For this reason, the preponderance of complaints against China from the United States and European Union should not be taken as evidence that other countries are pleased with China's trade practices. Trade-related action against smaller countries can be more devastating for their economies than anything China would do to the United States. When it involves the United States and European Union, China's behavior is free riding. In the case of smaller countries, it is intimidation, as WTO disputes never even materialize. Intimidating smaller neighbors is not just a trade issue; in a high-profile case, China meted out economic reprisals that induced South Korea to withdraw its plan to install an American THAAD missile defense system. South Korea reversed course again, but only after a ballistic missile test by North Korea. This Chinese intimidation has erupted again in 2022 with limited success.[5] South Korea is not the only case, and former U.S. Defense Secretary Mark Esper openly accused China of intimidating its neighbors in the South China Sea.[6]

4.5.3.3 Extortive joint ventures and foreign direct investment (FDI) practices

In many industries, foreign firms wishing to invest in China must do so as part of a joint venture with a Chinese firm, which has a CCP committee in its management structure. FDI operations that are not part of a joint venture are also required to have this CCP committee. Joint venture rules often require the transfer of proprietary technology to the Chinese firm, and thereby to CCP control (U.S. Department of State, 2019).

The prisoner's dilemma conundrum facing Western firms illustrates their incentive to participate in these joint ventures. Many American firms have complained about the practice, and the USTR has taken notice (Office of the United States Trade Representative, 2018). IP theft is hardly unique to China, and there are many ways for hostile foreign governments and firms to do it. China's government also employs other tactics to steal IP. This raises the question of why China chooses this joint venture system. One explanation is that it avoids the potential for WTO disputes. Forming a joint venture is always a complicated legal process, especially when it crosses international borders, and both firms have agreed to it in many steps along the way. The terms may be asymmetric, but they are voluntarily accepted, at least superficially. These joint venture requirements convert a general practice of stealing IP, which could be subject to WTO disputes, into one of case-by-case acceptance by victims, which rules out that remedy. Far from free riding on WTO rules, China simply avoids them.

China's joint venture rules are far from its only tactic. Foreign firms have established research and development centers in China because rules are structured to make the benefits exceed the cost of stolen IP. These rules include customs clearance facilitation and tax cuts for participation in government projects.[7] The tax and tariff terms can be very generous, but come with stiff compliance requirements, and government oversight is extensive.[8] These rules are not fully compliant with WTO principles and rules because the terms vary by industry according to China's state industrial policy and treatment is more preferential for firms using equipment made in China and for those that overtly transfer technology. The free riding dynamic is of the same prisoner's dilemma sort described above, but it is not clearly free riding on WTO rules.

4.5.3.4 Environmental and labor policies

China signed the Paris Agreement, yet its environmental pollution has continued unabated. Chinese President Xi Jinping pledged that China would build no new coal-fired power plants abroad, which it had been doing as part of the Belt and Road Initiative. He made no promises about financing new foreign coal power plants with Chinese money. Xi also made no promises about reducing the use of coal within China, and shortly before halting foreign construction, Chinese state firms announced plans to build 43 new coal-fired power plants and blast furnaces (Hillman and Sacks 2021).[9] From a cynical perspective, it makes sense that China would stop the coal-fired power plants where they are most salient to the West. From this same perspective, one could ask why it is in China's interest to be part of the Paris Agreement in the first place. Reducing the use of cheaper, carbon-intensive energy is expensive, and it will make goods produced in compliant countries more expensive, thereby expanding China's comparative advantage. China can point to some superficial, though very poorly disguised, compliance in arguing for continued trade.

This is just one example, but it shows the brazen nature of free riding. A clean environment is a common resource that is subject to free riding, and China has demonstrated that it will consume that environment while expecting others to maintain it. Although this is one of the clearest examples of free riding, it is not a WTO issue. Because the Paris Agreement is not a trade agreement, noncompliance cannot be addressed by the WTO dispute resolution system, even if it were fully operational. The Paris Agreement states that disputes are handled in accordance with the United Nations Framework Convention on Climate Change *mutatis mutandis*, which specifies that negotiation or peaceful means are to be used. Recourse to the International Court of Justice (ICJ) or arbitration is allowed if both parties have accepted jurisdiction.[10] Neither the United States nor China has accepted ICJ jurisdiction,[11] and even if both had, it cannot force a sovereign state to comply with its rulings.

4.5.4 Can this free riding be prevented?

China's own rules that govern its foreign trade and investment are nominally accepted by its trading partners. Their overriding spirit, however, runs counter to WTO principles, and China only induces compliance through economic might. Moreover, this is only possible because China has a nonmarket economy in which the state presents a unified front against trading partners with economies defined by independent, private enterprise. This is the nature of China's free riding, and it is more a matter of free riding on foreign economic institutions than on WTO rules. China's ability to prevent WTO disputes through superficial acquiescence is an element of free riding on WTO rules, but it is subordinate to free riding on foreign economic institutions.

Holmes et al. (2015) believe that, collectively, many Western firms have slowed their foreign direct investment in China because of China's policies. This is complicated by the fact that much FDI flows through tax havens like the British Virgin Islands or the Cayman Islands. Concerning China, historically, much FDI that comes ultimately from the West was funneled through Hong Kong, which was labeled as the source and may have been attributed to firms nominally based in Hong Kong. The assertion of Holmes et al. (2015) is tenuous, although the extent of China's behavior does lend some credence, implying that some in the West have sensed that the benefits of doing business with China no longer outweigh the costs. In further support of this idea, outbound FDI from the United States to China has decreased since 2019, but it has been skewed toward more technologically advanced industries that are the targets of IP theft. Inbound FDI from China has increased and is somewhat more focused on less sensitive areas from a regulatory and security perspective, potentially showing the American realization that geopolitical risks may exist from foreign control of sensitive sectors (Hanemann et al., 2021). The decline in outbound investment to China may reflect some firms' realization that the returns are not worth the costs. Conversely, ongoing grievances imply that this is still a problem, and waiting on private Western companies to leave China may not be effective as a means of stopping this free riding.

In addressing China's free riding, two points are critical. First, China does not uphold WTO rules or principles, and it does effectively deter retaliation. Second, China should not be in the WTO because it lacks commitment to WTO rules. Removing China from the WTO is almost certainly a non-starter. Many other countries would see near-term harm if this were to happen, even if there might be long-run benefits.

The WTO is not a government, so it lacks enforcement power. Beyond this, many things are not clearly defined, such as the definition of a developing country. More formal definitions and clearer rules may help to a small degree, but these would be difficult as any effort would lead to conflict among member states seeking their own advantages. In any case, China would certainly oppose any effort to reclassify it as a developed country. Given its long track record of noncompliance, it also seems unlikely that China would comply even if the rules were defined more clearly. As long as there is such a marked difference between the Chinese and Western economic systems, China will be able to induce acquiescence provided that its economic size offers enough near-term pecuniary benefit to the West. For the reasons outlined in this section, China's free riding cannot realistically be prevented if its trading partners continue to trade and maintain comparatively free market economic systems.

4.6 Conclusion

China has attracted plenty of criticism over its foreign trade practices, yet its trade with the world has steadily increased. China's trading partners, despite their rhetoric, have permitted this trade. Many complaints about China are well founded, but some are not. Frequently, trading partners have accused China of not complying with WTO rules, leading to talk about "free riding" on the global system in general and on WTO rules in particular.

Whether or not China free rides on WTO rules requires a definition of what free riding is. Most simply, it is consumption by those who do not pay. Extrapolating this definition to international trade, it is reaping the benefits of international trade without bearing the costs. China does this by imposing unfavorable terms on foreign *firms*, but not *governments*. These terms grant an asymmetric advantage to Chinese firms, all of which are influenced by the CCP (see Seaman's chapter in this book). This asymmetric advantage frequently takes the form of technology transfer to Chinese firms, though others exist. This dynamic exists because Western firms are not state controlled to the extent of Chinese firms; profits are to be had in trade with China, despite losses of technology. Foregoing these profits to avoid the losses of IP or other competitive advantage is not the best strategy for many Western firms if they have competitors who will earn profits in China despite the drawbacks. As a result, Western firms acquiesce to China, and this dynamic underpins the idea of free riding on economic institutions. This is possible because Western firms do not operate as part of a united political front that can resist Chinese influence.

As for free riding on WTO rules, China does practice it, but it is a secondary element of China's free riding. The effect of WTO membership is that more countries are open to trade with China, thus granting it more opportunities to free ride as described above. WTO rules require uniform treatment of all other WTO members absent a bilateral or multilateral trade agreement. China's extortive policies governing joint ventures, foreign direct investment, and market access are contrary to WTO principles. Its environmental and labor policies also confer an asymmetric advantage. Lastly, China presents itself as a developing country despite many reasons why it should not because WTO rules are more lenient toward developing countries. China's strategy has been "paper compliance" of saying it complies while substantively not complying. China's trading partners lack the resolve to resist, largely because of the near-term pecuniary benefits of this trade for their people. In conclusion, China does free ride on WTO rules, but this free riding is a magnification of the free riding on economic institutions and relationships described above, which could exist in a more limited form without the WTO.

Notes

1 See also https://www.trade.gov/nme-countries-list.
2 T. Miles, "U.S. Blocks WTO Judge Appointment as Dispute Settlement Crisis Looms," *Reuters*, 27 August 2018.
3 S. Nebehay, "U.S. Seals Demise of WTO Appeals Bench: Trade Officials," *Reuters*, 9 December 2019.
4 F. Russo, "Politics in the Boardroom: The Role of Chinese Communist Party Committees," *The Diplomat*, 24 December 2019.
5 T-H. Kim, "China, South Korea Clash over THAAD Anti-Missile System," *Defense News*, 10 August 2022.
6 R. Burns, "Esper Accuses China of Intimidating Smaller Asian Nations," *Associated Press*, 20 November 2019.
7 S. O'Farrell, "China in R&D Boost to Lure Foreign Businesses," *fDi Intelligence*, 24 March 2021.
8 L. Clowney, "China's R&D Policies Explained," *Cross Border Solutions*, 14 September 2021, available at https://crossborder.ai/white-paper/chinas-rd-policies-explained.
9 See also *Bloomberg News*, "China's Green Ambitions Aren't Halting New Coal and Steel Plans," 13 August 2021 and J. Hillman and D. Sacks, "Making Sense of China's Pledge to Stop Building Coal-Fired Power Plants Abroad," *Council on Foreign Relations*, 4 October 2021, available at https://www.cfr.org/blog/making-sense-chinas-pledge-stop-building-coal-fired-power-plants-abroad.
10 The Paris Agreement is available at https://unfccc.int/sites/default/files/english_paris_agreement.pdf. The article regarding the settlement of disputes (Art. 14) of

the United Nations Framework Convention on Climate Change is available at: https://unfccc.int/cop3/fccc/climate/conv_016.htm.

11 See https://www.icj-cij.org/en/declarations.

References

China Power Team (2020) "How Influential is China in the World Trade Organization?," *China Power*, available at https://chinapower.csis.org/china-world-trade-organization-wto.

Davey, W. J. (2009) "Compliance Problems in WTO Dispute Settlement," *Cornell International Law Journal*, Vol. 42, No. 1, pp. 119–128.

Gaillard, N. (2020) *Country Risk – The Bane of Foreign Investors*. Cham: Springer.

Gao, H. (2012) "China's Participation in WTO Negotiations," *China Perspectives*, 2012/1, pp. 59–65.

Gmeiner, R. J. (2021a) "International Free Riding on Institutions," *Economic Affairs*, Vol. 41, No. 1, pp. 123–140.

Gmeiner, R. J. (2021b) *How Trade with China Threatens Western Institutions: The Economic Roots of a Political Crisis*. Cham: Palgrave Macmillan.

Halverson, K. (2004) "China's WTO Accession: Economic, Legal, and Political Implications," *Boston College International and Comparative Law Review*, Vol. 27, No. 2, pp. 319–370.

Hanemann, T., Rosen, D. H., Witzke, M., Bennion, S. and Smith, E. (2021) *Two-Way Street: 2021 Update US-China Investment Trends*. Report by the U.S.-China Investment Project. New York City: National Committee on U.S.–China Relations and Rhodium Group.

Hart, N. M. and Murrill, B. J. (2021) *The World Trade Organization's (WTO's) Appellate Body: Key Disputes and Controversies*. CRS Report R46852. Washington, DC: Congressional Research Service.

Hillman, J. and Sacks, D. (2021) *China's Belt and Road – Implications for the United States*. Independent Task Force Report No. 79. New York City and Washington, DC: Council on Foreign Relations.

Holmes, T. J., McGrattan, E. R. and Prescott, E. C. (2015) "Quid Pro Quo: Technology Capital Transfers for Market Access in China," *Review of Economic Studies*, Vol. 82, No. 3, pp. 1154–1193.

Hu, W. (2019) "China as a WTO Developing Member, Is It a Problem?," *Centre for European Policy Studies, Policy Insights, No. 2019/16*.

Morrison, W. M. (2019) *China's Status as a Nonmarket Economy (NME)*. Report IF10385, 10 January. Washington, DC: Congressional Research Service.

Office of the United States Trade Representative (2018) *Findings of the Investigation into China's Acts, Policies, and Practices Related to Technology Transfer, Intellectual Property, and Innovation under Section 301 of the Trade Act of 1974*. Washington, DC: USTR.

Office of the United States Trade Representative (2022) *2021 Report to Congress on China's WTO Compliance*. Washington, DC: USTR.

Pillsbury, M. (2016) *The Hundred-Year Marathon: China's Secret Strategy to Replace America as the Global Superpower*. New York City: St. Martin's Griffin.

Scott, R. E. (1999) "China Can Wait: WTO Accession Deal Must Include Enforceable Labor Rights, Real Commercial Benefits," *Economic Policy Institute, Briefing Paper*.

Shaffer, G., Elsig, M. and Puig, S. (2016) "The Extensive (But Fragile) Authority of the WTO Appellate Body," *Law and Contemporary Problems*, Vol. 79, No. 1, pp. 237–273.

U.S. Department of State (2019) "2019 Investment Climate Statements: China," available at https://www.state.gov/reports/2019-investment-climate-statements/china.

Webster, T. (2013) "Paper Compliance: How China Implements WTO Decisions," *Michigan Journal of International Law*, Vol. 35, No. 3, pp. 525–578.

Wilson, B. (2007) "Compliance by WTO Members with Adverse WTO Dispute Settlement Rulings: The Record to Date," *Journal of International Economic Law*, Vol. 10, No. 2, pp. 397–403.

World Bank (1985) *China: Long-Term Development Issues and Options*. Baltimore (MD) and London: The Johns Hopkins University Press.

World Trade Organization (2001a) "China's Accession to the WTO and its Relationship to the Chinese Taipei Accession and to Hong Kong and Macau, China," available at https://www.wto.org/english/thewto_e/acc_e/chinabknot_feb01.doc.

World Trade Organization (2001b) "Report of the Working Party on the Accession of China," *WTO, Ministerial Conference, Fourth Session, 9–13 November 2001*, available at https://www.wto.org/english/thewto_e/acc_e/wp_acc_china_e.doc.

World Trade Organization (2022a) "Members Continue to Push to Commence Appellate Body Appointment Process," available at https://www.wto.org/english/news_e/news22_e/dsb_28mar22_e.htm.

World Trade Organization (2022b) "Principles of the Trading System," available at https://www.wto.org/english/thewto_e/whatis_e/tif_e/fact2_e.htm.

World Trade Organization (2022c) "The WTO General Council," available at https://www.wto.org/english/thewto_e/gcounc_e/gcounc_e.htm.

World Trade Organization (2022d) "Understanding on Rules and Procedures Governing the Settlement of Disputes," available at https://www.wto.org/english/docs_e/legal_e/28-dsu_e.htm.

World Trade Organization (2022e) "Who Are the Developing Countries in the WTO?," available at https://www.wto.org/english/tratop_e/devel_e/d1who_e.htm.

World Trade Organization (2022f) "Special and Differential Treatment Provisions," available at https://www.wto.org/english/tratop_e/devel_e/dev_special_differential_provisions_e.htm.

World Trade Organization (2022g) "Labour Standards: Consensus, Coherence, and Controversy," available at https://www.wto.org/english/thewto_e/whatis_e/tif_e/bey5_e.htm.

World Trade Organization (2022h) "Agreement on Trade-Related Aspects of Intellectual Property Rights as Amended by the 2005 Protocol Amending the TRIPS Agreement," available at https://www.wto.org/english/docs_e/legal_e/trips_e.htm.

5 The international financial architecture under pressure

Norbert Gaillard and Michael Waibel

The present international financial architecture (IFA) has been weakening since the early 2010s. Several factors have hindered the reorganization of the current IFA, accelerated the bipolarization of international financial relations, and reshaped the balance of power between sovereign debtors and creditors as well as between creditors themselves. The post-Bretton Woods IFA has been centered around the United States. The U.S. dollar has remained the world's most important reserve currency. The Federal Reserve and the U.S. Treasury have acted as the only reliable international lenders of last resort since 2008. Further, the United States has a veto at the International Monetary Fund. China has launched regional initiatives that threaten to fragment the IFA. It has signed central banks swaps agreements to prevent cross-border spillovers and internationalize the renminbi. The Asian Infrastructure Investment Bank is a key institution to support the Belt and Road Initiative. The New Development Bank is another innovative and independent institution. In fact, China is reshaping the IFA primarily through its sovereign lending and debt restructuring practices. Chinese contracts are built on harder terms than Western contracts, showing that China wants its creditors to obtain preferential treatment in the event of a default.

5.1 Introduction[1]

The international financial architecture (IFA) can be defined as the governance rules and practices established and implemented by formal and informal international financial organizations as well as by some powerful national institutions and firms (e.g., central banks, financial institutions, and credit rating agencies) to ensure an efficient, successful, and sustainable global monetary and financial system. The current IFA has evolved significantly since the Bretton Woods Agreement of 1944. The intensification of economic and financial relations between industrialized and emerging countries, the collapse of economic planning, the growing public and private debts in all regions of the world have made the IFA increasingly complex, all of which has led to heated debates.

DOI: 10.4324/9781003340430-7

For example, the key role played by the International Monetary Fund (IMF) since the 1980s has stirred controversy (Flores Zendejas and Gaillard, 2022). Second, the efficiency of macroprudential rules – established since the 2000s to preserve the stability of the banking system and fight systemic risk – has been seriously questioned (see Montanaro's chapter in this book). Third and more importantly, the increasing financialization of the U.S. economy (as well as other major economies) has been endangering the IFA since the late 2000s, which requires ambitious reforms to transform U.S. capitalism (Gaillard and Michalek, 2022b).[2]

However, the economic and political rise of the People's Republic of China (PRC) may also have destabilizing effects on the IFA. Echoing the arguments advanced in China and emerging countries, Chin and Thakur (2010, p. 119) point out that "the multilateral order cannot hold if the power and influence embedded in international institutions is significantly misaligned with the real distribution of power."

This chapter puts this statement into perspective and argues that the present IFA has been weakening since the early 2010s, partly because of the U.S.–China rivalry. Several factors have hindered the reorganization of the IFA, accelerated the bipolarization of international financial relations, and reshaped the balance of power between sovereign debtors and creditors as well as between creditors themselves.

Section 5.2 shows that the post-Bretton Woods IFA is centered around the United States. The U.S. dollar has remained by far the world's reserve currency while the largest credit rating agencies (e.g., Moody's and Standard & Poor's) and financial institutions (e.g., JPMorgan Chase and Bank of America) are headquartered in the United States. Next, the Federal Reserve and the U.S. Treasury have become more powerful than ever, acting as the only reliable international lenders of last resort (ILOLR) since the global financial crisis of 2008. Further, the United States has managed to keep its veto at the IMF and has prevented any large-scale reform. Lastly, Washington can exclude countries (e.g., Cuba, Iran, and Russia) from the international financial system by imposing economic and financial sanctions.

Section 5.3 argues that the PRC has challenged the international institutions promoting the existing liberal international order at the margins. China is now ranked third in terms of voting power at the IMF and the World Bank and self-classifies as a developing country at the World Trade Organization (WTO), but it is not a Paris Club member and does not participate in the Organisation for Economic Co-operation and Development's (OECD) Arrangement on Officially Supported Export Credits. Instead, China launched initiatives that may be fragmenting the IFA, reflecting a shift from a reformist to a revisionist stance (Nicolas, 2014). China signed central banks swaps agreements with East Asian, European, and Latin American authorities to prevent cross-border spillovers, preserve regional value chains, and internationalize the renminbi. Next, the BRICS (Brazil, Russia, India, China, and South Africa) Contingent Reserve Arrangement could become an alternative to the IMF in the medium to long term. Although the Asian Infrastructure Investment Bank (AIIB) is a key institution to support the Belt and Road Initiative (BRI), it works with the World Bank on various projects. The New Development Bank (NDB) is a more innovative and independent institution.

Section 5.4 investigates why and how China is reshaping the IFA through its sovereign lending and debt restructuring practices. Chinese contracts are built on harder terms (e. g., collateral arrangements, confidentiality, cancellation, acceleration, stabilization, and cross-default clauses) than Western contracts. Chinese interests abroad are also considered interdependent and "solidary" by the PRC, which involves diplomatic pressures on foreign debtors. In addition, the features of Chinese debt restructuring practices are idiosyncratic: "No Paris Club" clauses and the controversy regarding the status of China Development Bank show that the PRC wants its creditors to obtain preferential treatment in the event of a default.

Section 5.5 contends that the growing debt of developing countries, partly driven by the U.S.–China rivalry, may be the underrated weakness of the IFA. At least two nonexclusive scenarios can be envisaged in respect of the future path of debt in developing countries. The first is a possible "debt trap" caused by debt overhang, as illustrated by Sri Lanka and possibly several African countries. The second involves debtor and creditor moral hazard problems, which will inevitably weaken the position of certain creditors. In either case, developing economies may pay a high price for being at the fore of major geopolitical battles. Section 5.6 concludes.

5.2 How the United States defends the status quo

Since the collapse of the Bretton Woods system in 1973, the IFA has been largely dominated and centered around the United States. Concretely, Washington has managed to maintain the status of the U.S. dollar as the foremost international currency, ensured the globalization of the world economy, averted systemic risk, preserved its influence on key international financial institutions (especially the IMF), and sanctioned "delinquent" countries financially.

5.2.1 The U.S. dollar as the foremost international currency

The privileged status of the U.S. dollar (USD) is a fascinating and complex phenomenon. The U.S. currency is backed by the most powerful military in the world (thus reflecting the capacity to protect American vital interests worldwide), the largest economy in terms of gross domestic product (GDP), and a long-standing triple-A sovereign debt credit rating. As a result, it is not surprising that the USD accounted for more than 64% of the world's foreign exchange reserves, on average, between 1973 and 2021[3] and played an outsized role in the invoicing of global exports (Boz et al., 2020). It is also noteworthy that T-Bonds and T-Bills remain safe-haven assets during high-risk aversion periods. For instance, the market yield on the U.S. 10-year bond declined, on average, by more than 15% during the six domestic recessions observed since 1980.[4]

5.2.2 International finance and globalization

A second aspect of Washington's dominance is its unique capacity to enlarge the "battlefield" where it has a decisive competitive advantage: international finance. Several factors coalesced to boost world financial globalization and support the U.S. hegemony on the IFA. On the eve of the fall of communism, the "Washington Consensus" – a term coined by economist John Williamson (1990) – served as a macroeconomic roadmap for many governments in advanced as well as emerging countries. This Consensus spurred free trade, liberalization of inward foreign direct investments (FDI), privatization, and deregulation. Between 1990 and 2020, annual world trade volume and FDI stock jumped 4% and 10%, respectively.[5] The financialization of the world economy, especially through the development of derivatives markets and the decisive influence of the International Swaps and Derivatives Association, headquartered in New York City (Pistor, 2019), further strengthen this pattern.

In this context, the increasing accommodative monetary policy conducted by the Federal Reserve[6] has encouraged leverage strategies in the United States and abroad. Between 1990 and 2020, the total amount of international debt securities outstanding rose by a factor of 18, more than 42% of this debt being denominated in USD.[7]

In the meantime, globalization contributed to blur the lines between capital-exporting and capital-importing nations. It also entailed a high degree of interdependence and competition between economies (Gaillard, 2020). Thus, it is not surprising that the tight co-movement in the prices of international assets reinforced the global financial cycle among industrialized economies by synchronizing risk appetite and exacerbating potential contagion and spillover effects (see Jordà et al., 2018).

5.2.3 Fighting systemic risk

The latter point leads to the capacity of the United States to prevent major financial crises and fight systemic risk. The first "policy tool" used by Washington involves the credit rating agencies, such as Moody's and Standard & Poor's (S&P), two U.S. firms. The basic job of rating agencies is to assess credit risk. Their methodologies compel borrowers to remain solvent on their bond debt because debt restructurings or missed payments can be considered a default. The incorporation of credit ratings in international regulatory rules and investment funds' prudential rules (very frequent until recently) transformed credit rating agencies into gatekeepers of capital markets and drove up the cost of default.[8] Countries that failed to restore their credit position (such as Argentina and Venezuela) went through severe economic and political crises.

The second tool was the development of macroprudential policies in the aftermath of the global financial crisis (see Montanaro's chapter in this book). As early as 2009, the Financial Stability Forum (FSF) published a report designed to address procyclicality in the financial system (FSF, 2009).[9] This report was followed by a rich academic literature advocating the implementation of macroprudential rules (e.g., additional capital requirements; additional liquidity requirements; restrictions on assets, liabilities, or specific activities; and taxation) to fight systemic risk. These rules were (and are still) considered indispensable in times of high interconnectedness between too-big-to-fail (TBTF) banks and TBTF non-bank financial institutions.

The third tool was the extraordinary capacity of the United States to act as ILOLR. The first step occurred during the Mexican sovereign debt crisis in the second half of 1982. After hesitation to support Mexico and other Latin American economies in distress, President Ronald Reagan realized that a "laissez faire" stance was likely to endanger the U.S. banking system. As a result, within a few weeks, the White House approved a significant increase in IMF quotas, the Federal Reserve relaxed its monetary policy, U.S. commercial banks – main creditors of less developed countries – provided complementary financing to Mexico, and U.S. regulatory authorities agreed to classify Mexican debt as performing loans on the books of U.S. banks (Gaillard and Michalek, 2022a). These measures precluded the collapse of international financial markets, as had happened in the early 1930s.

In the subsequent years, Washington intervened in a timely manner to avert systemic risk. During the Asian crisis of 1997, the Clinton administration encouraged the IMF to rescue distressed countries[10] while the Federal Reserve arranged a bridge loan for Thailand and convinced U.S. banks to restructure the short-term debt owed by South Korea. This last move reduced risk aversion dramatically. During the global financial crisis and the COVID-19 pandemic, the Federal Reserve acted as ILOLR.[11] It conducted exceptional open market operations, both in terms of the amounts offered and the maturity of the securities. It also expanded its lending facilities and broadened the range of counterparties and eligible collateral. Next, it established dollar liquidity and foreign currency swap lines with the central banks of major industrialized and emerging countries. Lastly, it cut the funds rate to a range of 0%–0.25%. The U.S. accommodative monetary policy implemented between 2007 and 2021 eased access to capital markets and supported governments that borrowed in USD.

5.2.4 U.S. influence on the IMF

The status quo in the IFA has also been underpinned by the capacity of the United States to maintain its hegemony on Bretton Woods institutions. The most striking case is that of IMF governance. For decades, the United States has managed to keep its veto at the IMF (i.e., more than 15% of vote shares; see Hallaert, 2020; Shaffer and Waibel, 2015; Gu and Tong, 2022) while reforming the institution when necessary. For example, a general allocation of Special Drawing Rights equivalent to $650 billion was approved in August 2021 to boost global liquidity and fight the recessionary effects of the pandemic. The Biden administration was concerned that developing countries might turn to Chinese banks to meet their borrowing needs.[12] This strategy has reinforced the status of the IMF and complemented the ILOLR role played by the Federal Reserve.

Last but not least, a close examination of IMF loans with very soft conditionality[13] reveals that these are granted to U.S allies that implemented orthodox policies in recent decades (e.g., Colombia, Mexico, Morocco, and Poland).[14] Thus, the United States continues to exert a major influence on IMF policy.

5.2.5 U.S. financial and economic sanctions

An important yet overlooked dimension of the IFA involves U.S. economic sanctions against "delinquent" foreign governments. As of April 14th, 2023, the Office of Foreign Assets Control of the U.S. Department of the Treasury administered and enforced 38 sanctions programs. The most recent and most spectacular program, established in February 2022, has targeted Russia after its army invaded Ukraine. Numerous sanctions are directly related to the IFA.[15]

U.S. financial institutions were required to close many banks' accounts of Russian nationals and reject any future transactions while the U.S. Treasury froze their assets. Russian banks were also removed from SWIFT, the Western financial messaging system. The Central Bank of the Russian Federation was prevented from using its international reserves in many Western jurisdictions, including the United States. Lastly, the Treasury blocked Moscow from paying U.S. bondholders, which led to the historic default of Russia in June 2022.

The sanctions against Russia have shown that Washington can exclude a country from the international financial system and destroy its credit position. This "financial hyperpower" has been increasingly questioned and constitutes a key incentive for emerging economies to de-dollarize the global financial system (see Liu and Papa, 2022).

5.3 The "South–South" dynamics driven by China

The PRC did not actively challenge the U.S.-led IFA until the global financial crisis. It used complementary tactics to contest the U.S. hegemony and promote an alternative world economic order, in line with some form of "financial nationalism" (Helleiner and Wang, 2019). Chinese authorities refrained from joining several informal Western organizations to preserve their freedom of action and champion South–South cooperation. They also launched last-resort policy tools to support non-industrialized countries and built independent global payment infrastructures for international transactions. In addition, China established new development banks to promote its investments abroad and launched its own global financial infrastructures.

5.3.1 China as part of the "Global South"

Although it has been the second largest economic power in terms of GDP and a net capital exporter for a few years, China has repeatedly rejected the constraints that a classification as a "developed country" would have entailed. For example, as the PRC does not participate in the Arrangement on Officially Supported Export Credits,[16] it is not compelled to impose restrictions on the financing terms and conditions when providing official export credits. Next, China's persistent claim of its "developing member" status at the WTO aims to take advantage of the special and differential treatment provisions granted by the institution (see Gmeiner's chapter in this book).[17]

Particularly controversial is the PRC's decision to remain outside the Paris Club, despite its status as a top official creditor.[18] It seems that China has remained reluctant to submit to several key principles of the club, such as information sharing, conditionality, and the comparable treatment of public debts.

In fact, China's policy reflects a mix of ideological and pragmatic positioning. China is eager to preserve its image of "emerging country" to increase its geopolitical clout among the South. In the meantime, it systemically tries to be a rule-maker to maximize its economic and financial gains. This stance is consistent with the initiatives launched for a decade to break the perceived U.S. stranglehold on the IFA.

5.3.2 New facilities to provide liquidity to emerging and developing countries

China has promoted two significant international facilities that partly compete with the institutions and arrangements established by the present IFA: (i) bilateral and multilateral swap agreements and (ii) the so-called BRICS Contingent Reserve Arrangement (CRA).

The Chiang Mai Initiative (CMI) was launched in 2000 by the Association of Southeast Asian Nations (ASEAN),[19] plus China, Japan, and South Korea. This bilateral currency swap arrangement (CSA) was designed to address potential short-term liquidity difficulties in the aftermath of the Asian crisis. In 2010, the CMI Multilateralization (CMIM) succeeded the CMI: with current resources of $240 billion, this multilateral CSA is more ambitious: it aims to prevent balance-of-payments disturbances. Since the early 2010s, the People's Bank of China (PBOC) has also signed a growing number of bilateral swap lines with counterparts on five continents. In December 2020, China was involved in 31 bilateral CSAs amounting to the equivalent of $567 billion (Perks et al., 2021).[20] The development of these swap agreements has contributed to boost cross-border trade and internationalize the renminbi (Song and Xia, 2020).

The BRICS CRA was established in 2014 in reaction to the persistent underrepresentation of the BRICS (especially China) at the IMF. Contrary to the rules in force at the Washington-based institution, none of the five parties has a veto power. The committed resources of the CRA, which total $100 billion,[21] are split into two portions. The "de-linked portion," equal to 30% of the maximum access for each party, is available with limited conditionality. In contrast, the remaining 70% is contingent on an agreement with the IMF. This dichotomic scheme suggests that the BRICS CRA remains embedded in the present IFA. However, in the medium to long term, this emergency reserve fund could become a credible alternative to the IMF (see Würdemann, 2018).

The BRICS CRA and the currency swap agreements involving the PBOC have so far complemented rather than competed with the U.S.-led IFA. The ability of the PRC to create an alternative IFA fundamentally depends on its willingness to act as ILOLR, as Washington has done since the early 1980s.

5.3.3 The New Development Bank and the Asian Infrastructure Investment Bank

The NDB and the AIIB were established in 2014 to counter the influence of the Asian Development Bank and the World Bank, respectively, two institutions perceived to be spearheaded by Japan and Western countries. They also support the BRI, launched in 2013 by Chinese leader Xi Jinping. It created a hub-and-spoke network but one that is difficult to assess due to its fluidity and lack of transparency (Wang, 2019a; Lorenzo, 2021; Dreher et al., 2022). The examination of the governance, the objectives, and the lending policy of the NDB and the AIIB shows that these two entities have challenged the IFA on the margins.[22]

In 2020, the AIIB was composed of 83 members. Most industrialized countries have joined the bank, with Japan and the United States as exceptions. The PRC has a veto power, which mirrors the U.S. position in the Bretton Woods institutions. The founding members of the NDB are the BRICS: they have equal shareholding power and none of them has a veto.

During 2016–2020, 68% and 75% of the projects approved by the AIIB and the NDB, respectively, were sovereign loans. Around 52% of the AIIB projects and 75% of the NDB projects involved energy, water, transport infrastructures, and urban developments (AIIB, 2021a; NDB, 2021). The two institutions insist that there is no policy conditionality attached to their loans, contrary to the procedures applicable at the IMF, the World Bank, and multilateral development banks (Stephen and Skidmore, 2019; NDB, 2019). However, in practice, there may still be conditionality attached to lending along the BRI, and such lending may also create other types of dependency of borrowing countries. Neither the AIIB nor the NDB activities have contributed thus far to de-dollarize the world economy: in December 2020, 96% of total financial assets of the AIIB and 73% of the loans granted by the NDB were denominated in the U.S. currency (AIIB, 2021b; NDB, 2021).

The lesson is that the AIIB is not designed to upset the IFA but is part of a broader strategy to selectively reshape international economic institutions in China's favor (Wang, 2020). The numerous partnerships formed with the World Bank tend to support this view. The NDB may embody an alternative model soon, provided the BRICS manage to increase their lending facilities and use mostly local currencies (Wang, 2019b).

5.3.4 China's bank card network and international payment system

A remarkable evolution observed since the 2010s has been China's capacity to bypass U.S. global financial infrastructures. Two successful ventures deserve examination: UnionPay and Cross-Border Interbank Payment System (CIPS).

Launched in 2002, UnionPay is a Chinese financial services corporation headquartered in Shanghai and approved by the PBOC. It has become a major supplier of bank payment cards – ahead of Visa and MasterCard – and reports a high acceptance rate, ranging from 70% in Europe and North America to 90% in the Asia Pacific.[23] CIPS was established in 2015 as an alternative to SWIFT. Although CIPS conducts only $50 billion worth of volume daily, compared to $400 billion for SWIFT,[24] the growth of its coverage has been impressive (+900% between October 2015 and December 2020).[25]

UnionPay and CIPS promote broader international use of the renminbi. One may expect that this trend will continue in the coming years. As China is the top economic partner of many U.S.-sanctioned countries (e.g., Russia, Iran, Venezuela, North Korea, and Cuba),[26] those countries could complete the de-dollarization of their trade and financial system in the next years.

5.3.5 The limits of challenging the U.S.-led IFA

For a few years, Chinese authorities have had to endure the status quo on specific issues, either because it has been in their own interest to do so or because they did not manage to challenge U.S. leadership.

Consider the PRC's strategy regarding its holdings of U.S. Treasury securities. Between December 2017 and May 2022, China's percentage in all foreign holdings in federal debt declined from 19.1% ($1,185 billion) to 13.2% ($981 billion).[27] Although China will continue to diversify its foreign exchange reserves, there are few comparable alternative risk-free investments (He et al., 2016; Bernanke et al., 2011). Moreover, since the United States is China's largest customer, a massive selloff of T-Bonds and T-Bills could destabilize the two economies and lead Washington to retaliate by implementing new protectionist measures. In addition, such a move could signal a hardened geopolitical stance and increase the risk of a direct conflict between the two superpowers. For the moment, it seems that China is neither able nor eager to change the international reserve system.

Turn now to what has been the most spectacular setback suffered by China in the international financial field: namely, its failure to develop a credible international credit rating system. In the aftermath of the subprime crisis of 2007–2008, Chinese policy makers were critical of Moody's and S&P. Dagong – a rating firm headquartered in Beijing – made a breakthrough in the sovereign rating area (Bush, 2021). Dagong's credit opinions diverged from those of its U.S. competitors in the sense that emerging economies obtained much higher ratings whereas developed economies were rated lower (Gaillard, 2011). In fact, Dagong ratings, like those of other Chinese credit rating agencies, are too politicized and lack objectivity, which has prevented them from obtaining a regulatory license in the United States. Chinese authorities were so concerned by Chinese domestic credit rating agencies that they allowed S&P to rate domestic Chinese bonds in 2019.[28] This decision – unprecedented for a foreign firm – evidenced the low credibility of Chinese credit rating firms in their own domestic market.

5.4 Sovereign lending and debt restructuring practices: The Chinese way

Documentation of China's capital exports is opaque. China does not report on official lending and does not provide comprehensive standardized data on overseas debt stocks and flows. Credit rating agencies do not monitor sovereign borrowing from official lenders. Commercial providers such as Bloomberg and Dealogic do not track China's official overseas loans. The PBOC does not publish its sovereign bond purchases or the composition of its portfolio. China is not subject to standard disclosure requirements of the Paris Club, the OECD Creditor Reporting System, and the OECD Export Credit Group. China reports to the Bank for International Settlements (BIS), but the coverage is incomplete. As a result, the data and information used here come from a small set of research works. Although they may not match perfectly, they provide a good overview of the activities of Chinese creditors.

5.4.1 The features of Chinese lending practices

China's economic growth and enormous trade surpluses since the late 1990s have led to the accumulation of massive foreign exchange reserves available for use as a foreign policy tool (Horn et al., 2021; Dreher et al., 2022). Such global imbalances are not a new feature of the global economy but have raised tensions in the increasingly conflictual China–U.S. relationship (Frieden, 2009; Eichengreen, 2015; Shaffer and Waibel, 2016). Today, China is the world's largest creditor, far outstripping the combined Paris Club members. Over the last decade, non-Paris club members such as the PRC have become more important. In 2016, non-Paris Club debt accounted for 13% of low-income countries' public debt (Essl et al., 2019, p. 6). Besides, of the $45 billion in scheduled sovereign debt interest payments due in 2020, $6.2 billion was owed to Paris Club members and $11.4 billion to China.[29]

Research has shown that Chinese debt contracts are built on harder terms, including confidentiality clauses, collateral arrangements, cancellation, acceleration, and stabilization clauses. Chinese creditors have signed over 2000 loan agreements with developing countries since the early 2000s. Although these loan agreements are subject to far-reaching confidentiality clauses, Gelpern et al. (2021) obtained a sample of 100 contracts, based on which they found indications that Chinese entities use standardized contracts varying by lender. China's state-owned entities blend commercial and official lending terms and introduce novel ones to maximize commercial leverage over the sovereign borrower and secure repayment priority over other creditors. Around 30% of the contracts include a special bank account that effectively serves as security for debt repayment, an approach uncommon in sovereign lending since the early 20th century.[30] The consequence may be that a substantial share of debtor countries' revenues is under the secret effective control of a single creditor, resulting in countries having a servicing capacity less than, and a risk of debt distress greater than, those assessed by conventional measures based on publicly available sources (Gelpern et al., 2021, pp. 4–6). Loan agreements used by China Eximbank and China Development Bank (CDB) all include versions of a cross-default clause, standard in commercial debt but uncommon in the context of bilateral or multilateral official lending. Certain loan agreements also allow cross-default to be triggered by actions adverse to the interests of "a PRC entity" (Gelpern et al., 2021, p. 7).

Although Chinese domestic debates have often criticized IMF and World Bank conditionality in lending, Chinese lending shows forms of conditionality itself (Mattlin and Nojonen, 2015; Chesterman, 2016). Chinese-style conditionality comes in four varieties: First is political conditionality, including "basic diplomatic and political preconditions prior to receiving any funding," in respect of the diplomatic isolation of Taiwan. The second is embedded conditionality, including "project-related demands regarding, for example, the use of Chinese-sourced contractors, sub-contractors, technology, equipment suppliers, management and training, as well as a Chinese workforce," whereby "making aid conditional on the purchase of donor country products and technologies is one of the main economic aims of foreign aid." The third is cross-conditionality, making conditions established by other creditors de facto conditions for loan disbursements by a new creditor. Chinese interests abroad are thus considered interdependent and "solidary" by the PRC.[31] The fourth is emergent conditionality, describing the structural effects a history of funding and investment might create in the future, for example with Chinese-built infrastructure creating technological, financial, managerial, and educational dependencies of a host country on China (Mattlin and Nojonen, 2015).

Lastly, China has low involvement, for its size as a lender, in "vertical funds" combining private and public investment from multiple countries for sector-specific global development goals in such areas as agriculture, climate, education, health, and regional and national reconstruction (Morris et al., 2021, pp. 28–31). Stand-alone and "100% made in China" projects are prioritized.

5.4.2 The features of Chinese debt restructuring practices

China is not a member of the Paris Club: this poses major challenges for at least some restructurings, given the size of China's loans. Concretely, close to three quarters of the debt contracts reviewed by Gelpern et al. (2021) contain so-called "No Paris Club" clauses, expressly compelling the borrower to exclude Chinese debts from restructuring in the Paris Club and from comparable debt treatment. These clauses predate and are in tension with the PRC's commitments under the G20 Common Framework for Debt Treatments beyond the World Bank's Debt Service Suspension Initiative (DSSI) announced in November 2020, in particular the commitment of G20 governments to coordinate debt relief terms for eligible countries (Gelpern et al., 2021, pp. 6–7).

Consider CDB, the world's largest national development bank and China's largest institution for overseas investment. In 2019, CDB had total assets of $2.4 trillion. It typically lends at rates above those of the World Bank, although sometimes below in cases of political interest. Depending on context, CDB can act as both an official and a commercial creditor. CDB has the status of a development finance institution to support China's national initiatives and prioritize political objectives over profits. Unlike China Eximbank, CDB does not offer officially subsidized loans. Moreover, the Chinese government insists that CDB is not an official bilateral lender but instead a commercial bank under the DSSI. In development circles, CDB is seen as lacking international experience and credit risk management expertise, with less international staff than the PBOC (Rudyak and Chen, 2021, pp. 5–6).

Contrary to China Eximbank, CDB loan restructurings do not require a government-to-government agreement. Decisions are made within the bank and remain rather decentralized, partly because CDB has several regional branches. Debt renegotiations involving CDB most frequently lead to rescheduling. This outcome is less favorable than that observed for China Eximbank's and China International Development Cooperation Agency's restructured loans, which are likely to include not only maturity extension but also haircuts. In a few cases, the latter agency may concede write-offs (Rudyak and Chen, 2021, pp. 13–17).

According to Beers et al.'s (2022) database, at least 25 sovereign borrowers were in default on China's bilateral official loans in 2021.[32] Angola, the

Republic of the Congo, Pakistan, and Venezuela accounted for 87% of total defaulted debt to Chinese official creditors.[33] In general, the capacity of a distressed country to obtain a significant debt restructuring from China is contingent on several factors: the availability of alternative financing sources, a leadership change in the borrowing country, and tight bilateral relations between the borrower and China (Kratz et al., 2019).

Horn et al. (2021) consider that the geopolitical objectives of the Chinese government influence Chinese official lending. They also estimate that about 50% of China's lending may be "hidden." Despite significant Chinese lending to crisis countries such as Iran, Venezuela, and Zimbabwe over the past 15 years, China has not reported bank claims toward these countries to the BIS. Whereas other official creditors often lend to developing countries on concessionary terms with long maturities and at below-market rates, China often lends at market terms (with risk premia), with shorter maturities, and with collateral clauses that secure repayment through commodity export proceedings (e.g., oil and wheat), giving China a seniority among other creditors. In these regards, China's lending shows parallels with British, French, and German foreign lending in the 19th century.

5.5 The underrated weakness of the IFA: The growing debt of developing countries

At least two (nonexclusive) scenarios can be envisaged in respect of the future path of debt in developing countries. The first is a possible "debt trap" caused by debt overhang. The second involves the risk of debtor and creditor moral hazard. The short- and medium-term scenario is contingent on the future of the DSSI and the Common Framework.

5.5.1 Debt overhang

Aggressive lending practices by China have already drawn attention in cases of financially distressed states, such as Zambia and Sri Lanka, which have borrowed significantly from Chinese lenders, thus suggesting that the PRC is engaging in "debt trap diplomacy." This term was coined in 2017 by Brahma Chellaney, a professor of strategic studies at the New Delhi-based Center for Policy Research. He mentioned the China-Sri Lanka "debt for equity" deal for the port of Hambantota to popularize the notion that China engages in predatory lending.[34] The term has attained great popularity, generating nearly two million search hits on Google by 2018 as well as criticism that it has become a "meme" (Brautigam, 2020).

In the case of Sri Lanka, although Chinese investment as part of the BRI postdates Sri Lanka's reliance on debt to fund internal conflicts with Tamil groups, BRI investment has allowed China to build, then obtain majority shareholdings in, and a 99-year lease over, the port of Hambantota. In the case of Zambia, U.S. National Security Advisor John Bolton alleged in 2018 that China was making "strategic use of debt to hold states in Africa captive to Beijing's wishes and demands," including purported plans to take over Zambia's national power company and airport. In response to Bolton's comments, Zambia lodged an official protest with Washington, emphasizing in a press conference that Zambia did not use state assets or state enterprises as collateral for its loans with China (Brautigam, 2022, p. 1357).

The theory of "debt trap diplomacy" has also been expressed as a theory of "institutional eclipse," with China acting as an ILOLR, providing a bilateral alternative outside of the current IFA. In this view, China offers debtor states emergency lending on more favorable terms – or in any event with reduced or more attractive conditionality – than the IMF in exchange for economic and diplomatic advantages:

> Lending to countries across the developing world has assisted China's efforts to export construction services, import natural resources, and secure important votes in international fora, such as Cambodia's decision to block the Association of Southeast Asian Nations (ASEAN) from issuing a joint statement rejecting China's territorial claims in the South China Sea.
>
> (Sundquist, 2022)

Other authors express skepticism over the scope of any political or diplomatic ambitions behind Chinese lending. Brautigam argues that evidence remains "weak for the 'debt trap diplomacy' hypothesis, which asserts that China deliberately indebts countries for the purpose of acquiring leverage and strategic assets." She finds that, in the case of Zambia, China has exerted at most limited political pressure (and generated domestic political resistance) despite a large volume of lending. She also identifies potentially positive elements in the Chinese development philosophy, for example the critique by Li Ruogu, the former president of China Eximbank, that the IMF Debt Sustainability Analysis framework fails to consider what the debt is used for. China's BRI debt sustainability framework, announced in 2019, differs in its willingness to lend notwithstanding a high risk of debt distress in case of growth-oriented projects. Brautigam suggests that Chinese lenders may be "supporting Zambia's strategic vision, lending for projects with high growth potential" (Brautigam, 2022, pp. 1350–1351).

Regardless of whether borrowing from Chinese lenders entails an intentional loss of sovereignty in favor of China, it is uncontroversial that Chinese lenders routinely impose stricter and more expensive terms than peer official lenders, potentially leading to increased poverty in debtor states. Chinese banks structure their loans to give them discretion to trigger cancellation or default remedies, increasing economic pressure on debtors and the incentives to repay (Gelpern et al., 2021).

Another negative assessment draws on theories of debt dilution, according to which Chinese lending strategies intentionally exacerbate cooperation problems between creditors. In the absence of a sovereign insolvency mechanism (Flores Zendejas and Gaillard, 2022, pp. 95–96), lenders seek de facto seniority, for example by agreeing contractual terms that are difficult to restructure in a crisis. The stricter terms of newer loans will facilitate fresh lending but dilute the seniority of existing debt, resulting in a "bad" debt structure that is extremely hard to restructure (Gelpern et al., 2021). Note that this interpretation gels with the Chinese loan agreements reviewed, including the "No Paris Club" and special account (cash collateral) clauses, which are contractual terms effecting greater seniority and repayment advantages. As stated above, Chinese creditors provide debt relief predominantly through debt reprofiling, rather than face value debt reductions generally accepted by the Paris Club and private creditors, even in case of exogenous shocks such as the COVID-19 pandemic.[35] Lengthy renegotiations resulting at best in maturity extensions without interest or principal reductions can contribute to worsening debt overhang that is unresolved, hampers growth and sustains poverty for years or even decades.

5.5.2 Debtor and creditor moral hazard

The rivalry between the United States and China may encourage *debtor* moral hazard akin to what was observed in the second half of the 1970s, with debtors shopping for loans and exacerbating competition between lenders. For example, the Export–Import Bank of the United States (U.S. Eximbank) and China Eximbank may compete to provide lending for projects and states of questionable creditworthiness to pursue geopolitical aims. Darbellay and Gaillard (2022, pp. 69–71) give the example of U.S. Eximbank's approval of a $5 billion loan to Mozambique in 2019, the largest direct loan in its history, despite S&P rating Mozambique in "selective default" when the loan was approved. U.S. Eximbank emphasized its interest in the integrated liquefied natural gas project being carried out by U.S. companies, rather than by Chinese and Russian companies in the event of financing from those countries.

Creditor moral hazard has materialized among Western systemic banks since the 1980s (see Flores Zendejas and Gaillard, 2022), but it can arise within the institutional framework of Chinese lending as well. Erie (2021, p. 107) notes that, because state-owned enterprises "rely on the Party State for insurance and on the PRC government as an arbitrator in their disputes with the host government, they tend to take excessive risks." This problem arises with institutions in other countries, such as U.S. Eximbank, but it "is more pronounced in state capitalism given the muted role of independent decision-making. Moral hazard has long been a problem in the Chinese domestic economy: governmental guarantees to enterprises against insolvency de-incentivize firms from internalizing risk."

There is a growing risk of massive sovereign defaults and disorganized debt restructurings, as in the 1930s and 1940s (Wynne, 1951). An assessment of this risk is made difficult by the confidentiality clauses and secrecy of Chinese lenders, which in parallel appear to be contributing to tensions between the World Bank and the present IFA, on the one hand, and Chinese lenders, on the other. Chinese entities have already effectively diluted and antagonized the World Bank.

A recent World Bank publication urging "transaction-level debt transparency" mentions China only in passing, namely in the context of criticizing Chinese lending in Zambia, but it is difficult to read the publication other than as addressed to China, the global leader for confidential project finance in official lending. The World Bank authors emphasize that debt transparency is a critical basis for debt sustainability and creditworthiness assessments. Significantly, they also mention, without providing specifics, that their paper was "prompted by disclosure-related challenges and friction points that became evident during recent periods of widespread debt distress in developing countries." In particular, the authors mention instances of

> (i) the non-sharing of transaction-related information with IFIs that perform debt sustainability assessments and generate global debt information for stakeholders; (ii) revelations of 'surprise' and 'hidden' debt; (iii) undisclosed granting of collateral and quasi-collateral that, if disclosed, may impact creditor assessments of borrower liquidity or creditworthiness; and (iv) inter-creditor mistrust and tensions during debt restructurings.
>
> (Maslen and Aslan 2022, pp. 9 and 13)

This expresses succinctly four key categories of pressure exerted by Chinese lending on the current IFA today.

5.6 Conclusion

The IFA has gone through a series of substantial changes since 1944. They include (i) the shift to a floating exchange rates regime in the 1970s, (ii) the pervasive role played by the IMF, the Federal Reserve, and the U.S. Treasury since the 1980s, and (iii) the establishment of international micro-prudential and macroprudential rules since the advent of financial globalization in the 1990s. All these changes were spurred by U.S. authorities who have aimed to fight systemic risk and protect the rights of international creditors.

The emergence of China as a major commercial, economic, and financial power has exacerbated its rivalry with the United States and may be undermining the current IFA. The activities of the AIIB and the NDB – two China-based international institutions – do not seem to question fundamentally the present IFA. In contrast, Chinese sovereign lending and debt restructuring practices not only create coordination problems between creditors, but they also burden developing countries with debt. These two issues should be tackled right now to prevent economic and geopolitical crises.

Notes

1 Thanks to Benjamin Letzler for research assistance.
2 The U.S.-led IFA is also indirectly threatened by the mounting radical partisanship in U.S. politics (see Kalmoe and Mason, 2022).
3 Authors' computations based on IMF data. In 2021, the percentage reached 59%.
4 Authors' computations based on Federal Reserve data, see https://fred.stlouisfed.org/series/DGS10.
5 Authors' computations based on the United Nations Conference on Trade and Development (UNCTAD) and World Trade Organization (WTO) data.
6 U.S. real interest rates (i.e., the federal funds effective rate minus the Consumer Price Index growth rate) fell from 1.9% in the 1990s to 0.1% in the 2000s, and -1.1% in the 2010s. Authors' computations based on Federal Reserve data.
7 Authors' computations based on Bank for International Settlements (BIS) data.
8 European and U.S. lawmakers withdrew the references to credit ratings in their financial regulations in the early 2010s (Gaillard and Waibel, 2018). Yet the use of alternative credit measurements has proved difficult (Gaillard, 2016). Investors continue to extensively scrutinize credit ratings.
9 The FSF was a forum including international financial institutions (IFIs) and finance ministries and central bankers of the Group of Seven. It was succeeded by the Financial Stability Board (FSB) in 2009. When the FSF report was released, the United States was the country posting the highest number of financial institutions in the world's 30 largest banks by total assets, see www.gfmag.com.
10 The IMF lent a total of $35 billion to Indonesia, South Korea, and Thailand in 1997 (BIS, 1998, p. 134).
11 See Block (2022) for an overview of how U.S. authorities coped with the two crises.
12 The title of the *2021 IMF Annual Report* ("Build Forward Better") echoes the "Build Back Better" agenda promoted at the time by President Biden.
13 These specific loans include Flexible Credit Lines (FCLs) and Precautionary and Liquidity Lines (PLLs).
14 See the *IMF Annual Reports* published since 2012.
15 See https://home.treasury.gov/policy-issues/financial-sanctions/sanctions-programs-and-country-information.
16 This arrangement, set up by the OECD in 1978 to control export subsidies, brings together high-income economies.
17 In the meantime, Chinese authorities invest massively in building trade law capacity to defend their policy (Shaffer and Gao, 2021).
18 In 2017, emerging and developing countries owed $380 billion to China compared to $246 billion owed to the 22 Paris Club members (Horn et al., 2021).
19 The ASEAN is composed of ten countries: Indonesia, Malaysia, Philippines, Singapore, Thailand, Brunei Darussalam, Vietnam, Laos, Myanmar, and Cambodia.
20 More than 51% of these bilateral swap lines (in volume) were signed with Hong Kong, South Korea, Singapore, the Eurozone, and the United Kingdom.
21 The top contributing member is Beijing ($41 billion), ahead of New Delhi, Brasilia, and Moscow ($18 billion each), and Pretoria ($5 billion).
22 Skidmore's chapter in this book analyzes how the AIIB and the NDB compete with multilateral development banks and challenge the global development finance regime.
23 See https://www.unionpayintl.com/en/mediaCenter/newsCenter/companyNews/7374.shtml.
24 See https://asiatimes.com/2022/02/china-can-break-swift-sanctions-but-at-a-high-cost.

25 See https://www.cips.com.cn/cipsen/7050/index.html.
26 Authors' classification based on https://home.treasury.gov/policy-issues/financial-sanctions/sanctions-programs-and-country-information and https://oec.world.
27 Authors' calculations based on U.S. Treasury data, see https://ticdata.treasury.gov.
28 *PRNewswire*, "S&P Global Ratings receives first-of-its-kind approval to enter China domestic bond market," 28 January 2019.
29 https://www.imf.org/Publications/fandd/issues/2020/09/debt-relief-for-the-poorest-kevin-watkins.
30 An exception was the U.S. emergency loan to Mexico in 1995, requiring oil revenues to flow through an account at the Federal Reserve Bank of New York.
31 For example, Chinese creditors suspended billions in funding for Indonesian power projects pending resolution of a small dispute between the Indonesian government and a Chinese lender over a $232 million loan for the purchase of 15 civilian aircraft from a Chinese manufacturer. See Mattlin and Nojonen (2015).
32 Nearly two-thirds of these defaulting countries are African (Angola, Burundi, Cameroon, Cape Verde, Central African Republic, Chad, the Republic of the Congo, the Democratic Republic of the Congo, Djibouti, Ethiopia, Gabon, Kenya, Mauritania, Mozambique, Sierra Leone, and Zambia). Others are in Latin America, Asia, and Oceania (Dominica, Maldives, Pakistan, Papua New Guinea, Samoa, Tajikistan, Tonga, Venezuela, and Yemen).
33 Authors' calculation based on Beers et al.'s (2022) database.
34 B. Chellaney, "China's Debt-Trap Diplomacy," *Project Syndicate*, 23 January 2017, available at https://www.project-syndicate.org/commentary/china-one-belt-one-road-loans-debt-by-brahma-chellaney-2017-01.
35 Emmanuel's chapter in this book examines how China, the United States, and IFIs helped Latin America and the Caribbean fight the COVID-19 pandemic.

References

Asian Infrastructure Investment Bank (2021a) *2020 AIIB Annual Report*. Beijing: AIIB.

Asian Infrastructure Investment Bank (2021b) *Auditor's Reports and Financial Statements for the Year Ended Dec. 31, 2020*. Beijing: AIIB.

Bank for International Settlements (1998) *68th Annual Report*. Basel: Bank for International Settlements.

Beers, D., Jones, E., McDaniels, K. and Quiviger, Z. (2022) "BoC–BoE Sovereign Default Database: What's New in 2022?," *Bank of Canada and Bank of England*, available at https://www.bankofcanada.ca/2022/08/staff-analytical-note-2022-11.

Bernanke, B. S., Bertaut, C., Pounder DeMarco, L. and Kamin, S. B. (2011) "International Capital Flows and the Returns to Safe Assets in the United States, 2003–2007," *International Finance Discussion Paper No. 1014, Board of Governors of the Federal Reserve System*.

Block, C. (2022) "Design and Cost of U.S. Responses to the 2007–2009 Financial Crisis and the 2020 Covid-19 Pandemic," in Flores Zendejas, J., Gaillard, N. and Michalek, R. (Eds) *Moral Hazard – A Financial, Legal, and Economic Perspective*. Abingdon and New York City: Routledge.

Boz, E., Casas, C., Georgiadis, G., Gopinath, G., Le Mezo, H., Mehl, A. and Nguyen, T. (2020) "Patterns in Invoicing Currency in Global Trade," *IMF Working Paper WP/20/126*.

Brautigam, D. (2020) "A Critical Look at Chinese 'Debt-Trap Diplomacy': The Rise of a Meme," *Area Development and Policy*, Vol. 5, No. 1, pp. 1–14.
Brautigam, D. (2022) "China and Zambia: Creating a Sovereign Debt Crisis," *International Affairs*, Vol. 98, No. 4, pp. 1347–1365.
Bush, C. (2021) "The Rise and Fall of Dagong Global Credit Rating Agency: A Geopolitical Challenge for the Rating Industry," *Journal of Financial Regulation*, Vol. 7, No. 2, pp. 319–324.
Chesterman, S. (2016) "Asia's Ambivalence about International Law and Institutions: Past, Present and Futures," *European Journal of International Law*, Vol. 27, No. 4, pp. 945–978.
Chin, G. and Thakur, R. (2010) "Will China Change the Rules of Global Order?," *The Washington Quarterly*, Vol. 33, No. 4, pp. 119–138.
Darbellay, A. and Gaillard, N. (2022) "Moral Hazard in the Export Credit Industry," in Flores Zendejas, J., Gaillard, N. and Michalek, R. (Eds) *Moral Hazard – A Financial, Legal, and Economic Perspective*. Abingdon and New York City: Routledge.
Dreher, A., Fuchs, A., Parks, B., Strange, A. and Tierney, M. J. (2022) *Banking on Beijing: The Aims and Impacts of China's Overseas Development Program*. Cambridge: Cambridge University Press.
Eichengreen, B. (2015) *Hall of Mirrors: The Great Depression, the Great Recession, and the Uses and Misuses of History*. Oxford: Oxford University Press.
Erie, M. S. (2021) "Chinese Law and Development," *Harvard International Law Journal*, Vol. 62, No. 1, pp. 51–116.
Essl, S., Celik, S. K., Kirby, P. and Proite, A. (2019) "Debt in Low-Income Countries – Evolution, Implications, and Remedies," *World Bank Policy Research Working Paper No. 8794*.
Financial Stability Forum (2009) *Report of the Financial Stability Forum on Addressing Procyclicality in the Financial System*. Basel: Financial Stability Forum.
Flores Zendejas, J. and Gaillard, N. (2022) "The International Lender of Last Resort between Scylla and Charybdis," in Flores Zendejas, J., Gaillard, N. and Michalek, R. (Eds) *Moral Hazard – A Financial, Legal, and Economic Perspective*. Abingdon and New York City: Routledge.
Frieden, J. A. (2009) "Global Imbalances, National Rebalancing, and the Political Economy of Recovery," *Council on Foreign Relations, Center for Geoeconomic Studies*.
Gaillard, N. (2011) *A Century of Sovereign Ratings*. New York City: Springer.
Gaillard, N. (2016) "Coping with Reliance on Credit Ratings," *Banking & Financial Services Policy Report*, Vol. 35, No. 7, pp. 12–21.
Gaillard, N. (2020) *Country Risk: The Bane of Foreign Investors*. Cham: Springer.
Gaillard, N. and Michalek, R. (2022a) "The Institutionalization of Bailouts, 1970–1984," in Flores Zendejas, J., Gaillard, N. and Michalek, R. (Eds) *Moral Hazard – A Financial, Legal, and Economic Perspective*. Abingdon and New York City: Routledge.
Gaillard, N. and Michalek, R. (2022b) "Remarks and Policy Recommendations to Fight Moral Hazard," in Flores Zendejas, J., Gaillard, N. and Michalek, R. (Eds) *Moral Hazard – A Financial, Legal, and Economic Perspective*. Abingdon and New York City: Routledge.
Gaillard, N. and Waibel, M. (2018) "The Icarus Syndrome: How Credit Rating Agencies Lost Their Quasi Immunity," *SMU Law Review*, Vol. 71, No. 4, pp. 1077–1116.

Gelpern, A., Horn, S., Morris, S., Parks, B. and Trebesch, C. (2021) *How China Lends – A Rare Look into 100 Debt Contracts with Foreign Governments*. Williamsburg, Kiel, and Washington, DC: AidData at William & Mary, Kiel Institute for the World Economy, Center for Global Development, and Peterson Institute for International Economics.

Gu, B. and Liu, T. (2022) "Shareholding Formulas in International Financial Institutions: Learning from the Asian Infrastructure Investment Bank," *Journal of International Economic Law*, Vol. 25, No. 4, pp. 643–658.

Hallaert, J-J. (2020) "The Tragedy of International Organizations in a World Order in Turmoil," *ECIPE Policy Brief No. 5/2020, European Centre for International Political Economy*.

He, Z., Krishnamurthy, A. and Milbradt, K. (2016) "What Makes US Government Bonds Safe Assets?," *American Economic Review*, Vol. 106, No. 5, pp. 519–523.

Helleiner, E. and Wang, H. (2019) "The Richness of Financial Nationalism: The Case of China," *Pacific Affairs*, Vol. 92, No. 2, pp. 211–234.

Horn, S., Reinhart, C. M. and Trebesch, C. (2021) "China's Overseas Lending," *Journal of International Economics*, Vol. 133, 103539.

Jordà, Ò., Schularick, M., Taylor, A. and Ward, F. (2018) "Global Financial Cycles and Risk Premiums," *NBER Working Paper No. 24677*.

Kalmoe, N. P. and Mason, L. (2022) *Radical American Partisanship – Mapping Violent Hostility, Its Causes, and the Consequences for Democracy*. Chicago: University of Chicago Press.

Kratz, A., Feng, A. and Wright, L. (2019) "New Data on the "Debt Trap" Question," *Rhodium Group, Note*, available at https://rhg.com/research/new-data-on-the-debt-trap-question.

Liu, Z. and Papa, M. (2022) *Can BRICS De-dollarize the Global Financial System?* Cambridge: Cambridge University Press.

Lorenzo, J. A. P. (2021) "A Path Toward Sustainable Development Along the Belt and Road," *Journal of International Economic Law*, Vol. 24, No. 3, pp. 591–608.

Maslen, S. and Aslan, C. (2022) "Enhancing Debt Transparency by Strengthening Public Debt Transaction Disclosure Practices," *Equitable Growth, Finance & Institutions Insight, World Bank*.

Mattlin, M. and Nojonen, M. (2015) "Conditionality and Path Dependence in Chinese Lending," *Journal of Contemporary China*, Vol. 24, No. 94, pp. 701–720.

Morris, S., Rockafellow, R. and Rose, S. (2021) "Mapping China's Multilateralism: A Data Survey of China's Participation in Multilateral Development Institutions and Funds," *Center for Global Development Policy Paper No. 241*.

New Development Bank (2019) *New Development Bank Policy on Sovereign Loans & Loans with Sovereign Guarantee*. Shanghai: NDB.

New Development Bank (2021) *Annual Report 2020*. Shanghai: NDB.

Nicolas, F. (2014) "La Chine et les institutions économiques multilatérales, entre révisionnisme et 'statu quo'," *Politique étrangère*, Vol. 79, No. 3, pp. 49–61.

Perks, M., Rao, Y., Shin, J. and Tokuoka, K. (2021) "Evolution of Bilateral Swap Lines," *IMF Working Paper No. 2021/210*.

Pistor, K. (2019) *The Code of Capital: How the Law Creates Wealth and Inequality*. Princeton: Princeton University Press.

Rudyak, M. and Chen, Y. (2021) "China's Lending Landscape and Approach to Debt Relief," *Overseas Development Institute, Emerging Analysis*.

Shaffer, G. and Gao, H. (2021) "How China Took on the United States and Europe at the WTO," in Shaffer, G. (Ed) *Emerging Powers and the World Trading System: The Past and Future of International Economic Law*. Cambridge: Cambridge University Press.

Shaffer, G. and Waibel, M. (2015) "The (Mis)Alignment of the Trade and Monetary Legal Orders," in Halliday, T. C. and Shaffer, G. (Eds) *Transnational Legal Orders*. Cambridge: Cambridge University Press.

Shaffer, G. and Waibel, M. (2016) "The Rise and Fall of Trade and Monetary Legal Orders: From the Interwar Period to Today's Global Imbalances," in Mallard, G. and Sgard, J. (Eds) *Contractual Knowledge – One Hundred Years of Legal Experimentation in Global Markets*. Cambridge: Cambridge University Press.

Song, K. and Xia, L. (2020) "Bilateral Swap Agreement and Renminbi Settlement in Cross-Border Trade," *Economic and Political Studies*, Vol. 8, No. 3, pp. 355–373.

Stephen, M. D. and Skidmore, D. (2019) "The AIIB in the Liberal International Order," *The Chinese Journal of International Politics*. Vol. 12, No. 1, pp. 61–91.

Sundquist, J. (2022) "Institutional Eclipse: How Chinese Loans Substitute for IMF Assistance," *mimeo*, available at https://jamessundquist.github.io/website/docs/Sundquist_JMP.pdf.

Wang, H. (2019a) "China's Approach to the Belt and Road Initiative: Scope, Character and Sustainability," *Journal of International Economic Law*, Vol. 22, No. 1, pp. 29–55.

Wang, H. (2019b) "The New Development Bank and the Asian Infrastructure Investment Bank: China's Ambiguous Approach to Global Financial Governance," *Development and Change*, Vol. 50, No. 1, pp. 221–244.

Wang, H. (2020) "Selective Reshaping: China's Paradigm Shift in International Economic Governance," *Journal of International Economic Law*, Vol. 23, No. 3, pp. 583–606.

Williamson, J. (1990) "What Washington Means by Policy Reform," in Williamson, J. (Ed) *Latin American Adjustment: How Much Has Happened?* Washington, DC: Institute for International Economics.

Würdemann, A. I. (2018) "The BRICS Contingent Reserve Arrangement: A Subversive Power Against the IMF's Conditionality?," *Journal of World Investment & Trade*, Vol. 19, No. 3, pp. 570–593.

Wynne, W. (1951) *State Insolvency and Foreign Bondholders – Volume II*. New Haven: Yale University Press.

6 Twenty years of prudential rules

Unfulfilled promises and challenges ahead

Elisabetta Montanaro

Following Minsky's insights, this chapter analyzes the main strengths and weaknesses of the micro- and macroprudential approaches that have ruled the banking sector since the early 2000s. Despite the impressive succession of reforms, the ultimate objective of international financial regulation (i.e., safeguarding financial stability while fostering economic growth) has been missed. The reforms did not actually result in the radical changes needed to prevent the build-up of leverage and maturity mismatch within the global financial system. The more stringent capital requirements have increased neither the long-term solvency of Western and Chinese banks nor their ability to support the real economy. The fragility of their profitability, arising from the pressure exercised by shadow banking and the innovative intermediation circuits, demonstrates the flaws of the current regulatory framework. The new macroprudential paradigm has only consisted of enhancing micro-prudential tools and establishing new standards for large banks. More importantly, the absence of any formal enforcement mechanism or rescue framework capable of shrinking the systemic footprint of global financial actors and reducing the expectation that governments will ultimately bail out too-big-to-fail institutions has exacerbated moral hazard.

6.1 Introduction

This chapter examines the main strengths and weaknesses of the micro- and macroprudential approaches that have ruled the banking sector since the early 2000s.[1] The period covered starts from the years of the Great Moderation (Duffie, 2019). During this period – in line with Minsky's saying that "stability induces instability" – the vulnerabilities of the global financial system resulting from financial liberalization and deregulation have been dramatically amplified (Waibel, 2020, pp. 4–11). Even after the Global Financial Crisis (GFC), the overall market-friendly approach to financial regulation has been maintained (Tonveronachi, 2018), with the objective of enhancing the "level playing field" under the so called "home-country principle" (Persaud, 2010). The promises repeated every year at G20 meetings to contain the destabilizing effect of global private finance have been broken, as shown by the frequent financial crises in the

DOI: 10.4324/9781003340430-8

recent decades (Laeven and Valencia, 2020). In the absence of an official well-funded global lender of last resort, and in spite of the new "institutional view on capital flows" adopted by the International Monetary Fund (IMF), unregulated capital flows have created unsustainable global imbalances (Ocampo, 2017), recently made worse by the huge build-up of private and public debt and the increase of inequality generated by the COVID-19 pandemic and the war in Ukraine. Supply chain disruptions and the spike of energy and food prices, the combination of which hit hard the most vulnerable emerging markets, have heightened inflationary pressures, leading central banks to raise interest rates to their highest levels in 15 years and to scale back their bond holdings. The appreciation of the U.S. dollar and the slowdown of the largest economies have caused economic turmoil in many emerging countries (IMF, 2022a, p.18). The dominance of the dollar in cross-border bank loans and international debt securities (Flores Zendejas and Gaillard, 2022) had already exacerbated geopolitical risks, arising from the refusal of emerging countries to be maintained in a "colonial status" (Minsky, 1990, p. 11) and their desire to protect themselves from capital flow reversals (Zhou, 2009). The threats to global financial stability have escalated after the unanimous imposition of economic sanctions on Russia by the G10 countries (Fantacci et al., 2022; Galbraith, 2023).[2] In the current international setup, the asymmetries stemming from dollar hegemony meet increasing opposition from new global players, such as China (Carneiro and De Conti, 2022). Rising geopolitical tensions between the United States and China, especially after Russia's invasion of Ukraine in February 2022, reinforced by reshoring or friend-shoring policies, could lead to an East–West decoupling and a major trade fragmentation, resulting in sizable welfare losses (Attinasi et al., 2023; see also Gmeiner's and Gaillard's chapters in this book). In this scenario, an international financial fragmentation would be likely, with significant implications for global financial stability (IMF, 2023b, pp. 81–101).

This chapter will proceed as follows. Section 6.2 presents Minsky's approach to banking supervision and financial regulation – the theoretical foundation of my analysis. Section 6.3 shows that the growth of the financial sector and increased leverage in the last 20 years have affected major developed economies as well as China. Section 6.4 documents the main changes in micro-prudential regulation introduced by Basel III and finds that its complexity and high compliance costs will foster the development of shadow banking. Section 6.5 focuses on macroprudential regulation. Whereas the moral hazard problems arising from too-big-to-fail (TBTF) institutions remain unresolved, the wide discretionary powers delegated to supervisory authorities are inconsistent with the objective of establishing the international level playing field. Section 6.6 concludes.

6.2 Minsky's approach to financial supervision and regulation

According to Minsky, financial supervision and regulation should have two key objectives: (i) funding investments needed to support economic growth (at or near full employment) and (ii) maintaining a safe and secure payment system. The financial instability hypothesis helps understand these two contradictory objectives (Minsky, 1992d, 1994a, and 1994b). The rationale of the financial instability hypothesis is that the mutual interaction between financial and economic choices is characterized by endogenous processes leading to over-indebtedness, which amplify overall vulnerabilities (Minsky, 1992a). One of the main lessons of this theory is the pivotal role of the progressive accumulation of leverage by both financial and nonfinancial agents, making financial systems more fragile, especially after periods of excessive growth with financial deepening and over-investment.[3]

Financial fragility may materialize when borrowers have to make fixed payments: the ability to do so depends primarily on uncertain cash receipts, that is, from profits they expect to receive from underlying capital assets. If financial fragilities, due to debt overhang, affect large sectors of the economy, they can undermine financial stability due to the accumulation of losses on loans and other financial assets in banks' balance sheets. Because the desired level of leverage for investment financing depends on the expected value of future profits, both borrowers' and lenders' decisions are affected by intractable uncertainty (Roncaglia, 2013). Such decisions can only be conjectural and determined by conventions and experience of the past (Minsky, 1970, pp. 48–72, 1976, and 2008, pp. 191–218). Therefore, "acceptable liability structures are based upon some margins of safety so that expected cash flows, even in periods when the economy is not doing well, will cover contractual debt payments" (Minsky, 1977b, p. 24). These margins of safety are provided by the excess of current and expected profits over cash payment commitments, by cash and liquidity holdings and financial net worth: they allow borrowers and lenders to protect themselves against uncertainty of future profits and prevent or limit potential losses driven by unfavorable refinancing or sell-offs. The adequacy of these financial cushions depends on the monetary constraints arising from liability structures of financial and nonfinancial agents. The financial position of economic agents having to repay their debt can be classified into three categories: hedge, speculative, or Ponzi.

Hedge units are expected to always meet cash commitments. In contrast, speculative units are characterized by liquidity shortfalls, and need therefore to either constrain the ability of their creditors to call the obligation or refinance outstanding debts at market conditions as and when they become due. Hence, they are subject to financial risks. A hedge position can shift to speculative if its margin of safety falls short due to unexpected losses. Ponzi units are the most vulnerable ones because they are obliged to increase their indebtedness simply to meet outstanding commitments and interest charges. When Ponzi units become unable to carry additional debt, the liquidity problem leads to insolvency and default. Banks and other financial intermediaries engage in maturity and risk transformation: they are speculative or Ponzi units (Minsky, 2008, pp. 230–238; Kregel, 2013, pp. 165–167).

The fragility of a financial system can be measured by the size of cash flow shortfalls or interest-rate changes likely to cause a systemic distress. Every financial system consists of a mix of hedge, speculative and Ponzi finance units. During a period of expansion, the easy access to credit by borrowers and search for yield by investors reduces liquidity buffers and may transform not only speculative but also hedge liability structures into Ponzi ones. The increase of interest rates to contain inflationary risks accelerates the progressive erosion of the margins of safety, pushing financial and nonfinancial agents to meet commitments by selling out their positions (Minsky, 2008, pp. 232–245). Periodic debt crises due to the widespread inability of borrowers to fulfill their financial commitments generate liquidity shortfalls, which, if not promptly resolved by an accommodative central bank, can trigger a systemic crisis and an economic depression.

Two institutional mechanisms can contain systemic risk. The first is the countercyclical expansion of the fiscal deficit. This "Big Government" tool can smooth a downturn by preventing a reduction of aggregate profits and the subsequent decrease in aggregate investment and employment. In addition, the government may provide (i) a deposit insurance scheme that includes a fiscal backstop large enough to liquidate and pay off failed banks and (ii) a public agency sufficient "to handle institutions that are deemed too 'important' or too large to liquidate" (Minsky and Campbell, 1987, p. 263 and 1988; Minsky, 1995, pp. 89–90).

The second mechanism is the safety net provided by the central bank acting as lender of last resort (Minsky, 2008, pp. 205–244). According to Minsky, in order to stabilize the financial system with liquidity support, the central bank's discount window should be open not only to commercial banks, but also to secondary market primary dealers (Minsky, 1970) and all financial institutions that engage in maturity and risk transformation. These entities are susceptible to runs and generate contagion risks due to the connections with non-bank financial intermediaries (NBFIs) – the so-called "fringe banks" (Minsky, 2008, p. 351). However, widening the discount window to financial institutions engaged in speculative and Ponzi finance encourages "systemic moral hazard" (Minsky and Campbell, 1987, p. 257).[4] To address this issue, regulators should promote the exit of unviable financial firms in a timely manner (Minsky and Campbell, 1987, p. 261; Minsky, 2008, pp. 363–364).

6.2.1 *Cash flow-oriented bank examination: a macroeconomic tool for liquidity stress testing*

The analysis above stresses that, in the Minskyan perspective, financial stability crucially depends on the liquidity buffers available to speculative and Ponzi liability structures, which characterize banks and other financial intermediaries. The gap between expected and actual cash receipts, due to adverse economic conditions or inability to adjust profitability to rising refinancing costs, can deplete margins. Therefore, widespread liquidity shortfalls may compel financial firms "to make positions by selling positions" and cutting back on lending to real economy. Accordingly, the main result of the "cash flow-oriented bank examination" should be the estimate, through a scenario analysis, of the liquidity position of banks based on their ongoing activity, and the feasible "position making activities" needed to meet liquidity buffers due to operative and regulatory requirements (Minsky, 1967). Supervisory processes – at Minsky's time but also today – mainly focus on assessing the creditworthiness and the viability of banks through liquidity and capital ratios, and their compliance with the rule of conduct (Minsky, 1970, pp. 63–64 and 1975b, p. 5). To protect against these shortcomings, Minsky proposes the cash-flow analysis – an essential tool for monetary policy.

Minsky (1975a, pp. 154–155) advocates the adoption of the cash-flow analysis specifically for large banks, due to their connections with "fringe banks" and "various short-term financial markets." The purpose of this supervisory approach is

> to use the examination process to generate information on both the liquidity and solvency of particular institutions but also on threats, if any, to the stability of financial markets; this information was to be forward looking and to be such that the implications of alternative economic and policy scenarios could be investigated...The perspective underlying the suggestions was a dynamic, evolving set of financial institutions and relations.
>
> (Minsky, 1975a, p. 150)

As Kregel (2014) rightly points out, the cash-flow analysis suggested by Minsky is typically macroprudential: it is designed to prevent systemic risk caused by (i) the interconnectedness between financial institutions (Minsky, 1970, p. 73 and 1975b, pp. 2–3; Minsky and Campbell, 1987, p. 255) and (ii) the interactions between funding and market liquidity (Minsky, 1975b, p. 4). The same cash-flow analysis is the basis of the top-down liquidity stress tests recently performed by the IMF under the Financial Sector Assessment Program (FSAP) to assess funding and market liquidity risks as part of its mandate to monitor global financial stability (Adrian et al., 2020). It seems to me dispiriting that Minsky's proposal does not appear in the paper's rich bibliography. The significant difference between the stress test advanced by Minsky and the present macroprudential stress tests is presented in Section 6.5.

6.2.2 Financial regulation

According to Minsky (2008), instability is an endogenous characteristic of capitalism and financial regulation should limit its effects by jointly safeguarding financial stability and fostering economic growth. In a Minskyan perspective, the scope of financial policies is wider than what is traditionally attributed to regulatory bodies: they incorporate speculative and Ponzi financial structures, which involves the identification of excessive leverage, overinvestment in long-term capital assets, and growing financialization. My analysis of Minsky's proposals focuses on three points: (i) the speculative finance of large corporations; (ii) banking regulation in the strict sense; and (iii) the risks stemming from financial deepening and layering.

6.2.2.1 "Ordinary corporations as financial institutions" (Minsky, 2008)

The financial structure of large corporations is typically speculative, due to their high leverage and their need to refinance outstanding debt. In the short term, cash commitments are higher than expected profit obtained from long-term investments. Large corporations are frequently capital-intensive entities and their market power is supported by the Big Government's interventions, which ensure protection against financial and operational risks (Gaillard and Michalek, 2022a, pp. 134–139). Minsky therefore advances two main policies to eliminate the threats to financial stability. First, bankruptcy processes should be easy and cheap, so that "no organization can be so large that its bankruptcy is political unacceptable" (Minsky, 2008, p. 354). Second, in order to remove fiscal incentives to debt financing, the corporate income tax, which allows corporations to deduct interest paid on taxable income, should be replaced by "a full imputation of per-share income to the stockholders, regardless of whether or not dividends were paid" (Minsky, 2008, p. 241).

6.2.2.2 Banking regulation

The basic principles of banking regulation highlighted by Minsky are of extraordinary importance today. Banks should not be allowed to finance long-term capital assets with monetary liabilities protected by deposit insurance (Minsky, 1992b and 1994a). At the same time, regulation should protect commercial banks' "franchise value" and assure that commercial banking would always be profitable enough to build up adequate capital buffers (Minsky, 1992d). Regarding the TBTF and moral hazard problems, Minsky claims that "[t]he rule of thumb is that no bank or financial institution can be so big that the Federal Reserve would not allow the institution to fail" (Minsky, 1977a, p. 29 and 2008, pp. 222–223).[5] The need of a congruent financial regulation for NBFIs is pointed out by Minsky. Regulation of money market mutual funds "which looks at the assets they own and the liabilities they issue *must* identify the institutions as banks and their liabilities as money" (Minsky, 1982, p. 76). Minsky anticipates the procyclicality of bank capital requirements, arguing that "risk-adjusted capital requirements would be pro-cyclical, worsening the conditions of banks just when other operating costs are rising, and profits are being squeezed" (Minsky and Campbell, 1987, p. 258; Minsky, 1992d, p. 25).

The innovative character of Minsky's proposals for banking regulation deserves an in-depth analysis. The two main objectives of banking regulation should be to (i) promote a bigger role for small banks, which should provide loans to small firms and (ii) contain the growth of banks' assets, through leverage and pay-out ratios (Minsky, 2008, pp. 242–282, and pp. 354–358).

The first objective, aimed at reducing the increasing concentration in the banking system, should be pursued to enable small banks to offer investment and merchant banking services. Small banks should also be supported by the establishment of a uniform leverage ratio – assuming that, in the United States, their capitalization was higher than for large ones. Turning to the second objective, a uniform leverage ratio implies that monetary authorities can modify the increase in internal capital needed for every bank to support the growth of assets simply by modifying the pay-out ratio. When the growth of assets exceeds the non-inflationary rate of growth of nominal GDP, a bank should be obliged to increase its pay-out ratio "in order to have an internal rate of growth consistent with stable price" (Minsky, 2008, p. 357). Conversely, when credit growth rate is insufficient to support the desired increase in economic activity, the pay-out ratio should decline. A bank whose capitalization does not meet the required leverage ratio should be forbidden to remunerate shareholder with dividends and share buybacks (Montanaro and Tonveronachi, 2012). In a Minskyan perspective, higher capital ratios can only mitigate the economic and social costs of financial crises: instead, the main objective of banking regulation should be to control excessive credit growth and maturity mismatch (Jordà et al., 2021).

6.2.2.3 *Financial deepening and layering, and "money manager" capitalism*

Financial deepening is driven by the increase in the debt to GDP ratio and the availability of new financial markets and instruments which assure borrowers and lenders "that money will be available when needed as long they hold appropriate assets or have good profits" (Minsky, 2008, p. 242). Financial assets can therefore grow more than the monetary base when easy access to credit reduces liquidity buffers and increases the vulnerability of economic agents to financial risks. For that reason, Minsky was concerned by the expansion of institutional investors (money markets funds, pension funds and finance companies) and the decreasing weight of traditional commercial banks. This new financial structure where NBFIs "have given rise to a new layer of financial intermediation" was called "money manager capitalism" (Minsky, 1992c, p. 7, 1993 and 1995, p. 92). According to Minsky (1992e), two main factors fostered the growth of "money manager capitalism": the inability of banks to compete with these new intermediaries eager to make payment services a profit center, and the increase in public debt. The objective of these institutional investors was (and is) not the healthy capital development of the economy, which needs relationship banking, but the maximization of "shareholder value" focusing on high short-term returns and speculative gains across various capital markets (Rajan, 2005; Lazonick, 2013).

Let's conclude with one of Minsky's most important messages:

> The impact of money market capitalism has heightened uncertainty... Institutional innovations that help to offset the impact of uncertainty are needed as the losers in the gambles imposed by uncertainty can become alienated and become potential recruits for an alternative to democracy.
>
> (Minsky, 1996, p. 365)

6.3 Leverage and financial deepening in the last 20 years

Figures 6.1–6.3 present, respectively, the massive surge in private debt, and public debt, and the growth of non-bank credit to private non-financial sector in the United Kingdom, the United States, China, and the Euro area. Figure 6.4 plots the rising use of leverage within the financial system through over-the-counter (OTC) derivatives.

Figures 6.1 and 6.2 show two significant trends since 2002. First, private and public debts have risen in all major economies, partly under the effect

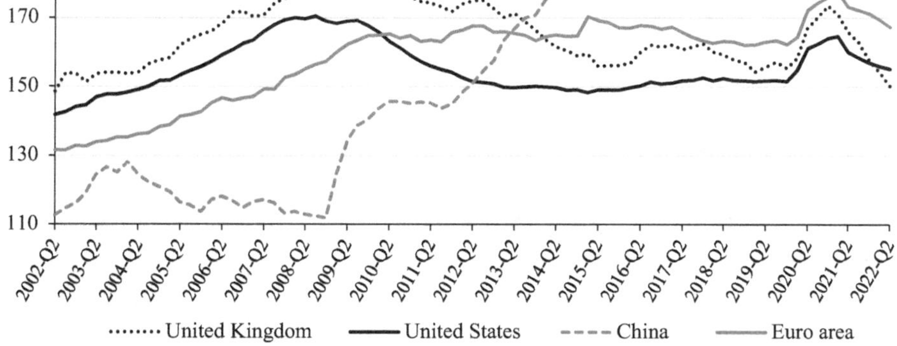

Figure 6.1 Total credit to private non-financial sector (in % of GDP), 2002Q2–2022Q2

Source: Bank for International Settlements (BIS) Statistics Warehouse.

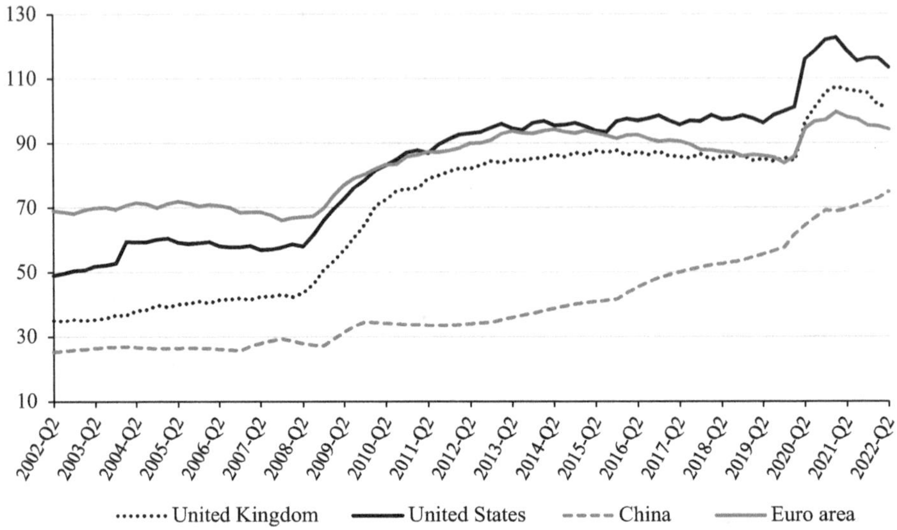

Figure 6.2 Total credit to the government sector at nominal value (in % of GDP), 2002Q2–2022Q2

Source: BIS Statistics Warehouse.

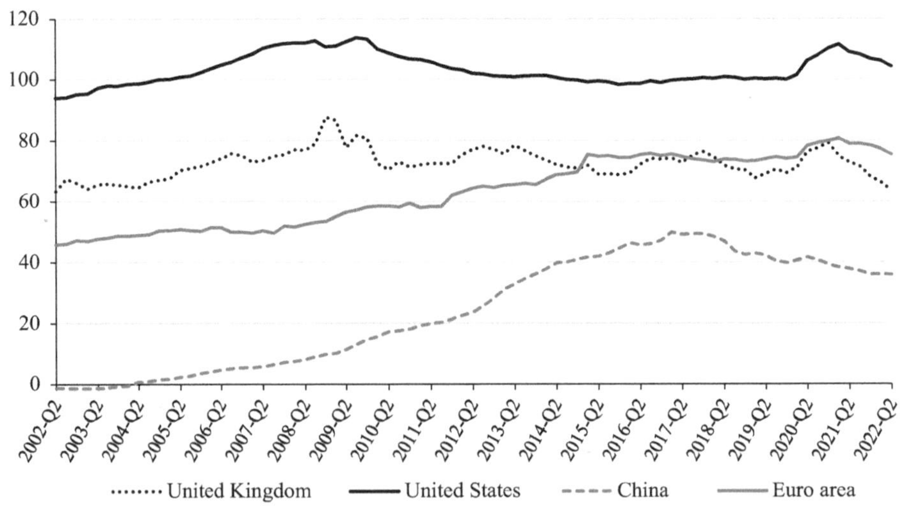

Figure 6.3 Non-bank credit to private non-financial sector (in % of GDP), 2002Q2–2022Q2

Source: BIS Statistics Warehouse.

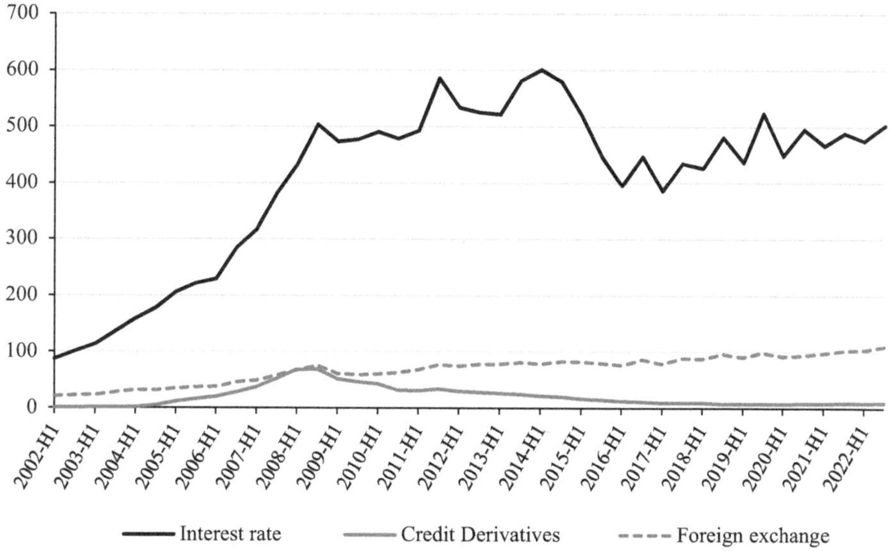

Figure 6.4 Notional value of OTC derivatives (US$ tn), 2002H1–2022H1

Source: BIS, OTC derivatives statistics.

of accommodative monetary policies. The spectacular tightening of monetary policies and the new geopolitical risks observed since 2022 have increased debt service cost, especially for governments and non-financial companies. They have also affected the quality of banks' assets and exacerbated the vulnerabilities of NBFIs (Financial Stability Board, 2023; Minsky, 2008, pp. 232–245). Second, China's public and private debts have grown at a much higher rate than major developed countries. This evolution, which has been partly driven by the progressive opening of China's capital account and its destabilizing effects, reflects the financialization of the Chinese economy. More than ever, Chinese and Western economies share common vulnerabilities.[6]

In its latest report on China, the IMF (2023a, pp. 4–6) stresses that the country's financial vulnerabilities have increased dramatically. The main causes are the large debt overhang of the household and corporate sector, the unresolved crisis of the Ponzi-like property developers,[7] the surge in non-performing loans (NPLs), and the undercapitalization of many small- and medium-sized banks. The shadow banking to GDP ratio grew from 5.3% in 2002 to 59.8% in 2020, with a significant growth of the riskiest components – i.e., open-ended and money market funds (Financial Stability Board, 2022c). According to Bellavite Pellegrini et al. (2022), the "too big to fail" and "too important to fail" issues remain a persistent threat to state-owned banks in an environment where Chinese authorities play a key role to ensure financial stability.[8] At the same time, the high leverage of real estate finance services and shadow banking firms is set to contribute significantly to the increased systemic risk of China's financial system. Financial stability could also be undermined by the rapid growth of Big Tech credit (Cornelli et al., 2023).

Figure 6.3 reflects financial deepening and, to some extent, systemic risk, which partly arises from short-term funding (Duffie, 2019). In the two market-based financial systems (i.e., the United States and the United Kingdom), non-bank financing has remained relatively stable since the end of the GFC. In contrast, the growth of market financing has been sustained for China and the Euro area. One more time, this suggests that the lessons from past crises are quickly forgotten.

The GFC demonstrated that the OTC derivative markets, due to the network connections between banks and NBFIs, can nurture systemic risk dramatically (Ellul and Kim, 2021). Notwithstanding, as supported by Figure 6.4, the size of OTC derivative market has rebounded since the mid-2010s, mainly for interest rate and foreign exchange derivatives, whose risks have grown due to heightened volatility, higher margin requirements, and deteriorating market liquidity.

6.4 Basel III micro-prudential regulation

Basel III standards were the response to the regulatory and supervisory shortcomings observed during the GFC.[9] The new rules, which apply to internationally active banks, consist of strengthening present requirements, limiting the use of unreliable models based on value-at-risk (Aymanns et al., 2016), and establishing macroprudential frameworks. However, global regulators have continued to privilege a market-friendly approach to address banking and financial issues (Tonveronachi, 2010). Although the improvements in micro-prudential regulation have been far-reaching, Basel III does not reduce supervisors' large discretionary powers in terms of approving and validating internal models and fixing the various add-ons to capital requirements (Haldane, 2014). Despite the G20 leaders' willingness that the definition of capital should be harmonized to achieve consistent measures of capital and capital adequacy (G20, 2008), the size of bank capital remains opaque. Why? Because of the divergence between regulatory and accounting rules and the wide range of eligible hybrid instruments whose loss-absorbing capacity may be overestimated for periods of stress (European Central Bank, 2022, p. 2).

From a micro-prudential perspective, the main objectives of Basel III have been to cut the excessive variability of risk-weighted assets' valuations and increase the level and quality of capital most capable of absorbing losses (Acharya et al., 2022). The risk sensitivity of the standardized approach has been enhanced, and the use of internal models has been constrained by (i) setting higher limits ("input floors") to the main determinants of risk-weight values and (ii) removing the internal rating-based approach for credit exposures to banks and corporate firms and for operational risk. Besides, risk-weighted assets computed with internal models cannot fall below the "output floor." Concretely, the outcome of the bank's total risk-weighted assets when using internal models cannot be lower than 72.5% of what it would have been if the bank had used standardized methods. Due to the strong opposition of European banks to the output floor (Mérö, 2021), the European Commission has proposed a longer transitional period and a narrow implementation of this rule – at the consolidated level only. The opposition of the banking industry is understandable as banks have invested a lot to establish and implement internal models. Those have been promoted by regulators to "improve risk-market efficiency," so "that regulatory capital is both adequate and closer to economic capital" (Caruana, 2005).[10]

A non-risk-weighted leverage ratio has been introduced, aimed at restricting the build-up of leverage in the banking sector and reinforcing the risk-based requirements with a simple, non-risk-based "backstop measure." The objectives of the new leverage ratio are jointly micro- and macroprudential. From a micro-prudential perspective, the leverage ratio should contain the variability of the valuation of risk-weighted assets. From a macroprudential perspective, the leverage ratio – if rightly measured – should limit the procyclical effects arising from risk weights.

In 2019, the rules for large exposures – defined as exposures to a counterparty or to a group of connected counterparties – entered into force. They establish the maximum allowable amount in percent of highest quality of capital, as a "backstop" to risk-based capital requirements. Two liquidity ratios have been added: the liquidity coverage ratio (LCR) and the net stable funding ratio (NSFR). The first addresses the bank funding liquidity risk, and the second aims at reducing incentives to maturity transformation. These two ratios are a huge step forward looking at the micro-dimension of prudential regulation and should contribute to tackle liquidity risk in a macroprudential perspective. However, Minsky's arguments make it clear that – considering the interconnectedness between financial intermediaries and the linkages between funding and market risks – only a systemic approach to liquidity risk can prevent the threat to the overall financial stability. The March 2023 failures of Silicon Valley Bank (SVB) and Signature Bank (partly caused by their exposure to the crypto sector) and the related market turmoil confirm Minsky's approach to liquidity risk. Finally, capital requirements for the trading book have been rewritten to limit regulatory arbitrage generated by the progress in financial engineering and the misuse of internal models. In addition, the main problem of these prudential rules, namely the fictitious distinction between the banking and the trading book, has not been solved.

Even though many new tools relating to the micro-prudential reforms have not been finalized yet, a preliminary assessment can be made. First, once again, the Basel Committee reacted to the complexity of banking by increasing the complexity of the regulatory framework: the last version of Basel III counts 1518 pages, compared to 347 pages for Basel II. This complex set of rules is very likely to encourage evasion and regulatory arbitrage and evasion (Schenk, 2021, p.11). Second, the more stringent capital ratios and higher compliance costs could undermine a bank's "franchise value" which runs counter to the main objectives of banking regulation (Minsky, 1992b). Without a holistic perspective among financial supervisors, systemic risk stemming from interlinkages across financial institutions and countries may be amplified by the more severe micro-prudential requirements. The unintended consequences would be the decrease of bank lending to riskier companies (De Jonghe et al., 2020), and the further development and expansion of shadow banking (Irani et al., 2021), including crypto-assets,[11] widely considered a potential source of systemic risk (Financial Stability Board, 2022b).[12] Third, because the principle of proportionality remains at national supervisors' discretion, smaller banks will be the most penalized, which may lead to a higher concentration of banking systems (Minsky, 2008). Fourth, in spite of some macroprudential adjustments, the procyclical effect of risk-adjusted capital requirements remains significant, amplifying the procyclicality of leverage. Minsky and Campbell (1987) warned regulators to be careful on this issue. Finally, the effective implementation of the more basic rules of micro-prudential regulation continues to be constrained by "economic nationalism" (Waibel, 2020, p. 41) and ongoing lobbying efforts (Redert, 2022). In light of the large discretionary powers granted to national supervisors, the "international convergence of capital measurement and capital standards" remains unaccomplished. This evolution questions the appropriateness and feasibility of the one-size-fits-all approach (Tonveronachi, 2020, Hertogen, 2020).

6.5 The macroprudential perspective of the new regulatory framework

Financial instability is an endogenous feature of capitalism. It can be contained by reducing the weight of speculative and Ponzi finance structures and breaking the opaque and extended linkages between banks and shadow institutions and markets. Therefore, a true macroprudential perspective implies not only a systemic approach, but also a greater ability of supervisors and regulators to go beyond non-binding recommendations (Aikman et al., 2019, p. 127) and enforce the structural changes needed to shift to the cash-flow approach advanced by Minsky.

The regulatory tools labeled as macroprudential and added to the regulatory framework were designed to address the systemic risk issue caused by the TBTF problem and enhance micro-prudential requirements. Among these micro-macro measures, capital buffers are the most significant regulatory innovation. Their purposes are to contain the procyclicality of capital requirements and force banks to build up higher margins of safety during low-aversion periods, which can be drawn down to hedge losses in recessionary times. As a result, banks must progressively restrict the pay-out ratio if their capital goes below the required buffers, for which only the capital of highest quality is eligible. Amidst the COVID-19 pandemic, regulators relaxed constraints regarding capital and liquidity buffers and allowed banks to delay loss recognition for distressed borrowers (Drehmann et al., 2020). Yet, "only a few banks' capital ratios have fallen below their regulatory capital buffer levels to date, while many banks maintained substantial capital buffers" (Hernández de Cos, 2021, p. 9). Banks' decisions – driven by the uncertainty over the level of future profits needed to rebuild the buffers – confirm the difficulty of pursuing macroprudential objectives with micro-prudential tools (White, 2019). Banks have also learned that, during high risk-aversion periods, prudential authorities are prone to use their large discretionary powers and adopt accommodative policies. For example, they are prompt to relax the provisioning of NPLs, which may amplify moral hazard problems (Gaillard and Michalek, 2022b, p. 203).[13]

The Financial Stability Board (FSB) has been tasked with implementing the macroprudential package related to the TBTF problem: the new framework has been applied to the global banks defined as "systemically important" (G-SIBs) by the Basel Committee's methodology. These TBTF institutions are subjected to higher capital requirements and to "enhanced supervision" through stress tests and the validation of resolution plans. The objective of stress tests is to (i) measure the impact of adverse macroeconomic scenarios on large banks' solvency, profitability and lending activity following a top-down or a hybrid approach (top-down and bottom-up), and (ii) oblige the banks that present a capital shortfall to raise additional capital or restrict the pay-out ratio. These scenarios are based on external shocks only, such as a prolonged recession. They overlook endogenous fragilities, which arise from interactions between vulnerabilities of the financial and real estate sectors as well as the need to contain them through structural interventions. Moreover, stress tests do not "incorporate *indirect* risks to bank capital through channels such as market-wide funding and liquidity disruptions, fire sales and so on" (Tarullo, 2016, p. 7). The new crisis procedure for G-SIBs is a resolution regime that allows authorities to take control of a failing bank in order to restore its viability or, if the bank is no more viable, to write down specific classes of liabilities and convert creditor claims into equity or other capital instruments (bail-in). In both cases, the resolution authorities may resort to a mandatory resolution fund financed by all banks. G-SIBs must (i) have an adequate amount of financing instruments, (ii) check that those are suitable for a bail-in, and (iii) meet additional financial requirements, labeled "total loss absorbing capacity" (TLAC). Because at least one third of TLAC must be fulfilled with long-term debt, it is questionable that these financial instruments "will actually absorb losses in a time of market stress, since it has not done so in the past" (Federal Reserve Bank of Minneapolis, 2017, p. 18). As the resources needed for an orderly resolution may exceed the available TLAC, the authorities can utilize the resolution fund. In the event of a systemic crisis or in case of distress of a large bank, the resolution fund may become underfunded. Recovering financial resources *ex post* through levies on the financial industry may amplify the downturn. Ultimately, investors are encouraged to prioritize G-SIBs, thus increasing the TBTF distortion (Tonveronachi, 2020, p. 22).

More than a decade after the GFC, the FSB (2021) highlights several disappointing outcomes. The funding cost advantages of G-SIBs remain at least as high as they were before the 2007–2008 crisis (FSB, 2021, p. 3), demonstrating the low credibility of the reforms in terms of market valuation. At the same time, the complexity of the TBTF banks has increased: the average G-SIB has over a thousand subsidiaries in more than 40 jurisdictions (FSB, 2021, p. 4; Gaillard and Michalek's chapter in this book). The degree of concentration of financial systems has not been reduced, and banking sectors are still characterized by a dominant set of a few very large banks and many small- and medium-size banks (FSB, 2021, p. 5; Gaillard and Michalek's chapter in this book). Whereas the effectiveness of resolution regimes in systemic crises remains untested, government support for failing banks has continued (FSB, 2021, p. 7). Because supervisors provide extensive forbearance and tend to intervene too late, the bail-in design will not become a credible alternative to a bailout in the event of a financial crisis or the failure of a TBTF financial institution, as the March 2023 case of Credit Suisse demonstrates.

The absence of any formal rescue and enforcement framework capable of shrinking the systemic footprint of global financial actors combined with the expectation that governments will ultimately bail out TBTF institutions have exacerbated moral hazard. The objective of setting an international level playing field for national supervisors and financial actors has not been achieved. In fact, the one-size-fits-all approach is a mistake as global regulators are unable to overcome the resistance of national supervisors against international constraints on their policy autonomy. Moreover, the substantial discretion afforded by the new regulatory framework to supervisory authorities encourages financial firms' lobbying and leads to competitive deregulation pressures. Lastly, "macroprudential measures are largely bank-based, so that they miss the growing non-bank forms of financial intermediation" (Bank for International Settlements, 2022, p. 10). Despite the broad consensus that the shadow banking system was one of the main causes of the GFC (Tarullo, 2019), it remains outside the regulatory perimeter (G20, 2022; FSB, 2022a).

6.6 Conclusion

Despite the painful social and economic costs of financial crises, the prudential framework that has ruled the banking sector since the early 2000s has been unable to limit the rise of public and private debts and the growth of financial deepening. As the SVB and Credit Suisse crises have shown, "banking is suddenly at inflection point. It is now clear how essentially vulnerable the sector is no matter what the capital and liquidity ratios say."[14] Micro- and macroprudential rules have become increasingly complex and their efficacy is very questionable. This is worrying at the time when global financial regulators have to tackle new tail risks – e.g., climate and cyber risks and the systemic risk arising from artificial intelligence (Daníelsson et al., 2022).

As Minsky (1986, p. 14) taught us, "regulatory changes follow, rather than lead, changes in market practices. Successful avoidance of old regulations is usually a prerequisite to the promulgation of new (and more) liberalized ones." Since the 2010s, the deregulatory pressure has shifted from the banking sector to NBFIs.

Next, contrary to what many policy makers promised, the international playing field has remained unleveled and the cost of financial globalization is unevenly distributed within and across countries. Minsky clearly understood many years ago that

> global financial stability also requires agreed domain of responsibility for each key central bank when it acts as a lender of last resort to the international financial community. The need for a clarification of international lender of last resort responsibilities implies that the development of regulations and interventions required for the proper functioning of a globally integrated financial structure should be on the 'agenda'.
>
> (Minsky, 1986, p. 33)

Since a global safety net does not exist, simplifying and de-globalizing financial regulation remain major challenges. Following Minsky's proposals, several structural financial regulations should be introduced to shrink financial intermediation and reduce the financialization of large companies. These interventions could help achieve financial stability and induce supervisors to prevent and penalize banking mismanagement.

Notes

1 I thank Mario Tonveronachi for his invaluable suggestions that helped improve a previous draft. The usual caveats apply.

2 The G10 includes 11 members: Belgium, Canada, France, Germany, Italy, Japan, the Netherlands, Sweden, Switzerland, the United Kingdom, and the United States. See https://www.imf.org/en/About/Factsheets/A-Guide-to-Committees-Groups-and-Clubs.

3 Financial deepening can be defined as the increase in the ratio of a country's financial assets to its GDP (Moore, 1986).

4 Minsky examines the need for central banks to extend the access to the discount window even to the financial intermediaries which are now defined as shadow banks. One the most interesting examples is the episode of the run on REITs (Real Estate Investment Trusts) which was resolved by the intervention of the Federal Reserve in 1974–1975 (Minsky, 2008, pp. 50–68). This episode is remarkably similar to what occurred in the so-called "dash-for-cash" episode in March 2020, during the COVID-19 pandemic. On this occasion the Federal Open Market Committee intervened with massive purchases of mortgage-backed securities

(MBS). This injection of liquidity preserved financial stability and averted contagion risk deriving from the strong connections between REITs and other entities holding MBS with the banking sector (Financial Stability Board, 2020; Metrick and Tarullo, 2021). According to the IMF (2023b, p. 78), "opening access to central bank liquidity to NBFIs could be necessary if there is a high risk of contagion either to systemically important institutions or markets or if the sector or entities are important for financial intermediation and credit provision."

5 According to Minsky (1992c, pp. 5–6), the bailout of Continental Illinois in 1984 gave rise to the "too big to fail doctrine." See also Gaillard and Michalek (2022a).

6 In the early 2010s, China posted a primary fiscal surplus. According to the IMF (2022b), its primary fiscal deficit has become structural and was projected to increase from 5.2% of GDP in 2021 to 7.9% in 2022.

7 Chinese property developers usually cover contractual spending commitments and net interest payments by additional borrowing and presales of unfinished properties. The default of Evergrande and other Chinese property developers confirms the fragility of these firms' liability structure.

8 In my opinion, it would be right for every government to have a dominant role in pursuing financial stability.

9 It is interesting that China was prompt to adopt and implement Basel III standards (see Xi, 2016; IMF, 2017). This implies that the shortcomings of Basel III identified here are likely to affect not only Western but also Chinese banks.

10 On November 8th, 2022, the Council of the European Union (second regulator) proposed to the European Parliament the full implementation of the output floor both at the banking group level and at the individual bank level. Yet, it left to Member States the discretion to apply the floor at the highest level of consolidation for banks operating in their country. Therefore, the issue remains unresolved.

11 Crypto-assets can be considered a sort of private money (Garratt and Shun, 2023).

12 The Basel Committee on Banking Supervision published in December 2022 the final standard on the prudential treatment of crypto-asset exposure, to be implemented from January 1st, 2025. The collapse of the crypto company FTX and the related turmoil in financial markets have highlighted the risks of cryptocurrencies.

13 The so-called borrower-based measures, such as stricter risk weights applied to exposures to the real estate sector or caps for loan-to-income and debt service-to-income ratios, seem to be much more robust. According to Aikman et al. (2019, p. 119), these measures, if applied before the GFC, "would have helped to reduce the build-up of household debt vulnerabilities in the run-up to the crisis." Their implementation is however uneven and left to the discretion of national supervisors.

14 *Euromoney*, "The Banking Crisis and its Consequences," 20 March 2023.

References

Acharya, V. V., Gujral, I., Kulkarni, N. Shin, H. S. (2022) "Dividends and Bank Capital in the Global Financial Crisis of 2007–2009," *Journal of Financial Crises*, Vol. 4, No. 2, pp. 1–39.

Adrian, T., Morsink, J. and Schumacher, L. (2020) *Stress Testing at the IMF*. International Monetary Fund, Monetary and Capital Markets Department, Report No. 20/04. Washington, DC: IMF.

Aikman, D., Bridges, J., Kashyap, A. and Siegert, C. (2019) "Would Macroprudential Regulation Have Prevented the Last Crisis?," *Journal of Economic Perspectives*, Vol. 33, No. 1, pp. 107–130.

Attinasi, M.-G., Boeckelmann, L. and Meunier, B. (2023) "Friend-Shoring Global Value Chains: A Model-Based Assessment," *European Central Bank, Economic Bulletin*, Vol. 2023, No. 2, pp. 59–66.

Aymanns, C., Caccioli, F., Farmer, J. D. and Tan, V. W. C. (2016) "Taming the Basel Leverage Cycle," *Journal of Financial Stability*, Vol. 27, December, pp. 263–277.

Bank for International Settlements (2022) *Macro-Financial Stability Frameworks and External Financial Conditions*. Report Submitted to the G20 Finance Ministers and Central Bank Governors. July. Basel: Bank for International Settlements.

Bellavite Pellegrini, C., Cincinelli, P., Meoli, M. and Urga, G. (2022) "The Contribution of (Shadow) Banks and Real Estate to Systemic Risk in China," *Journal of Financial Stability*, Vol. 60, 101018.

Carneiro, R. and De Conti, B. (2022) "Exorbitant Privilege and Compulsory Duty: The Two Faces of the Financialised IMS," *Cambridge Journal of Economics*, Vol. 46, No. 4, pp. 735–752.

Caruana, J. (2005) "Basel II – Back to the Future," *Speech delivered at the 7th HKMA Distinguished Lecture, "Basel II – Back to the Future", Hong Kong, 4 February*, available at https://www.bis.org/review/r050216c.pdf.

Cornelli, G., Frost, J., Gambacorta, L., Rau, P. R., Wardrop, R. and Ziegler, T. (2023) "Fintech and Big Tech Credit: Drivers of the Growth of Digital Lending," *Journal of Banking & Finance*, Vol. 148, 106742.

Daníelsson, J., Macrae, R. and Uthemann, A. (2022) "Artificial Intelligence and Systemic Risk," *Journal of Banking & Finance*, Vol. 140, 106290.

De Jonghe, O., Dewachter, H. and Ongena, S. (2020) "Bank Capital (Requirements) and Credit Supply: Evidence from Pillar 2 Decisions," *Journal of Corporate Finance*, Vol. 60, No. C, pp. 1–28.

Drehmann, M., Farag, M., Tarashev, N. and Tsatsaronis, K. (2020) "Buffering Covid-19 Losses – The Role of Prudential Policy," *BIS Bulletin No. 9*, 24 April.

Duffie, D. (2019) "Prone to Fail: The Pre-Crisis Financial System," *Journal of Economic Perspectives*, Vol. 33, No. 1, pp. 81–106.

Ellul, A. and Kim, D. (2021) "Counterparty Choice, Bank Interconnectedness, and Systemic Risk," *Office of Financial Research, Working Paper 21-03*.

European Central Bank (2022) *ECB Response to the European Commission's Call for Advice on the Review of the EU Macroprudential Framework*. March. Frankfurt: European Central Bank.

Fantacci, L., Gobbi, L. and Luciani, D. (2022) "Global Public Good or Financial Weapon? Dollar Hegemony to the Test of Sanctions," *Moneta e Credito*, Vol. 75, No. 298, pp. 123–147.

Federal Reserve Bank of Minneapolis (2017) *The Minneapolis Plan to End Too Big to Fail*. December. Minneapolis: Federal Reserve Bank of Minneapolis.

Financial Stability Board (2020) *Holistic Review of the March Market Turmoil*. 17 November. Basel: Financial Stability Board.

Financial Stability Board (2021) *Evaluation of the Effects of Too-Big-To-Fail Reforms. Final Report*. 31 March. Basel: Financial Stability Board.

Financial Stability Board (2022a) *To G20 Finance Ministers and Central Bank Governors*. 14 February. Basel: Financial Stability Board.

Financial Stability Board (2022b) *Assessment of Risks to Financial Stability from Crypto-Assets*. 16 February. Basel: Financial Stability Board.

Financial Stability Board (2022c) *Global Monitoring Report on Non-Bank Financial Intermediation 2022*. 20 December. Basel: Financial Stability Board.

Financial Stability Board (2023) *To G20 Finance Ministers and Central Bank Governors*. 6 April. Basel: Financial Stability Board.

Flores Zendejas, J. and Gaillard, N. (2022) "The International Lender of Last Resort between Scylla and Charybdis," in Flores Zendejas, J., Gaillard, N. and Michalek, R. (Eds) *Moral Hazard – A Financial, Legal and Economic Perspective*. Abingdon and New York City: Routledge.

G20 (2008) "Declaration of the Summit on Financial Markets and the World Economy – Washington, DC, 15 November," available at http://www.g20.utoronto.ca/2008/2008declaration1115.html.

G20 (2022) "Communiqué – G20 Finance Ministers and Central Bank Governors Meeting, 17–18 February, Jakarta, Indonesia," available at https://www.banque-france.fr/sites/default/files/media/2022/02/22/g20_fmcbg_communique_jakarta_17-18_february_2022.pdf.

Gaillard, N. and Michalek, R. (2022a) "The Institutionalization of Bailouts, 1970–1984," in Flores Zendejas, J., Gaillard, N. and Michalek, R. (Eds) *Moral Hazard – A Financial, Legal and Economic Perspective*. Abingdon and New York City: Routledge.

Gaillard, N. and Michalek, R. (2022b) "Remarks and Policy Recommendations to Fight Moral Hazard," in Flores Zendejas, J., Gaillard, N. and Michalek, R. (Eds) *Moral Hazard – A Financial, Legal and Economic Perspective*. Abingdon and New York City: Routledge.

Galbraith, J. K. (2023) "The Gift of Sanctions: An Analysis of Assessments of the Russian Economy, 2022–2023," *Institute for New Economic Thinking, Working Paper No. 204, 10 April*.

Garratt, R. and Shun, H. S. (2023) "Stablecoins versus Tokenised Deposits: Implications for the Singleness of Money," *BIS Bulletin No. 73*, 11 April.

Haldane, A. G. (2014) "Constraining Discretion in Banking Regulation," in Goodhart, C., Gabor, D., Vestergaard, J. and Ertürk, I. (Eds) *Central Banking at a Crossroads – Europe and Beyond*. London and New York City: Anthem Press.

Hernández de Cos (2021) "Evaluating the Effectiveness of Basel III during Covid-19 and Beyond," *Keynote address at the BCBS-Bundesbank-CEPR workshop on evaluating financial regulation, 20 April*, available at https://www.bis.org/speeches/sp210420.htm.

Hertogen, A. (2020) "The Legal Implications of the Global Financial Crisis for Financial Services Liberalization," in Waibel, M. (Ed) *The Legal Implications of Global Financial Crises*. Leiden and Boston: Brill Nijhoff.

International Monetary Fund (2017) *People's Republic of China – Financial Sector Assessment Program – Detailed Assessment of Observance of Basel Core Principles for Effective Banking Supervision*. IMF Country Report No. 17/403. Washington, DC: IMF.

International Monetary Fund (2022a) *World Economic Outlook – Countering the Cost-of-Living Crisis*. October. Washington, DC: IMF.

International Monetary Fund (2022b) *G-20 Report on Strong, Sustainable, Balanced, and Inclusive Growth*. November. Washington, DC: IMF.

International Monetary Fund (2023a) *People's Republic of China*. IMF Country Report No. 23/67. Washington, DC: IMF.

International Monetary Fund (2023b) *Global Financial Stability Report – Safeguarding Financial Stability amid High Inflation and Geopolitical Risks*. April. Washington, DC: IMF.

Irani, R. M., Iyer, R., Meisenzahl, R. R. and Peydró, J-L. (2021) "The Rise of Shadow Banking: Evidence from Capital Regulation," *Review of Financial Studies*, Vol. 34, No. 5, pp. 2181–2235.

Jordà, Ò., Richter, B., Schularick, M. and Taylor, A. M. (2021) "Bank Capital Redux: Solvency, Liquidity, and Crisis," *Review of Economic Studies*, Vol. 88, No. 1, pp. 260–286.

Kregel, J. (2013) "Political Economy Approaches to Financial Crisis: Hyman Minsky's Financial Fragility Hypothesis," in Wolfson, M. H. and Epstein, G. A. (Eds) *The Handbook of the Political Economy of Financial Crises*. New York City: Oxford University Press.

Kregel, J. (2014) "Minsky and Dynamic Macroprudential Regulation," *Levy Economics Institute of Bard College, Public Policy Brief No. 131.*

Laeven, L. and Valencia, F. (2020) "Systemic Banking Crises Database II," *IMF Economic Review*, Vol. 68, No. 2, pp. 307–361.

Lazonick, W. (2013) "From Innovation to Financialization. How Shareholder Value Ideology is Destroying the US Economy," in Wolfson, M. H. and Epstein, G. A. (Eds) *The Handbook of the Political Economy of Financial Crises*. New York City: Oxford University Press.

Mérö, K. (2021) "The Ascent and Descent of Banks' Risk-Based Capital Regulation," *Journal of Banking Regulation*, Vol. 22, pp. 308–318.

Metrick, A. and Tarullo, D. K. (2021) "Congruent Financial Regulation," *Brookings Papers on Economic Activity*, Spring, pp. 143–181.

Minsky, H. P. (1967) "Suggestions for a Cash Flow Oriented Bank Examination", *Hyman Minsky Archive, Paper 175.*

Minsky, H. P. (1970) "Financial Instability Revisited: The Economics of Disaster," *Hyman P. Minsky Archive, Paper 80.*

Minsky, H. P. (1975a) "Suggestions for a Cash Flow-Oriented Bank Examination," *Hyman P. Minsky Archive, Paper 17.*

Minsky, H. P. (1975b) "Notes on: Suggestions for a Cash Flow Oriented Bank Examination," *Hyman P. Minsky Archive, Paper 176.*

Minsky, H. P. (1976) "Banking and a Fragile Financial Environment," *Hyman P. Minsky Archive, Paper 405.*

Minsky, H. P. (1977a) "How "Standard" is Standard Economics," *Hyman P. Minsky Archive, Paper 39.*

Minsky, H. P. (1977b) "The Financial Instability Hypothesis: An Interpretation of Keynes and an Alternative to 'Standard' Theory," *Challenge*, Vol. 20, No 1, pp. 20–27, reprinted in Minsky (1982), pp. 59–70.

Minsky, H. P. (1982) *Can "It" Happen again – Essays on Instability and Finance*. Armonk (NY): M.E. Sharpe.

Minsky, H. P. (1986) "Global Consequences of Financial Deregulation," *Hyman P. Minsky Archive, Paper 378.*

Minsky, H. P. (1990) "The Global Economy: The Vision from the North," *Hyman P. Minsky Archive, Paper 211.*

Minsky, H. P. (1992a) "The Financial Instability Hypothesis," *Levy Economics Institute of Bard College, Working Paper No. 74, May.*

Minsky, H. P. (1992b) "The Capital Development of the Economy and the Structure of Financial Institutions," *Hyman Minsky Archive, Paper 179.*
Minsky, H. P. (1992c) "Reconstituting the Financial Structure: The United States," *Hyman Minsky Archive, Paper 18.*
Minsky, H. P. (1992d) "Financial Instability and APT Bank Supervision," *Hyman P. Minsky Archive, Paper 470.*
Minsky, H. P. (1992e) "Schumpeter and Finance", *Hyman P. Minsky Archive, Paper 280.*
Minsky, H. P. (1993) "The Economic Problem at the End of the Second Millenium: Creating Capitalism, Reforming Capitalism, Making Capitalism Work," *Hyman P. Minsky Archive, Paper 101.*
Minsky, H. P. (1994a) "Issues in Bank Regulation and Supervision," *Hyman P. Minsky Archive, Paper 72.*
Minsky, H. P. (1994b) "Outine for Issues in Bank Regulation and Supervision," *Hyman P. Minsky Archive, Paper 73.*
Minsky, H. P. (1995) "Longer Waves in Financial Relations: Financial Factors in the More Severe Depressions II," *Journal of Economic Issues*, Vol. 29, No. 1, pp. 83–96.
Minsky, H. P. (1996) "Uncertainty and the Institutional Structure of Capitalist Economies," *Hyman P. Minsky Archive, Paper 24.*
Minsky, H. P. (2008, 1986) *Stabilizing an Unstable Economy*. New York City: McGraw-Hill.
Minsky, H. P. and Campbell, C. (1987) "How to Get Off the Back of a Tiger, Or, Do Initial Conditions Constrain Deposit Insurance Reform," *Hyman P. Minsky Archive, Paper 70.*
Minsky, H. P. and Campbell, C. (1988) "Getting of the Back of a Tiger: The Deposit Insurance Crisis in the United States," *Hyman P. Minsky Archive, Paper 67.*
Montanaro, E. and Tonveronachi, M. (2012) "Financial Re-regulation at a Crossroads: How the European Experience Strengthens the Case for a Radical Reform Built on Minsky's Approach," *PSL Quarterly Review*, Vol. 65, No. 263, pp. 335–383.
Moore, B. J. (1986) "Inflation and Financial Deepening," *Journal of Development Economics*, Vol. 20, No. 1, pp. 125–133.
Ocampo, J. A. (2017) *Resetting the International Monetary (Non)System*. Oxford: Oxford University Press.
Persaud, A. (2010) "The Locus of Financial Regulation: Home Versus Host," *International Affairs*, Vol. 86, No. 3, pp. 637–646.
Rajan, R. G. (2005) "Has Financial Development Made the World Riskier?," *NBER Working Paper No. 11728.*
Redert, B. (2022) "From Clubs to Hubs: Analysing Lobbying Networks in EU Financial Regulation after Crisis," *Journal of Public Policy*, Vol. 42, No. 2, pp. 390–408.
Roncaglia, A. (2013) "Hyman Minsky's Monetary Production Economy," *PSL Quarterly Review*, Vol. 66, No. 265, pp. 77–94.
Schenk, C. N. (2021) "The Global Financial Crisis and Banking Regulation: Another Turn of the Wheel?," *Journal of Modern European History*, Vol. 19, No. 1, pp. 8–13.
Tarullo, D. K. (2016) "Next Steps in the Evolution of Stress Testing," *Remarks at Yale University School of Management Leaders Forum, Yale University, New*

Haven, Connecticut, 16 September, available at https://www.federalreserve.gov/newsevents/speech/files/tarullo20160926a.pdf.

Tarullo, D. K. (2019) "Financial Regulation: Still Unsettled a Decade After the Crisis," *Journal of Economic Perspectives*, Vol. 33, No. 1, pp. 61–80.

Tonveronachi, M. (2010) "Financial Innovation and System Design," *PSL Quarterly Review*, Vol. 63, No. 253, pp. 131–144.

Tonveronachi, M. (2018) "Ending Laissez-Faire Finance," in Corsi, M., Kregel, J. and D'Ippoliti, C. (Eds) *Classical Economics Today. Essays in Honour of Alessandro Roncaglia*. London: Anthem Press.

Tonveronachi, M. (2020) "Ages of Financial Instability," *Journal of Post Keynesian Economics*, Vol. 43, No. 2, pp. 169–209.

Waibel, M. (2020) "Financial Crises and International Law," in Waibel, M. (Ed) *The Legal Implications of Global Financial Crises*. Leiden and Boston: Brill Nijhoff.

White, W. R. (2019) "The Limits of Macroprudential Policy," *The International Economy*, Winter, pp. 52–55.

Xi, C. (2016) "Why Has Basel III Become Hard Law for China? The Domestic Political Economy of International Financial Law," in Buckley, R. P., Avgouleas, E. and Arner, D. W. (Eds) *Reconceptualising Global Finance and its Regulation*. Cambridge: Cambridge University Press.

Zhou, X. (2009) "Reform the International Monetary System," 23 March, available at https://www.bis.org/review/r090402c.pdf.

7 China, technical standardization, and the future of globalization

John Seaman

As the global economy sits at a crossroad between connectivity-driven globalization and strategic decoupling, technical standardization provides a valuable measure of where we are headed. Long thought of as a benign, apolitical defining of baseline processes, products, and services, standardization has ballooned into a field of geopolitical competition, particularly as the United States, China, Europe, and others wrestle over technological leadership in the industries of the future. Driven largely by private enterprise initiatives, the West has long held the high ground in setting technical standards. While China is a newcomer to the field, it has grand ambitions of becoming a premier purveyor of global standards and has laid the groundwork for building out a more China-centered ecosystem through efforts such as the Belt and Road Initiative. In this context, the "twin transitions" toward a low-carbon and digital future, where many standards remain to be set, offer an opportunity for Beijing. Ultimately, whether China chooses a collaborative path with the West on standards development, how the latter respond to China's initiatives, and whether multistakeholder, consensus-based standardization processes can resist the push and pull of geopolitics will go a long way to determining the degree of cohesion and fragmentation in the global economy for decades to come.

7.1 Introduction

As discussed throughout this book, the liberal international order (LIO) is coming under increasing strain as a result of a shifting balance of power and the growing forces of geopolitical competition, particularly between the United States and China. The realm of technical standardization is one area where this strain is clearly evident, as China has sought to play a more proactive role in international standard setting. Broad trends toward harmonization of technical standards have helped facilitate market integration and drive globalization, for instance in the realm of telecommunications with the advent of standardized third generation (3G) technology. But geopolitical tensions risk fragmentation of the standardization space. For example, when the U.S. government levied sanctions on Huawei in 2019, the Chinese

DOI: 10.4324/9781003340430-9

telecoms manufacturer found itself barred from a number of U.S.-based standard-setting forums, including the Institute of Electrical and Electronics Engineers (IEEE). While the Trump administration's decision on standardization was quickly reversed following outcry from industry, American suspicions around Chinese participation in standardization have not. In a November 2022 speech laying out Washington's vision of economic competition with China, U.S. Secretary of Commerce Gina Raimondo accused China of "gaming the system" on technical standards (Raimondo, 2022). As Washington moves toward a broader strategy of limiting China's technological development in critical sectors such as semiconductor manufacturing, questions have once again risen about whether cooperation on technical standards, particularly in cutting-edge sectors such as Artificial Intelligence (AI), will be allowed to continue. Indeed, the implications for the future of the global economic order are significant.

Technical standards are definitions of processes or technical specifications for products and services. Functionally, a standard seeks to improve a product or service's quality, security, or interoperability. Illustrative examples include the size and shape of electric sockets and standard-sized sheets of paper, the width of railway gauges or the specifications of Internet Protocol. While standard setting is often overlooked, the implications are potentially wide-ranging in that standards functionally define technologies, shape markets, and in many ways reflect the worldviews of those who develop them. Admittedly, the geopolitical implications of A4 size paper or NEMA 5-15 electrical outlets are minimal. Standardized railway gauges, on the other hand, have shaped regional transportation networks and market connectivity, whereas Internet Protocol standards (TCP/IP) have not only defined the technical baseline for how the Internet functions, but also reflect a values-based vision of a free, open, and global network. As sociologist Laurence Busch (2013) explains, standards are "recipes for reality" that are intimately linked to the definition and exercise of power. Who defines technical standards therefore can have implications for how power is distributed in a political system, locally, nationally, or internationally.

The setting of voluntary international technical standards has largely been steered since the late 19th century by Western actors, particularly in the United States and Europe, and has helped form the bedrock of market integration and the global economy as we know it (Yates and Murphy, 2019). For much of this time, the process has been driven primarily by private actors, in particular enterprises or industry associations. In essence, standardization has become a form of industry self-regulation, or governance by market actors, that has helped to define and drive globalization, forming a pillar of the LIO (Busch 2013, p. 27; Büthe and Mattli, 2011). Against the backdrop of a broader questioning of the current global economic order, what becomes of the practice of standardization – how China approaches it and how established players in the field adapt – will play a significant role in shaping the contours of the global economy and the broader international system moving forward.

The analysis in this chapter begins by detailing why technical standard setting is important not only from an economic, but also from a political perspective and how standardization fits into today's broader competition for geo-economic and geopolitical power and influence. It defines the established models through which voluntary technical standards are developed and adopted internationally. In particular, it underlines the fact that the international rules overseeing how standards are made today, rules which functionally restrain political influence on the standardization process, are a structural part of the international trade architecture, which itself is a pillar of the LIO as we know it.

Second, the chapter traces China's evolution from a global standards taker to an increasingly influential standards maker. It explores the drivers behind this shift and the distance China has come so far. It details the domestic reforms meant to improve China's ability to develop standards nationally, and the measures China has taken to integrate international standard-setting regimes even as it lays the groundwork for the development of more China-centered standardization processes.

Finally, the chapter explores the various pathways along which the international standardization system might evolve in light of increased geopolitical tensions – including those that would lead toward a greater convergence that would strengthen global connectivity, those that lead toward a bifurcation centered primarily around Chinese and American standardization ecosystems, and those leading toward a broader fragmentation that could result in a more multipolar economic order.

7.2 Technical standards: what they are, why they matter, and how they are made

Technical standards provide baseline definitions of processes, methodologies, terminologies or specifications for products and services. ISO/IEC 8802-11,[1] for instance, is a family of standards that define wireless connections commonly known as WiFi. EN71 is a group of European standards defining safety parameters for toys, including mechanical and physical properties, chemical compounds, and flammability. International Financial Reporting Standards (IFRS), meanwhile, establish common definitions and procedures for accounting and reporting that now set the baseline for most major financial markets throughout the world. Standards allow for quality assurance, set the bar for safety, and ensure interoperability. They are voluntary in nature, but if widely adopted they can increase economies of scale and create lock-in effects that effectively shape and define markets.

7.2.1 Why standards matter

There are hundreds of thousands of standards scattered across the globe today, and the vast majority appear to sit well outside of the realm of great power politics. Technical standardization is considered by many to be a field reserved for engineers or technical experts, far removed from the consideration of high politics and diplomacy. As Busch (2013, p. 28) notes, although "many standards appear to be neutral, benign, merely technical, obscure and removed from daily life, they are … largely an unrecognized but extremely important and growing source of social, political and economic relations of power." This is particularly true in the case of emerging technologies, such as 5G and 6G telecommunications, electric vehicles, the Internet of Things (IoT), AI, and other technologies and industries of the future. Rühlig (2021) notes four broad dimensions – economic, legal, political, and ideational – of what he terms "technical standards power," which make standardization particularly relevant in today's increasingly tense geopolitical context.

7.2.1.1 *Economic importance*

Standards impact growth, trade, innovation, and competitiveness. There is a clear economic logic behind standard setting related to interoperability and market connectivity, network effects, growing economies of scale, supply chain efficiency, and consumer trust. While detailed figures to illustrate the macroeconomic impacts are rare, standards are found to have facilitated over 23% of France's economic growth between 1950–2007, over 27% of Germany's growth from 1960–1990, and over 63% from 1990–2006, following the country's reunification (Blind et al., 2011). Standards today are intricately related to trade, with an estimated 93% of global economic exchanges being affected by standards and technical regulations (Okun-Kozlowicki, 2016). Moreover, there is a clear incentive to shaping global standards in that they establish technological pathways that can provide comparative advantages to those capable of achieving them. In some industries, in particular information and communications technologies (ICT), standardization can open important revenue streams for companies able to standardize patented technology. For instance, in 2017, revenue from Qualcomm-registered standard-essential patents (SEPs) reportedly reached €5.2 billion, representing 20% of the company's annual revenue.[2] Companies can then reinvest these revenue streams into research and development, creating a virtuous cycle for innovation. Indeed, there is a direct correlation between the involvement of companies in standardization, their spending on R&D, and their ultimate output of innovative products (Blind, 2016). Firms that do not, or are not able to standardize their technology, on the other hand, run the risk of being isolated from global technological trends and shoulder high adaptation costs (Ezell and Atkinson, 2014). At scale, this can impact a country's economic competitiveness as a whole, either in a positive or a negative sense.

7.2.1.2 *Legal importance*

While voluntary in nature, standards have also entered into the legal architecture of trade and regulation. While standardization can help facilitate trade, standards can also be used as protectionist measures, creating barriers to market entry. As such, the Agreement on Technical Barriers to Trade (TBT) within the framework of the World Trade Organization (WTO) has established a basis (further detailed below) for recognizing the weight of standards within international trade law. Furthermore, in some cases, technical standards are intricately related to regulation. Standards can be used, or standards bodies can be called upon, to develop harmonized standards to ensure regulatory conformity. For example, Europe's Directive 2009/48/EC paved the way for the EN71 standards on toy safety, cited above. Applying a standard, therefore, provides a fast track for products to conform with regulatory requirements set by governments. Producers that cannot certify the use of EN71 standards can still access Europe's toy market, but would need to prove conformity with regulations, a potentially costly endeavor. In the case of more sensitive sectors such as medical devices, this may even require revealing proprietary information.

7.2.1.3 Political importance

In some areas, particularly involving critical infrastructure, standards can also generate dependencies and exacerbate strategic competition. While standardization can facilitate market connectivity, it can also create lock-in effects that benefit dominant market players and functionally create political spheres of influence. In the early 20th century, for instance, competing British and German telegraph standards, which defined the workings of telecommunications networks of the day, proved to be not only of great economic but also strategic significance leading up to and during the First World War (Brunnermeier et al., 2018). Today, standards competition in areas such as ultra-high voltage (UHV) power transmission (Argonne National Laboratory, 2015), 5G telecommunications, high-speed rail, and cloud computing can lock markets into structural dependencies on industrial ecosystems that are derived from a particular standard (Rühlig, 2021). For instance, whether standards for UHV transmissions systems are built on alternate current (AC) or direct current (DC) has important implications for suppliers – whereas Western firms have comparative advantages in AC, Chinese firms largely dominate the market for DC technologies. In a broad sense, such dependencies open the space for vulnerabilities that can impact policy choices in that they change the calculation of interest on the part of decision-makers.

7.2.1.4 Ideational importance

Finally, standards can reflect underlying political and ethical values. Indeed, standards are shaped by the set of worldviews and values held by their developers; they can subsequently influence the way in which such values are reflected back onto society by way of the products and processes that they define. As noted in the introduction, Internet Protocol, the standardized architecture of today's Internet, is built around a principle of free and open participation by users. Data privacy and user anonymity are areas where competing standards reflect competing political ideologies. Today's WiFi standard, adopted by the International Organization for Standardization (ISO), allows internet users a high degree of anonymity and privacy protection. In 2006, China proposed an alternative standard in the ISO, known as WAPI, which functionally allows for a greater degree of oversight and control of users and user activity, which can be leveraged by administrators and governments alike. The ISO declined the WAPI standard by majority voting, with some raising concerns over secrecy and the existence of an undisclosed algorithm written into the protocol (Kroeber, 2007). WAPI is still the applied technical standard for wireless area networks in China today. Another important contemporary debate surrounds the standards for developing AI, particularly on ethical issues such as algorithmic bias and the definitions of "human-centered" AI, wherein standards will define what these concepts mean and the technical parameters around which AI will develop.[3]

7.2.2 How standards are made

With such broad-ranging importance of standards, the processes through which they are developed and set are also highly significant. The practice of standardization at the international level has evolved over time, but the complex system as we know it today derived largely from the initiative of engineers, industry and technical experts that sought to develop standard practices in the wake of the industrial revolution in the 19th century, and the desires of states to defend economic interests and manage cross-border trade and infrastructure development. In essence, there are two extremes to standards development: at one end, standardization that is de-facto driven by dominant market players – e.g., Microsoft or Apple – and at the other, standards developed, imposed, or negotiated by states. While some standards are indeed developed at these extremes, the vast majority of standardization work, particularly with regard to international standards, happens as a collaborative process somewhere in the middle.

Indeed, the need to define common standards gave rise to some of the first modern-day multilateral institutions. The International Telecommunications Union (ITU), which is incorporated within the United Nations framework, was founded in 1865 to manage international telegraph networks. Today, its responsibilities include developing global ICT standards. While the ITU includes multi-stakeholder participation with over 900 private-sector participants, particularly from industry, it is functionally a state-driven forum centered around 193 member states wherein politics and diplomacy play an important role. In practice, the ITU model is rare in the standard setting world. By comparison, two of the premier standards development bodies, the ISO and the International Electrotechnical Commission (IEC), are private institutions whose representatives are comprised mostly of private standards bodies. The American National Standards Institute (ANSI), the French

Association for Standardization (AFNOR) and the German Institute for Standardization (DIN), for instance, are all non-governmental organizations whose members are comprised of private entities, primarily companies. Furthermore, a large body of international standardization work is done by independent associations such as the IEEE, the Internet Engineering Task Force (IETF), or the Third Generation Partnership Project (3GPP), wherein participation is open to a broad range of stakeholders, independent of national origin.

With such a broad diversity of forums, and potentially such high economic and political stakes, the impetus for manipulation and "gaming the system" is high. As such, various rules have been established to ensure that standardization work remains fair and open, couched namely with the architecture of international trade rules of the General Agreement on Trade and Tariffs (GATT). In particular, the Agreement on Technical Barriers to Trade identifies a set of procedural principles (i.e., transparency, openness, impartiality and consensus, effectiveness and relevance, coherence, and openness to developing states) that standards development organizations (SDOs) must meet in order not to have their standards deemed as obstructive to global trade (Dackö, 2021).

The international trade architecture is a key pillar upon which the LIO has been constructed. Incorporating rules for standard setting into this trade architecture has effectively allowed for a set of principles that manage competition over technical standardization – allowing standards to be developed based more on their technical merits than on degrees of political influence. As cracks form in the international trade architecture more broadly, international technical standards development may be one victim. At the same time, technical standardization itself has become the target of geopolitical forces that are functionally unravelling the LIO, particularly as China has sought to play a more active and increasingly central role in international technical standardization.

7.3 China's role in shaping international standardization: from standards taker to standards maker

China is a latecomer to the field of international technical standard setting, but its companies and political leaders have quickly become attuned to the importance of this practice. As China develops into a formidable global actor and a leader in technological development, from telecommunications to AI to clean and renewable energies, it has found itself in a stronger position to shape international technical standards and has honed a strategy to establish itself as a major player in the field (Fägersten and Rühlig, 2019). Through state-driven initiatives and engagement by Chinese companies, Beijing is increasingly present and proactive in international standards development, on par with many of its Western counterparts. Yet, it is still far from dominant and has encountered both pitfalls and resistance along the way (Seaman, 2020). Reviewing what drives China in this domain, what makes its approach different, and how it has served to both integrate and circumvent established standard-setting fora will provide a basis for reflecting on how the international standards arena may evolve in the future.

7.3.1 What motivates China's interest in standardization

China's approach to standardization, both domestically and at the international level, is intricately related to its economic development and the evolution of how the Chinese leadership sees the country's place in the world. Over much of the last forty years since China launched its reform and opening up movement, standards have played an important, though sometimes contradictory role in the nation's development. Competing pressures from Chinese industry actors have historically presented standards in contradictory ways, often reflecting the differing priorities between the "old economy" (i.e., inefficient, state-owned industries that must be protected), and the "new economy," namely the more innovative, cutting-edge firms that seek to compete in the global marketplace. More than simply setting technical standards to limit market access at the border, local and provincial governments in the past used competing standards to protect local industries from other Chinese competitors (Peyrat, 2012). Ultimately, external and top-down pressures resulting from WTO accession starting in 2001 and bottom-up pressures from export-oriented industries, particularly as export-driven growth became a major factor of economic development, helped to push China toward more convergence with international standards (Ernst, 2011; Wang and Zheng, 2018). China's official adoption rate of ISO standards today is 79%, and as high as 95% in standards related to consumer goods.

Beyond trade and market access, standardization came to be seen in China as a springboard for innovation and an important step on the path toward greater economic and technological competitiveness. Technical standards are both a tool for facilitating innovation – avoiding a duplication of efforts and providing for gains in efficiency – and a reflection of quality and technological leadership. Indeed, a popular saying has emerged in China, which has been attributed to the Sony Corporation, explaining that "third-tier companies make products, second-tier companies make technology, top-tier companies make standards,"[4] an image that adequately reflects the goals of China's economic development strategy. In this light, standardization has become a core component of China's economic development strategy, from the "Made in China 2025" plan released in 2015 to the 14th Five-Year Plan (2021–2025), and even including specific policies related to standard setting in domains such as AI (Exovera, 2022). Indeed, China's National Standardization Development Outline, published by the State Council in October 2021, identifies standardization as a key pillar driving the development of Chinese competitiveness in the industries of the future, including AI, quantum technologies, integrated circuits, health and biotechnologies, smart cities, and the Internet of Things (Chinese Communist Party Central Committee and State Council, 2021).

Underlying Beijing's emphasis on the importance of standards is also a reflection on China's vulnerability, autonomy, and power. China's dependence on foreign suppliers of technology results in part from its reliance on foreign standards. This became evident in the 1990s and early 2000s as telecom markets became structured around Western standards such as GSM (Global System for Mobile) and CDMA (Code Division Multiple Access), and China's efforts to develop its own standard failed.[5] Such failures ultimately reflected back on the country's inability to secure its own information networks and were considered a source of critical vulnerability, highlighting the need to invest more structurally in critical industries of the future (Ernst, 2011). China's failure to push through the adoption of its WAPI standard at the international level was further interpreted as a sign of its ineffectiveness at international standard setting, and ultimately emphasized the need to formulate a more proactive approach at the international level (Gao, 2008). Now, as Chinese firms move closer to the technological cutting edge, international standardization is seen as an opportunity to shape the industries of the future, carve out a place for China in the global economy and consequently shape the international order (Seaman, 2020). The turning of the tables can be observed in the case of 5G, for instance, where Chinese firms (namely, Huawei) are responsible for one third of 5G standards contributions – more than any other country (Pohlmann and Buggenhagen, 2022, p. 5). Xi Jinping, China's leader, has framed the current moment of technological, environmental, and geopolitical transformation as "changes unseen in a century," underscoring not only the risks for China inherent in such changes, but also the opportunities that they present for claiming the mantel of global leadership (Doshi, 2021, pp. 261–329). China's proactive efforts to shape international technical standards are thus an important piece of achieving its larger strategic vision for its place in the world.

7.3.2 China's approach to standard setting

In 2015, China's State Council, the country's highest governing body, began a process of deep reforms aimed at re-structuring the way that standards are developed and set in China.[6] Indeed, China's role in global standard setting has been historically weak, not only because its innovative capacity was lagging, but because the way it approached standardization failed to capture the innovative capacity of Chinese firms. Rather than facilitate market integration and catalyze innovation, standards in China proved to be a hindrance. Standardization was a state-driven process, incorporating ministries and government agencies at the national, provincial, local and industrial level, often leading to a proliferation of ineffectual, and sometimes even contradictory standards (Wang and Zheng, 2018). By 2012, the country counted over 150,000 technical standards, or seven times the number in the European Union (Peyrat, 2012). If China were to compete globally on standards, it would first need to find a better way of going about standardization at home.

The reforms launched by the State Council ultimately gave way in January 2018 to a new standardization law, replacing the previous legislation adopted in 1989. On one hand, the reforms reconfirmed the central role played by the state in the standards development process. The number and type of standards – national, sectoral, industrial – were rationalized and streamlined, but state agencies maintained a fundamental role in defining them. The Standardization Administration of China (SAC), the body tasked with broad-level coordination of standards in China and representing the country in international standards forums such as the ISO and IEC, is an administrative branch of the State Administration for Market Regulation (SAMR), an organ of the State Council.[7] Furthermore, relevant ministries, technical government agencies, and state-owned enterprises in a given sector also play an important role in organizing and carrying out the work of technical standardization committees in China.[8]

This central role played by the state differs fundamentally from how standards development is carried out in Europe or the United States, where standardization is driven by private-sector initiatives involving independent stakeholders. In Europe, national (e.g., AFNOR and DIN) and international standardization organizations (e.g., the European Telecommunications Standards Institute, ETSI) are independent associations made up of private companies and stakeholders. State actors may be members of these associations, but the organizations themselves are independent and driven by private-sector engagement. While they may be mandated by the governments to elaborate standards that align with state regulations (e.g., harmonize standards in the case of the toy safety), they effectively remain non-governmental actors. In the United States, the process is even more decentralized, with hundreds of independent associations such as the IEEE, the IETF or the American Society for Testing and Materials (ASTM) forming around specific industries or issue sets with no formal links to the government. Some of these organizations have gained such notoriety that they effectively produce international standards in their own right. Internet Protocol standards, for instance, were developed and set by the IETF, with offices in California and Delaware. In standards bodies such as the ISO and IEC, American interests are represented by the ANSI. While standards development in the United States is predominantly market and industry driven, the National Institute for Standards and Technology (NIST), an agency of the U.S. Department of Commerce, plays an important role in supporting and fostering standards development in coordination with the federal government.

Meanwhile, in contrast to the existing state-driven standardization process, China's 2018 reforms opened up a new category of market-driven standards, known as association standards. In essence, association standards are designed to provide more flexibility to industry actors, interest groups and non-governmental organizations to organize and advance standardization work independently of the oft bureaucratically burdensome government-directed processes. A key goal is to leverage private-sector and market-driven initiatives to more effectively advance and standardize solutions to technical problems in China. Functionally, in this respect, China's new association standards resemble the American standards ecosystem. Another important development coupled with this process was the 2017 Foreign Investment Law, stipulating that the work of standardization bodies in China must be equally open to Chinese and foreign participants on a non-discriminatory basis – further aligning its practices with TBT rules.

While the role of the state is marginalized with the advent of association standards, a major difference with American and European models persists in the Chinese context regarding the role that the Chinese Communist Party increasingly plays in the workings of private corporations and industry today. It is reported that 92% of China's 500 largest corporations host Party cells, and since 2018 Beijing has required that all domestically listed companies, regardless of size, establish a party unit.[9] While China has turned to market forces in an effort to improve the quality and competitiveness of the standards it develops, standardization is a key pillar of public policy and can scarcely escape the long arms of the state and the Party.[10]

The 2018 reforms were only the beginning of a longer-term process of re-tooling standardization in China. A two-year collaborative review process piloted by the SAC in conjunction with the Chinese Academy of Sciences, referred to as "China Standards 2035," subsequently gave way to the State Council's National Standardization Development Outline, published in 2021. The Outline reiterates the need to continue domestic reforms to bolster the development and competitiveness of domestic Chinese standards and a professional class capable of developing them, particularly by leveraging the competencies of Chinese industry and the private sector. However, the Outline is unambiguous about the central role of the state in the process. As mentioned above, it further ties standards to China's broader development goals and underlines the importance of generating Chinese standards in fields related to strategic and high-tech sectors, and more broadly associates standard setting with virtually every aspect of society. Moreover, the Outline increases its emphasis on the investments that China must make into international standards development.

7.3.3 China and international standards development

Starting from a late-comer position, Chinese state and corporate actors have made concerted efforts over the last two decades to engage more proactively in the international standard-setting arena, efforts which have been redoubled in recent years. Broadly, these efforts follow a dual path. On the one hand, China is proactively engaging with and integrating existing international standard-setting forums. On the other hand, it is simultaneously pursuing bilateral arrangements and exploring the development of parallel multilateral forums, namely within the context of the Belt and Road Initiative (BRI), and incubating industry-led standards associations within China, all of which serve to improve China's standing and advance Chinese standards internationally.

Over the last 15 years, China has integrated the existing framework of international standards development at all levels – a reflection of China's increasingly central importance in the global economy and Beijing's ambition. At the ISO, for instance, China became the sixth permanent member of the organization's Council in 2008, and in 2013 joined France, Germany, Japan, the United Kingdom, and the United States as a permanent member of the ISO's Technical Management Board. Two years later, Zhang Xiaogang was elected to a three-year term as president of the ISO, a first for a Chinese national. Chinese nationals would also take up the top leadership positions in the ITU in 2015 and the IEC in 2020. At the working level, China has also boosted its overall participation, created working groups and technical committees and secured chairmanship positions, notably in areas such as critical raw materials, industrial machinery, smart grids, e-commerce and electrical systems all of which relate to Beijing's broader industrial strategy (Rühlig 2021, p. 25). Chinese companies have also been increasingly active members in industry-led initiatives, such as ETSI and 3GPP for telecommunications, based in the EU, and in U.S.-based organizations such as the IEEE Standards Association, the Car Connectivity Consortium, or JEDEC (Joint Electron Device Engineering Council), which develops standards for microelectronics (Neaher et al. 2021, p. 12).

While its participation has risen and Chinese actors have become more active, China does not dominate international standard setting. Its total level of active membership participation in ISO technical committees has risen from roughly under 500 in 2007 to over 650 in the early 2020s, but it remains on par with others, such as the United Kingdom, Germany, France, and the United States. Meanwhile, it held 68 technical committee secretariats in the ISO in 2021, but this was still far less than Germany's 132, the U.S.'s 98, or Japan's 80 (Rühlig 2021, pp. 24–26). China's active participation has certainly led to some notable successes in standards development, particularly in the field of 5G, as cited above, or the in the realm of IoT, where in 2018 Chinese companies successfully sponsored the standardization of a reference architecture for IoT in the ISO (Seaman, 2020). Still, other initiatives, starting with the failed attempt to validate WAPI as an international standard at the ISO, or rebuffed attempts to open discussions on a new Internet Protocol (i.e., the "New IP") in the ITU suggest that China's influence is moderated (Voo and Creemers, 2021). Indeed, despite a high level of engagement, and contrary to the concerns of many, and perhaps even to Beijing's own ambitions, China has not dominated international standard-setting forums to the degree some have feared. Much of this can be credited to the governance rules by which standards organizations abide, notably the key principles of technical barriers to trade mentioned above, and the importance that standards development organizations place on credibility and trustworthiness in the standardization process (Baron and Kanevskaia, 2021). China has played by the rules in these institutions and, until now, has not sought to fundamentally change them. In effect, these rules appear to have fulfilled their objective in buffering standards development within these forums from outsized influence – in this case from China (Kratz and Seaman, 2023).

Outside the realm of international standards development organizations, however, China continues to explore ways to advance its interests and gain acceptance for its role as a standard setter. In particular, where established international technical standards do not yet exist or have yet to be settled, in areas such as high-speed rail or smart cities, there is a broad space for developing acceptance for one's own technical standards in foreign markets, and Beijing is seeking to fill this space. These efforts have largely taken shape through de-facto standards diffusion, the multiplication of bilateral agreements and the development of the BRI as a platform for standards development and diffusion. De-facto standards diffusion refers to the adoption of standards as a result of a high market penetration on the part of a specific technology, company or set of corporate actors, especially in sectors where switching costs are high, such as high-speed rail or smart cities. As of 2020, 106 countries had reportedly already played host to some form of smart city project that incorporated Chinese technologies, such as technologies developed by Huawei or ZTE (Atha et al., 2020). Subsequently, as the standards for smart city concepts, designs and technologies are discussed in forums such as the ISO and the ITU, existing market penetration for associated technologies can bolster the case for a particular standard within standards body deliberations (Russel and Berger, 2021). At the same time, China has pursued bilateral standards recognition agreements with a broad range of countries. By 2019, China had concluded 90 such agreements with 52 countries, mostly in the form of non-binding memorandums of understanding (Rühlig, 2020). While most of these lack substance, some cooperation has begun to take shape. For example, the China-ASEAN (Association of Southeast Asian Nations) International Standardization Forum in 2021 unveiled a China-ASEAN Standard Cloud Platform and initiated an International Standardization Training Center in Nanning, China.[11] Since 2015, China's SAC has also issued multiple plans to integrate standardization within the framework of the BRI, and, within the context of the "China Standards 2035," the idea of a Belt and Road Standards Forum was explored (Rühlig, 2020).[12] While the BRI currently seems to have fallen off Beijing's policy radar, that the creation of such a forum was considered at all speaks to China's willingness to explore international technical standardization outside the current, established frameworks.

The fact that countries pursue their own path to advance the adoption of technical standards which serve their industrial interests is nothing new. For instance, during the 1990s and early 2000s, the United States and the European Union often lobbied in third markets for the adoption of competing CDMA and GSM telecom standards, and in the run-up to China's accession to the WTO, Washington even secured concessions from Beijing to adopt the CDMA standard in a portion of its own market. Such competitive practices continue today, particularly in sectors where international standards have yet to be defined. What has changed is the context and the highly strategic way in which China frames standard setting. Indeed, the central role that the Chinese state plays in standards development and policy and the high-level recognition by the Chinese authorities of the important role that standards play in the pursuit of broader, more strategic policy goals sets China apart. Set against a backdrop of strategic competition and geo-economic and geopolitical friction, particularly between Beijing and Washington, and the broader questioning of the LIO, the future of inclusive, collaborative international standards development looks increasingly uncertain.

7.4 How might international standardization evolve in an era of strategic competition?

China's activism in the technical standardization arena has prompted others, notably the United States and European policy makers, to think more strategically about their engagement in standard setting. Bipartisan coalitions in the U.S. Congress, for instance led in March 2020 by Senators Bob Portman (R-OH) and Mark Warner (D-VA), have expressed concern that "China is currently working to use standards setting bodies to gain the imprimatur of international legitimacy and support across a range of emerging technologies," with a particular concern for surveillance technologies and the use of AI, and underlining the risk that China could "use the ITU to advance its techno-nationalist agenda."[13] Senators ultimately called for the United States to further engage in the international standard setting arena and commissioned a study to assess China's influence in the field (Exovera, 2022). The call for further American engagement was answered by a campaign to support the election of the U.S. national Doreen Bogdan-Martin as the successor to Houlin Zhao at the head of the ITU in September 2022. Meanwhile, the European Union, as part of a broader push to be more geopolitical, edited a standardization strategy in February 2022 aiming for "a new approach to enable global leadership of EU standards" that seeks to leverage standardization to successfully achieve Europe's strategic goals for the "twin transition" toward a green and digital future (European Commission, 2022a).

As technical standardization is increasingly perceived within the context of strategic policy and great power competition, three possible pathways emerge for how the field may further develop: i) a bifurcation of technical standards into competing spheres led at opposing ends by Washington and Beijing; ii) a broader fragmentation of technical standards development, with additional, distinctive roles played by the European Union and key players such as India and Japan, ultimately reflecting a more multipolar composition of the international system; and iii) a continued convergence of global technical standards and the global economy, through strengthened institutions and technological interoperability.

In the first instance, both Beijing and Washington have pursued targeted policies in recent years that effectively amount to a broader decoupling agenda in strategic, notably high-tech sectors. While China has sought to pursue a path of greater self-reliance, the United States has turned toward an approach that would not only boost its technological competitiveness but also stymie China's own progress in cutting edge fields such as advanced semiconductors, AI and quantum communications (Bateman, 2022). Such efforts may already be forging divergences at the pre-standardization phase of technological development, making technological solutions and associated standards increasingly incompatible. For example, the Next G Alliance, a U.S.-based industrial consortium to develop technologies for 6G telecommunications already explicitly excludes participation from Chinese firms.[14]

At the diplomatic level, the United States has also sought to reinforce dialogue on technical standards with allies and partners through minilateral initiatives. In a joint statement in May 2022, QUAD country leaders (Australia, India, Japan, and the United States) called for the creation of an International Standards Cooperation Network (ISCN) to "help ensure technology development in the region is guided by our shared democratic values" (White House, 2022). Within the Trade and Technology Council (TTC), the United States and EU have also formed a working group on technical standardization to include coordinated standards work in the field of AI, quantum technologies, Internet of Things and electro-mobility charging infrastructure. The TTC has also developed a Strategic Standardization Information (SSI) mechanism to "share information about international standardization activities and promptly react to common strategic issues," which include efforts to "help shape global standards at international institutions such as the International Telecommunication Union (ITU)" (European Commission, 2022b). Such developments are surely meant to coordinate action in response to China's increased activism in the field.

If such efforts result in the increasing isolation of China within standards development organizations, China is likely to pursue more vigorously alternative options for standards diffusion at the minilateral level, for instance with ASEAN countries, or within the context of the BRI. Chinese industry groups are also likely to further develop along the lines of the American model, with China-domiciled associations adopting an international agenda and developing standards of international relevance. A world of competing technical standards will lead to compatibility issues between technologies created in China, on one hand, and in the West on the other, further anchoring the emergence of dichotomous geopolitical spheres with distinctive technological features.

Beyond simple bifurcation, a broader fragmentation of technical standardization is also a possibility. In addition to the push factors driving strategic decoupling between the United States and China, other global players, to include Europe and India, have been keen to pursue their own paths toward bolstering strategic autonomy and avoiding a binary strategic choice between

Washington and Beijing. India, for instance, has tried – though ultimately failed – to develop its own standard for 5G, known as 5Gi, which Indian Prime Minister Narendra Modi has framed within the context of the country's ambitions for Aatmanirbharta (self-sufficiency). As Trisha Ray explains, India's ambitions demonstrate that, when it comes to standards cooperation in the QUAD, "shared values will not always translate into frictionless cooperation given the specific quandaries each country faces, and the distinct, privileged positions some hold."[15] Europe's own standards strategy, meanwhile, is also linked to broader quest for strategic autonomy and digital sovereignty. In this context, frictions have already become apparent with regard to the internal governance of European standards development organizations and the inclusion of foreign-headquartered companies such as Microsoft or Huawei to participate in standardization work on key issues like AI.[16] A push by the United States to support an alternative framework for 5G standards development, known as the Open Radio Access Network (O-RAN), has also met with skepticism in Europe and elsewhere as an attempt to skirt the established processes of the 3GPP in favor of American industrial interests (Kleinhans and Rühlig, 2022).

Still, despite the pressures of strategic competition and decoupling, standardization continues to be a space where technical collaboration can and does happen. For the time being, while major powers have integrated more strategic thinking into their approaches to standards development, their strategies continue to call for more engagement within international standards development organizations, not less. The United States has increasingly levied sanctions on Chinese firms, tightened restrictions on collaboration through Entity Lists, and sharpened its export control regime to include a broader range of technologies and restrictions (see Gaillard's chapter in this book). A notable carve-out is consistently made to allow for a level of collaboration with blacklisted entities within the realm of technical standards development. This means that for the time being standards development organizations are likely to be witness to geopolitical tensions and maneuvering. Crucially, it is ensuring broad-based, multistakeholder participation in global standard-setting forums and an adherence to the WTO's TBT rules that will help to mitigate this strategic competition in the standardization space (Kratz and Seaman, 2023).

The frictions that increasingly beset the realm of technical standards ultimately take place against the backdrop of shifting attitudes toward global trade and the process of globalization more broadly. While legitimate critiques have been levied on China for years over distortionary trade practices and the lack of a level playing field (see Gmeiner's chapter in this book), including with regard to standard setting, the United States, Europe, and others are now also evolving more in the direction of protectionist trade measures and proactive industrial policies. With regard to technical standards, it is the attacks on the WTO framework in particular and the underlying principles of globalization that may threaten these collaborative frameworks most. Indeed, the golden age of global standards is closely linked to trade liberalization and, more importantly, to the rules designed to moderate unfair, distortionary practices. When it comes to technical standards, such practices lead to sub-optimal outcomes in that they skew standards development in favor of industrial interests and power politics rather than technical competence and the broader societal good. Ultimately, the future trends of globalization, post-globalization, or de-globalization, and the shape of the global economy rests in part upon whether technical standardization remains an open, collaborative process or whether it becomes yet another tool of strategic rivalry and great power competition.

Notes

1 It is also registered and originally developed as IEEE 802.11.
2 D. Strumpf, "Where China Dominates in 5G Technology," *Wall Street Journal*, 26 February 2019.
3 M. Hauri, "Technical Standards: From Track Gauge to Ethics of AI," *DecodeTech*, 7 July 2022, available at https://decodetech.eu/post/technical-standards-from-track-gauge-to-ethics-of-ai.
4 Testimony of J. Olthoff before the House Committee on Science, Space, and Technology, Subcommittee on Research and Technology on *Setting the Standards: Strengthening U.S. Leadership in Technical Standards*, 17 March 2022, available at https://docs.house.gov/meetings/SY/SY15/20220317/114508/HHRG-117-SY15-Wstate-OlthoffJ-20220317.pdf.
5 J. D. Ma, "From Windfalls to Pitfalls: Qualcomm's China Conundrum," *MacroPolo*, 14 November 2018, available at https://macropolo.org/analysis/from-windfalls-to-pitfalls-qualcomms-china-conundrum.
6 See http://www.sac.gov.cn/sacen/Features/201602/t20160204_201329.htm.
7 The SAMR was formed as a result of further governmental reforms set in place in 2018. Previously, the SAC was attached to the AQSIQ, which was also an agency under the authority of the State Council.
8 M. Sheehan, "Standards Bearer? A Case Study of China's Leadership in Autonomous Vehicle Standards," *MacroPolo*, 3 June 2021, available at https://macropolo.org/analysis/standards-bearer-a-case-study-of-chinas-leadership-in-autonomous-vehicle-standards.
9 J. Doyon, "Influence without Ownership: The Chinese Communist Party Targets the Private Sector," *Institut Montaigne*, 21 January 2021, available at https://www.institutmontaigne.org/en/analysis/influence-without-ownership-chinese-communist-party-targets-private-sector.
10 M. Sheehan, M. Blumenthal, and M. R. Nelson, "Three Takeaways From China's New Standards Strategy," *Carnegie Endowment for International Peace*, 28 October 2021, available at https://carnegieendowment.org/2021/10/28/three-takeaways-from-china-s-new-standards-strategy-pub-85678.
11 See http://www.sac.gov.cn/sacen/events/photonew/202110/t20211009_348057.htm.
12 Skidmore's chapter in this book documents the numerous opportunities offered by the BRI. See also International Institute for Strategic Studies (2023).
13 See https://www.warner.senate.gov/public/index.cfm/2020/3/portman-warner-bipartisan-colleagues-express-concern-about-china-s-use-of-artificial-intelligence-based-technologies-to-oppress-uyghur-muslims-urge-secretary-pompeo-to-work-with-allies-to-prevent-its-spread-internationally.

14 R. Clark, "China Rails at Foreign 6G Partnerships," *Light Reading*, 1 November 2022, available at https://www.lightreading.com/6g/china-rails-at-foreign-6g-partnerships/d/d-id/774509.

15 T. Ray, "The Quad and The Wicked Problem of Tech Standards," *Observer Research Foundation*, 1 June 2022, available at https://www.orfonline.org/expert-speak/the-quad-and-the-wicked-problem-of-tech-standards.

16 L. Bertuzzi, "Commission Leaves European Standardisation Body out of AI Standard-Setting," *Euractiv*, 7 December 2022, available at https://www.euractiv.com/section/artificial-intelligence/news/commission-leaves-european-standardisation-body-out-of-ai-standard-setting.

References

Argonne National Laboratory (2015) *Power Play: China's Ultra High Voltage Technology and Global Standards*. Paulson Papers on Standards. Chicago: Paulson Institute.

Atha, K., Callahan, J., Chen, J., Drun, J., Green, K., Lafferty, B., McReynolds, J., Mulvenon, J., Rosen, B. and Walz, E. (2020) *China's Smart Cities Development*. Research Report Prepared on Behalf of the U.S.–China Economic and Security Review Commission, available at https://www.uscc.gov/sites/default/files/2020-04/China_Smart_Cities_Development.pdf.

Baron, J. and Kanevskaia, O. (2021) "Global Competition for Leadership Positions in Standards Development Organizations," *mimeo*, available at https://dspace.library.uu.nl/bitstream/handle/1874/415150/SSRN_id3818143.pdf.

Bateman, J. (2022) "Biden is Now All-In on Taking Out China," *Foreign Policy*, 12 October, available at https://foreignpolicy.com/2022/10/12/biden-china-semiconductor-chips-exports-decouple.

Blind, K., Jungmittag, A. and Mangelsdorf, A. (2011) *The Economic Benefits of Standardization*. Berlin: DIN German Institute for Standardization.

Blind, K. (2016) "The Impact of Standardisation and Standards on Innovation," in Edler, J., Cunningham, P., Gök, A. and Shapira, P. (Eds) *Handbook of Innovation Policy Impact*. Cheltenham and Northampton (MA): Edward Elgar Publishing.

Brunnermeier, M., Doshi, R. and James, H. (2018) "Beijing's Bismarckian Ghosts: How Great Powers Compete Economically," *Washington Quarterly*, Vol. 41, No. 3, pp. 161–176.

Busch, L. (2013) *Standards: Recipes for Reality*. Cambridge (MA): MIT Press.

Büthe, T. and Mattli, W. (2011) *The New Global Rulers: The Privatization of Regulation in the World Economy*. Princeton: Princeton University Press.

Chinese Communist Party Central Committee and State Council (2021) "National Standardization Development Outline," available at https://cset.georgetown.edu/wp-content/uploads/t0406_standardization_outline_EN.pdf.

Dackö, C. (2021) "What Makes a Technical Specification a WTO Compliant Standard?," *Mannheimer Swartling*, April, available at https://www.mannheimerswartling.se/app/uploads/2021/04/what-makes-a-technical-specification-a-wto-compliant-standard.pdf.

Doshi, R. (2021) *The Long Game: China's Grand Strategy to Displace American Order*. New York City: Oxford University Press.

Ernst, D. (2011) "Toward Greater Pragmatism? China's Approach to Innovation and Standardization," *Brief No. 18, Institute on Global Conflict and Cooperation*.

European Commission (2022a) *An EU Strategy on Standardisation: Setting Global Standards in Support of a Resilient, Green and Digital EU Single Market.* Communication from the Commission to the European Parliament, the Council, the European Economic and Social Committee and the Committee of the Regions, 2 February. Brussels: European Commission.

European Commission (2022b) *EU–US Joint Statement of the Trade and Technology Council.* Statement, 5 December. Brussels: European Commission.

Exovera (2022) *A New "Great Game?": China's Role in International Standards for Emerging Technologies.* Center for Intelligence Research and Analysis, Exovera, August, available at https://cira.exovera.com/wp-content/uploads/2022/08/NIST-Final-Report.pdf.

Ezell, S. J. and Atkinson, R. D. (2014) "The Middle Kingdom Galapagos Island Syndrome: The Cul-De-Sac of Chinese Technology Standards," *Information Technology & Innovation Foundation*, December, available at https://www2.itif.org/2014-galapagos-chinese-ict.pdf.

Fägersten, B. and Rühlig, T. (2019) "China's Standard Power and its Geopolitical Implications for Europe," *Brief 2/2019, Swedish Institute of International Affairs.*

Gao, P. (2008) "WAPI: A Chinese Attempt to Establish Wireless Standards and the International Coalition that Resisted," *Communications of the Association for Information Systems*, Vol. 23, Art. 8, pp. 151–162.

International Institute for Strategic Studies (2023) *China's Belt and Road Initiative – A Geopolitical and Geo-economic Assessment.* London: Routledge.

Kleinhans, J.-P.. and Rühlig, T. (2022) "The False Promise of Open RAN. Why Open RAN Does Not Solve the '5G China Challenge'," *Digital Power China*, August, available at https://timruhlig.eu/ctf/assets/x93kiko5rt7l/2VmWvuXxKdqdTuwkLSWUSQ/b48a2ffe9e42dc3a3b09d4c35b1c802e/DPC-Open_RAN_-_FULL_REPORT_-_FINAL.pdf

Kratz, A. and Seaman, J. (2023) "Strengthening US-EU Cooperation on Technical Standards in an Era of Strategic Competition," *Policy Brief, German Marshall Fund of the United States, 26 May.*

Kroeber, A. (2007) "China's Push to Innovate in Information Technology," in Jakobsen, L. (Ed) *Innovation with Chinese Characteristics – High-Tech Research in China.* Basingstoke: Palgrave Macmillan.

Neaher, G., Bray, D. A., Mueller-Kaler, J. and Schatz, B. (2021) *Standardizing the Future: How Can the United States Navigate the Geopolitics of International Technology Standards?* Washington, DC: Atlantic Council.

Okun-Kozlowicki, J. (2016) "Standards and Regulations: Measuring the Link to Goods Trade," *International Trade Administration, U.S. Department of Commerce*, available at https://legacy.trade.gov/td/osip/documents/osip_standards_trade_full_paper.pdf.

Peyrat, O. (2012) "China's Standardization Strategies," *ParisTech Review*, 9 October, available at https://www.paristechreview.com/2012/10/09/china-standardization.

Pohlmann, T. and Buggenhagen, M. (2022) "Who Is Leading the 5G Patent Race?," *IPlytics*, June, available at https://www.iplytics.com/wp-content/uploads/2022/06/5G-patent-race-June-2022_website.pdf.

Raimondo, G. M. (2022) "Remarks by U.S. Secretary of Commerce Gina Raimondo on the U.S. Competitiveness and the China Challenge," 30 November, available at https://www.commerce.gov/news/speeches/2022/11/remarks-us-secretary-commerce-gina-raimondo-us-competitiveness-and-china.

Rühlig, T. (2020) "Technical Standardisation, China and the Future International Order – A European Perspective," *E-Paper, Heinrich Böll Stiftung*, February, available at https://eu.boell.org/sites/default/files/2020-03/HBS-Techn%20Stand-A4%20web-030320.pdf.

Rühlig, T. (2021) "The Shape of Things to Come: The Race to Control Technical Standardisation," *European Union Chamber of Commerce in China*, available at https://static.europeanchamber.com.cn/upload/documents/documents/The_Shape_of_Things_to_Come_English_Final%5b966%5d.pdf.

Russel, D. R. and Berger, B. H. (2021) *Stacking the Deck: China's Influence in International Technology Standards Setting*. New York City and Washington, DC: Asia Society Policy Institute.

Seaman, J. (2020) "China and the New Geopolitics of Technical Standardization," *Notes de l'Ifri, French Institute of International Relations (Ifri)*, January.

Voo, J. and Creemers, R. (2021) "China's Role in Digital Standards for Emerging Technologies – Impacts on the Netherlands and Europe," *Leiden Asia Centre, Leiden University*, May, available at https://leidenasiacentre.nl/wp-content/uploads/2021/05/Chinas-Role-in-Digital-Standards-for-Emerging-Technologies-1.pdf.

Wang, P. and Zheng, L. (2018) "Beyond Government Control of China's Standardization System – History, Current Status, and Reform Suggestions," in Ernst, D. and Plummer, M. G. (Eds) *Megaregionalism 2.0 – Trade and Innovation within Global Networks*. Singapore: World Scientific.

White House (2022) "Quad Joint Leaders' Statement", *Statements and Releases*, 24 May, available at https://www.whitehouse.gov/briefing-room/statements-releases/2022/05/24/quad-joint-leaders-statement.

Yates, J. and Murphy, C. N. (2019) *Engineering Rules – Global Standard Setting since 1880*. Baltimore (MD): Johns Hopkins University Press.

Part III

Competition and rivalry between China and the United States

8 China's challenge to the global development finance regime and the Western response

David Skidmore

The global development finance regime has been transformed by China's emergence as the largest and most consequential source of development funding. At the multilateral level, China's impact has been incremental and largely consistent with existing norms. Regarding bilateral development finance, China has operated outside of the Western-dominated regime of Official Development Assistance as represented by the Development Assistance Committee (DAC). Instead, China's Belt and Road Initiative serves to export China's own post-2008 model of infrastructure-led development. Western responses to Chinese development finance have denounced China's norm-breaking behavior while seeking to compete on the ground of infrastructure development, which remains attractive to recipient countries. Beijing, in turn, has gradually adapted some of its policies in response to both Western and recipient country criticism. As a result, a process of competitive convergence points toward an evolving development finance regime that reaffirms many of the procedural and institutional norms of the past while broadening the substantive vision of development beyond neoliberalism to encompass a stronger state role resembling the embedded liberal norms of the early Bretton Woods order.

8.1 Introduction

China is a deeply invested stakeholder in the existing global economic order. China benefits from an open, stable and well-functioning system of complex interdependence. China is also a profoundly illiberal power rising within the liberal international order (LIO) and a country that seeks to export aspects of its own state-driven political economy. The tensions between these realities have defined the complexities of China's impact upon the international regime for official development finance.

Over the past decade, China has become the world's largest source of public finance for development, despite some lessening of flows in recent years. In some respects, China's intervention has been incremental and conformist; producing "norm-governed" regime change, in John Gerard Ruggie's (1982) evocative phrasing. This is especially the case with respect to both

DOI: 10.4324/9781003340430-11

new and established multilateral institutions. In other ways, China's impact upon the pre-existing official development regime has been disruptive, especially with respect to bilateral flows through the Belt and Road Initiative (Wang, 2022).

Overall, the official development regime is being profoundly transformed through a still unfolding process of mutual interaction among China, Western donors, legacy institutions, and recipient countries. Western moves to compete with China's Belt and Road Initiative (BRI) combined with Chinese efforts to correct some of the shortcomings in its own lending practices are producing competitive convergence around a new post-neoliberal equilibrium. A relatively homogenous post-1980 neoliberal regime is being replaced by a more fragmented, heterogenous development finance regime that allows space for state-led development paths resembling those more commonly associated with the early Bretton Woods era. While transformational with respect to a fading neoliberal era, the emerging order nevertheless falls within the parameters of the LIO envisioned by its founders.

As defined here, the term development finance refers to international loans or grants issued by governments or multilateral agencies for the purpose of promoting economic and social development in low- and middle-income countries. Excluded are official financial flows aimed at managing balance of payments problems, such as International Monetary Fund (IMF) lending or World Bank structural adjustment loans. Also excluded are foreign direct investment (FDI) flows, even when undertaken by state-owned enterprises.

Development finance may be offered on concessional or commercial terms. Development finance encompasses, but is broader than, Official Development Assistance (ODA), which, by the traditional criteria of the Organisation for Economic Co-operation and Development (OECD)'s Development Assistance Committee (DAC), must include a concessional element equal to 25% or more of total value.

Only one tenth of China's overall official financing for development, including the BRI, is provided on concessional terms (Dreher et al., 2022, p. 309). BRI lending is developmental in purpose but offered on commercial or near-commercial terms. Much of China's development finance is similar to that of the International Bank for Reconstruction and Development (IBRD), the World Bank's main lending facility that serves middle-income countries, but different from the Bank's International Development Agency (IDA) or the bilateral programs of DAC member states that offer grants or concessional loans.

The chapter begins with a description of the post-World War II development finance regime followed by a discussion of China's independent path outside of that regime. We then examine China's recent challenges to the neoliberal development finance regime at both the multilateral and bilateral levels. The multilateral challenge includes China's sponsorship of the Asian Infrastructure Investment Bank (AIIB) and co-sponsorship of the New Development Bank (NDB) along with Chinese calls for reform of legacy multilateral development banks (MDBs), especially the World Bank. The challenge to the existing bilateral development finance regime represented by the OECD's DAC takes the form of China's BRI.

We offer an analysis of how the China challenge differs at the multilateral and bilateral levels, but also what each share: a focus on state-led infrastructure development. This development model offers a sharp contrast with the neoliberal model that has dominated the Western development finance regime since the 1980s (Chin and Gallagher, 2019).

The concluding sections of the chapter consider Western responses to the China challenge, how China has dealt with these responses and how this competitive process of move and countermove has transformed the development finance regime. While the China challenge has further undermined an already weakened neoliberal consensus, it has also in some degree been reconciled with the broader embedded liberal normative structure of the Bretton Woods order as conceived after World War II. The new equilibrium will feature greater competition over control of development finance flows and institutions even as a degree of convergence emerges around norms of multilateralism, the key role of infrastructure in development and greater state involvement in economic management.

8.2 The development finance regime

The Bretton Woods conference that created the World Bank and the IMF, thus establishing the foundations for the post-war international development aid regime, constituted, according to Eric Helleiner, "a form of institutionalized liberal multilateralism that was compatible with various kinds of active public management of the economy (Helleiner, 2019, p. 1113)." The architects of Bretton Woods rejected the classical liberalism of the 19th century in favor of what John Gerard Ruggie (1982) has labeled "embedded liberalism." The designers of the World Bank were influenced by New Deal thinking and by the experience of state war-time economic mobilization (Helleiner, 2016).

As Helleiner (2019, p. 1114) notes, the pre-1980 Bretton Woods order was "both more contested and more malleable in its content than is often recognized." During the 1950s, for example, World Bank and U.S. Treasury Department advisers promoted active state economic intervention in developing countries, including the promotion of import-substitution industrialization (Maxfield and Nolt, 1990). The World Bank in its early decades focused heavily upon publicly funded and managed infrastructure development.

This changed with the end of the Cold War and the consolidation of American hegemony. Under the pressure of the Latin American debt crisis of the 1980s and ideological shifts in the United States and United Kingdom, embedded liberalism gave way to neoliberalism. The new orthodoxy was accompanied by two sets of conditionalities: structural adjustment lending to debtor countries was conditioned upon deregulation and cuts to the public sector while official development assistance was conditioned upon good governance reforms. Foreign aid became less oriented to growth, now left to markets, and more focused on the amelioration of poverty, disease, ignorance, inequality, and environmental degradation (Babb, 2013). The latter emphasis on "soft" development received the imprimatur of the United Nations (UN) with the launch of the Millennium Development Goals in 2000.

Although anti-poverty programs were not new, the deepened priority given to ameliorative ODA was intimately connected with the neoliberal, anti-statist turn of the 1980s and 1990s in two specific ways. First, the austerity measures that the IMF and World Bank imposed upon debtor countries as a condition for lending exacted punishing hardships on the poor. Seeking to avert social instability, donors directed an increased proportion of aid to those harmed by austerity policies. Second, previously favored types of aid that supported active state intervention in support of growth strategies, such as infrastructure development or industrial policies, were deemed ideologically incompatible with neoliberalism. Anti-poverty programs, however, were recognized as necessary to meet the needs of those left behind by market-led development and to prepare the poor to become productive market participants in the future. It was this development finance regime that China set out to challenge in the years following the global financial crisis.

8.3 The multilateral challenge: the Asian Infrastructure Investment Bank and New Development Bank

China's sponsorship of the Asian Infrastructure Investment Bank (AIIB) represents an example of norm-governed change within the confines of the existing development finance regime (Stephen and Skidmore, 2019; Helleiner, 2019, p. 1128). As such, it is illustrative of China's investment in and desire to deepen its influence within the normative and institutional structures of the existing system, including the mechanisms of multilateral development finance (Lairson, 2018; see also Gaillard and Waibel's chapter in this book).

The AIIB was initially conceived as a relatively direct extension of Chinese foreign economic policy and a vehicle for recycling China's dollar surplus through the BRI. After Great Britain and other Western countries showed interest in joining as members, Beijing reconceived of the AIIB as a genuinely multilateral institution on par with existing MDBs (He, 2016, p. 12).

This move dovetailed with a growing sense among top Chinese officials that the Western global governance system had "malfunctioned" and required reform. Following two high-level work conferences on global governance in 2015 and 2016, Xi Jinping publicly declared that China "must make the international order more reasonable and just to protect the common interests of China and other developing countries" (Heath, 2018; Zeng, 2019).

A more specific motivation for launching the AIIB was Beijing's frustration with China's meager voting share at the World Bank despite China's rise to become the world's second largest economy (Pratt, 2020; Urpelainen and de Graaf, 2015). Even after a 2010 World Bank reform package marginally raised China's share from 2.8% to 4.4% (Chin, 2012, p. 219), implementation was delayed until the United States Congress finally gave assent in 2015. Further action raised China's share to 6.1% in 2018, still far below China's share of the global economy (Humphrey and Chen, 2021, p. 10).

By contrast, China is the AIIB's single largest shareholder with a 26.57% voting share and effective veto power over major policy decisions.[1] Moreover, the AIIB is headquartered in Beijing with a Chinese national as president. While the AIIB is a genuinely multilateral bank with around 100 members, China remains a dominant player.

China also criticized the World Bank as overly bureaucratic, encumbered by costly overhead and painfully slow in project approval and implementation. Beijing considered the World Bank's lending priorities unfocused, with too little emphasis on economic growth in favor of expansive social and environmental initiatives. China sold the AIIB, by contrast, as lean, nimble, and focused on the massive infrastructure needs of the Asian region, which China viewed as key to removing major bottlenecks to development. In contrast with Western-centered MDBs, the AIIB does not attach governance conditions related to democratic reforms or human rights. This is consistent with Beijing's insistence that multilateral institutions respect the sovereignty and political independence of member states.

Yet AIIB hardly poses a systemic challenge to the existing MDBs or the norms of the development regime. Many of the AIIB's personnel as well as the rule sets that make up the Bank's charter and regulations were drawn from the World Bank, the Asian Development Bank (ADB) and other MDBs. Worries that the AIIB would undercut existing MDBs by offering loans with lenient social and environmental conditions have proven unfounded. Indeed, many of the AIIB's loans, especially in its early years, have been made in co-sponsorship with other MDBs with the usual social and environmental standards attached (Stephen and Skidmore, 2019).

In other respects, the AIIB is norm-governed. As mentioned, membership is broad and includes many Western countries. The AIIB raises capital on international bond markets and its securities are subject to scrutiny by the major ratings agencies, which have so far rated them high investment grade. Loans are made in dollar, rather than renminbi. Political considerations do not appear a major constraint on lending. For instance, India, a major rival of China, is the largest recipient of AIIB loans.[2] Firms from non-member countries may bid for contracts on AIIB-funded projects (Humphrey and Chen, 2021, p. 26; Morris et al., 2021, p. 19).

Many of the design features that differentiate the AIIB from the World Bank, such as streamlined loan procedures with greater borrower input and quicker project implementation, mirror prior recommendations of the

High-Level Commission on Modernization of World Bank Group Governance chaired by former President of Mexico Ernesto Zedillo, which criticized the World Bank for bloat and inefficiency.[3] Indeed, perhaps in response to the challenge presented by the AIIB, both the World Bank and the ADB have promised to speed up project approval, reduce overhead costs and allocate greater resources to infrastructure development. The ADB, for instance, has streamlined its loan approval process from two years to six months (Yamamoto, 2020, p. 336).

While these may be considered positive reforms, there is also evidence that direct Chinese competition may have prompted the World Bank to lower its lending standards. One study of 54 African countries between 1980 and 2013 found that the World Bank imposed fewer conditions on its loans in cases where the country was also the recipient of Chinese loans. The effect was greatest for low-income countries (Hernandez, 2016).

The design of the New Development Bank (NDB) represents a more significant departure from MDB precedents. A so-called South-South bank founded in 2016, the NDB has so far limited membership to the original five co-sponsors: China, Russia, Brazil, South Africa and India. Capital contributions and voting shares are distributed equally among the charter members and decisions are made by consensus. Unlike the AIIB and other MDBs, the NDB relies upon the regulatory and legal frameworks of borrower countries and has adopted only skeletal safeguard policies. Staff are drawn exclusively from member countries and the NDB both raises and dispenses funds exclusively within member countries. While the NDB represents a more radical break with the established multilateral development finance regime than the AIIB, the challenge is limited by the NDB's small size and scope. Moreover, the NDB has entered into regular collaborations and information-sharing arrangements with the major MDBs (Humphrey and Chen, 2021; He, 2016; Gaillard and Waibel's chapter in this book).

China's creation of parallel institutions has not lessened its investment in legacy MDBs. Despite Beijing's unhappiness with its underrepresentation and with some of the policies of the World Bank, its engagement with the Bank has remained deep. This is not surprising considering that China is the second largest recipient, following India, of World Bank lending over the latter's more than seven-decade history despite only joining the Bank in 1980. China graduated from IDA funding eligibility in 1999 but remains one of the largest recipients of IBRD lending.[4]

While China's capital share of the World Bank remains far below its relative size in the world economy and its contributions to the IDA are modest, China supplements World Bank resources in other ways. China established a co-financing fund – essentially a line of credit – of $3 billion with the World Bank's International Finance Corporation (IFC) to support lending to private entities. Chinese funds do not count as paid-in capital and no voting rights are attached. China can turn down projects, but otherwise has no direct influence over project selection, approval, implementation, or procurement.

In practice, China's criterion for project approval has focused on financial viability rather than political factors; an emphasis consistent with China's apparent motivation for the project, which is to find a profitable outlet for recycling surplus dollar reserves. This arrangement served as a model for the IFC's Managed Co-Lending Portfolio Program, which seeks to attract private investment funds to co-finance IFC projects. China has partnered with smaller, regional MDBs on similar co-financing arrangements (Humphrey and Chen, 2021).

China's stake in the World Bank also extends to the profitable opportunities afforded to Chinese firms through participation in World Bank projects. Chinese firms consistently rank at the top in the value of procurement contracts issued by the World Bank and captured 20% of World Bank contracts by value between 2010 and 2020 (Morris et al., 2021, p. 20).

China has used its heavy engagement with the World Bank – as a contributor, borrower, and contractor – to exert leverage. For instance, as early as 2007, China successfully pressured the World Bank to enter a memorandum of understanding (MOU) accepting China as an equal partner in co-sponsoring loan projects as opposed to the usual practice wherein the World Bank would serve as the lead partner when co-financing with bilateral donors (Chin, 2012, p. 211).

8.4 The bilateral challenge: The Belt and Road Initiative

Launched in 2013, the BRI is a massive program of development finance that has already distributed more than $850 billion in lending through the developing world, mostly in support of infrastructure projects: roads, railways, ports, airports, electric grids, dams, power plants, pipelines, etc.[5]

The BRI is representative of China's new-found willingness to promote its own political and economic model as an example for developing countries (Skidmore, 2021). In his address to the 19th Chinese Communist Party Congress in October 2017, President Xi Jinping argued that China's successful development experience was "blazing a new trail for other developing countries to achieve modernization." Xi added that the Chinese model "offers a new option for other countries and nations who want to speed up their development while preserving their independence."[6]

Compared with the AIIB, China's Belt and Road Initiative offers a stark contrast with the principles and rules of the pre-existing aid regime. The OECD's Development Assistance Committee, which coordinates policies among major donor countries, serves as the organizational core of the bilateral ODA regime.[7] While China's official financial development lending has in recent years exceeded that of all DAC members combined, it has refused to join the DAC, although it has participated in a DAC-China Study Group. China has also rejected invitations to join the Paris Club, the OECD Creditor Reporting Group, the International Aid Transparency Initiative, and a multilateral effort to place limits on export financing (Dreher et al., 2022, pp. 65

and 292). In general, China has intentionally elected to remain an outsider with respect to multilateral institutions designed to coordinate the efforts of bilateral development finance.

This stance arises in part from China's long-standing rejection of the West's model of aid, which the Chinese interpret as the extension of a lingering colonial mentality. From a Chinese perspective, the Western donor-recipient model is inherently unequal, allowing the donor to set the terms of the relationship, and thus giving rise to an unhealthy degree of dependence. In principle, the Chinese model instead emphasizes "win-win" or "mutual benefit" exchanges among equals: "cooperation" rather than "aid" (Chin, 2012, p. 220; Humphrey and Chen, 2021, p. 5).

Most DAC assistance takes the form of grants and is offered untied – recipients are not required to source inputs from the donor. Donors commit to stringent standards regarding transparency, anti-corruption, competitive bidding, and social and environmental safeguards. Aid is conditioned upon the democratic and human rights performance of recipients. Substantively, DAC countries have focused upon ameliorating poverty, disease, ignorance, and environmental threats.

By contrast, the vast majority of BRI financing takes the form of loans offered through one of China's two main policy banks – the China Development Bank and the China Export-Import Bank – on commercial or near-commercial terms. The bidding process is closed, non-competitive, and the contracts include non-disclosure clauses. Loans are generally tied to the hiring of Chinese firms, the purchase of Chinese-made goods, and the use of Chinese services and labor. Controls on corruption or the implementation of social and environmental safeguards depend upon local regulations. China abstains from imposing conditions relating to democracy, human rights, or good governance (Dreher et al., 2022, p. 22; Skidmore, 2021).

China often describes BRI contracts as akin to commercial transactions that should not be held to the same standards as concessional aid. Indeed, the way Chinese banks and firms do business through the BRI mirrors commercial practices at home. As Batson (2019) puts it:

> The Belt and Road is really the expansion of a specific part of China's domestic political economy to the rest of the world. That is the nexus between state-owned contractors and state-owned banks, which formed in the domestic infrastructure building spree construction that began after the 2008 global financial crisis.[8]

Many of the players are the same abroad as in China, including local and provincial governments. Also consistent is the laxity of centralized control over infrastructure development both domestically and internationally. With respect to the BRI, Xi Jinping provided what Jones and Zou (2017) have referred to as a "policy envelope," or general policy guidance, which varied actors at all levels of the Chinese political and economic system hastened to fill with projects that might plausibly align with the broad objectives outlined at the top. Especially in the early years of the BRI, the result was a poorly coordinated rush to secure and implement projects while the funding spigot remained open (Jones and Zeng, 2019).

Unsurprisingly, the BRI became subject to many of the same problems abroad that plagued the excessive expansion of domestic infrastructure at home over the past decade and more: overpriced contracts, high levels of corruption, serious environmental consequences, lack of transparency and accountability and unsustainable debt. Jones (2020) argues that while the BRI is largely pro-market and pro-globalization, it nevertheless challenges the LIO because "China's internal governance structure is ... highly fragmented and operates in ways that frequently ignore and violate existing governance regimes around development financing, environmental and social protection, and corporate governance."[9]

China has implicitly acknowledged some of the problems raised by critics of the BRI. At the Second BRI Forum in 2019, Xi Jinping reassured the audience that BRI projects would henceforth "deliver true benefits to the people of participating countries" while also meeting the standards of "commercial and fiscal sustainability."[10] New regulations were aimed at compelling Chinese actors to pay more attention to social, financial and environmental risks, to hire both Chinese and host country consultants to assess risks, and to not only follow local laws but also meet international standards.[11] As always, however, enforcing such regulations on far-flung investments around the world against the immediate interests of the actors involved poses a challenge.

At the Second Forum, China launched the Debt Sustainability Framework (DSF) as an answer to charges that the BRI encourages reckless borrowing. Largely modeled after those designed by the IMF and the World Bank, the DSF was presented as a set of criteria for developing countries and lenders to assess the sustainability of proposed borrowing (World Bank, 2019, p. 104).

China has also taken tentative steps toward building multilateral elements into the Belt and Road in order to share risk, leverage resources and reduce friction with partners and rivals. An example is the Forum on China-Africa Cooperation (FOCAC), which has convened summits of China with African countries every three years since 2000. In 2018, summit participants declared that FOCAC would henceforth serve as a platform for BRI coordination (Murphy, 2022, p. 244).

On a larger scale, the BRI Forums that Beijing convened in 2017 and 2019 brought together hundreds of heads of state and officials from developing countries and international organizations associated with the BRI. The Forums allowed the informal sharing of ideas and information across the "spokes" of the hub-and-spoke structure that makes up the BRI. The multinational expert group that helped set the agenda for the second BRI Forum made further multilateralization of the BRI a centerpiece of their recommendations. In his address to the second BRI Forum in 2019, Xi cited the "need to earnestly advance... institution-building for Belt and Road Cooperation" in a "spirit of multilateralism."[12]

In 2018 came the launch of the China-IMF Capacity Development Center, with the goal of training officials from China and BRI countries on issues related to debt sustainability (Dreher et al., 2022, p. 290). Another example is the Multilateral Cooperation Center for Development Finance (MCDF), inaugurated in July 2020. Initiated by China's Ministry of Finance and hosted by the AIIB, the Center is touted as a vehicle for sharing information, building capacity, and facilitating feasibility and preparation studies for infrastructure projects through collaboration among the eight MDBs that signed the original MOUs in 2017 or 2019. An initial infusion of $180 million in funding was provided by China, Egypt, Saudi Arabia, Hungary, Cambodia, and the Philippines (Nedopil et al., 2022).

In an address to the United Nations General Assembly in September 2021, Xi Jinping announced the Global Development Initiative (GDI) which is aimed at supporting the UN's 2030 Sustainable Development Goals. Over the following year, 60 countries and international organizations joined the Group of Friends of the GDI (Refinitiv, 2022). As troubles with the BRI have forced China into a "defensive crouch,"[13] mentions of what was once Xi Jinping's flagship initiative have virtually vanished from his speeches in favor of the GDI.[14]

The goals, purposes, and mechanisms of the GDI remain pitched in general and abstract terms, as is common with new Chinese initiatives. While Chinese officials have been at pains to distinguish between the BRI and the GDI, it seems apparent that the latter is aimed in part at steering attention away from the growing problems and criticism associated with the BRI. With the GDI, China seeks to stake out a leadership role in defining the development agenda beyond infrastructure and to do so through engagement with the UN system, where China enjoys considerable strength and credibility.

The GDI can also be seen as a rejoinder to the various initiatives that the U.S. and other Western countries have launched to counter the BRI. China intends to show that it can, through the GDI, compete with the West on the ground of "soft" infrastructure and other poverty- and health-related initiatives.

Another area where China has shown some bend in its aloof stance toward existing institutions concerns negotiations with debtor countries. The combined fallout from the Covid pandemic, supply chain disruptions, the war in Ukraine, and rising inflation have pitched 60% of low-income countries and 30% of emerging market countries into debt distress, according to the IMF.[15] Many countries, including some that borrowed heavily from China, are at risk of default and in need of debt relief or restructuring (Horn et al., 2021). The Paris Club coordinates negotiations with debtor countries on behalf of sovereign creditors. Members of the Paris Club agree to act collectively, to make decisions by consensus, to share information, to insist upon common conditions, and to require that debtors not accept treatment from non-Paris Club creditors that is less favorable than the terms agreed to with the Paris Club.

Unlike Paris Club members, China has typically insisted that borrower governments provide collateral to back loans from Chinese banks. While collateral has sometimes taken the form of hard assets or future commodity streams, more commonly the debtor is required to deposit hard currency in an escrow account controlled by China.[16] China's access to collateral in case of default ensures that it will receive preferential treatment over Paris Club or commercial creditors. Indeed, BRI contracts typically include "anti-Paris Club" clauses through which borrowers promise that Chinese debt will not be subject to Paris Club rescheduling agreements (Dreher, et al., 2022, p. 300, fn. 59). These arrangements have proven a serious sticking point in debt negotiations as other creditors object to China receiving preferential treatment (see Gaillard and Waibel's chapter in this book).

China has shown some flexibility. In November 2020, China backed the Common Framework developed between the G20 and the Paris Club on the terms of relief for distressed debtor countries.[17] China agreed to co-chair, along with France, creditor committees in negotiations with Zambia and Ethiopia[18] and has participated in "1+6" roundtable discussions with leaders of major international economic institutions on debt rescheduling and other topics. Nonetheless, the logjam persisted as no countries had yet succeeded in negotiating a debt rescheduling or restructuring agreement through the Common Framework some two years after its announcement. In a November 2022 report, Fitch Ratings predicted more defaults among emerging market countries in 2023 and declared that the Common Framework "is not proving effective in resolving crises quickly.[19]

8.5 The statist challenge

China's multilateral and bilateral interventions in development finance differ. The former has been incremental and norm-governed while the latter has been disruptive to existing norms. Both, however, promote a development pathway that depends upon high degrees of state economic intervention in the form of infrastructure development. This represents a significant challenge to the neoliberal ODA regime that has reigned since the 1980s. The latter model treats the private sector, not the state, as the primary agent of economic growth. Moreover, Western aid programs often bypass weak or corrupt states bureaucracies, instead routing resources through non-governmental organizations (NGOs), international agencies or private contractors. By contrast, Chinese development finance centers the state in the process of development and privileges state-state ties.

Although China's statist approach to development finance thus challenges neoliberal precepts, it has roots in the more expansive liberalism of the early Bretton Woods order as well as the "East Asian Model" pioneered by Japan.

Indeed, the BRI was largely modeled on Japanese aid to China during the latter's early reform period.

Japan took out its first World Bank loan for infrastructure development in 1953, launching the country on its way to becoming known as a "construction state" (Yamamoto, 2020, p. 328). Once Japan became a significant aid donor, it focused on financing infrastructure in East and Southeast Asia in support of networks for trade and raw materials. Like China's contemporary BRI, Japan offered loans on largely commercial terms tied to purchases of Japanese goods made without political conditions.

Japan made its first infrastructure project loan to China in 1978. Japanese assistance to China was substantial during the 1980s, as were both official and semi-official efforts to promote Japan's model of infrastructure-led development in China. Japanese aid familiarized Chinese officials with other aspects of Japan's state-led approach to industrial development: state credit allocation, export promotion, the nurturing of infant industries, and the spurring of technological innovation (Sasada, 2019, p. 1048).

In the 1980s and early 1990s, Japan's infrastructure-heavy financing came under criticism from the United States and Europe. Moreover, some projects were plagued by the kinds of problems that now accompany BRI loans, leading to pushback within some recipient societies. In response to these pressures, Japan altered its foreign assistance programs in the early 1990s to conform more closely to DAC norms.[20] This included a reduction in infrastructure spending in favor of programs aimed at fighting poverty, supporting democracy and human rights, improving the environment, and promoting market principles. Japan also untied its aid and shifted from loans to grants (Jain, 2016, pp. 98–100; Jiang, 2019, p. 785; Sasada, 2019, pp. 1045 and 1050; Katada and Liao, 2020, pp. 454–458; Liao and Katada, 2021).

Yet the impact of Japan's earlier aid approach proved lasting as a model for China's domestic and international behavior. For instance, China's "Going Global" campaign of the late 1990s – a precursor of the BRI – was fashioned after Japan's state-supported efforts to internationalize Japanese firms decades earlier. The AIIB itself is China's answer to Japan's 1966 move to establish the Asian Development Bank, which also focused heavily upon infrastructure lending.

China's BRI has prompted Japan to shift back toward its pre-1992 approach to aid.[21] In 2015, Japanese Prime Minister Shinzo Abe announced the Quality Infrastructure Investment Initiative, pledging $110 billion in infrastructure investment to Asian countries over the coming five years through both bilateral and multilateral programs (Yamamoto, 2020). The next year, Abe unveiled the Expanded Partnership for Quality Infrastructure, which promised $200 billion in infrastructure investment globally over five years (Kikuchi and Unzaki, 2019). Like China, Japan seeks international outlets for overcapacity in Japanese construction firms. While Japan's domestic infrastructure is largely built out, overseas infrastructure sales by Japanese firms doubled from 2010 to 2016 (Kikuchi and Unzaki, 2019). In 2013, an official Japan Revitalization Strategy set a goal of tripling Japanese infrastructure exports by 2020 (Trinidad, 2019, p. 92). Japan and China are now engaged in competitive infrastructure-building projects across Southeast Asia that have both economic and political ramifications (Zhao, 2019).

8.6 Western responses to the China challenge

Western responses to China's growing role in global development finance have been divided and incoherent. The United States adopted a reflexively negative attitude toward the AIIB, depicting it as a direct challenge to the World Bank that would undercut lending standards and initiate a race to the bottom. Indeed, Washington sought to isolate the AIIB and counseled other countries against joining.[22] Excepting Japan, American allies largely rejected this approach; instead opting to influence the new institution's evolution from within. In so doing, the involvement of many traditional donor countries in the AIIB likely helped steer it toward convergence with traditional norms while also bestowing international legitimacy on Beijing's creation.

The United States treated the BRI as not only a challenge to the norms of the existing development finance regime, but as a national security threat. The 2017 National Security Strategy labeled the BRI as part of a China's revisionist strategy to reshape the global order (Ashbee, 2021, p. 135). Washington's efforts to build an international coalition aligned against the BRI were somewhat more successful, especially as problems with many BRI projects became evident and strategic tensions with China intensified.

U.S. criticisms of the BRI, sometimes seconded by allied countries, ranged widely. China was accused of setting "debt traps" for borrower countries in order to grab control over strategic assets.[23] American officials decried the lack of transparency of the BRI, the allegedly poor quality of the infrastructure projects, the tough financing terms, hidden corruption and the social and environmental costs accompanying poorly planned projects. China was accused of using the BRI to lay the groundwork for expanded military influence or supporting authoritarian governments.

In Europe, early support for the BRI, especially in Eastern Europe, eroded over time due to the lack of concrete benefits along with rising security concerns. In 2012, China launched the 16+1 Initiative which promised to funnel infrastructure investments to participating countries through the BRI. With the addition of Greece in 2019, the association became 17+1, including twelve EU members. The European Union, although sending an observer to meetings of the group, criticized the project as an attempt to divide the EU. The initiative was slow to produce results, however, as only four of forty announced projects had reached completion by 2020. Lithuania withdrew in 2021 after a row with China over its ties with Taiwan. Estonia and Latvia quit the group in 2022 after Chinese President Xi Jinping pledged a "no limits" partnership with Russia shortly before the Russian invasion of Ukraine. As an alternative, the United States and the EU offered support for the Three Seas Initiative among a group of state in southeastern Europe to develop infrastructure connectivity free of dependence upon China or Russia.[24]

Implicitly, however, the United States and the European Union eventually acknowledged that dire warnings about the dangers and drawbacks of entanglement with the BRI were insufficient to sway developing countries in other regions while the latter's need for infrastructure development remained unmet through other avenues. Indeed, Western responses to the BRI rarely defended the lending priorities that had directed most development financing since the early 1990s. Instead of doubling down on soft development aid, the West aimed to compete with Beijing on China's own terms by offering a better pathway to meeting the infrastructure needs of developing countries.

In the space of a few years, the United States, the EU and the G7 have unveiled a succession of initiatives directed at the infrastructure space. Taken together, Western initiatives have promised to: (i) marshal the necessary funds and expertise to meet the South's infrastructure needs through public-private partnerships placing commercial actors in lead roles; (ii) ensure high-quality infrastructure that meets stringent social and environmental standards; (iii) offer transparent and sustainable financial terms; and (iv) broaden the scope of "infrastructure" to include strengthened "soft" social and technological capacities beyond "hard" physical construction.

First up was the $60 billion BUILD Act, passed by the U.S. Congress in 2018,[25] which provided loans to private firms engaged in infrastructure projects in developing countries. The Act created a new International Development Finance Corporation (IDFC), which largely took over the functions of the former Overseas Private Investment Corporation (OPIC). Although IDFC funding was twice the level of OPIC, it was nevertheless a small fraction of the financial heft represented by China's BRI. A similar measure was the creation of the China and Transformation Exports Program (CTEP) within the U.S. Export-Import Bank. Congress mandated that the Eximbank allocate at least 20% of its $135 billion financing authority to CTEP, through which companies in certain targeted sectors could request support to counter Chinese export subsidies when competing in foreign markets (see Gaillard's chapter in this book).

The United States, Australia, and Japan announced the Blue Dot Network (BDN) at the Indo-Pacific Business Forum on the sidelines of ASEAN's 35th summit meeting in November 2019. The main purpose of the BDN was to expose and highlight the BRI's alleged low standards with respect to design and construction quality and social and environmental safeguards. BDN would serve as a sort of ratings agency, providing assessments of the quality of proposed infrastructure projects and certifying those that passed muster. Certification, in turn, would reassure investors that the project carried acceptable levels of risk and uncertainty, thus attracting funds at reduced interest rates. It was also hoped that the certification process would produce a virtuous race to the top in project quality (Ashbee, 2021).

BDN proved a bust and was later merged into the OECD Trust in Business Initiative. Countries were reluctant to submit projects for certification due to fear of associating with an initiative Beijing considered antagonistic to China, concern that applications for certification may be rejected, resulting in political humiliation, and resentment that the initiative implicitly cast disrepute upon projects not carrying certification (Ashbee, 2021).

U.S. President Joseph Biden and other leaders unveiled the Build Back Better World (B3W) initiative at the G7 Summit in June 2021. The announcement offered vague suggestions that existing funds channeled through various foreign assistance agencies of the G7 member states would provide leverage to mobilize private investment in infrastructure projects in the developing world. Priority would be given to soft infrastructure areas such as climate, health, digital technology and gender equity. B3W failed to attract private funding and, within a year, had "sunk without a trace."[26]

Much the same was true of the European Union's Global Gateway initiative, announced in December 2021 with promises of $318 billion in infrastructure investment by 2027. A year later, EU officials could cite no new projects attributable to the Global Gateway and Vincent Grimaud, Acting Director of the European Commission Department for International Partnerships, admitted: "Global Gateway does not bring new financial means – there is no additional money when it comes to the EU level."[27]

The latest rebranding is the Partnership for Global Infrastructure and Investment (PGII), launched at the June 2022 G7 Summit. This time the assembled countries pledged to marshal $600 billion in "comprehensive, transparent and values-driven" infrastructure investment by 2027 including public and private sources.[28] Once again, the focus will be on soft infrastructure rather than the massive construction projects characteristic of China's BRI. The United States followed up at a Washington D.C. summit with African leaders by pledging $55 billion over five years as part of its PGII commitment.[29] At this point, however, the credibility of Western commitments remains in question.

8.7 Conclusion

China's emergence as the largest provider of official development finance has shaken the pre-existing regime. Even as China trims the size of the BRI, it will remain a major source of development finance for developing countries and will likely diversify its portfolio of supported projects through the Global Development Initiative.

China's impact has not only been quantitative, but also qualitative. Chinese development finance is offered on different terms and for different sorts of projects than traditional Western ODA. BRI funding is attractive to states that view large scale infrastructure development as a way to remove bottlenecks that stand in the way of economic growth. China thus offers an alternative to the predominately ameliorative types of aid on offer from Western donors. China's approach also serves as a statist contrast with the pro-market, private sector-oriented, neoliberal model of development for so long promoted by Western governments and MDBs.

Yet the challenge China poses to the Western development finance regime is not undifferentiated, but instead varies with the institutional context (Wang, 2020). At the multilateral level, China has sought incremental change to existing norms while at the bilateral level it has posed more fundamental challenges to the existing rules of the game.[30] This variegated challenge to the existing development finance regime has led to greater institutional fragmentation, ideological pluralism and normative complexity. Nevertheless, there are indications that a new, more heterogenous equilibrium may emerge through a process we refer to as competitive convergence.

China has reaffirmed a commitment to multilateralism both by seeking increased influence within legacy MDBs and building parallel institutions of its own initiative. The latter have replicated many procedural and substantive norms associated with legacy institutions. This underlines China's entanglement with the existing LIO. In order to play within the multilateral space, China faced the necessity of engaging with varied stakeholders, including potential capital contributors, bond markets, ratings agencies, borrower governments, and partner MDBs. Building new lending institutions that would be accepted as credible and legitimate within this world requires a good deal of conformity with existing norms.

At the same time, the AIIB and the NDB engaged in brand differentiation, selling themselves as speedier, nimbler, less bureaucratic alternatives to the legacy MDBs. The latter, in turn, responded by reducing loan processing times and cutting overhead costs. The World Bank and regional development banks also increased lending for infrastructure development to compete with the new kids on the block. Indeed, World Bank funding for infrastructure development shows the greatest growth in countries that have previously received increased Chinese infrastructure loans (Zeitz, 2021).

These dynamics of competitive convergence are most evident within the multilateral space, where the initial challenge was modest, as was the adaptive response of the legacy institutions. As Chin (2012, p. 211) has noted, the socialization process between China and legacy MDBs has run both ways.

Yet by far the greater part of the China challenge to the pre-existing development finance regime has taken place at the bilateral level through the BRI. The financial sums involved in the BRI dwarf those available through the AIIB and NDB. The political import of bilateral lending is also far greater, especially given the vast disparity in size and power between China and BRI recipient countries.

The incentives for China to conform to the norms of the DAC have been far less compelling than those that operate in the multilateral space. As Wang (2022) argues, China's Jekyll and Hyde approach to development finance reflects its diverse interests. Alignment with multilateral institutions reflects China's deep investment in the existing LIO, while it simultaneously rejects

DAC norms that grate against longstanding Chinese principles of solidaristic cooperation with fellow developing countries. The goals of the BRI also align with strong domestic imperatives – the needs to recycle dollar surpluses, to export overcapacity in construction industries, to enhance access to raw materials abroad, and to promote growth in China's underdeveloped Western provinces (Lai, 2021) – while the business methods reproduce those of the domestic debt-development complex that emerged in China following the 2008 financial crisis. Furthermore, the "fragmented authoritarianism" (Lieberthal and Lampton, 1992) of the Chinese political system renders it difficult for Beijing to exercise greater centralized discipline over BRI projects despite the manifest drawbacks of "business as usual."

Even so, China has undertaken modest efforts to respond to criticisms of the BRI. These have included steps toward multilateralizing aspects of the BRI. Beijing has reduced the pace of BRI lending and rescheduled the debt of some distressed debtors. The Global Development Initiative represents an effort to compete on the "soft" development ground that was long the focus of Western ODA. Nevertheless, as Dreher et al. (2022, p. 291) point out, the willingness of other countries and international organizations to embrace China's tentative moves to multilateralize aspects of the BRI or follow-on initiatives may be constrained by a lack of trust owing to China's poor record of compliance with international rules and norms of the international development regime.

Meanwhile, Western responses to the BRI have embraced China's vision of infrastructure-led development even while rejecting Beijing's model for accomplishing this vision. Japan has moved most aggressively, putting significant money on the table for hard infrastructure and tying loans more closely to Japanese commercial interests than other DAC members. Other Western initiatives have been less coherent, often lacking in real money and focusing on "soft" infrastructure rather than competing head-to-head on the kind of large-scale projects funded through the BRI. Western promises to mobilize private investment or to offer higher quality at reasonable cost and speed are yet to be realized at scale. Moreover, in the rush to compete with China through emulation rather differentiation, traditional donors may reinforce a development path that is poorly suited to the needs of the least developed countries, where investments in agricultural productivity rather than massive infrastructure projects may best correlate with these nation's financial capacities and comparative advantages (Ndii, 2022).

Yet it remains significant that, in order to compete with China, the West is embracing development models that once more re-center the state, as governments will inevitably play large roles in expanded infrastructure even if in partnership with the private sector. Similarly, the United States has turned to high-tech industrial policy and large-scale infrastructure spending at home to better compete with China.[31]

The emerging development finance regime is one featuring intense competition between China and the West. But this very competition is driving each side, in iterative fashion, to adapt and emulate one another in ways that may produce convergence around a post-neoliberal order that values types and degrees of state economic intervention that were discouraged by the Washington Consensus that prevailed from the 1990s through the 2008 financial crisis. The emerging regime will be more institutionally fragmented, with greater divergence between its multilateral and bilateral wings, increased diversity within the "West" (e.g., Japan's divergence from DAC norms), and continued rivalry between China and the United States.

This new regime will pose both opportunities and risks for developing countries. There will be a broader diversity of choices, both in sources of funding and policy pathways. But there will also be greater political pressures as big countries push small countries to pick sides in a deepening great power rivalry. Just as the Bretton Woods regime was nested within a Cold War, so might its ideological successor.

Notes

1 See https://www.aiib.org/en/about-aiib/governance/members-of-bank/index.html.
2 S. Babones, "China's AIIB Expected to Lend $10-15B a Year, But Has Only Managed $4.4B in 2 Years," *Forbes*, 16 January 2018.
3 L. Martinez-Diaz, "Toward a Grand Bargain on World Bank Reform," *Brookings*, 16 December 2009, available at https://www.brookings.edu/articles/toward-a-grand-bargain-on-world-bank-reform.
4 Although China ostensibly graduated from IBRD eligibility in 2016 based upon per capita income thresholds set by the Bank, continued lending of $7.8 billion between 2016 and 2018 was justified by reference to exceptional borrowing categories involving either capacity-building or global public goods, though outside observers questioned these judgments; see https://www.cgdev.org/blog/closer-look-world-banks-sizable-china-portfolio.
5 See International Institute for Strategic Studies (2023) and https://podcasts.apple.com/us/podcast/banking-on-beijing-the-aims-and-impacts-of/id1569469267?i=1000571198187.
6 The full text of Xi Jinping's report at 19th CPC National Congress is available at http://www.xinhuanet.com/english/download/Xi_Jinping's_report_at_19th_CPC_National_Congress.pdf.
7 See https://www.oecd.org/dac/development-assistance-committee.
8 See https://andrewbatson.com/2019/05/02/the-belt-and-road-is-about-domestic-interest-groups-not-development.
9 Jones (2020) reports that, according to official Chinese sources, "58 per cent of Chinese firms operating in BRI countries have never published any corporate social responsibility or sustainability reports; half fail to conduct social impact assessments before commencing projects; over a third neglect EIAs."
10 See http://www.beltandroadforum.org/english/n100/2019/0429/c22-1392.html.
11 J. Horsley, "Can China Deliver a Better Belt and Road?," *Foreign Policy*, 22 April 2019, available at https://foreignpolicy.com/2019/04/22/965685-china-beltandroad-governance.
12 See http://www.beltandroadforum.org/english/n100/2019/0429/c22-1392.html.
13 See https://podcasts.apple.com/us/podcast/banking-on-beijing-the-aims-and-impacts-of/id1569469267?i=1000571198187.
14 A. Brînză, "What Happened to the Belt and Road Initiative?," *The Diplomat*, 6 September 2022.

15 P. Coy, "China is Playing Hardball with Troubled Debtors. That's Dangerous for All of Us," *New York Times*, 22 July 2022.
16 See https://podcasts.apple.com/us/podcast/banking-on-beijing-the-aims-and-impacts-of/id1569469267?i=1000571198187.
17 *The Economist*, "The Pandemic is Hurting China's Belt and Road Initiative," 4 June 2020.
18 *The Economist*, "Faced with an Overseas Debt Crisis, Will China Change Its Ways?," 24 August 2022.
19 A. Rappeport, "Defaults Loom as Poor Countries Face an Economic Storm," *New York Times*, 3 December 2022.
20 This was one among a series of confrontations between the United States and Japan during this era. Washington not only perceived Japan of the 1980s and 1990s, like China today, as a challenge to U.S. economic predominance, but also considered Japan's statist economic model – once acceptable under the terms of embedded liberalism – as now intolerable under the tenets of newly ascendant neoliberalism. Japan pushed back against U.S. pressures in various ways – defending the legitimacy of industrial policy, shaping a World Bank report (World Bank, 1993) sympathetic to a Japan-led East Asian model of development and, in response to the Asian financial crisis of the late 1990s, proposing an Asian Monetary Fund. Nevertheless, Japan was compelled to accept "voluntary export restraints" on auto exports to the U.S. market, appreciate the value of the Yen as part of the 1985 Plaza Accord (leading to Japan's asset bubble and financial crisis of later that decade), and suffer rejection of its proposal for an Asian Monetary Fund.
21 T. Harris, "'Quality Infrastructure': Japan's Robust Challenge to China's Belt and Road," *War on the Rocks*, 9 April 2019.
22 J. Perlez, "China Creates a World Bank of Its Own, and the U.S. Balks," *New York Times*, 4 December 2015.
23 U.S. Secretary of State Mike Pompeo charged that China proffered "corrupt infrastructure deals in exchange for political influence" and used "bribe-fuelled debt-trap diplomacy." See *Reuters*, "China Says 'Fed Up' with Hearing U.S. Complaints on Belt and Road," 9 May 2019. The claim that China set deliberate debt-traps through BRI lending has been questioned; see D. Brautigam, "Is China the World's Loan Shark?," *New York Times*, 26 April 2019.
24 See A. Brînză, A., "Central and Eastern Europe is Not in Bed with China," *The Diplomat*, 3 July 2020; A. Brînză, "How China's 17+1 Became a Zombie Mechanism," *The Diplomat*, 10 February 2021; M. Nikolova, "As China's 17+1 Forum Crumbles, the Three Seas Initiative is Increasingly Relevant," *Emerging Europe*, 14 July 2021; S. Lau, "Down to 14+1: Estonia and Latvia Quit China's Club in Eastern Europe," *Politico*, 11 August 2022.
25 See https://www.whitehouse.gov/briefing-room/presidential-actions/2022/06/26/memorandum-on-the-partnership-for-global-infrastructure-and-investment.
26 S. Paduano, "The G-7 Infrastructure Plan Won't Succeed Unless It Learns from Past Failures," *Foreign Policy*, 18 July 2022, available at https://foreignpolicy.com/2022/07/18/the-g-7-infrastructure-plan-wont-succeed-unless-it-learns-from-past-failures.
27 F. Bermingham and J. Nyabiage, "1 Year On, EU Alternative to China's Belt and Road Fails to Deliver," *South China Morning Post*, 31 December 2022.
28 See https://www.whitehouse.gov/briefing-room/presidential-actions/2022/06/26/memorandum-on-the-partnership-for-global-infrastructure-and-investment and S. Paduano, "The G-7 Infrastructure Plan Won't Succeed Unless It Learns from Past Failures," *Foreign Policy*, 18 July 2022, available at https://foreignpolicy.com/2022/07/18/the-g-7-infrastructure-plan-wont-succeed-unless-it-learns-from-past-failures.

29 J. Nyabiage, "Africa Has 'More Options on the Table' as US Seeks to Reset Ties," *South China Morning Post*, 17 December 2022.
30 In line with the latter point, Seaman's chapter in this book examines China's ambition of becoming a premier purveyor of global standards.
31 A. Swanson, "Biden Administration Releases Plan for $50 Billion Investment in Chips," *New York Times*, 6 September 2022.

References

Ashbee, E. (2021) "The Blue Dot Network, Economic Power, and China's Belt & Road Initiative," *Asian Affairs: An American Review*, Vol. 48, No. 2, pp. 133–149.

Babb, S. (2013) "The Washington Consensus as Transnational Policy Paradigm: Its Origins, Trajectory and Likely Successor," *Review of International Political Economy*, Vol. 20, No. 2, pp. 268–297.

Chin, G. T. (2012) "Two-Way Socialization: China, the World Bank, and Hegemonic Weakening," *Brown Journal of World Affairs*, Vol. 19, No. 1, pp. 211–230.

Chin, G. T. and Gallagher, K. P. (2019) "Coordinated Credit Spaces: The Globalization of Chinese Development Finance," *Development and Change*, Vol. 50, No. 1, pp. 245–274.

Dreher, A., Fuchs, A., Parks, B., Strange, A. and Tierney, M. J. (2022) *Banking on Beijing: The Aims and Impacts of China's Overseas Development Program*. Cambridge: Cambridge University Press.

He, A. (2016) "China in the International Financial System: A Study of the NDB and the AIIB," *Centre for International Governance Innovation Paper No. 106*, June.

Heath, T. R. (2018) "China Prepares for an International Order After U.S. Leadership," *Lawfare*, 1 August, available at https://www.lawfareblog.com/china-prepares-international-order-after-us-leadership.

Helleiner, E. (2016) *Forgotten Foundations of Bretton Woods – International Development and the Making of the Postwar Order*. Ithaca (NY) and London: Cornell University Press.

Helleiner, E. (2019) "The Life and Times of Embedded Liberalism: Legacies and Innovations since Bretton Woods," *Review of International Political Economy*, Vol. 26, No. 6, pp. 1112–1135.

Hernandez, D. (2016) "Are 'New' Donors Challenging World Bank Conditionality?," *AidData Working Paper No. 19*, January.

Horn, S., Reinhart, C. M. and Trebesch, C. (2021) "China's Overseas Lending," *Journal of International Economics*, Vol. 133, 103539.

Humphrey, C. and Chen, Y. (2021) *China in the Multilateral Development Banks – Evolving Strategies of a New Power*. Report. London: Overseas Development Institute.

International Institute for Strategic Studies (2023) *China's Belt and Road Initiative – A Geopolitical and Geo-economic Assessment*. London: Routledge.

Jain, P. (2016) "Japan's Foreign Aid: Old and New Contests," *The Pacific Review*, Vol. 29, No. 1, pp. 93–113.

Jiang, Y. (2019) "Competitive Partners in Development Financing: China and Japan Expanding Overseas Infrastructure Investment," *The Pacific Review*, Vol. 32, No. 5, pp. 778–808.

Jones, L. (2020) "Does China's Belt and Road Initiative Challenge the Liberal, Rules-Based Order?," *Fudan Journal of the Humanities and Social Sciences*, Vol. 13, pp. 113–133.

Jones, L. and Zeng, J. (2019) "Understanding China's 'Belt and Road Initiative': Beyond 'Grand Strategy' to A State Transformation Analysis," *Third World Quarterly*, Vol. 40, No. 8, pp. 1415–1439.

Jones, L. and Zou, Y. (2017) "Rethinking the Role of State-owned Enterprises in China's Rise," *New Political Economy*, Vol. 22, No. 6, pp. 743–760.

Katada, S. N. and Liao, J. (2020) "China and Japan in Pursuit of Infrastructure Investment Leadership in Asia," *Global Governance: A Review of Multilateralism and International Organizations*, Vol. 26, No. 3, pp. 449–472.

Kikuchi, T. and Unzaki, S. (2019) "Japanese Infrastructure Investment in Southeast Asia," *Journal of Infrastructure, Policy and Development*, Vol. 3, No. 1, pp. 129–138.

Lai, H. (2021) "The Rationale and Effects of China's Belt and Road Initiative: Reducing Vulnerabilities in Domestic Political Economy," *Journal of Contemporary China*, Vol. 30, No. 128, pp. 330–347.

Lairson, T. D. (2018) "The Global Strategic Environment of the BRI: Deep Interdependence and Structural Power," in Zhang, W., Alon, I. and Lattemann, C. (Eds), *China's Belt and Road Initiative: Changing the Rules of Globalization*. London: Palgrave Macmillan.

Liao, J. C. and Katada, S. N. (2021) "Institutions, Ideation, and Diffusion of Japan's and China's Overseas Infrastructure Promotion Policies," *New Political Economy*, Vol. 27, No. 6, pp. 944–957.

Lieberthal, K. G. and Lampton, D. M. (Eds) (1992) *Bureaucracy, Politics, and Decision Making in Post-Mao China*. Berkeley: University of California Press.

Maxfield, S. and Nolt, J. H. (1990) "Protectionism and the Internationalization of Capital: U.S. Sponsorship of Import Substitution Industrialization in the Philippines, Turkey and Argentina," *International Studies Quarterly*, Vol. 34, No. 1, pp. 49–81.

Morris, S., Rockafellow, R. and Rose, S. (2021) "Mapping China's Multilateralism: A Data Survey of China's Participation in Multilateral Development Institutions and Funds," *Center for Global Development, CGD Policy Paper 241*.

Murphy, D. C. (2022) *China's Rise in the Global South – The Middle East, Africa, and Beijing's Alternative World Order*. Stanford: Stanford University Press.

Ndii, D. (2022) *Africa's Infrastructure-Led Growth Experiment is Faltering. It is Time to Focus on Agriculture*. Washington, DC: Carnegie Endowment for International Peace.

Nedopil, C., Larsen, M. L., Yue, M. and Wang, Y. (2022) "Prospects of the Multilateral Cooperation Center for Development Finance (MCDF) to Catalyze Infrastructure Financing," *Asia & the Pacific Policy Studies*, Vol. 9, No. 1, pp. 81–110.

Pratt, T. (2020) "Angling for Influence: Institutional Proliferation in Development Banking," *International Studies Quarterly*, Vol. 65, No. 1, pp. 95–108.

Refinitiv (2022) *Infrastructure 360 Review – BRI Focus / Second Edition: The Great BRI Reset*. London and New York City: Refinitiv.

Ruggie, J. G. (1982) "International Regimes, Transactions and Change: Embedded Liberalism in the Postwar Economic Order," *International Organization*, Vol. 36, No. 2, pp. 379–415.

Sasada, H. (2019) "Resurgence of the 'Japan Model'?," *Asian Survey*, Vol. 59, No. 6, pp. 1044–1069.

Skidmore, D. (2021) "Searching for a 'China Model' along the Belt and Road," *Asian Politics & Policy*, Vol. 13, No. 3, pp. 326–348.

Stephen, M. D. and Skidmore, D. (2019) "The AIIB in the Liberal International Order," *Chinese Journal of International Politics*, Vol. 12, No. 1, pp. 61–91.

Trinidad, D. (2019) "Strategic Foreign Aid Competition: Japanese and Chinese Assistance in the Philippine Infrastructure Sector," *Asian Affairs: An American Review*, Vol. 46, No. 4, pp. 89–122.

Urpelainen, J. and Van de Graaf, T. (2015) "Your Place or Mine? Institutional Capture and the Creation of Overlapping International Institutions," *British Journal of Political Science*, Vol. 45, No. 4, pp. 799–827.

Wang, H. (2020) "Selective Reshaping: China's Paradigm Shift in International Economic Governance," *Journal of International Economic Law*, Vol. 23, No. 3, pp. 583–606.

Wang, H. (2022) "Regime Complexity and Complex Foreign Policy: China in International Development Finance Governance," *Global Policy*, Vol. 12, No. S4, pp. 69–79.

World Bank (1993) *The East Asian Miracle: Economic Growth and Public Policy*. Oxford: Oxford University Press.

World Bank (2019) *Belt and Road Economics: Opportunities and Risks of Transport Corridors*. Washington, DC: World Bank.

Yamamoto, R. (2020) "China's Development Assistance in Southeast Asia: A Threat to Japanese Interests?," *Asian Survey*, Vol. 60, No. 2, pp. 323–346.

Zeitz, A. O. (2021) "Emulate or Differentiate? Chinese Development Finance, Competition, and World Bank Infrastructure Funding," *Review of International Organizations*, Vol. 16, pp. 265–292.

Zeng, J. (2019) "Chinese Views of Global Economic Governance," *Third World Quarterly*, Vol. 40, No. 3, pp. 578–594.

Zhao, H. (2019) "China–Japan Compete for Infrastructure Investment in Southeast Asia: Geopolitical Rivalry or Healthy Competition?," *Journal of Contemporary China*, Vol. 28, No. 118, pp. 558–574.

9 Belt and Road Initiative and the Indo-Pacific strategy

Coexistence of a sino-centered regional order with the current alignment of like-minded liberal democracies

Tai Wei Lim

The American-led Indo-Pacific order consists of preserving a status quo based on free trade, freedom of navigation, international law, and a series of regional arrangements and alliances. The Quadrilateral Security Dialogue (involving Australia, India, Japan, and the United States) was reinvigorated in 2017 to manage China militarily and diplomatically. Since 2021, the United States, the United Kingdom, and Australia have engaged in an emerging Anglo-centered military alliance (AUKUS), featuring nuclear-powered submarines. President Biden's objectives are to affirm America's return to multilateralism, the staying power of its military strength, and the reversal of former President Trump's unilateralism. China's regional order building is boosted by its perception that the United States is declining in the region. In contrast, China appears as a rising economic, military, diplomatic, and political power with a greater influence on multilateral international organizations. A centerpiece of Chinese economic power is the Belt and Road Initiative (BRI). Launched in 2013, the BRI is China's most important economic diplomatic initiative. Its focus on infrastructure construction and connectivity has appealed to many developing economies which are less concerned about geopolitical issues unless their national interests are threatened in a direct manner.

9.1 Introduction

Henry Kissinger (2014, p. 9) defines the term "order" in international relations as "a set of commonly accepted rules that define the limits of permissible action and a balance of power that enforces restraint when rules break down, preventing one political unit from subjugating all others." Kissinger articulated these features of a world order again in a 2016 interview when he said:

> The world is in chaos. Fundamental upheavals are occurring in many parts of the world simultaneously, most of which are governed by disparate principles. We are therefore faced with two problems: first, how

DOI: 10.4324/9781003340430-12

to reduce regional chaos; second, how to create a coherent world order based on agreed-upon principles that are necessary for the operation of the entire system.[1]

The Indo-Pacific is certainly one of the world regions that requires the re-introduction of order and a coherent international framework to reduce regional disruptions and recalibrate the world system. Taking Kissinger's definition into account, it is possible to argue that the world order evolved from the Cold War-era bipolar order in place between 1947 and 1991 to a unipolar moment when the United States, a hyperpower in the 1990s, forged a new world order. The unipolar moment gradually transitioned to a world characterized with the "rise of the rest" in which large emerging economies have closed the gap with the United States and other G7 economies. Finally, it has led to the current situation where, in the Asian hemisphere at large, there appears to be a fragile coexistence between a U.S.-envisioned Indo-Pacific order and an emerging Chinese regional order (Turner et al., 2023).

As for the liberal international order (LIO), John Ikenberry defines it as "a distinctive type of order, organised around open markets, multilateral institutions, cooperative security, alliance partnership, democratic solidarity and United States hegemonic leadership" which aligns with the idea of a "rules-based order" (Wilkins, 2021). Ikenberry (2018, p. 7) describes the current Western LIO as 70 years of age with its foundations based on multilateral institutions (e.g., the North Atlantic Treaty Organization – NATO – and the World Trade Organization) led by the U.S. and joined by its principal partners of Western Europe and Japan stabilizing the world economy.

In East Asia and the Asia-Pacific, Japan and South Korea are crucial U.S. allies which host American air bases. South Korea hosts the THAAD (Terminal High Altitude Area Defense) missile systems that can intercept long-range missiles fired from North Korea or even China. The United States, Japan, and South Korea are also engaged in a trilateral intelligence-sharing pact known as General Security of Military Information Agreement. The United States has also approved South Korea's development of longer-range missiles that can eventually reach into China. Besides, Japan has altered its peace constitution to allow Japanese Self-Defense Forces to come to the collective defense of its allies (including the United States) if they were under attack.

The immediate post-Cold War world order, underpinned by U.S. leadership and its alliance network, eventually extended to former communist regions in East Asia, Eastern Europe, and Latin America that democratized and joined the existing order. For the American-led Indo-Pacific order, the stakes are high in the superpower competition against China: this region is a major engine of world economic growth and includes eminent global sea lanes of communication. Any contestation of these "assets" has led to speculation over the emergence of a new Cold War with flashpoints in the South China Sea, Taiwan Strait, Korean Peninsula and East China Sea.

9.2 Literature review

An important literature investigates these developments from different perspectives. Kurt Campbell and Jake Sullivan (2019), both policy practitioners, provide valuable insights on how to formulate long-term policies towards China. They argue that the United States has reached an increasingly clear consensus that the period of engagement is over and the next phase shuttles between exercising strategic patience and strategic ambiguity. In addition, Campbell and Sullivan agree that, when they survey the spectrum of opinions related to U.S.-China relationship, the consensus is that the two superpowers have to coexist with each other. For the U.S., they suspect that it may not mean military dominance but deterrence to prevent any Chinese aggression. They also advocate for the U.S. to set the rules and standards for technological development with U.S. allies and partners.[2] A veteran diplomat from Singapore, Kishore Mahbubani advises American policy makers to consider the purpose of their policy towards China while resolving urgently their domestic challenges.[3]

The complexity of formulating a policy designed to manage rivalry with China extends even to outer space, as pointed out by Marc Julienne (2021a). Next, pushing back against the hawks, Julienne (2021b) disagrees with the establishment of the AUKUS – the trilateral security pact between Australia, the United Kingdom, and the United States. He argues that it has led to ambivalent reactions from ASEAN (Association of Southeast Asian Nations) leaders,[4] upset French sentiments and isolated New Zealand. However, Julienne's piece was written at the start of the AUKUS formation: regional views, with the exception of China's, have moderated since then. Moreover, the new Labour government in Australia may have a comparatively softer approach to China.

Sino-U.S. rivalry also extends to a battle for the hearts and minds of less developed countries. For Nadège Rolland (2022b), Beijing is utilizing the Global South to contain U.S. influence. Rolland explains that, for a few years, China has intensified its influence in the developing world. Neglected by Western media and policy makers, this evolution was identified by Western security agencies and led to public warnings. Rolland (2022a) argues that Chinese activities spread to regions like the African continent using various techniques (e.g., cultural diplomacy, political lobbying, elimination of vocal critics of the regime, etc.). In her view, all these initiatives aim at securing a favorable external environment that would support China's efforts to ostracize Taiwan.

Nicholas Burns, U.S. ambassador to China, advocates a tougher line against Beijing, focusing on human rights issues in Xinjiang, Tibet, and Hong Kong as well as on Chinese nuclear build-up and Taiwan bullying.[5] He is also keen on working with allies and partners to cope with China's ambitions. He thinks that countering China involves technological and economic competitiveness rather than pure military strength.

Nicholas Burns is joined by Matt Pottinger, who is considered a hawk in Washington. Pottinger (2021) believes that there is little leverage over Beijing and Americans deceived themselves into thinking that China would liberalize its political system once it became a wealthy nation. According to Pottinger, the Chinese Communist Party (CCP) hid its true intentions after studying the collapse of the Soviet Union. It borrowed the free-market system to reinforce the authoritarian system by raising its standards of living before reverting back to authoritarianism.

The doubts raised by American policy makers and scholars about how to deal with their major competitor have been very similar to those observed among Chinese scholars. He and Li (2020) note that, since 2010, the concept of "Indo-Pacific" has been inevitably tied to the foreign policies of Australia, India, Japan, and the United States, i.e., the countries belonging to the Quadrilateral Security Dialogue (also known as the "Quad"). However, China is reluctant to identify itself as part of the Indo-Pacific, stating that this is a strategic framework designed to fight Chinese ambitions. The Indo-Pacific concept has therefore led to a competition between the U.S. open Indo-Pacific strategy and China's preference for the traditional Asia-Pacific conceptualization of its strategic space. It is interesting that, in the Asia-Pacific region, the fears of overreliance on China have convinced a country like South Korea to embark on its New Southern Policy (NSP) to deepen its relationships with ASEAN countries and India. Yet, as Françoise Nicolas (2021), an expert on East Asian issues, argues, the two first trade partners of South Korea remain China and the United States and Korea-ASEAN trade is increasingly skewed towards Vietnam.

Other Asian countries are also re-examining their position in the great Sino-U.S. rivalry. Medcalf (2019b) insists that the Indo-Pacific concept "renews the region's enduring maritime and multipolar character." He thinks that the Indo-Pacific may dilute Chinese influence, partly because of the scale of the region, its diversity, and the fact that national approaches may emerge to address common issues. Medcalf (2019a) documents the Australian perspective of the U.S.-Australia alliance designed to counter China. He argues that Washington cannot simply assume that Canberra will align with all U.S. strategic priorities. Therefore, a new narrative to shape the alliance is needed to make it more pragmatic and sustainable. Sustainability is important given that U.S.-China rivalry may be a long one. For Medcalf, intelligence-sharing and military interoperability will be the pillars of the bilateral relationship particularly given the U.S. Marines' rotational presence in Darwin. In his view, Australia will decouple in some selective areas of bilateral exchanges with China, because of its own national interests.

9.3 The Chinese regional order

Chinese regional order building is based on the Chinese perception (and certain mistaken East Asian perceptions) that the United States is on a relative decline in the region whereas China is increasing its economic, military, diplomatic, and political power and has been exerting a prominent influence on multilateral international organizations. The exercise of Chinese power has been nuanced: sometimes charming, sometimes abrasive (when its core interests are at stake) and generally adaptive to changing circumstances. A couple of decades ago, many Asian nations saw China as "a good neighbor, a constructive partner, a careful listener, and a nonthreatening regional power" (Shambaugh, 2005, p. 64). However, the image of Beijing in the region has changed dramatically since the rise of Xi Jinping.

After perceiving China as a communist hegemon, East Asian economies were attracted by its economic success, with that attraction now subdued by China's growing diplomatic and military power. Many East Asian policy makers have openly declared that they do not intend to take sides in the Sino-U.S. rivalry, but they quietly hedge against both in the economic and security spheres. This is especially prevalent amongst ASEAN leaders. Take Indonesia, frequently considered the most powerful country in the ASEAN. At the IISS (International Institute for Strategic Studies) Shangri-La Dialogue, in June 2022, Indonesia's Minister of Defense Prabowo Subianto – who accepted his party's nomination to run in the 2024 presidential election – declared:

> [Southeast Asia] has been for many centuries the crossroad of imperialism, big power domination and exploitation. We understand the rivalry between the established world power and the rising world power... [Southeast Asian countries are] the most affected by big powers' competition [but] we've come to our own ASEAN way of resolving challenges... Indonesia opted to be not engaged in any military alliance.[6]

In fact, ASEAN countries are progressively realigning their military and economic systems to fit new realities. Whereas they used to be careful not to undermine U.S. national interests, East Asian governments now take Chinese interests into consideration and tend to give them growing or equal weight to those of the United States.

9.3.1 Trade interdependence

The Regional Comprehensive Economic Partnership (RCEP) is a free trade treaty signed in 2020.[7] While it enjoys the ASEAN support, it reflects the central position of China. In fact, Beijing's economic strength and resilience, in particular during the COVID-19 pandemic years, contrasts with the perception that Western nations failed to contain the virus, even though the West developed world-class vaccines, donated medical equipment to developing and emerging countries, and provided scientific advice. The Trump-era signing of the "phase-one" U.S. trade deal with China in January 2021 did not prevent the bilateral trade relations from deteriorating further, especially after the Trump administration held China responsible for the pandemic. The

Biden administration has tried to restart from where the Trump administration left off, but China has the upper hand now, or at least perceives it so. Chinese state media decode the idea of "creating a safe supply chain" as an attempt to weaken China by establishing an alternative supply chain of key technologies that gets around mainland Chinese manufacturers, especially the semiconductor industry.[8]

From the Chinese perspective, "the new Indo-Pacific economic framework only serves the geopolitical calculation of the US."[9] In addition, Washington lacks commitment, as evidenced by its refusal to join the Comprehensive and Progressive Agreement for Trans-Pacific Partnership (CPTPP), an agreement very similar to the Obama-era Trans-Pacific Partnership (TPP). To sum up, China perceives Washington's basic objective to be to "undermine regional economic cooperation initiatives proposed by China."[10]

Even in the arena of vaccine assistance to the world, Chinese policy makers have been critical of what they have perceived as U.S. vaccine nationalism (see Emmanuel's chapter in this book). They insist that Beijing provided more than 480 million doses of COVID-19 vaccines to approximately 100 countries within 6 months.[11] The reality is somewhat different. Until 13 June 2022, the United States had delivered more than 550 million vaccines all over the world without any pre-condition and the Biden administration aimed to provide more than 1.2 billion doses eventually.[12] Besides, U.S. mRNA (messenger ribonucleic acid) vaccines – namely, Pfizer and Moderna – are widely acknowledged as the most effective vaccines in the world. On its side, China donated approximately 190 million doses of Chinese vaccines between December 2020 and March 2022.[13]

9.3.2 The Belt and Road Initiative

Launched in 2013, the Belt and Road Initiative (BRI) is China's most important economic and diplomatic initiative (see Skidmore's chapter in this book). In addition to supporting Chinese economic resilience, the BRI focuses on infrastructure construction and connectivity. This approach attracts many developing economies which are less concerned about geopolitical issues unless their national interests are at risk in a direct manner. The biannual BRI summits in China have gathered Central Asian, African, and Latin American leaders, rather than major European or North American leaders.[14] The Chinese infrastructure funding filled in the developing economies' infrastructure gap but with mixed results due to what critics charged as possible debt traps, environmental concerns, conflicts with local communities, etc. Despite these challenges, Chinese authorities have learnt from their BRI's experience and adapted to local conditions as well as global sentiments.

Within the past few decades, China has surpassed both the economic strength of Japan and the naval forces (in quantitative terms) of the United States. This success has reinforced China's self-confidence and spurred nationalism among policy makers and citizens after what it perceives as a century of humiliation (from the Opium War to the Sino-Japanese Wars), which led Wright and Cartwright (1908, p. 773) to call China the "sick man of the Far East" at that point of history. Aware of its newfound strength and without any regional challenger during the "peaceful rise" of the 1990s and 2000s, China has had more leeway in shaping the regional order and stepping into its traditional role as an Asian dominant power, as happened during the Han, Tang, Yuan, and Ming dynasties.

For now, China sees itself as a peer rival to the United States and a *primus inter pares* among major emerging countries. China considers U.S. allies in Asia mere appendages of U.S. power (at least in its nationalistic narrative and propaganda) and seeks to convert some of these Asian allies through a combination of sticks and carrots. The Chinese trump card is its competitive economy and the tight interdependence in which it has enmeshed large and small Asian countries (Ekman et al., 2019, pp. 86–94). The regional economic order that Beijing has been implementing through the BRI creates great opportunities for Chinese firms. By the same token, the regional institutions that were built up by Washington are increasingly mature and autonomous of U.S. resources and influence.

The BRI seems to have unleased some form of autonomy assertion by some Southeast Asian players. They are cautious when taking sides between China and the United States and focus primarily on their national interests. More crucially, several regional players have become client states, facilitators and even allies of China. These countries include Cambodia, Iran, Laos (somewhat), North Korea, Pakistan, Russia, and some argue that post-coup Myanmar and Afghanistan are likely to join this group. Regarding the Iranian nuclear issue, Wang Yi – who served as Foreign Minister until December 2022 – blamed the U.S. unilateral withdrawal from the Joint Comprehensive Plan of Action (JCPOA, or Iran Nuclear Deal) and its ongoing pressure on Tehran.[15] There are forces in Malaysia, Nepal, and Sri Lanka that are friendly to China as well. They are much more aligned with China's interests, though they also have their own agendas with the U.S.-led Western network. One may assume that the interdependence stemming from the BRI could eventually result in a coalition around China.

9.3.3 China's military capabilities

For Zhao Lijian, former spokesperson of the Ministry of Foreign Affairs and a well-known "wolf warrior," the AUKUS "seriously undermines regional peace and stability," thus reflecting a "Cold War mentality."[16] However, China's military power may outgrow AUKUS capabilities soon. By 2017, the People's Liberation Army (PLA) had expanded its reach as far as Eastern Africa in Djibouti – the PLA's first overseas military base. The U.S. and its alliance network are scrutinizing the recent Chinese construction of the Ream naval base in Cambodia, the consequences of the security pact signed with Solomon Islands, and responding to speculations of a possible Chinese naval base in Equatorial Guinea. Chinese advancements in artificial intelligence (AI) and AI-based weapons systems, space, cyberspace, electromagnetic spectrum, military drones, hypersonic weapons, ballistic missiles, aircraft carriers, and stealth fighters have enhanced PLA capabilities dramatically.[17]

Operationally, China's anti-access/area denial (A2/AD) strategy to stop enemies from reaching a specific territory (anti-access) and deny their freedom of movement on the battlefield (area denial) is buttressed by naval and air defense systems. Area and access denial weapons may include strategic weapons like the DF-26 "Guam killer" ballistic missiles. China is also strengthening its strategic presence and tactical capabilities in the Taiwan Strait, the Spratly Islands, the Paracel Islands, and the Senkaku/Diaoyu Islands. The hardware acquired by the Chinese is also paired off with requisite legal regulations to permit self-defense.

In February 2021, the Chinese authorities enacted a new Coast Guard Law that gives the Chinese Coast Guard more leeway to utilize their weapons in conflict situations. Beijing has converted rocks and shoals in the Spratly Islands into significant artificial island bases armed with fighter jet hangars, surface to air missiles, missile silos, and land bombers. In fact, the PLA has become a de facto dominant naval power in the region, contested only by Trump and Biden administrations' freedom of navigation operations and joint allied maneuvers. In the meantime, ASEAN countries have attempted to reach an accord on the Code of Conduct discussions. Tensions between the two superpowers make the South China Sea a tinderbox for a high-intensity conflict. Publicly, Chinese leaders have sought to portray a peaceful and non-hegemonic public image. In the opening ceremony of the 9th World Peace Forum organized by Tsinghua University and the Chinese People's Institute of Foreign Affairs in July 2021, Wang Yi declared that

> the CPC [Communist Party of China] will never seek hegemony and will never engage in expansionism. For a century, the CPC has always adhered to fairness and justice, and has been unremittingly promoting the freedom and liberation of human being.[18]

9.3.4 Chinese perceptions of the Quad and the Indo-Pacific strategy

Yang Xiyu, senior research fellow at the China Institute of International Studies in Beijing, considers that the Quad and AUKUS are now two pillars of the U.S. Indo-Pacific strategy. From the Chinese perspective, the Quad is a containment device against China. Chinese state media questioned the amount of "money the U.S. will invest in the plan to promote regional cooperation [for the Quad and the Indo-Pacific strategy]" and, given the present U.S. financial difficulties, wondered how it can be possible to "invest heavily in regional economic initiatives" and whether it will "be sustained over the long term."[19] Overall, the Chinese political elites have had harsh words over the Indo-Pacific strategy. Wang Yi called the U.S.-led Indo-Pacific strategy a "regression of history that should be swept into the dustbin."[20]

European Union (EU) countries – most of which are NATO members – have coordinated with the United States to draw up a strategic plan to "recommit to the [Indo-Pacific]'s stability, security and prosperity based on the promotion of democracy, rule of law, human rights and international law."[21] Although the EU explained that this move is not an "anti-China" stance, Beijing continues to deem it "as a reinforcement of a strategic focus to counter China's rising profile in the region."[22] Chinese state media believe that the EU intends to enhance its trade status in the region, intensify its investments with the Quad, and raise human rights issues (e.g., regarding Hong Kong and Xinjiang) while working towards the Comprehensive Agreement on Investment with China. Yet, unlike its narrative and rhetoric related to competition with the U.S., Beijing considers that the "consensus between China and the EU is far greater than differences, and cooperation far exceeds confrontation."[23]

9.4 The American pacific alignment

9.4.1 The Indo-Pacific strategy

The Western vision of the Indo-Pacific strategy consists of preserving the U.S. status quo, i.e., the freedom of navigation, free trade, transparent trade rules, etc. The Free and Open Indo-Pacific (FOIP) scheme was integrated into the U.S. Indo-Pacific strategy in 2019 by the administration of then-President Trump. The U.S. Congress displayed bipartisan support for the Trump administration's strategy by approving the Asia Reassurance Initiative Act of 2018 and the BUILD Act of 2018 which formulated the U.S. International Development Finance Corporation. The U.S.-led order is not compatible with China's rejection of the Hague arbitral ruling on the maritime dispute between China and the Philippines, China's recourse to economic sanctions against several Asian economies (e.g., South Korea and Taiwan), Beijing's debt trap diplomacy (Kratz et al., 2019), and so on.

European Union partners (e.g., Germany, France, the Netherlands, and Sweden) have expressed their concerns about Chinese unilateralism in the region.[24] Officially, the Indo-Pacific strategy is not targeted at a specific country. Instead, it is designed to deal with numerous threats, including piracy, terrorism, proliferation of weapons of mass destruction, natural disasters, and illegal fishing. In geopolitical terms, the FOIP concept confronts traditional maritime security threats through active interoperability, joint exercises, and improved Maritime Domain Awareness against "gray area" incursions (Wilkins, 2021).

Beyond the Indo-Pacific strategy, from 2021, the Biden administration sought to revive the Western LIO, which started fading in the 2000s and was substantially weakened by anti-globalization and populist movements in Anglo-Saxon nations (e.g., Brexit and "Make America Great Again"). The West has now realized that integrating Beijing into the globalized world economy did not create a more liberal or democratic China (Pottinger, 2021). It is now confronted with a systemic rival that is more powerful and authoritarian than ever, especially after the Western setbacks in the Middle East and Afghanistan (the longest military conflict in American history). Washington spent exorbitant financial resources in the so-called "War on Terror" while Beijing expanded its influence worldwide through its economic and cultural soft power, the BRI, and the launching of the Asian Infrastructure Investment Bank and of the New Development Bank. Ironically, the United States has now to adjust to a global order where China plays a key role in global value chains and Washington Consensus-based policies have enabled several emerging economies to enhance their competitiveness and increase their GDP (gross domestic product) per capita significantly (Gaillard, 2020, pp. 53–74).

9.4.2 The AUKUS alliance

Whereas they decried the chaotic way in which the United States left Afghanistan, U.S. allies and partners welcomed AUKUS. Even Indonesia, which initially expressed reservation, relaxed its opposition, and said it understood the nuclear submarine deal within AUKUS. The United States, Britain, and Australia engaged in an emerging U.S.-centered AUKUS military alliance, featuring nuclear-powered (not nuclear-armed) submarines, thereby assuaging regional concerns and aligning with non-proliferation principles.[25] These three countries, which have been traditional allied nations for a century, remain central to the Five Eyes intelligence pact (with Canada and New Zealand) and to the core of the Western order defending a "free and open Indo-Pacific."

AUKUS reflects President Biden's willingness to (i) balance the world and regional order and (ii) reject Trumpism. It is also designed to quiet the allies worried about America's withdrawal from Afghanistan and possible global isolationism, but it has also triggered domestic critics regarding U.S. imperial overstretch.[26] Whereas former President Trump argued that its allies should take up a larger share of the defense and security burden, President Biden has preferred gentle and moral suasion under the umbrella of consultative multilateralism to nudge allies to do the same.

The U.S. army is also working hard on new weapon systems, like mid-range missiles penetrating Chinese A2/AD shield in the South China Sea and AI-powered autonomous weapons systems to counter Chinese weaponry designed to outdo the United States.[27] U.S. Strategic Command is also aware of advanced Chinese strategic weapons: namely, the hypersonic glide vehicles DF-17, nuclear warheads mounted on long-range missiles, and the Chinese Fractional Orbital Bombardment System, which circumnavigated the world twice in 2021. This was coined by some in the media as a "Sputnik moment."

In reaction, it is not surprising that the U.S. wants to spur its own military industrial complex to overtake its principal rivals' weapon systems.

At the same time, U.S. allies/partners' defensive and military capabilities have expanded. South Korea and Taiwan got the green light to build long-range and cruise missiles to penetrate China's A2/AD sphere/shield and counter Beijing's inexorable expansion. Western analysts conceptualized China's expansion and exploitation of territorial disputes: they called it the "salami-slicing tactics" (Barnett, 2021, p. 52). At large, salami slicing refers to cutting off piece by piece another nation's territory. This may also involve undermining the enemies' capabilities so gradually and incrementally that the evolution is almost unnoticeable but becomes significant. As the PLA is slowly eroding American military superiority in the Western Pacific, the United States is clearly engaged in an arms race with China. Washington must maintain military presence in the region and use adequate deterrence tools against China and Russia. By the same token, Washington preserves its East Asian alliance network with Japan, the Philippines, South Korea, and Thailand.

9.4.3 The Quad

The Quadrilateral Security Dialogue was reinvigorated in 2017 to focus on regional issues beyond the forum discussing disaster-relief efforts. The Quad is an informal cooperation platform, described by some observers as "Washington's Chinese-containment policy."[28] Because of growing Chinese power and the reluctance of Southeast Asian states to confront China, the United States needed to expand its alliances further away from East Asia and into the Indo-Pacific. This initiative brought in "natural" partners with enough weight and aligned interests to work with Washington.

The March 2021 Quad meeting at the top level declared that its members were "united in a shared vision for the free and open Indo-Pacific" and committed to "promoting a free, open rules-based order, rooted in international law to advance security and prosperity and counter threats to both in the Indo-Pacific and beyond" (Wilkins, 2021). During the meeting, U.S. President Joe Biden, then Japan's Prime Minister Yoshihide Suga, then Australia's Prime Minister Scott Morrison, and India's Prime Minister Narendra Modi affirmed their commitment to multilateralism.

9.4.4 India, an autonomous player

Unlike other Southeast Asian states, India has the bulk and the potential strength to resist Chinese overreach. Its military capacities exceed by far those of South Korea, the Philippines, Thailand, Australia, and Japan. India relishes its geopolitical autonomy: its time-tested friendship with the Russian military-industrial complex makes it less dependent on the United States for security needs. Yet, New Delhi's special relationship with Moscow is ambiguous. On the one hand, the Sino-Russian partnership is partly designed to lure India away from the U.S. orbit. On the other hand, the West can weaponize its strong economic and diplomatic ties with India to outreach Russia in containing China.

India and China have frequent border disputes[29] and their interests are conflicting in the Indian Ocean maritime area. India and Western powers are concerned about perceived Chinese "String of Pearls" strategy, which consists of establishing points in the Indian Ocean through funding port developments from Hong Kong to Sudan, thereby encircling India.[30] It seems obvious that the West should work with New Delhi. India constitutes a key participant in global value chains and a major market (with a growing middle class) likely to be a long-term alternative to China.

9.4.5 ASEAN nations

Beijing has a great knowledge of historical facts and is eager to elicit respect from surrounding states. Yet, China has failed to fully appreciate the strategic rise of other powers in the region. In the last golden age of Asian power, before the onset of Western industrial revolution, imperialism, and colonialism, the three great Asian powers were the Ottoman Empire, Ming China, and Moghul India. Beijing alienated India during their border disputes, just as it stepped on Australia/South Korea and Japan by, respectively, exerting economic pressures and recalling the Sino-Japanese Wars. Beijing has also resorted to various provocative strategies against ASEAN nations, such as incursions in Indonesian Natuna waters and boundary disputes involving Vietnam. Consequently, these latter two nations could be considered "Quad-lite" candidates. Like many other Asian countries, they may simply prefer to maintain the status quo and the regional and global rules-based order so that they can trade freely and thrive in a stable environment. As Kenichirō Sasae, President of the Japan Institute of International Affairs, bemoaned: "in the field of diplomacy, the "rules-based international order," that until recently had been functioning despite its incompleteness, is under unprecedented strain" (Wilkins, 2021).

In fact, the U.S.-led regional order may need to take into account the idea of ASEAN centricity (and its associated neutrality). This is reflected in Rodrigo Duterte's and "Bongbong" Marcos's diplomacies. Both have balanced between Chinese and U.S. interests, although the Filipino bureaucracy and army are perceived to remain pro-U.S. or at least more cautious towards China. Myanmar and Thailand are two tricky cases for Washington. "Tatmadaw" – Myanmar's military – has a strongman tradition of cracking down on protesters and opponents whereas the 2020–2021 Thai protests led to a hardening of that nation's military elites that see themselves as self-appointed guardians of the monarchical regime. Washington can rely on Tokyo, its loyal ally, to maintain communication and dialogue with Naypyidaw and Bangkok.

9.4.6 *Japan's military evolution*

In the present geopolitical context, the Kishida administration has increased Japan's defense budget. It will rise to approximately 2% of GDP in 2027, from 1% in 2022. This fiscal effort should boost scientific research and cybertechnology and upgrade the quality of military infrastructure and Japan Coast Guard's capabilities.[31] This move is consistent with the recent announcements made by NATO members (e.g., Germany) and other U.S. allies like South Korea. Tokyo will also reform its military organization so that all departments are involved in national security. To fund these additional military expenditures, the Kishida administration will expand its government bond issuance and implement a budgetary reform.

Japan's rearmament is in line with what Christopher Hughes (2022, p. 73) calls the "grand strategy," which implies a centralized U.S.-Japan alliance and more maritime collaboration with other Quad members (e.g., through "Exercise Malabar"). As the United States organizes its alliance network for the FOIP, U.S. allies and partners express their support for a continued U.S. presence in the region. South Korea and Japan are no exception to this development as both face a nuclear-armed North Korea which tested a record number of ballistic missiles in 2022 (including two that flew over Japan's airspace). North Korea's hostile actions have generated strong support among the Japanese public opinion for a more robust defense system against Pyongyang's intercontinental ballistic missiles (ICBMs).

Japan's security posture is naturally oriented towards its homeland defense. The continued dependence on the U.S. implies that only the alliance with Washington is likely to deter belligerent states like North Korea (Hughes, 2022, p. 75). Given this subordination, Japan has to contribute to the regional alliance to manage provocations. In the meantime, one observes that many U.S. allies and partners in the Indo-Pacific region try to take advantage of U.S. efforts to contain China's tactical maneuvers, what Hughes describes as the tendency to "plug into the U.S. security system" (Hughes, 2022, p. 76).

9.4.7 *The trans-Pacific trade agreements remain at a standstill*

Some policy makers argued that U.S.-allied nations formulated the TPP to rebalance international trade and prevent the dominance of a potential hegemon like China. This view was held by former Republican Senator Bob Corker (chairperson of the Senate Committee on Foreign Relations during 2015–2019) who pointed out that the TPP covered nearly 40% of the global economy and excluded China. Corker encouraged the Biden administration to rebuild an "alliance" comparable to the TPP.[32] However, some experts saw the TPP as an attempt to level the playing field for all by setting higher standards for social rights and environment standards and regulating the status of state-owned enterprises. For Aaron Connelly (then Director of the Lowy

Institute's Southeast Asia Project), the TPP was a unique tool to go beyond tariff issues and adapt global trade rules to technological advancements.[33]

By withdrawing from the TPP in 2017, the Trump administration gave up U.S. leadership in designing multilateral rules and institutions and regulating regional trade (an Obama-era objective). Instead, it raised suspicion among its East Asian allies about U.S. commitment to free trade regionalism and offered China an opportunity to increase its influence in the region. The Trump administration's decision constrained Canberra and Tokyo to sustain the TPP in a modified version, known as the CPTPP, to keep their aspirations alive. In October 2021, U.S. Secretary of Commerce Gina Raimondo announced that Washington intends to kick-start "a formal process" to formulate the Indo-Pacific economic framework through a "coalition of democracies" for trade.[34]

The TPP and CPTPP schemes were supported by bilateral initiatives like the Economic Partnership Agreement (EPA) signed in 2018 by the European Union and Japan (and complemented with the EU–Japan Strategic Partnership Agreement), reinforcing existing EPAs (e.g., Australia–Japan EPA). In fact, since the COVID-19 pandemic, the United States and its allies have recalibrated their objectives. Through the World Bank, the Asian Development Bank, Indo-Pacific institutions, the Quad, and the G7-backed B3W (Build Back Better World), the West has focused on high-quality infrastructure programs, which promote local hiring, sustainable development, and equitable funding conditions.

Despite the contradictions in its economic and trade policies, the United States is still perceived as a relatively benign power by many Southeast Asian countries. Its pragmatic approach, soft power, and technological savoir-faire attract many people in the world, regardless of ideological affiliation and religious belief. Although the U.S. by itself cannot balance against multiple challenges in the international system, the Indo-Pacific institutions, the Quad, AUKUS, and existing multilateral and bilateral alliances constitute a robust network likely to counter a rising rival that is also building its own network and regional institutions.

9.5 Concluding remarks

The outbreak of the Russo-Ukrainian War may not have changed Beijing's timetable or views on Taiwan, but it awakened Taipei, Seoul, and Tokyo to the possibility that a similar scenario might happen in East Asia. This risk was examined by South Korea's and Japan's leaders at the IISS Shangri-La Dialogue in Singapore, in June 2022, convincing the two countries and Taiwan to increase their military budget. Taiwanese policy makers are studying the Ukrainian resistance and therefore preparing their citizens for firearms training. Washington is also advising Taiwanese authorities to consider the purchase of light and nimble arms like those used by the Ukrainian army. In June 2022, South Korea launched eight missiles in response to North

Korea's own firing of eight ballistic missiles. These tit-for-tat retaliatory actions against Pyongyang have prevented a high-intensity war so far. Lastly, though Japan remains limited by Article 9 of its Constitution,[35] it is increasing its defensive military budget to take into account changing geopolitical climate in East Asia.

For several years, China has significantly toughened its military stance. The PLA General and National Defense Minister Wei Fenghe declared at the Shangri-La Dialogue that China will fight to the very end to take back Taiwan. Simultaneously, a Chinese air force jet fighter released aluminum chaffs that were ingested by an Australia naval plane patrolling over the South China Sea while Canadian aircrafts enforcing United Nations sanctions against North Korea were buzzed by PLA fighters. When President Biden visited Tokyo in May 2022, the PLA air force carried out joint patrols with Russian nuclear bombers near Japan and South Korea. The Russo-Ukrainian War has toughened the stance of U.S. allies in the region and convinced like-minded democracies to support the Indo-Pacific strategy. All these events appear to have significantly increased tensions in the region and prompted U.S. liberal democratic allies and partners to revise their geopolitical ambitions.

The present rivalry between China and the United States has materialized so far through trade confrontation, which undermines three decades of growing economic interdependence (see Gaillard's chapter in this book). In the meantime, the diplomatic and military alliances have developed piecemeal as some countries do their best to preserve their geopolitical autonomy. Two potential flashpoints for conflict have emerged: Taiwan and North Korea. The North Korean threat is a double-edge sword that can be converted into an opportunity for China as well as the United States. Taiwan seems to carry the real danger of a high-intensity war between the two superpowers.

Beijing's strength lies in the fact that it has unambiguously stated its willingness to reunify Taiwan, by force, if necessary. To achieve this goal, Beijing has modernized its army and espoused a military strategy to "prepare, fight, and win wars," especially in South China Sea. In contrast, the U.S. policy has been unclear and at times contradictory, largely driven by its "strategic ambiguity" over Taiwan.[36] Taipei's de facto self-governance encourages Washington to opt for the status quo and support a one-China policy, a persistent stance from the Trump to Biden administrations.

Just as the United States and Western powers underestimated the rise of China, they also underestimated North Korean military capabilities whose weapon developments now include hydrogen bombs, cruise missiles, short-range ballistic missiles, ICBM prototypes, and even hypersonic prototypes. The U.S. defense and security establishment carefully monitors Pyongyang's interactions with Beijing and Moscow. Former Foreign Minister (now State Councillor) Wang Yi advised his American counterparts that "the old dream of Cold War hegemony will not help win a promising future, let alone building a better world."[37] In fact, Chinese leaders believe that regional opinions are on their side and wish more cooperation between the two superpowers:

> The most important thing is that the position of the overwhelming majority of members of the region is to hope that the US regional economic strategy will abandon the narrow consideration of competing with China and instead will earnestly cooperate with China. China-US cooperation is in the common interest of most countries in the region. If the US cannot get rid of old thinking, no matter how it adjusts, it will be heading in the wrong direction.[38]

Turn finally to the U.S. viewpoint. U.S. partners and allies have informed Washington that they have been consistently intimidated by Beijing who seeks military parity with Washington. Some Chinese military and security tactics utilized in the superpower rivalry are unacceptable to Washington and threaten its national interests, in the Indo-Pacific area and beyond. More than ever, U.S. policy makers expect a Chinese de-escalation, but this accommodative move seems unlikely in the short term.

Notes

1 J. Goldberg, "World Chaos and World Order: Conversations with Henry Kissinger," *The Atlantic*, 10 November 2016, available at https://www.theatlantic.com/international/archive/2016/11/kissinger-order-and-chaos/506876.
2 "Transcript: Jake Sullivan and Kurt Campbell talk with Michael Morell on 'Intelligence Matters'," *CBS News*, 9 October 2019, available at https://www.cbsnews.com/news/transcript-jake-sullivan-and-kurt-campbell-talk-with-michael-morell-on-intelligence-matters.
3 *National Committee on U.S.-China Relations*, "Has China Won?: The Chinese Challenge to American Primacy with Kishore Mahbubani," 15 October 2020, available at https://www.youtube.com/watch?v=v1Nrgw37If0.
4 ASEAN member states are Brunei, Cambodia, Indonesia, Laos, Malaysia, Myanmar, the Philippines, Singapore, Thailand, and Vietnam.
5 P. Zengerle and M. Martina, "U.S. China Ambassador Nominee Burns Takes Tough Line on Dealings with Beijing," *Reuters*, 21 October 2021.
6 RFA Staff, "ASEAN States Unlikely to Choose Sides between US and China, say Officials and Experts," *Radio Free Asia (RFA)*, 12 June 2022, available at https://www.rfa.org/english/news/china/asean-usa-06122022074314.html.
7 The RCEP includes Australia, Brunei, Cambodia, China, Indonesia, Japan, South Korea, Laos, Malaysia, Myanmar, New Zealand, the Philippines, Singapore, Thailand, and Vietnam.
8 *Global Times*, "Quad Mechanism Turning into 'Sinister Gang of Indo-Pacific': Global Times Editorial," 23 September 2021, available at https://www.globaltimes.cn/page/202109/1234988.shtml.
9 G. Song, "US' Indo-Pacific Economic Framework to Be Judged on Actions," *Global Times*, 18 November 2021, available at https://www.globaltimes.cn/page/202111/1239326.shtml.
10 Idem.
11 Q. Li and Y. Lu, "US' Indo-Pacific Strategy a 'Regression of History,' Should Be Swept into Dustbin: Wang Yi," *Global Times*, 3 July 2021, available at https://www.globaltimes.cn/page/202107/1227701.shtml.
12 See https://www.state.gov/covid-19-recovery/vaccine-deliveries.

13 See https://www.statista.com/statistics/1297752/china-covid-19-vaccine-doses-international-donations-by-region.
14 K. Brown, "The Indo-Pacific, the Quad and the Reality of Chinese Power," *East Asia Forum*, 23 September 2021, available at https://www.eastasiaforum.org/2021/09/23/the-indo-pacific-the-quad-and-the-reality-of-chinese-power.
15 Q. Li and Y. Lu, "US' Indo-Pacific Strategy a 'Regression of History,' Should Be Swept into Dustbin: Wang Yi," *Global Times*, 3 July 2021, available at https://www.globaltimes.cn/page/202107/1227701.shtml.
16 T. McTague, "Joe Biden's New World Order," *The Atlantic*, 16 September 2021, available at https://www.theatlantic.com/international/archive/2021/09/us-uk-australia-china/620094.
17 D. Akimoto, "China's Grand Strategy and the Emergence of Indo-Pacific Alignments," *Institute for Security and Development Policy*, 14 April 2021, available at https://isdp.eu/chinas-grand-strategy-and-the-emergence-of-indo-pacific-alignments.
18 Q. Li and Y. Lu, "US' Indo-Pacific Strategy a 'Regression of History,' Should Be Swept into Dustbin: Wang Yi," *Global Times*, 3 July 2021, available at https://www.globaltimes.cn/page/202107/1227701.shtml.
19 G. Song, "US' Indo-Pacific Economic Framework to Be Judged on Actions," *Global Times*, 18 November 2021, available at https://www.globaltimes.cn/page/202111/1239326.shtml.
20 Q. Li and Y. Lu, "US' Indo-Pacific Strategy a 'Regression of History,' Should Be Swept into Dustbin: Wang Yi," *Global Times*, 3 July 2021, available at https://www.globaltimes.cn/page/202107/1227701.shtml.
21 "EU Should Play a Constructive Role in Indo-Pacific to Avoid Tension with China," *Global Times*, 20 April 2021, available at https://www.globaltimes.cn/page/202104/1221611.shtml.
22 Idem.
23 Idem.
24 D. Akimoto, "China's Grand Strategy and the Emergence of Indo-Pacific Alignments," *Institute for Security and Development Policy*, 14 April 2021, available at https://isdp.eu/chinas-grand-strategy-and-the-emergence-of-indo-pacific-alignments.
25 T. McTague, "Joe Biden's New World Order," *The Atlantic*, 16 September 2021, available at https://www.theatlantic.com/international/archive/2021/09/us-uk-australia-china/620094.
26 Idem.
27 D. Akimoto, "China's Grand Strategy and the Emergence of Indo-Pacific Alignments," *Institute for Security and Development Policy*, 14 April 2021, available at https://isdp.eu/chinas-grand-strategy-and-the-emergence-of-indo-pacific-alignments.
28 T. McTague, "Joe Biden's New World Order," *The Atlantic*, 16 September 2021, available at https://www.theatlantic.com/international/archive/2021/09/us-uk-australia-china/620094.
29 Beijing considers that the Sino-Indian boundary dispute can be settled through bilateral negotiations and that any third-party involvement may be negative.
30 D. Akimoto, "China's Grand Strategy and the Emergence of Indo-Pacific Alignments," *Institute for Security and Development Policy*, 14 April 2021, available at https://isdp.eu/chinas-grand-strategy-and-the-emergence-of-indo-pacific-alignments.
31 Nikkei Staff Writers, "Japan Set to Increase Defense Budget to 2% of GDP in 2027," *Nikkei Asia*, 28 November 2022, available at https://asia.nikkei.com/Politics/Japan-set-to-increase-defense-budget-to-2-of-GDP-in-2027.

32 Y. N. Lee, "U.S. Missed an Opportunity to 'Put a Lot of Pressure' on China, Says Former Senator," *CNBC*, 8 December 2020, available at https://www.cnbc.com/2020/12/08/tpp-was-missed-opportunity-for-us-to-pressure-china-bob-corker.html.
33 A. L. Connelly, "The TPP Is Not a Containment Strategy," *The Interpreter, Lowy Institute*, 9 October 2015, available at https://www.lowyinstitute.org/the-interpreter/tpp-not-containment-strategy.
34 G. Song, "US' Indo-Pacific Economic Framework to Be Judged on Actions," *Global Times*, 18 November 2021, available at https://www.globaltimes.cn/page/202111/1239326.shtml.
35 Article 9 stipulates that: "Aspiring sincerely to an international peace based on justice and order, the Japanese people forever renounce war as a sovereign right of the nation and the threat or use of force as means of settling international disputes," see https://japan.kantei.go.jp/constitution_and_government_of_japan/constitution_e.html.
36 The last time this strategic ambiguity led to war was when the United States did not make it clear that it was incorporating the Korean Peninsula into its post-WWII sphere of influence. Soviet Union leaders perceived a space into which they could move, which led to the Korean War (1950–1953).
37 Q. Li and Y. Lu, "US' Indo-Pacific Strategy a 'Regression of History,' Should Be Swept into Dustbin: Wang Yi," *Global Times*, 3 July 2021, available at https://www.globaltimes.cn/page/202107/1227701.shtml.
38 G. Song, "US' Indo-Pacific Economic Framework to Be Judged on Actions," *Global Times*, 18 November 2021, available at https://www.globaltimes.cn/page/202111/1239326.shtml.

References

Barnett, R. (2021) "Nibble Like a Silkworm, Swallow Like a Whale," *Foreign Policy*, Vol. 241, pp. 47–54.

Campbell, K. M. and Sullivan, J. (2019) "Competition Without Catastrophe," *Foreign Affairs*, Vol. 98, No. 5, pp. 96–111.

Ekman, A. (Ed), Nicolas, F., Pajon, C., Seaman, J., Saint-Mézard, I., Boisseau du Rocher, S., Kastouéva-Jean, T. (2019) "China's Belt & Road and the World: Competing Forms of Globalization," *Etudes de l'Ifri, French Institute of International Relations*, April, available at https://www.ifri.org/sites/default/files/atoms/files/ekman_china_belt_road_world_2019.pdf.

Gaillard, N. (2020) *Country Risk – The Bane of Foreign Investors*. Cham: Springer.

He, K. and Li, M. (2020) "Understanding the Dynamics of the Indo-Pacific: US–China Strategic Competition, Regional Actors, and Beyond," *International Affairs*, Vol. 96, No. 1, pp. 1–7.

Hughes, C. W. (2022) *Japan as a Global Military Power*. Cambridge: Cambridge University Press.

Ikenberry, G. J. (2018) "The End of Liberal International Order?," *International Affairs*, Vol. 94, No. 1, pp. 7–23.

Julienne, M. (2021a) "China's Ambitions in Space – The Sky's The Limit," *Etudes de l'IFRI, French Institute of International Relations*, January, available at https://www.ifri.org/sites/default/files/atoms/files/julienne_china_ambitions_space_2021.pdf.

Julienne, M. (2021b) "AUKUS Rocks the Boat in the Indo-Pacific, And It's Not Good News," *Lettre du Centre Asie, French Institute of International Relations*,

29 September, available at https://www.ifri.org/en/publications/editoriaux-de-lifri/lettre-centre-asie/aukus-rocks-boat-indo-pacific-and-its-not-good.

Kissinger, H. (2014) *World Order*. New York City: Penguin Books.

Kratz, A., Feng, A. and Wright, L. (2019) "New Data on the 'Debt Trap' Question," *Rhodium Group*, 29 April, available at https://rhg.com/research/new-data-on-the-debt-trap-question.

Medcalf, R. (2019a) "Toward a Shared Alliance Strategy in a Contested Indo-Pacific – A View from Australia," *National Bureau of Asian Research*, 21 May, available at https://www.nbr.org/publication/toward-a-shared-alliance-strategy-in-a-contested-indo-pacific-a-view-from-australia.

Medcalf, R. (2019b) "Indo-Pacific Visions: Giving Solidarity a Chance," *Asia Policy*, Vol. 14 No. 3, pp. 79–96.

Nicolas, F. (2021) "The Economic Pillar of Korea's New Southern Policy: Building on Existing Assets," *Asie.Visions, No. 120, French Institute of International Relations*, February, available at https://www.ifri.org/sites/default/files/atoms/files/nicolas_economic_pillar_korea_2021.pdf.

Pottinger, M. (2021) "Beijing's American Hustle: How Chinese Grand Strategy Exploits U.S. Power," *Foreign Affairs*, Vol. 100, No. 5, pp. 102–114.

Rolland, N. (2022a) "Introduction," in Rolland, N. (Ed) *Political Front Lines – China's Pursuit of Influence in Africa*. Seattle: National Bureau of Asian Research.

Rolland, N. (2022b) "China's Southern Strategy," *Foreign Affairs*, 9 June, available at https://www.foreignaffairs.com/articles/china/2022-06-09/chinas-southern-strategy.

Shambaugh, D. (2005) "China Engages Asia – Reshaping the Regional Order," *International Security*, Vol. 29, No. 3, pp. 64–99.

Turner, O., Nymalm, N. and Aslam, W. (Eds) (2023) *The Routledge Handbook of US Foreign Policy in the Indo-Pacific*. Abingdon and New York City: Routledge.

Wilkins, T. (2021) "Japan as a Contributor to the Rules-Based Order in the Indo-Pacific," *Sasakawa Peace Foundation*, 22 September, available at https://www.spf.org/iina/en/articles/thomas_02.html.

Wright, A. and Cartwright, H. A. (Eds) (1908) *Twentieth Century Impressions of Hong Kong, Shanghai, and other Treaty Ports of China: Their History, People, Commerce, Industries, and Resources*. London: Lloyd's Greater Britain Publishing Company.

10 Latin American and Caribbean cooperation with China and the United States during the COVID-19 pandemic

Kim Emmanuel

The COVID-19 crisis raised fundamental questions over the resilience of the liberal international order (LIO). At first glance, the early part of the crisis seemed to have substantiated the Realist proposition that, faced with a risk of anarchy, states pursue their national interests to ensure their survival. This vision involves that competitive and even antagonistic dynamics between states may exacerbate and jeopardize the LIO. The pandemic restricted inter-state interactions but, more dramatically, the relations between the United States and China became increasingly contentious. However, nationalistic stances reached their limits within a few months. Once severely affected by the COVID-19 pandemic, Latin American and Caribbean developing states advocated and followed a well-tested approach to overcome the crisis: they actively cooperated with the two superpowers and international financial institutions (IFIs). During this process, China, the U.S., and IFIs played a pivotal role and shaped regional responses to the pandemic. Despite obvious tensions within the LIO, this evolution has highlighted the strength and resilience of liberal principles.

10.1 Introduction

John Ikenberry (2010, p. 512) defines the liberal international order (LIO) as "a distinctive type of order, organised around open markets, multilateral institutions, cooperative security, alliance partnership, democratic solidarity and United States hegemonic leadership." The LIO has largely shaped the world economy and international relations, especially since the collapse of the Soviet Union in 1991. However, it appears that the COVID-19 crisis challenged the very foundations of the LIO. As the pandemic rapidly spread around the world, states cited national security concerns to tighten border controls and curtail international exchanges. In the meantime, the rivalry between the United States and China heightened as the two powers sought to develop their own narratives regarding the emergence and management of the virus. These tensions had implicit consequences for developing countries like Latin America and the Caribbean (LAC). These countries were hit hard by the pandemic but to what extent has the health crisis affected the LIO,

DOI: 10.4324/9781003340430-13

especially when accounting for Latin American and Caribbean states' responses to the pandemic? This chapter answers this question.

Rather than reflecting a potential decline of the LIO, the COVID-19 crisis required a liberal response: namely, cooperation. To address the health and economic effects of the crisis, it is argued that LAC governments worked in close collaboration with the United States and China and increased their partnerships with international financial institutions (IFIs) like the World Bank and the International Monetary Fund (IMF). Ensconced within various strands of Liberalism is the idea that international cooperation engenders mutual gains (Ruggie, 1992; Jervis, 1999; Haas, 2008). For the proponents of "complex interdependence," states are connected through a web of interactions that makes cooperation a feasible and rational choice for actors. Cooperation may be considered a process of policy coordination which seeks to maximize gains while aiming to minimize negative effects and outcomes. In seeking to formulate and implement agendas for the pursuit of common goals, states focus on building or upholding partnerships (Milner, 1997, pp. 8–9). However, the agendas on which they cooperate are affected by international and domestic problems (Keohane and Nye, 2012, p. 27). The need for international cooperation to contain and control infectious diseases has long been recognized through the establishment of institutional mechanisms and partnerships designed to advance public health solutions (Haas, 2008, p. 35).

In Latin America and the Caribbean, an intricate web of interdependencies and asymmetrical dynamics prompted a pragmatic response to the crisis. However, this response is contingent on the position of the countries. At this stage, there is a distinction to be made between sensitivity and vulnerability. Sensitivity denotes the degree and extent of costly effects even if policies may be implemented to alter or change the situation. Vulnerability indicates that states may face costs imposed by external events or forces without being equipped to effectively respond or change policies (Keohane and Nye, 2012, p. 13). The pandemic did shake all LAC countries but their capabilities to cope with the sanitary crisis varied to a large degree.

The pandemic pushed Latin American and Caribbean states to the brink, revealing the inadequacy of their healthcare systems, and increasing their vulnerabilities. Although LAC countries make up 8% of the world population, they accounted for about 28% of deaths worldwide (Schwalb et al., 2022). The effects of the coronavirus crisis on the region raised awareness among policy makers and within public opinion that collective action was key to addressing the pandemic. In a survey conducted by the Organisation for Economic Co-operation and Development (OECD) and the Economic Commission for Latin America and the Caribbean (ECLAC), 70% of Latin Americans thought that cooperation was essential to deal with the challenges brought about by the COVID-19 crisis (OECD et al., 2021, p. 198). This sentiment was echoed by the head of the Pan American Health Organization (PAHO), who concluded that countries are unable to overcome global challenges alone (PAHO, 2022).

The need for cooperation was highlighted throughout much of the region's responses to the pandemic. China proved to be a vital partner during the first phase of the crisis (i.e., from the second quarter of 2020 to the first quarter of 2021) and played a key role in promoting access to its vaccines. With the advent of the Biden administration, the United States broadened its cooperation with the region. The U.S. expanded access to its own vaccines in 2021–2022 and boosted vaccine coverage dramatically. Moreover, LAC states turned to several multilateral institutions, including the World Bank and the IMF, to obtain emergency loans.

10.2 Cooperation with China

China has long viewed developing states as central to its global strategy.[1] Cooperation with Latin America and the Caribbean to combat the COVID-19 crisis was therefore at the forefront of Beijing's engagement in the region. China's assistance first consisted of providing medical supplies and equipment and later shifted to promoting vaccine diplomacy. This outreach was consistent with China's pre-COVID emphasis on technical and financial assistance in the public health area. Beijing's foreign policy studies on Latin America and the Caribbean in the late 2000s noted that the Chinese government should share experience and carry out cooperation in areas such as disease control and responses to public health emergencies. These priorities were confirmed shortly before the pandemic. China has not only embarked on promoting exchanges through the deployment of health personnel, but it has also spent millions of U.S. dollars in upgrading health facilities.

In March 2020, at the G20 Extraordinary Virtual Leaders' Summit on COVID-19, President Xi Jinping delivered a speech entitled "Working Together to Defeat the COVID-19 Outbreak." He explained that major

> infectious disease is the enemy of all. As we speak, the COVID-19 outbreak is spreading worldwide, posing enormous threat to life and health and bringing formidable challenge to global public health security... We must comprehensively step up international cooperation and foster greater synergy so that humanity as one could win the battle.[2]

In the meantime, Chinese officials and medical personnel conducted a video conference with Latin American and Caribbean states. International representatives from the World Health Organization (WHO) and the PAHO had also joined the event. During the conference, China reiterated its commitment to enhancing cooperation with LAC states in an effort to address the challenges brought about by the COVID-19 virus.[3] China later pledged financial assistance amounting to $1 billion for pandemic response in the region.[4]

China's focus on cooperation was partly driven by the necessity to enhance its international status and restore its image amidst conflicting views over its transparency and reactivity at the very beginning of the pandemic (Lee, 2021). For Peeri et al. (2020), limited information flows on the magnitude of the disaster unfolding in Wuhan in January 2020 hampered early steps to curtail the spread of the pathogen. A study conducted by Andrade et al. (2021) in Brazil in March–April 2020 showed mixed sentiments about China. Next, a Pew survey conducted from June to August 2020 found that China's reputational power had been adversely affected in Australia, Japan, and the European Union. In Australia, unfavorable perceptions reached historic highs (Silver et al., 2020, p.4).

However, in most Latin American and Caribbean states, the perception of China was more nuanced. As emphasized by the China Institute of International Studies, many countries in the LAC region expressed their sympathy for China when the pandemic struck and thus offered their assistance.[5] Even in the case of Brazil where conflictual responses emerged during the first months of the crisis, cooperation was the norm rather than the exception. President Bolsonaro was dissatisfied with China's handling of the crisis but, for many observers, his stance was especially risky in an environment where cooperation was essential (Amorim and Ferreira-Pereira, 2021; Ponce, 2020).

The sanitary crisis exacerbated many of the region's vulnerabilities and partnering with China to contain the devastating effects of the pandemic enabled a greater response to the emergency. Like many other emerging and developing regions, Latin America and the Caribbean suffered from a wave of protectionist policies during the initial phase of the pandemic. In advanced economies, export authorizations were required for the sale of medical protective equipment, including face masks, protective suits, and the critically important ventilators. Such measures had an adverse impact on the health sector of the most vulnerable developing countries (Schmucker, 2020).

In the midst of these challenges, Beijing expanded its collaboration with various countries and became the top supplier of medical equipment to LAC states. It is estimated that China's medical aid to Latin America and the Caribbean amounted to $215 million at the height of the crisis (Ray et al., 2021, p. 1). In Brazil, China proved to be among the earliest international responders in terms of aid assistance. Beijing provided Brasilia with personal protection equipment (PPE), including 5,000 protective garments, 50,000 surgical masks, and other medical supplies.[6] It is interesting that China's assistance to Venezuela (still under Western sanctions) exceeded $100 million, accounting for nearly half of the total amount to Latin America and the Caribbean (Ray et al., 2021, p. 1).

A wide range of actors were involved in assisting the LAC region. China's commercial, subnational, and local organizations "followed the flag" and promoted aid allocations, in line with the central government's priorities. The city of São Paulo in Brazil received masks directly from the municipality of Shanghai, a sister city since 1988. Local organizations in China also embarked on their own donation strategies. For example, a major Chinese association of journalists donated 200,000 masks to the Union of Press Workers of Buenos Aires.[7]

China's substantial role in Latin America and the Caribbean was also partly related to its position as leading world producer and supplier of medical equipment. So, it is not surprising that Beijing managed to boost the production of surgical masks and other PPE (Campbell and Doshi, 2020). China also enjoyed a strong position as a manufacturing hub. During the first weeks of the pandemic, Mexico ordered $56 million worth of PPE while Argentina received tens of thousands of test kits and hundreds of thousands of medical face masks.[8] Such capabilities provided much leverage in China's foreign policy outreach to developing countries. Chinese assistance to LAC was usually accompanied with wide media coverage (Brizuela de Ávila et al., 2022).

Recall that industrialized countries with research and development (R&D) capacity engaged in what was seen as "vaccine nationalism": they preempted millions of doses of new vaccines for domestic use only, which triggered an international public health crisis (Rutschman, 2021, p. 9). This practice was harmful to many developing states and led to some criticism. The WHO outlined the disastrous effects of hoarding vaccine supplies amid the pandemic. Leaders in the LAC region, such as Mexico's President Andrés Manuel López Obrador and Jamaica's Prime Minister Andrew Holness also decried vaccine nationalism. Regional organizations shared their concerns. The Community of Latin American and Caribbean States (CELAC) released a collective statement on the need for equitable access to vaccines (Mowla and Zhang, 2022).

In contrast, China sought to fill the vaccine gap quickly. It emphasized cooperation and announced that the vaccines developed by its laboratories would be made available as a "global public good" and that credit would be provided to Latin American and Caribbean countries to get the vaccines (Sanborn, 2020, p. 7). Beijing was thus considered a key ally for many LAC states.

The case of Chile is very illustrative. Chile faced significant shortfalls in its vaccine program. By December 2020, Chile had received only 150,000 out of the 10 million doses ordered from Pfizer, the U.S. pharmaceutical company. Santiago then turned to Beijing for much-needed vaccine supplies and China managed to deliver 4 million doses within a month.[9] CoronaVac vaccine accounted for 75% of vaccine doses administered in Chile during December 2020–July 2021.[10] By May 2021, China had committed to shipping more than 143 million vaccine doses to the ten most populous LAC nations.[11]

Although the cooperation of LAC countries with China was comprehensive in scope, Beijing's vaccine diplomacy differed across states. In the Caribbean Community (CARICOM) region, the vaccine developed by the United Kingdom's pharmaceutical company, AstraZeneca, received early approval and was widely used in 2021 (Griffith, 2021, pp. 13–14). The shift to U.S. vaccines – i.e., Pfizer, Moderna, and Johnson & Johnson – was progressive and did not occur until the second half of 2021. China's vaccine diplomacy was almost absent in the American, British, and European

Caribbean territories, which obtained the vaccines developed by Western pharmaceutical firms.

China's assistance programs were largely underpinned by the "One-China" principle. Myers (2021, p. 6) points out that China's medical supplies were directed nearly exclusively to diplomatic allies and Beijing's vaccine diplomacy was weaponized to isolate Taiwan from its LAC partners. Guatemala, Honduras, Nicaragua, and Paraguay, which recognized Taiwan over China, did not receive Chinese vaccines. In these countries, Taipei sought to provide medical assistance, concentrating its efforts on technical support, especially at the height of the crisis. Taiwan also helped Paraguay secure 2 million doses of India's COVAXIN.[12]

Regardless of the pro-Taiwan governments, China made a major contribution to pandemic responses in the LAC region, especially during the first year of the crisis. In light of its longstanding policy of health cooperation with Latin America and the Caribbean, Beijing has laid concrete plans for intensifying its partnership in the region. It has taken steps to further scientific collaboration while reinforcing its commitment to public health assistance. Chinese vaccine manufacturer, Sinovac, pledged investments amounting to $60 million in a vaccine facility and R&D center in Chile.[13] This complemented earlier efforts by China to strengthen scientific collaboration with countries like Cuba and Brazil. Early in the crisis, Brazil's Instituto Butantan – a famous biologic research center – agreed to cooperate with China to produce and market its Sinovac vaccine.[14] Cuba developed its own vaccine, Abdala, and partnered with China on possible treatments for COVID-19 through a joint venture (the ChangHeber plant in Jilin). An antiviral treatment, Interferon Alfa-2B, was produced as part of this collaboration. The treatment became part of the medicines selected by the Chinese National Heath Commission to fight COVID-19 infection in China.[15] To help reaffirm its commitment to health cooperation in the region, China agreed to provide technical and financial assistance at the virtual China–CELAC summit in 2021. Such initiatives illustrate the continuity in China's development cooperation with the region.

10.3 Cooperation with the United States

There was a real concern among U.S. policy makers that failing to respond to the crisis in Latin America and the Caribbean would undermine U.S. efforts to contain it domestically, given the tight cultural, social, and economic relations between North and South America. As the pandemic spread, 34 civil society groups in the United States gathered and pressed Congress to provide humanitarian assistance to LAC states.[16] Several months later, U.S. Senators worried that China sought to make gains in the LAC region through a bold vaccine diplomacy, much more efficient than the American's. They insisted that the vaccines to send to the south should have a clear "made-in-the-USA" label.[17]

The short-lived U.S. passivity partly traces its roots in Donald Trump's worldview. His administration lessened the emphasis on alliances and collective approaches when addressing common security threats, including pandemic and sanitary risks. This temporary deviation from established liberal principles of cooperation did not preclude the U.S. engagement with Latin America and Caribbean states. During the initial phase of the crisis, the Trump administration committed to providing bilateral assistance to LAC states. Once Joe Biden entered the White House in January 2021, there was an obvious return to international partnerships (Marczak and Guevara, 2021, p. 11).

The focus on cooperation by the Biden administration had wider implications for the LIO. One of President Biden's first initiatives was to retract the Trump administration's decision to withdraw from the WHO. This move not only signaled a dissatisfaction with his predecessor's approach to health crises, but it was also designed to reassure state and non-state actors that the U.S. intended to take back its leading role in international affairs. He reiterated this message in a speech delivered in February 2021. He emphasized the importance of alliances whilst indicating to the world that "America is back."[18] In line with this more proactive involvement in international partnerships, the United States assumed henceforth a far more visible role in pandemic responses.

The U.S. cooperation with Latin America and the Caribbean initially revolved around the management of COVID-19 at the local level and later shifted to vaccine delivery and support. Various U.S. government agencies and programs were involved to provide medical assistance to the region: e.g., the Humanitarian Assistance Program (HAP), the U.S. Agency for International Development (USAID), and the State Department's Bureau of Population, Refugees, and Migration (PRM). Although somewhat siloed in terms of expertise, these agencies are robustly interconnected not only with one another but also with other organizations seeking to defend U.S. security interests (Pforzheimer, 2021, pp. 1–2).

Under the broader mandate of the PRM, the U.S. provided $1.8 million in support to states like Mexico for aiding refugees, asylum seekers and other vulnerable migrants. The assistance was geared toward providing sanitation and personal hygiene supplies at shelters and migratory stations. USAID made technical and pandemic-related equipment donations to the Western Hemisphere in 2020. It provided a total of 3,486 ventilators to 13 LAC states – Bolivia, Brazil, Colombia, the Dominican Republic, Ecuador, El Salvador, Guatemala, Haiti, Honduras, Panama, Paraguay, Peru and St. Kitts & Nevis (Pforzheimer, 2021, p. 3). The aid provided by USAID in Latin America and the Caribbean amounted $110 million in 2020 (Pforzheimer, 2021, p. 1).

During the first months of the crisis, the HAP funded about 290 projects in 28 LAC nations amounting to $16 million.[19] These projects included field hospitals which addressed pandemic emergency as well as structural health issues. According to the WHO, very few LAC states reached the world average of 2.9 hospital beds per 1,000 inhabitants and intensive care units in the region were far below the bare minimum of 6 per 100,000 inhabitants (Schwalb et al., 2022, p. 410). While countries such as Argentina surpassed the world average, Central American and Caribbean states had to increase their health capacities significantly to manage the effects of the virus. Through the various U.S. initiatives, some of the most acute shortages in healthcare facilities were averted. Costa Rica benefited from four field hospitals at a cost of $1.1 million each. Between the outbreak of COVID-19 and January 2021, the U.S. administration spent $112 million for the Western Hemisphere countries and over $22 million for El Salvador, Guatemala, Honduras, and Mexico (U.S. Department of State, 2021).

The United States relied on a wide array of cooperative strategies to strengthen its vaccine diplomacy in LAC states and compete efficiently with China. Washington played a more formal role in collective endeavors such as COVAX, a worldwide initiative designed to promote vaccine equity and access in developing countries.[20] It also partnered directly with regional entities in vaccination drives and further reappraised the role of the PAHO in pandemic responses across the region. In the process, the U.S. became a critical partner in the fight against COVID-19 in Latin America and the Caribbean.

Led by a public-private partnership including the WHO, the United Nations Children Fund (UNICEF), the PAHO as well as the Global Alliance for Vaccine and Immunization (GAVI) and the Coalition for Epidemic Preparedness Innovations (CEPI), COVAX is an invaluable facility for developing states with little R&D capacity. Under the Biden administration, the United States became a top contributor to the facility. In March 2022, considering donations and pledges, Washington had committed to providing 900 million vaccine doses to the COVAX facility, compared to 527 million for the European Union.[21]

To advance its vaccine diplomacy in the region, Washington significantly increased its donation drives across LAC states. Between June and August 2021, the U.S. donated more than 27 million doses of the Moderna and Pfizer vaccines to Argentina, Colombia, Costa Rica, Ecuador, El Salvador, Guatemala, Haiti, Honduras, Mexico, Panama, Paraguay, Peru, and Uruguay, and nearly 8 million doses of the Johnson & Johnson vaccine to Brazil, Bolivia, Colombia, and Mexico.[22] It also gifted 5.5 million doses of Pfizer vaccines and 3 million ancillary kits to CARICOM states.[23] By January 2022, Washington had shipped over 50 million doses developed by U.S. pharmaceutical companies.[24] This focus on donations contrasted with China's vaccine diplomacy, which was often linked to various funding arrangements aimed at facilitating purchases from China. These diverging strategies may explain that U.S. contribution to fight the pandemic dwarfed China's. For example, in Central America, U.S. donations (including those through COVAX) totaled 16.8 million doses compared to 1.75 million doses from China (Brizuela de Ávila et al., 2022, p. 4).

The impressive development of mRNA (messenger ribonucleic acid) research in the United States has enabled U.S. pharmaceutical firms to dominate the vaccine race. Whereas China is frequently perceived as rising power, research advances in this area have been clearly associated with the West, thus influencing and shaping public preferences in the developing as well as advanced economies. Studies showed that a government's willingness to accept a specific vaccine was positively correlated with its high efficacy, its low incidence of major adverse effects, its production patterns, and its endorsement from medical organizations (see Argote et al., 2021, p. 1). So far, vaccine research efforts by Western states have tended to boost efficacy rates. Very high efficacy rates were observed for Moderna and Pfizer-BioNTech vaccines – 94% and 95%, respectively (Iqbal et al., 2022). Chinese vaccines showed lower efficacy rates, ranging from 50% to 70% (Damasceno et al., 2022).

In addition, the vaccines produced by Western firms obtained wider global approval for emergency use. The Pfizer BioNTech vaccine – developed by the United States and Germany – and British AstraZeneca vaccine got the highest approval rates while Chinese vaccines remained well behind.[25] Although widely used in Latin America and the Caribbean – due to their cost-effectiveness and easier storage – China's vaccines had to cope with the wider availability of their U.S. contenders. The scientific advance ascribed to the U.S. in terms of vaccine development is incontestable and has contributed to increase substantially worldwide vaccine coverage. In fact, the alliances built through various cooperative efforts have been fruitful. Latin America and the Caribbean has become one of the most vaccinated regions in the world, with over 60% of the population being inoculated as of January 2022, as compared to just 15% in July 2021 (Jaramillo, 2022a).

Unlike China who early on had put public health issues on top of its development cooperation agenda, the U.S. previously privileged border security, democracy, and governance issues. Following the pandemic, Washington has identified additional areas for possible collaboration and engagement. For example, it is envisaged that, by spurring greater investment in the health sector and strengthening supply chains in the Western Hemisphere, the U.S. could help facilitate more effective responses to present and future pandemics.[26]

Established in 1902 by Washington in reaction to the yellow fever that swept the Americas, the PAHO has been a key organization for articulating and implementing partnerships between the U.S. and LAC nations. The PAHO supports health ministries and other government institutions throughout the region to help strengthen surveillance, testing and laboratory capacities. It also bolsters health care services in the region. In an effort to deepen U.S. engagement in health cooperation, the PAHO has called for increased collaboration in terms of R&D in the Americas.

The organization has not been without challenges in responding to the pandemic across Latin America and the Caribbean. The U.S. hardline attitude toward multilateral cooperation under the Trump administration led to criticism of the actions undertaken by the PAHO. During the initial phase of the pandemic in 2020, U.S. Secretary of State, Mike Pompeo, attacked the PAHO's role in "Mais Médicos," a medical program which deployed Cuban doctors to underserved communities in Brazil. The dispute triggered the suspension of U.S. contribution to the PAHO. It was reinstated a few months later in October 2020 (Pforzheimer, 2021). Despite all, the Pan-American organization has re-emerged as an important pillar in fighting the pandemic.

To enhance cooperation with the United States, the PAHO made a formal call for building vaccine manufacturing capacity in LAC countries at the Global COVID-19 summit. This summit, held in September 2021 and hosted by President Joe Biden, was entitled "Ending the Pandemic and Building Back Better Health Security to Prepare for the Next." In the meantime, the PAHO launched the "Regional Platform to Advance the Manufacturing of COVID-19 Vaccines and other Health Technologies in the Americas." This platform is aimed at fostering research and incentivizing the development and manufacturing of essential and strategic health technologies within the Americas. It is envisaged that this would not only promote broader cooperation in the hemisphere but would also give rise to increased synergies between the public and private sectors as well as between the health industry and the science and technology sectors (PAHO, 2022). Although it remains to be seen whether these specific endeavors will bear fruit, these initiatives could pave the way to greater cooperation between the U.S. and LAC states in the broader health sector.

10.4 Cooperation with international financial institutions

The notions of "institution" and "cooperation" are strongly interconnected (Jervis, 1999, p. 43), institutions (especially international ones) being vital for addressing common global challenges. To help combat a multitude of risks stemming from the pandemic, Latin American and Caribbean states expanded partnerships with the IMF, the World Bank, and major regional development banks. By May 2021, these IFIs had approved about \$103 billion in funding for the Americas, including the LAC region (Segal, 2021). Cooperation efforts were aimed at building more resilient health systems, contributing to vaccine equity, and minimizing the economic fallout from the pandemic.

Keep in mind that, in Latin America and the Caribbean, the pandemic occurred in a complex social and economic environment. Like in most developing countries, the health sector had been structurally underfunded. In the LAC region, total public expenditure on health stood at 3.8% of GDP (gross domestic product) in 2020, well below the OECD average which reached 6.6% (OECD, 2020a, p. 11). However, these percentages varied across countries. In Cuba, well known for its health diplomacy in other developing states, the percentage was almost 12% of GDP while, for Venezuela, health expenditure had declined to 1.1% because of social unrest and economic sanctions (OECD, 2020a, p. 134). A fundamental weakness of Latin America and the Caribbean is the lack of access to health services. In terms of health personnel, the region has an average of two doctors per 1,000 population, compared to 3.5 for OECD members (OECD, 2020a, pp. 9–10).

The Latin American and Caribbean countries also suffer from several other persistent weaknesses. Their economies depend on commodity exports and a few sectors like tourism. Next, their high debt to GDP ratio worries international creditors. Last, illegal work and the lack of efficient social protection schemes for the most vulnerable exacerbate social inequality. The informal sector represents 58% of the labor force and at least 65% of those workers receive no form of social protection (OECD et al., 2021, p. 200). Therefore, workers not only failed to benefit from formal social or economic support, but they were also very vulnerable to health risks like COVID-19.

In this context, the virus undermined the fragile public health systems of the region. As early as May 2020, the WHO declared that Latin America and the Caribbean was the most affected region, accounting for more than 30% of the world's reported COVID-19 deaths (OECD, 2020b, p. 2). The outbreak of the pandemic triggered a deep recession. The region's GDP contracted by 7.4% in 2020. In the Caribbean countries relying heavily on tourism, GDP plunged by 10% (Werner et al., 2021). This economic shock occurred amid a sluggish economic period: GDP growth during 2014–2019 had reached the lowest level recorded since the 1950s (ECLAC, 2020, p. 1).

Unlike most advanced economies, LAC governments were unable to provide immediate and significant financial support to citizens and firms through stimulus packages, subsidies, tax deferrals, and enhanced social benefits. In fact, Latin American and Caribbean countries managed to offset the cost of the pandemic and hasten economic recovery thanks largely to the IFIs and their swift response to liquidity demands. The region confirmed that it could rely on traditional partners like the World Bank and the IMF.

10.4.1 The World Bank

During the first days of the crisis, in March 2020, the World Bank authorized the establishment of the "Fast Track COVID-19 Facility" to assist eligible countries in addressing the pandemic. With this facility, the Washington-based institution approved the first set of global emergency support operations for developing countries.[27] World Bank's commitments for the 12-month period in fiscal year 2021 totaled $98.8 billion. Around 18% of this amount was directed to Latin America and the Caribbean (World Bank, 2021, p. 3).[28] The Bank cooperated with LAC governments on their COVID-19 emergency responses as well as with a broad range of international institutions (e.g., the CEPI, the GAVI, the IMF, the UNICEF, the WHO, and the World Trade Organization).

During the early phase of the pandemic, the World Bank contributed to building more resilient health systems and laid the groundwork for assisting in vaccination efforts. As early as October 2020, the World Bank Board had approved a $12 billion package to finance the acquisition and distribution of COVID-19 vaccines for all developing countries (World Bank, 2020). In the LAC region, the World Bank contributed to accelerate vaccination campaigns. For example, in Peru, it provided a $500 million loan to strengthen Lima's vaccination plan through the procurement of 40 million vaccine doses. The aim was to vaccinate 20 million people, about 62% of Peru's population. In December 2021, the vaccination rate in Peru reached 69.7%.[29] Similarly, another $500 million was provided to Argentina to boost its vaccination rate.[30]

10.4.2 The IMF

The IMF has been intervening as lender of last resort for several decades to avert systemic risk and support distressed countries (Flores Zendejas and Gaillard, 2022, pp. 87–97). So, it is not surprising that the institution played a major role in the pandemic response. In January 2021, the Fund had already committed $66.5 billion to Latin America and the Caribbean. This represented 63% of its total disbursement to 85 economies in the developing world (ECLAC, 2021, p. 5).

To cope with this crisis, the IMF used several financial facilities, some of which had been established in the aftermath of the global financial turmoil of 2008 (IMF, 2012, pp. 18–22). The Rapid Credit Facility (RCF) and the Stand-By Credit Facility (SCF) are designed to resolve short-term balance-of-payments problems in low-income countries. The conditionality attached to the former loan type is softer. The aim of the Rapid Financing Instrument (RFI) is to meet urgent financial needs. The RFI was the facility most used in the LAC region in 2020–2021. The Flexible Credit Lines (FCL) facility was available to countries with very strong macroeconomic fundamentals, economic policy framework, and policy track record. The Extended Fund Facility (EFF), Stand-By Arrangement (SBA), and Precautionary and Liquidity Line (PLL) provide medium-term financial assistance. As Table 10.1 shows, the IMF lent to 21 Latin American and Caribbean economies during April 2020–December 2021.

10.4.3 What results?

The assistance provided by the IMF and other IFIs enabled Latin American and Caribbean governments to fight the recessionary effects of the pandemic through more expansive fiscal policies. They implemented measures designed to (i) support households, firms, and banks, (ii) restore health systems, and (iii) extend social safety nets (Elgin et al., 2020). However, these measures varied across LAC countries.

Table 10.1 IMF's COVID-19 financial assistance for member countries, April 2020–December 2021

Country	*Type of emergency financing*	*Amount approved (in $ mil.)*	*Date approved*
Bahamas	RFI	250	June 1, 2020
Barbados	Augmentation of EFF	91	June 3, 2020
	Augmentation of EFF	69	December 9, 2020
Bolivia	RFI	327	April 17, 2020
Chile	FCL	23,930	May 29, 2020
Colombia	FCL	10,748	May 1, 2020
	Augmentation of FCL	6,200	September 25, 2020
Costa Rica	RFI	508	April 29, 2020
	EFF	1,778	March 1, 2021
Dominica	RCF	14	April 28, 2020
Dominican Republic	RFI	650	April 29, 2020
Ecuador	RFI	643	May 1, 2020
	EFF	6,500	September 30, 2020
El Salvador	RFI	389	April 14, 2020
Grenada	RCF	22	April 28, 2020
Haiti	RCF	112	April 17, 2020
Honduras	Augmentation of SBA & SCF	223	June 1, 2020
	SBA & Arrangement under SCF	216	September 13, 2021
Jamaica	RFI	520	May 15, 2020
Mexico	FCL	50,000	November 19, 2021
Nicaragua	RFI	124	November 20, 2020
	RCF	62	
Panama	RFI	515	April 15, 2020
	PLL	2,700	January 19, 2021
Peru	FCL	11,000	May 28, 2020
St. Lucia	RCF	29	April 28, 2020
St. Vincent and the Grenadines	RCF	16	May 20, 2020
	RCF	12	July 1, 2021
Suriname	EFF	668	December 22, 2021

Source: https://www.imf.org/en/Topics/imf-and-COVID19/COVID-Lending-Tracker#WHD.

In Brazil, the Bolsonaro administration lifted the obligation to comply with the primary balance target in 2020. It increased healthcare spending and provided temporary income support to vulnerable households, especially informal and low-income workers. Argentina made significant efforts to improve its healthcare system: it sought to have much better virus diagnostics and engaged in the construction of hospitals. In addition, it gave assistance to poor workers and vulnerable groups through increased social transfers and supported hard-hit sectors by covering payroll costs and granting subsidized loans. In Costa Rica, increased public health spending was complemented with a moratorium on the payment of value-added taxes, business income taxes, and customs duties. Mexican authorities implemented measures aimed to ensure that the Ministry of Health would have sufficient financial resources in the short term. They also granted loans with optional repayments to family business and small- and medium-sized enterprises that maintained employees on payroll.[31]

The results of all these interventions have been mixed. With the assistance of the IFIs, the coverage of income support programs in the LAC region increased from 22% of all households before the pandemic to nearly 50% in March 2022. The coverage exceeded the two thirds of households in El Salvador, Bolivia, Guyana, Panama, and Chile. Estimates suggest that 28 million more people would have slipped into poverty in 2020 without these measures (Jaramillo, 2022b). Those were especially helpful for LAC countries with a large informal sector.

However, broader concerns remain. Recessions caused by epidemics are among the textbook examples for causing large fiscal deficits and massive public debts (Baldwin and Werder di Mauro, 2020, p. 17). In 2022, the ratio of general government gross debt to GDP was forecast to be higher than its pre-pandemic level in 80% of LAC countries (see Table 10.2). In the medium term, external financing may fuel dependencies and further limit spending on essential public services, including healthcare and social programs. As Stubbs et al. (2021) point out: "under current restrictions on cumulative use, the rapid [IMF] low-conditionality loans will need to be repaid within 3 to 10 years." As a result, massive sovereign defaults and significant debt reliefs may occur very soon.

10.5 Conclusion

The pandemic underscored the critical role of China, the United States, and the IFIs (including the World Bank and the IMF) in shaping responses to the health and economic crises in the LAC region. China played a vital role in medical aid and vaccine diplomacy, especially during the first phase of the crisis (i.e., until the first quarter of 2021). The U.S. intensified its support and imposed its vaccine diplomacy during the second phase of the crisis (i.e., during 2021–2022). Contrary to what could be feared at the onset of the

Table 10.2 General government gross debt to GDP ratios for LAC countries

	2019	*2020*	*2022 (forecast)*
Antigua & Barbuda	81.3	101.5	91.2
Argentina	88.8	102.8	76.0
Aruba	71.6	110.1	95.0
Bahamas	59.7	75.0	90.7
Barbados	123.2	147.0	117.9
Belize	79.0	104.5	76.3
Bolivia	59.3	78.0	82.6
Brazil	87.9	98.7	88.2
Chile	28.3	32.6	36.2
Colombia	52.4	65.7	61.1
Costa Rica	56.4	67.2	67.6
Dominica	97.9	114.5	102.8
Dominican Republic	53.6	71.5	58.4
Ecuador	51.4	60.9	58.9
El Salvador	71.3	89.4	80.3
Grenada	58.5	71.4	68.9
Guatemala	26.4	31.5	30.1
Guyana	43.6	51.1	22.8
Haiti	25.8	21.3	23.1
Honduras	42.9	52.4	Not Applicable
Jamaica	94.3	108.1	86.2
Mexico	53.3	60.1	56.8
Nicaragua	41.7	48.0	47.0
Panama	41.9	65.6	55.6
Paraguay	25.8	36.9	39.3
Peru	26.9	35.0	34.8
St. Kitts & Nevis	51.5	56.8	56.5
St. Lucia	62.1	96.9	90.1
St. Vincent & the Grenadines	68.1	79.2	87.9
Suriname	85.2	146.1	134.0
Trinidad & Tobago	45.4	59.3	54.7
Uruguay	61.0	68.3	61.2
Venezuela	201.4	319.1	Not Applicable

Source: IMF (2022).

pandemic, the two superpowers cooperated extensively with LAC governments and coordinated with IFIs. Paradoxically, it seems that the liberal principle of cooperation was reinvigorated during the pandemic episode.

As Ikenberry (2020) analyzes, liberal norms have long defined the international order and offer a set of ideas for mutual gain despite underlying rivalries. For their part, IFIs collaborated closely with developing countries' governments, advancing public health solutions and facilitating economic recovery. They have invariably strengthened liberal principles amidst tensions within the LIO.[32]

Notes

1 Kellner and Wintgens (2021) investigate the relationships between China and Latin America and the Caribbean during the 2010s. Skidmore's chapter in this book focuses on the Belt and Road Initiative.
2 "Full Text of Xi's Remarks at Extraordinary G20 Leaders' Summit," *Xinhuanet*, 27 March 2020, available at http://www.xinhuanet.com/english/2020-03/27/c_138920767.htm.
3 See the Foreign Ministry Spokesperson Geng Shuang's regular press conference, 24 March 24 2020, available at https://www.fmprc.gov.cn/mfa_eng/xwfw_665399/s2510_665401/2511_665403/202003/t20200324_693148.html.
4 D. Oré, "Mexico Says China Plans $1 Billion Loan to Ease Latam Access to Virus Vaccine," *Reuters*, 23 July 2020, available at https://www.reuters.com/article/us-health-coronavirus-mexico-china-idUSKCN24O08L.
5 See https://www.ciis.org.cn/english/lbt/202008/t20200825_7203.html.
6 "Chinese Embassy Delivers Donation of Medical Supplies to Brazil," *Xinhuanet*, 4 July 2020, available at http://www.xinhuanet.com/english/2020-07/04/c_139187100.htm.
7 F. Harmitton and M. Camoletto, "Argentina–China: Cooperate in Adverse Times," *Fundeps*, 13 August 2020, available at https://fundeps.org/en/argentina-china-cooperate-in-adverse-times.
8 M. Myers and R. Barrios, "China's Medical Outreach in LAC: Facts and Features," *The Dialogue*, 22 May 2020, available at https://www.thedialogue.org/blogs/2020/05/chinas-medical-outreach-in-lac-facts-and-features.
9 H. Wu and K. Gelineau, "Chinese Vaccines Sweep Much of the World, Despite Concerns," *Medical Xpress*, 2 March 2021, available at https://medicalxpress.com/news/2021-03-chinese-vaccines-world.html.
10 J. Rolnick and G. Voss, "In China We Trust: Field-testing CoronaVac in Chile," *Wilson Center*, 23 July 2021, available at https://www.wilsoncenter.org/blog-post/china-we-trust-field-testing-coronavac-chile.
11 M. Stott, B. Harris, M. Pooler, G. Long. B. Mander and J. Webber, "Chinese Jabs Dominate Latin American Vaccination Campaigns," *Financial Times*, 9 May 2021, available at https://www.ft.com/content/511d3cee-b388-4eb5-a667-e693349ad564.
12 C Harrison, "Vaccines Reignite China vs. Taiwan Debate in Latin America," *Americas Society/Council of the Americas*, 12 May 2021, available at https://www.as-coa.org/articles/vaccines-reignite-china-vs-taiwan-debate-latin-america.
13 "Coronavirus: China's Sinovac Investing US$60 Million in Chile Vaccine Facility," *South China Morning Post*, 5 August 2021, available at https://www.scmp.com/news/world/americas/article/3143853/coronavirus-chinas-sinovac-investing-us60-million-chile-vaccine.
14 "Coronavirus: Brazil's Butantan Institute to Sell Sinovac Shots Abroad After Jair Bolsonaro Rebuffs 'Chinese Vaccine'," *South China Morning Post*, 30 September 2021, available at https://www.scmp.com/news/world/americas/article/3150646/coronavirus-brazils-butantan-institute-sell-sinovac-shots.
15 M. Myers and R. Barrios, "China's Medical Outreach in LAC: Facts and Features," *The Dialogue*, 22 May 2020, available at https://www.thedialogue.org/blogs/2020/05/chinas-medical-outreach-in-lac-facts-and-features.
16 "Congress Should Approve Aid for COVID-19's New Epicenter: Latin America and the Caribbean," *Reliefweb*, 1 July 2020, available at https://reliefweb.int/report/world/congress-should-approve-aid-covid-19-s-new-epicenter-latin-america-and-caribbean.

17 G. Weeks, "U.S. Vaccine Diplomacy in Latin America is Failing," *Global Americans*, 27 May 2021, available at https://theglobalamericans.org/2021/05/u-s-vaccine-diplomacy-failing.
18 See https://www.whitehouse.gov/briefing-room/speeches-remarks/2021/02/04/remarks-by-president-biden-on-americas-place-in-the-world.
19 U.S. Southern Command, "SOUTHCOM Donates Field Hospitals to Support COVID-19 Response in Costa Rica; 24 Field Hospitals to be Donated in the Region," *DVIDS*, 24 August 2020, available at https://www.dvidshub.net/news/376704/southcom-donates-field-hospitals-support-covid-19-response-costa-rica-24-field-hospitals-donated.
20 President Biden announced that the United States would join the COVAX vaccine facility when he took office; see S. Nebehay, "U.S., Staying in WHO, To Join COVID Vaccine Push for Poor Nations: Fauci," *Reuters*, 21 January 2021, available at https://www.reuters.com/article/us-health-coronavirus-who-usa-idUSKBN29Q12B.
21 See https://ourworldindata.org/grapher/covax-donations?country=FRA~ESP~SWE~USA~CAN~NOR~NZL~GBR~DNK~CHE~ITA~DEU~PRT~BEL~European+Union~JPN~NLD~FIN~HKG~IRL~AUT~BRA~SVK~SVN~KOR~MEX~GRC.
22 G. Voss, J. Zhou and H. Shuldiner, "'Vaccine Diplomacy' in Latin America," *Wilson Center*, 1 October 2021, available at https://www.wilsoncenter.org/blog-post/vaccine-diplomacy-latin-america.
23 "The US Government Donates 5.5 Million Pfizer Vaccines to the Caribbean Community (CARICOM)," *Reliefweb*, 13 August 2021, available at https://reliefweb.int/report/haiti/us-government-donates-55-million-pfizer-vaccines-caribbean-community-caricom.
24 H. Shuldiner, "'Vaccine Diplomacy,' the Final Frontier," *Wilson Center*, 21 January 2022, available at https://www.wilsoncenter.org/blog-post/vaccine-diplomacy-final-frontier.
25 See https://covid19.trackvaccines.org/agency/who.
26 See https://www.congress.gov/event/117th-congress/house-event/LC67773/text.
27 World Bank, "World Bank Group Launches First Operations for Covid-19 (Coronavirus) Emergency Health Support, Strengthening Developing Country Responses," *Press Release*, 2 April 2020, available at https://www.worldbank.org/en/news/press-release/2020/04/02/world-bank-group-launches-first-operations-for-covid-19-coronavirus-emergency-health-support-strengthening-developing-country-responses.
28 It is interesting that all the World Bank's organizations were involved: namely, the International Bank for Reconstruction and Development, the International Development Association, the International Finance Corporation, and the Multilateral Investment Guarantee Agency.
29 World Bank, "The World Bank Will Finance COVID-19 Vaccines for 20 Million Peruvians," *Press Release*, 20 December 2021, available at https://www.worldbank.org/en/news/press-release/2021/12/20/the-world-bank-will-finance-covid-19-vaccines-for-20-million-peruvians.
30 World Bank, "The World Bank Provides US$ 500 Million to Strengthen Argentina's COVID-19 Vaccination Plan," *Press Release*, 1 October 2021, available at https://www.worldbank.org/en/news/press-release/2021/10/01/el-banco-mundial-refuerza-con-us-500-millones-el-plan-de-vacunaci-n-contra-la-covid-19-en-argentina.
31 See https://www.imf.org/en/Topics/imf-and-covid19/Policy-Responses-to-COVID-19.
32 Lim's chapter in this book investigates the Sino-U.S. rivalry in the Indo-Pacific region and its consequences on the LIO.

References

Amorim, S. C. and Ferreira-Pereira, L. C. (2021) "Brazil's Quest for Autonomy in Asia: The Role of Strategic Partnerships with China and Japan," *Revista Brasileira de Política Internacional*, Vol. 64, No. 2, pp. 1–21.

Andrade, F. M. R., Barreto, T. B., Herrera-Feligreras, A., Ugolini, A. and Lu, Y-T. (2021) "Twitter in Brazil: Discourses on China in Times of Coronavirus," *Social Sciences & Humanities Open*, Vol. 3, No. 1, 100118.

Argote, P., Barham, E., Daly, S. Z., Gerez, J. E., Marshall, J. and Pocasangre, O. (2021) "The Shot, the Message, and the Messenger: COVID-19 Vaccine Acceptance in Latin America," *NPJ Vaccines*, Vol. 6, No. 1, pp. 118–126.

Baldwin, R. and Weder di Mauro, B. (2020) "Introduction," in Baldwin, R. and Weder di Mauro, B. (Eds) *Mitigating the COVID Economic Crisis: Act Fast and Do Whatever It Takes*. London: CEPR Press.

Brizuela de Ávila, M. E., Insanally, R., Trevisan, C., Marti, B. and Mowla, W. (Ed) (2022) "US–China Vaccine Diplomacy: Lessons from Latin America and the Caribbean," *Atlantic Council*, available at https://www.atlanticcouncil.org/wp-content/uploads/2022/02/US-China-vaccine-diplomacy-Lessons-from-Latin-America-and-the-Caribbean.pdf.

Campbell, K. M. and Doshi, R. (2020) "The Coronavirus Could Reshape Global Order," *Foreign Affairs*, 18 March, available at https://www.foreignaffairs.com/articles/china/2020-03-18/coronavirus-could-reshape-global-order.

Damasceno, D. H. P., Amaral, A. A., Silva, C. A., and Simões e Silva, A. C. (2022) "The Impact of Vaccination Worldwide on SARS-CoV-2 Infection: A Review on Vaccine Mechanisms, Results of Clinical Trials, Vaccinal Coverage and Interactions with Novel Variants," *Current Medicinal Chemistry*, Vol. 29, No. 15, pp. 2673–2690.

Economic Commission for Latin America and the Caribbean (2020) "Measuring the Impact of COVID-19 with a View to Reactivation," *Special Report COVID-19*, No. 2, 21 April, available at https://repositorio.cepal.org/bitstream/handle/11362/45477/S2000285_en.pdf.

Economic Commission for Latin America and the Caribbean (2021) "Financing for Development in the Era of COVID-19 and Beyond – Priorities of Latin America and the Caribbean in Relation to the Financing for Development Global Policy Agenda," *Special Report COVID-19*, No. 10, 11 March, available at https://repositorio.cepal.org/bitstream/handle/11362/46711/1/S2100063_en.pdf

Elgin, C., Basbug, G., and Yalaman, A. (2020) "Economic Policy Responses to a Pandemic: Developing the COVID-19 Economic Stimulus Index," *COVID Economics*, No. 3, 10 April, pp. 40–53.

Flores Zendejas, J. and Gaillard, N. (2022) "The International Lender of Last Resort between Scylla and Charybdis," in Flores Zendejas, J., Gaillard, N. and Michalek, R. (Eds) *Moral Hazard – A Financial, Legal and Economic Perspective*. Abingdon and New York City: Routledge.

Griffith, I. (2021) "Vaccination and Vaccine Diplomacy in the Caribbean," *Global Americans*, available at https://theglobalamericans.org/wp-content/uploads/2021/12/Vaccines-and-Vaccine-Diplomacy-in-the-Caribbean.pdf.

Haas, E. B. (2008) *Beyond the Nation-State – Functionalism and International Organization*. Colchester: ECPR Press.

Ikenberry, G. J. (2010) "The Liberal International Order and Its Discontents," *Millennium*, Vol. 38, No. 3, pp. 509–521.

Ikenberry, G. J. (2020) *A World Safe for Democracy: Liberal Internationalism and the Crises of Global Order*. New Haven: Yale University Press.

International Monetary Fund (2012) *Annual Report 2012 – Working Together to Support Global Recovery*. Washington, DC: IMF.

International Monetary Fund (2022) *World Economic Outlook – Countering the Cost-of-Living Crisis*. October 2022. Washington, DC: IMF.

Iqbal, T., Imran, S., Tye, G., Zaman, K. and Nordin, F. (2022) "COVID-19 Vaccination Effectiveness: A Review in Early Vaccine Adopters in Asian Countries," *European Review for Medical and Pharmacological Sciences*, Vol. 26, pp. 4902–4925.

Jaramillo, C. (2022a) "Four New Year's Resolution Ideas for Latin America and the Caribbean," *World Bank Blogs*, 2 February, available at https://blogs.worldbank.org/latinamerica/four-new-years-resolution-ideas-latin-america-and-caribbean.

Jaramillo, C. (2022b) "Social Protection and COVID-19 in Latin America: Building on Achievements," *World Bank Blogs*, 15 March, available at https://blogs.worldbank.org/latinamerica/social-protection-and-COVID-19-latin-america-building-achievements.

Jervis, R. (1999) "Realism, Neoliberalism, and Cooperation – Understanding the Debate," *International Security*, Vol. 24, No. 1, pp. 42–63.

Kellner, T. and Wintgens, S. (Eds) (2021) *China–Latin America and the Caribbean – Assessment and Outlook*. London and New York City: Routledge.

Keohane, R. and Nye, J. (2012) *Power and Interdependence* (Fourth Edition). Boston and New York City: Longman.

Lee, S. T. (2021) "Vaccine Diplomacy: Nation Branding and China's COVID-19 Soft Power Play," *Place Branding and Public Diplomacy*, available at https://link.springer.com/article/10.1057/s41254-021-00224-4.

Marczak, J. and Guevara, C. (2021) *COVID-19 Recovery in Latin America and the Caribbean – A Partnership Strategy for the Biden Administration*. Washington, DC: Atlantic Council.

Milner, H. V. (1997) *Interests, Institutions, and Information: Domestic Politics and International Relations*. Princeton: Princeton University Press.

Mowla, W. and Zhang, P. (2022) "Latin America and the Caribbean's Asymmetrical Engagement with China during the COVID-19 Pandemic," *Georgetown Journal of International Affairs*, 18 January, available at https://gjia.georgetown.edu/2022/01/18/latin-america-and-the-caribbeans-asymmetrical-engagement-with-china-during-the-COVID-19-pandemic.

Myers, M. (2021) "China's COVID-19 Diplomacy in Latin America and the Caribbean: Motivations and Methods," *Jack D. Gordon Institute for Public Policy* and *The Dialogue*, available at https://digitalcommons.fiu.edu/cgi/viewcontent.cgi?article=1039&context=jgi_research.

Organisation for Economic Co-operation and Development (2020a) *Health at a Glance: Latin America and the Caribbean 2020*. Paris: OECD.

Organisation for Economic Co-operation and Development (2020b) *COVID-19 in Latin America and the Caribbean: An Overview of Government Responses to the Crisis*. Paris: OECD.

Organisation for Economic Co-operation and Development, Economic Commission for Latin America and the Caribbean, Development Bank of Latin America, and

European Commission (2021) *Latin American Economic Outlook 2021: Working Together for a Better Recovery*. Paris: OECD.

Pan American Health Organization (2022) *Pan American Health Organization Response to COVID-19, January–June 2022 – Mid-Year Summary Report, Key Indicators and Selected Highlights*. Washington, DC: PAHO.

Peeri, N. C., Shrestha, N., Rahman, M. S., Zaki, R., Tan, Z., Bibi, S., Baghbanzadeh, M., Aghamohammadi, N., Zhang, W. and Haque, U. (2020) "The SARS, MERS and Novel Coronavirus (COVID-19) Epidemics, the Newest and Biggest Global Health Threats: What Lessons Have We Learned?," *International Journal of Epidemiology*, Vol. 49, No. 3, pp. 717–726.

Pforzheimer, A. (2021) "Pandemic Help to Latin America and the Caribbean: The Roles of USAID and the Department of State," *Wilson Center's Latin American Program*, available at https://www.wilsoncenter.org/publication/pandemic-help-latin-america-and-caribbean-roles-usaid-and-department-state.

Ponce, D. (2020) "The Impact of Coronavirus in Brazil: Politics and the Pandemic," *Nature Reviews Nephrology*, Vol. 16, No. 9, p. 483.

Ray, R., Albright, Z. C. and Wang, K. (2021) *China–Latin America Economic Bulletin – 2021 Edition*. Boston: Global Development Policy Center.

Ruggie, J. G. (1992) "Multilateralism: The Anatomy of an Institution," *International Organization*, Vol. 46, No. 3, pp. 561–598.

Rutschman, A. S. (2021) "Is There a Cure for Vaccine Nationalism?," *Current History*, Vol. 120, No. 822, pp. 9–14.

Sanborn, C. (2020) "Latin America and China in Times of COVID-19," *Wilson Center's Latin American Program* and *Kissinger Institute on China and the United States*, available at https://www.wilsoncenter.org/sites/default/files/media/uploads/documents/FINAL%20Updated%20Sanborn%20Article.pdf.

Schmucker, C. (2020) "The Effects of the COVID-19 Pandemic on US and European Commitment to the Multilateral Economic Order," *Istituto Affari Internazionali (IAI), Paper 20/39*.

Schwalb, A., Armyra, E., Méndez-Aranda, M. and Ugarte-Gil, C. (2022) "COVID-19 in Latin America and the Caribbean: Two Years of the Pandemic," *Journal of Internal Medicine*, Vol. 292, No. 3, pp. 409–427.

Segal, S. (2021) "International Financial Institutions' COVID-19 Approvals through Q1 2021 Surpass $260 Billion," *Center for Strategic & International Studies*, 4 May, available at https://www.csis.org/analysis/international-financial-institutions-COVID-19-approvals-through-q1-2021-surpass-260.

Silver, L., Devlin, K. and Huang, C. (2020) "Unfavorable Views of China Reach Historic Highs in Many Countries," *Pew Research Center*, 6 October, available at https://www.pewresearch.org/global/2020/10/06/unfavorable-views-of-china-reach-historic-highs-in-many-countries.

Stubbs, T., Kring, W., Laskaridis, C., Kentikelenis, A. and Gallagher, K. (2021) "Whatever It Takes? The Global Financial Safety Net, COVID-19, and Developing Countries," *World Development*, Vol. 137, 105171.

U.S. Department of State (2021) "U.S. Government Support to El Salvador, Guatemala, Honduras, and Mexico During the COVID-19 Pandemic," 20 January, available at https://www.state.gov/u-s-government-support-to-el-salvador-guatemala-honduras-and-mexico-during-the-COVID-19-pandemic.

Werner, A., Ivanova, A. and Komatsuzaki, T. (2021) "Latin America and Caribbean's Winding Road to Recovery," *IMF Blog*, 8 February, available at https://www.imf.org/en/Blogs/Articles/2021/02/08/blog-latin-america-and-caribbeans-winding-road-to-recovery.

World Bank (2020) "World Bank Support for Country Access to COVID-19 Vaccines," available at https://www.worldbank.org/en/who-we-are/news/coronavirus-COVID19/world-bank-support-for-country-access-to-COVID-19-vaccines.

World Bank (2021) "The World Bank Group Responding to the COVID-19 Pandemic and Rebuilding Better," available at https://thedocs.worldbank.org/en/doc/bb1b191f6b1bd1f932d0ddc5492987ec-0090012021/original/WBG-Responding-to-the-COVID-19-Pandemic-and-Rebuilding-Better.pdf

Part IV

Revamping the liberal international order

11 Global climate change governance

Three models into one?

Andy Hira and Ronaldo Au-Yeung

The central challenge for global climate change governance is to overcome negative externalities and create collective action. The current voluntary agreements have failed to stem temperature increases. In this chapter, we examine how China, the United States, and the European Union – the largest greenhouse gas (GHG) emitters – have fought global warming. The European Union is the undisputed leader of GHG emissions reduction owing to a strong domestic support and the development of green jobs. In the United States, the lobbying power of the fossil fuel industry has stymied policy progress at the national level. In fact, climate change policies have flourished within U.S. states. China presents the clearest path for emissions reduction by responding to the enormous domestic costs of climate change through centralized as well as decentralized planning. However, this approach has been complicated by China's economic development. We find lessons for a more effective global system. These include transparency on climate change costs and GHG emissions reduction, the value of policy experimentation, the payoff of integrating energy markets, the business opportunities created by the green transition, and the need to subsidize the losers of this transition.

11.1 Climate change as a collective action problem

In this chapter, we review the challenge of climate change in the context of the emerging tripolar world order of the 21st century, with the United States, China, and the European Union playing crucial roles in the global response to climate change. By its nature, climate change is an existential threat of global proportions, with unique historical characteristics that require a unique global response. Responding effectively to climate change will stretch global governance arrangements beyond the patchwork of regimes designed primarily around facilitating global trade and finance.

The Intergovernmental Panel on Climate Change (IPCC), a global group of scientists who gather under the umbrella of the United Nations (UN), is considered the foremost authority on research into climate change. The IPCC estimates that the Earth has already warmed up 1.07°C from 1900 to 2019. It points to shifts in weather patterns and the melting of the polar ice caps

DOI: 10.4324/9781003340430-15

among the many resulting changes from global warming. There are a plethora of well-known negative effects that will manifest as warming continues, including sea level rises wiping out low-lying countries, regions, and cities; changes in precipitation patterns, with some areas becoming wetter and others much drier, disrupting food production and ecosystems more generally; ocean acidification with major impacts on marine life; a higher frequency of severe weather events; and, if the "tipping point" of 2°C is surpassed, there could be long-term shifts in weather patterns (IPCC, 2021).

Reviewing a few key concepts from environmental economics helps to explain the nature of the governance challenge. The first and foremost challenge, externalities, are costs (or benefits) not borne by the producer or consumer (Pigou, 1920). A classic example of a negative externality is pollution. A related concept is the overestimated "discount rate," where future costs are underestimated by current market participants. Climate change is a classic example where rationality fails because of myopic understanding of discount rates. Finally, there is the key concept of the "tragedy of the commons," where publicly shared spaces tend to deteriorate as no particular user is responsible for their maintenance (Hardin, 1968). This is exemplified by the overfishing in international waters. The complications around climate change clearly fit within the externality, discount rate, and commons issues. The challenge is thus a collective action or public goods problem: no state is incentivized to reduce its greenhouse gas (GHG) emissions as long as available alternative energy sources are more costly than fossil fuels. All the major emitting states must agree to reduce emission simultaneously in order to avoid the "free rider" problem, whereby an individual state can cheat while still enjoying the collective good (Olson, 1965). The conditions often described as necessary for collective goods provision – whether we are posing the question in terms of common pool resource management, "polycentric governance," "adaptive governance," or "socio-ecological systems" – are transparency, monitoring, and enforcement, together with a relatively slow depletion of resources (Dietz et al., 2003; Chaffin et al., 2014). Currently, all of the above conditions are missing from global climate change governance.

Two sets of solutions are suggested for improving climate change governance. The first is to essentially rely on markets, or rather on adjustments within the financial and insurance markets following anticipated technological breakthroughs that will offer less harmful substitutes to fossil fuels. However, the IPCC's warnings suggest that relying on a road with indeterminate timing would risk the future of the planet given the urgency of the issue. The other solution is regulation, which can take on a very wide array of forms, from outright bans (such as those on harmful chlorofluorocarbon production), to requiring lower emission standards, providing subsidies for new technologies, changing production systems through carbon taxes and "internalizing" negative externalities, thus reflecting their true price to society and the individual consumers (Pigou, 1920; Coase, 1960). One market-based regulatory pathway is the "cap and trade" model. This approach would enforce a cap on externalities but then allow trading between those with room "under their cap" with those whose cap is limiting their current production processes. One would slowly lower the cap over time, thus incentivizing innovation in pollution-reducing devices by the private sector (Jaffe et al., 2005). The bottom line is clear: unless there is a global governance framework in place – one that addresses the challenges of enforcement, international competition, and the uneven distribution of technology and resources – no effective regulation can be created.

11.2 Climate change as a global governance problem

Existing regulatory solutions have failed to reverse GHG emissions because of two major factors. The first is the power of lobbying groups. In line with collective action theory, vested existing interests are far more powerful than dispersed potential ones, even if the benefits stemming from the latter outweigh the costs stemming from the former. This reflects the reality of fossil fuels and carbon "lock in" whereby the sunk costs of a fossil fuel-based economy (and the habits and routines linked to it) give it huge advantages beyond price differences from substitutes (Unruh, 2000). The second factor is the focus of this chapter: namely, the difficulty in creating a global governance framework that can generate regulatory action across regions in a way that stimulates collective action. Collective action theory tells us that transparency and enforceability problems are the key obstacles to steady provision. Transparency in this case includes not only being able to measure emission levels but also some rewards or at least recognition for countries willing to take positive steps toward transforming their economies. Table 11.1 presents a breakdown of GHG emissions. Approximately 50% of global emissions come from China, the United States, and the European Union.

In theory, the global regimes around climate change, such as the IPCC, could serve as quasi-institutions for collective action, monitoring information and using it to "enforce" compliance (Abbott, 2012). After the demise of the 1997 Kyoto Protocol because of U.S. withdrawal, the EU-based idea of binding targets has shifted toward voluntary national commitments.

Table 11.1 Top emissions sources in the world, 2010–2018, and their evolution during 1990–2018

	% of world emissions, 2010–2018 average	*% change during 1990–2018*
China	26.3%	+559.3%
United States	13.8%	+11.5%
European Union	8.4%	-22.4%
India	6.7%	+352.1%
Russian Federation	5.7%	+13.5%

Source: Authors calculations based on World Bank's World Development Indicators.

As Biermann et al. (2009) point out, the current global governance system is based primarily on getting countries to accept norms and principles around the facts of climate change and, by implication, the need for action upon it, as reflected in the 1992 UN Framework Convention on Climate Change. As such, the current targets are built with limited formal roles anticipated for international organizations; action depends on individual governments as reflected in the term, "common but differentiated responsibilities and respective capabilities" (CBDRRC). This approach was strengthened in the 1997 Kyoto Protocol, the 2016 Paris Agreement, and the 2021 Glasgow Agreement. The principles for action depend on "nationally determined contributions" – each country volunteering a level of reduction to which it would pledge. A secondary principle was the substantial reduction, mitigation, and adaptation assistance from the northern hemisphere (North) to the southern hemisphere (South). Targeted promises of assistance are estimated at around $100 billion per year, but with just a fraction of that being actually committed. The voluntary nature of these agreements was underscored when the United States pulled out during the Trump administration. Beyond the problematic collective action aspects of voluntary commitments without enforcement are three other serious issues: the lack of transparency over compliance; the lack of clear roadmaps to achieve the targets; and the lack of capacity of many states in the South toward climate change emissions reduction, and mitigation and adaptation.

The global governance regime depends on voluntary action by the major "sub-units" (i.e., nations and regions). China, the United States, and the European Union can act upon climate change: they have accepted the reality publicly; they have the financial and technical resources to act; and they have the institutions to enact sweeping new national or regional regulations (Eisenack et al., 2014). Despite its junior geopolitical status (see Gaillard and Waibel's and Lim's chapters in this book), the EU has been the leader in global climate governance issues and is the only major region that has managed to cut its emissions since the 1990s.

In sum, while formal multi-level and multi-actor coordination is required, developing a global authority around harmonized regulation seems currently beyond reach. Some experts posit that a global authority may not be necessary if multiple actors at different levels ("polycentricity") are all working in the same direction on climate change (Sovacool, 2011). We argue that the problem and its solution are analogous to the efforts in the EU and the United States to coordinate different countries and states, respectively. Next, we contrast these polycentric systems with the centralized one in China for lessons on governance.

11.3 Three different approaches to climate change

11.3.1 Overview

In this section, we explore climate change governance strategies in the European Union, the United States, and China. We see each of these strategies as attempts to solve collective action problems by coordinating, respectively, the member nations, the states, and the provinces, toward a common aim of reducing emissions and meeting targets. In fact, two different systems of decision-making emerge, which is a central obstacle to moving toward a global authority on climate change (Bernauer, 2013). As democracies, the EU and the U.S. struggle to plan over the long term. Their decisions tend to be made according to election cycles of 5 years or less. Moreover, elections themselves mean that politicians and regulators may be subject to "capture" by lobbying groups from fossil fuel and other industries eager to preserve the status quo.

By the same token, as private market economies, the EU and the United States face domestic collective action issues. They simply cannot match the ability of China to impose regulations (regardless of popular support or the lack thereof) in line with long-term development plans. They face serious incumbent lobbies in the fossil fuel sector. However, private markets have historically been more innovative, responding to the exigencies of competition. They likely offer a possibility for solutions financed in part by private capital and benefitting from greater scrutiny and testing through market competition. Moreover, the greater freedom given to civil society in the West allows the potential for social movements and activists, such as Greenpeace and Greta Thunberg, to work to change public values, creating support for policy shifts. In contrast, the non-governmental organizations (NGOs) in China are at best understood as persuaders and lobbyists, but not "watchdogs," given their political environment (Liu et al., 2017). In the sense that Western political systems are, by design, polycentric, there is greater ability for individual cities and regions to lead national policy, creating the space for diverse policy experimentation and local tailoring. But such systems allow the chance for others to lag and free ride. Conflict over the distribution of costs and benefits of adaptation are more likely as well (Carlisle and Gruby, 2019). While important, the "democracy vs. authoritarian regime" dichotomy fails to explain the EU's superior response to climate change, which suggests that other factors must be at work. As Kuzemko et al. (2016) point out, governance systems and resource and energy systems go together. The nature of the existing energy systems and the availability of resources constrain such systems and enable them to adapt. Contextual factors are highlighted as we review governance in each region.

11.3.2 The European Union

The EU's active efforts toward climate change began around the 1992 United Nations Framework Convention on Climate Change (UNFCCC). Since then, the green movements have gained strength in the region and grown through the opportunities provided by proportional representation (PR) voting systems. The EU has been a consistent champion of global climate change agreements, including the 1997 Kyoto Protocol. That Protocol set out voluntary emissions reduction commitments but was throttled by the U.S. withdrawal from the agreement in 2001. The EU nonetheless committed to follow the Protocol, accepting to cut emissions by 8% of 1990 levels by 2010 (Schreurs and Tiberghien, 2007). In 2009, it advanced the even more ambitious target of an 80–95% reduction in GHG by 2050 compared to 1990 levels. In line with this, it set out targets for renewable energy, including 20% of all energy and at least 34% of electricity (Jägemann et al., 2013).

The EU has a unique system of "supranational" governance. While member states retain full sovereignty and control over national laws, the EU allows them to come together to create "common" policies. The EU is composed of three principal bodies: the European Commission, the European Parliament, and the Council of the European Union. The Commission, which has representatives from each state and is headed by a President, is the key initiator of legislation, and the main enforcement body. The initiatives proposed by the Commission are then moved to the Council, which negotiates and adopts legislative acts together with the European Parliament (this is also called the "codecision" principle). The EU's overall decision-making process has been analyzed extensively, reflecting various concepts, from "elite bargaining" to "neofunctionalism" and "liberal intergovernmentalism" (Dupont, 2015, pp. 9–11 and 44–46).

On a supranational level, authors argue that EU elites saw the issue of climate governance as a way to assert European leadership and reinforce international law and norms. The nature of the EU as a community of states is the foundation for their global approach, as internal decision-making requires reaching fully voluntary agreement among member states. This is partly accomplished by differentiating burdens for a large number of member states. Therefore, much of the impetus has to be linked to the leadership of the dominant economies – i.e., Germany, the United Kingdom (a member until recently), and France, who have embraced proactive climate change policies (Schreurs and Tiberghien, 2007).

It is also important to point to the domestic pressures in key EU states regarding climate change. In Germany, the Netherlands, and Scandinavian countries, there are strong green party movements which have taken advantage of PR voting systems to promote climate change policy. The advances made to fight global warming have occurred despite the powerful dependence on foreign fossil fuel, highlighted by the dilemma posed by how to handle Russian oil and gas imports following the invasion of Ukraine. Beyond these negative forces lies the incentive of developing leadership in emerging green industries under the general banner of the "Green New Deal" (Bloomfield and Steward, 2020). However, the green transition is still subject to claims of an environment-industry trade-off, especially among populist and alt-right parties (Jahn, 2021). Ultimately, stronger support for green values underlies the contrast between the EU and the United States (Grant and Tilley, 2019).

The lack of a robust fossil fuel sector outside of the North Sea region also differentiates the EU from the United States, home to some of the largest private oil companies. By the same token, EU countries do not have the plethora of state-owned oil industries active in China, India, Russia, and throughout the Middle East. Perhaps equally important are the roles of industry and public opinion in influencing the EU's championing of climate change policy. Public opinion is far more supportive of climate change policies in the EU, owing to the rise of the Green party in Germany, the experience of the OPEC oil crisis and the clear dependence on fossil fuel imports that continues today. The Chernobyl nuclear disaster also exerted a significant influence, helping to spark a search for "clean" renewable energy. The EU has endeavored to harness the power of public opinion and has formally tried to marshal civil society and business leaders through its Climate Change Programme (Jordan et al., 2012). However, the power of industry lobby groups is not entirely absent, as seen in the slow drawdown of the coal sector in Germany and part of Eastern Europe; they are just less powerful than the other groups.

The primary mechanisms within the EU for emissions reduction are voluntary national commitments. In fact, Helm (2014) points out that there are two broad mechanisms: the internal energy market (IEM) and the climate change package (CCP). The IEM includes measures to allow for the creation of market-based mechanisms, such as unbundling and third-party access within member states with an aim toward harmonization of regulations. This should promote a harmonized competitive energy market, engendering economies of scale and enabling access to diverse renewable energy sources. However, harmonization has been plodding, and basic issues such as infrastructure connections still lag (Helm, 2014). The CCP includes support for renewables and relies on the Emissions Trading System (ETS). The ETS, which sets a long-term cap that reduces overall emissions over time and allows for companies to trade permits, has had a limited effectiveness so far. Several explanations can be advanced: it only covers large industry installations; initial market distortions remain significant; the price for emissions has been set too low; and reductions that would likely have already taken place (such as coal plants closing) now receive additional payments (Böhringer et al., 2009).

The EU shows remarkable success in terms of emissions reduction for its member states, but it does not provide a clear model for global governance of climate change. Its models of transition were based on the expectation that (i) fossil fuel prices would rise quickly and (ii) those of alternatives and renewables would decline sufficiently to make them competitive (Helm, 2014). This has hardly proven to be the case, due in part to the development of "fracking" and offshore drilling bringing new supply to the fossil fuel market. Dreams of large competitive green energy companies to rival those of the fossil fuel industry have only been partly realized, with the EU's early leaders such as offshore wind leader Vestas losing market share over time to its Chinese competitors. The EU's efforts to enforce membership commitments have also been haphazard, with the incentive of creating a unified energy market falling short due to the resistance of national authorities and to the EU Commission lacking enough fiscal space to incentivize harmonization in renewables promotion. More importantly, there are no real mechanisms by which to reduce fossil fuel dependence outside the core leadership states. In Germany, the Nordstream deal for Russian natural gas – which was seriously impaired by the explosion of one of the two critical pipelines as well as by political pressures due to the Ukraine War – and the temporary shift back to coal and liquefied natural gas suggests that the transition away from fossil fuel-based energy has been painful. As discussed, the failure of the ETS raises additional doubts. Finally, the rise of populism in Europe has been a significant slowing factor, but, overall, there remains a strong commitment to region-wide climate change policies.

The effective ongoing green shift in Western EU states does set an example for the rest of the world on how to use policy instruments – such as feed-in tariffs, higher petrol and parking taxes, and subsidies for public transportation – to close the remaining cost gaps between fossil fuels and renewables. The fact the EU is the largest global market gives it a significant advantage to shift action in the rest of the world. The subsidies provided under the European Green Deal will help to spur private sector adaptation and innovation toward broader circular economic objectives.[1] Abundant resources have been applied to assuage reluctant and fossil fuel-dependent Eastern European members to sign on to EU-level goals. Market access in the future will be shaped by sustainability standards, particularly the carbon border tax, which will impose levies on all imports based upon their level of carbon inputs.[2]

11.3.3 The United States

Hayes and Knox-Hayes (2014) argue that the principal difference in the way the U.S. administration has approached climate change compared to the EU is that Washington has posited it largely as a security challenge, not an environmental necessity or economic opportunity. This is supported by the fact that the Pentagon has cited climate change in its security threat reports (U.S. Department of Defense, 2021).

The reasons can be traced to the well-publicized role of U.S. oil companies in promoting climate change denial (Supran, 2021), an effort that has been supported by a wide range of Republican candidates – including former presidents Bush Jr. and Trump, who were responsible for withdrawing from the Kyoto Protocol and the Paris Agreement, respectively. Such messaging is rife throughout the United States, propagated by leading right-wing news outlets, such as Fox News and a variety of think tanks reflecting powerful corporate neoliberal perspectives (Hein and Jenkins, 2017). Not only are the oil and gas sector and their allies powerful, but governance arrangements in the United States inhibit decisive action. The Senate reflects geographical, not popular, representation, thus giving outsized influence to oil- and gas-producing states such as Texas, Louisiana, Oklahoma, and North Dakota. Passage of foreign treaties requires the support of two-thirds of the members of the Senate.

Besides, there are major regulatory limitations to what the federal government can do to create an integrated electricity market across the states. The landscape remains a byzantine patchwork of haphazard regional trading arrangements (Welton, 2021).

Despite these formidable obstacles, the United States has been a supporter of global climate change transition in important ways. It has been a major contributor to the IPCC. It has helped to promote new policy implementation ideas, including emissions trading and joint implementation. With the arrival of the Biden administration in 2021, the United States rejoined the Paris Agreement and supported the Glasgow Agreement, while reaching a bilateral accord on climate change with China related to the efforts of the diplomatic envoy John Kerry (Bang and Schreurs, 2017).[3]

Domestic federal regulation has been stymied by Republican opposition. Therefore, the Obama administration relied primarily on executive orders to move forward climate actions, such as increasing fuel economy standards for vehicles. The Environmental Protection Agency, with the authority to regulate GHG emissions, was a primary regulatory vehicle. Obama's willingness to sign the Paris Agreement followed the fracking revolution of the 2000s, when plentiful natural gas with lower emissions began to undercut the economic viability of coal. Many of the executive orders were rapidly undone by the subsequent Trump administration, and then resurrected under Biden. President Biden's $1.2 trillion infrastructure package, passed in November 2021, contained significant funding for public transit and incentives for the manufacture and purchase of electric vehicles (EVs). Biden's proposed Build Back Better legislation contains substantial funding for climate change transition, mirroring the political preference for inducements such as spending projects, as opposed to disincentives, such as taxes. Biden has cleverly tied climate change, following the EU example, to the promise of green jobs. This is reflected in proposed policies such as those around "critical supply chains" promoting US-based EV battery development (Reinsch and Benson, 2021).

The challenges at the federal level mean that many significant climate actions have occurred under individual state leadership. Most states have adopted some measures, such as renewable portfolio standards, which require their utilities to create a certain percentage of their electricity over time from renewable energy. In the Northeast, the governors have set up a regional cap-and-trade emissions system. The foremost example of state leadership is California, which raised fuel economy standards and offers a range of support to promote the transition to EVs.[4] California also created an emissions trading system in 2012, shared with Québec, under which a ceiling for carbon emissions slowly declines over time.[5] The variation of activities in states and cities can be linked to partisanship (consistent with income and citizens' values), state level administrative capacity (tied to income and tax receipts), local presence of fossil fuel industries, and a state's vulnerability to climate change and increasing frequency of extreme weather events (Miao, 2019; Bromley-Trujillo and Holman, 2020). The last factor may help to explain why Texas is a leader in renewable energy, particularly in creating large wind farms over the past decade. Several authors argue that states that have unbundled their utility monopolies have more robust climate change policies because this move has reduced incumbent interest groups' power (Lee, 2020; Culhane et al., 2021).

The main lesson from the review of American climate policy is that, even in the face of intransigent opposition for national level action, large subnational actors can push action forward. Their regulatory initiatives, as illustrated in California, can create regulatory waves in other states.

11.3.4 China

China is both the largest developing country and a geopolitical superpower, with economic might to rival the United States and the European Union. As seen in Figure 11.1, the main source of China's domestic electricity is coal, a major cause of GHG emissions. Yet, China reduced its reliance on coal, from a peak of 79% of electricity generation in 2005 to 63.5% in 2020. Natural gas as a fuel increased significantly, but only accounted for 3% of electricity generation in 2020, less than the 6% from wind, 4.7% from nuclear, and 3.4% from solar.

In fact, China has been aggressive in taking climate actions. While historically opposing strong climate actions and giving top priority to the CBDRRC principle espoused within the UNFCCC, China officially started its "green revolution" in 2007 with the publication of its first *National Climate Change Program* and has since then been following a transitional path to sustainable

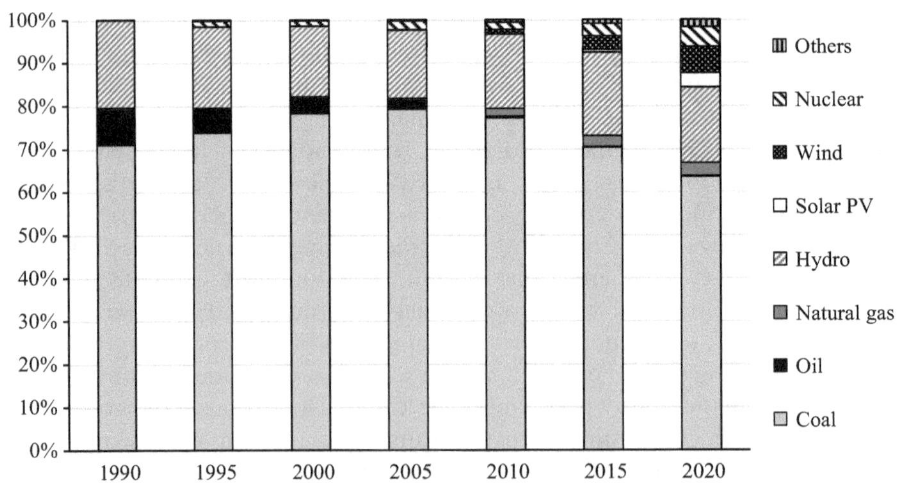

Figure 11.1 China's electricity generation by source, 1990–2020

Source: https://www.iea.org/countries/china.

development. Since 2008, it has been publishing annual white papers on *Policies and Actions for Addressing Climate Change* to announce the outcome of its climate actions. In 2009, prior the Copenhagen Conference, it pledged to reduce GHG emissions by 40–45% by 2020, a target that was achieved 3 years ahead of schedule.[6] In 2014, Beijing issued its *National Climate Change Plan (2014–2020)*. Recently, it has committed to the "two carbon goals": peaking GHG emissions by 2030 and achieving carbon neutrality in 2060.

The first part of the explanation about China's U-turn in its climate policy direction is the change in China's self-perception from a developing country during the 1990s to a global superpower with responsibilities under President Xi Jinping from 2013. Climate actions are increasingly regarded as a critical component of China's image in the world (Kuhn, 2015). In taking strong climate actions, China also attempts to delegitimize the Pax Americana, especially after the United States withdrew from the Paris Agreement (Hodzi and Yu-Wen, 2018). This shift in China's self-perception is reflected in its efforts to organize a sub-group: the so-called "BASIC" (for Brazil, South Africa, India, and China) to work as a coalition in global climate change negotiations. It has also offered climate change assistance of $3.1 billion in 2015 to provide the South with climate change adaptation policies. They complement the efforts made through the Asian Infrastructure Investment Bank and the New Development Bank (which China primarily finances) to support green infrastructure initiatives (Li, 2016) and the Belt and Road Initiative.

Another part of the explanation on China's climate policy shift is related to international pressures (Schroeder, 2008; Heggelund et al., 2010). These pressures are mainly manifested during diplomatic exchanges. While they often fail to make tangible behavioral change of the Chinese government in such issues as human rights (Wachman, 2001), such pressures arguably helped alter China's climate policy direction, as one interview by Schroeder (2008, p. 515) with a representative of an international environmental NGO in China suggests:

> Every time foreign leaders come to China, they want to discuss climate change. Every time Hu Jintao goes abroad, foreign leaders want to discuss climate change. It is really getting on his nerves. The Chinese delegation submitted this very constructive proposal to the Bali COP/MOP, because the leader had said "you must do something to reduce the pressure on my shoulders."

China's *National Climate Change Program* published in 2007 may also be interpreted as a reaction to rising international concerns over the country's significant GHG emissions (Heggelund et al., 2010). China's participation in climate negotiations sought to demonstrate its re-emergence on the international stage after gaining its permanent seat at the UN Security Council following Resolution 2758 of 1971 (Kuhn, 2015). Before 2007, its efforts remained most evident in climate negotiations (particularly about the CBDRRC principle) but much less in enduring behavioral changes. When the Kyoto Protocol was tabled in 1997, Beijing showed fervent allegiance to the CBDRRC principle, arguing it would not consider emissions reduction obligations until becoming a "medium level developed country in the middle of the 21st century" (cited in Zhang, 2007). While China continues to claim proportional climate responsibilities according to "national conditions" up to Glasgow,[7] the "medium level developed country" argument has lost its credibility and is now rarely heard (Heggelund et al., 2010). In fact, China has changed its climate negotiation position in 2008, now pointing out that "climate change arises out of development and should thus be solved along with development" (Information Office of the State Council of the People's Republic of China, 2008).

The third part of the explanation relates to the role of NGOs (Wang et al., 2018; Liu et al., 2017). Chinese environmental NGOs primarily function to influence the state's climate policy through persuasion. Given China's political environment, they are mainly lobbyists and implementers – as opposed to activists and watchdogs. Their persuasion strategy appears to have paid off. Following the 2004 "26-Degree Campaign" organized by six NGOs that advocated that air conditioners should be set at 26°C in the summer for energy savings, the State Council accepted the suggestion with an additional requirement that all air conditioners in public space not exceed 20°C in the winter (Wang et al., 2018).

Perhaps the best explanation for the shift in China's climate policy direction is the "internalization" of the externalities associated with climate change at the national level. China is among the most climate vulnerable countries, a fact that has greatly changed China's sentiment about climate change. This perception is well-reflected in Xi's opening statement at Paris. He remarked:

> In the past few decades, China has seen rapid economic growth and significant improvement in people's lives. However, this has taken a toll on the environment and resources. Having learned the lesson, China is vigorously making ecological endeavors to promote green, circular, and low-carbon growth.[8]

Among these lessons learned is the recognition that China has the highest global exposure to sea level rise (Asian Development Bank, 2015). From 1951 to 2020, China's average temperature has increased by 0.26°C every decade, significantly higher than the global average and causing an annual sea level rising rate of 3.4 mm (National Climate Center, 2021). Up to 57 million people in coastal China – especially in Shanghai and Guangdong – could be displaced by the end of the century, according to recent scientific research (Kulp and Strauss, 2019). Moreover, the intensity and severity of extreme events in China has increased (National Climate Center, 2021).

In August 2021 alone, the Chinese Meteorological Administration issued 48,496 disaster warnings (Information Office of the State Council of the People's Republic of China, 2021), not to mention the Henan floods. These disasters cost 156 human lives as well as a direct economic loss of $6.4 billion in the first half of 2021.[9]

In addition to extreme events, higher temperatures and changes in precipitation pose further threats to human security. It is estimated that China's agricultural productivity will decline by 10%, with up to a 40% reduction in rice production by the mid-century due to climate change (Asian Development Bank, 2015; King et al., 2015). Chinese scholars expect a decreasing amount of water available for distribution through the South-to-North Water Diversion Project (Tan et al., 2017). Furthermore, glacial melt in the Qinghai-Tibet Plateau is also causing additional concerns about human security. A scientific study reveals that a temperature increase of 1–2°C would result in up to 30 cm sag of the permafrost in which the Qinghai-Tibet Railway are built on (Tan et al., 2017). Disruptions of the railway could obstruct the movement of agricultural goods (Asian Development Bank, 2015) and of lithium – which is mainly located in Southwest China and is required for a transition to a green economy (Wang, 2016).

China also sees the payoffs for a green industrial policy. Approximately 75% of its oil usage relies on imports,[10] but it is the world's largest renewable energy investor and producer of green technologies. It also has one of the largest lithium reserves in the world, ranking only behind the "Lithium Triangle" and the United States (Wang, 2016). Its renewable energy sector has, either directly or indirectly, created more than 4.7 million employment opportunities (International Renewable Energy Agency and International Labour Organization, 2021). According to China's 5-year plans, such industries are critical to its future economic well-being, particularly its ability to continue to lead in EVs. As early as 2009, the *Policies and Actions for Addressing Climate Change* report recognized new energy vehicles as a "breakthrough point" to develop circular economy (Information Office of the State Council of the People's Republic of China, 2009). More recently, President Xi Jinping pushed even harder to promote car electrification (State Council, 2020).

However, it bears mentioning that Beijing's decision-making is more decentralized than often realized, despite single-party rule (Tan, 2014, 2020, 2021; see also Gotoh and Li's chapter in this book). In fact, the climate policy responses of the central and subnational governments differ substantially with some subnational administrations having limited incentives to implement national policies to address climate change (Teng and Wang, 2021). Yet, China's polycentric decision-making process does not seem to weaken its climate responses on the global stage. On the contrary, the national government in Beijing is likely to adopt more ambitious climate policies to offset possible non-compliance of state directions at provincial and local levels, as it was observed in response to World Trade Organization entry (Tan 2020, 2021).

Although China has a strong record of upholding its climate commitments internationally (e.g., China's Copenhagen target) and recently pledged the "two carbon goals," it remains unclear how China plans to peak emissions by 2030 and become carbon-neutral by 2060. The success of future international climate negotiation is therefore dependent on a more transparent collaboration that is at the same time acceptable to China who favors a self-monitored approach to uphold climate commitments.

The key points from our review of China's policies are that global governance can be presented as a major opportunity for economic development, and "leapfrogging" to green industries. Even in an authoritarian regime, global pressures do affect policy decisions. Perhaps the most important inducement is awareness of the threats of climate change to national security and the opportunities for economic growth in emerging green sectors.

11.4 How to strengthen global climate change architecture and cooperation

How could we move from disparate national systems toward greater coordination in emissions reduction? Hale and Roger (2014) suggest "orchestration" is the right metaphor in a polycentric world. The term implies the attempt to move toward harmonization of efforts over time, to reduce redundancies and to create the possibilities for learning from the different players. Orchestration understands that international organizations (IOs) lack the authority to lead in climate change. Creating transparency around individual activities is a good starting point to avoiding collective action dilemmas, thus IOs might potentially play the role of information broker, if given sufficient autonomy and resources. IOs could also serve as arenas for discussion and negotiation, potentially leading in the direction of global policy consensus. In this way, the aspiration is that a "loose" and relatively uncoordinated polycentric system evolves into a tighter one over time. Transparency of national emissions would reduce free rider problems and reward reductions.

In line with this, the vital factor of knowledge cannot be underestimated. IPCC publications and reports presenting global effects of climate change are a starting point. However, more detailed national-level studies of the projected costs of adaptation would be more persuasive to countries in the South, as shown by the Chinese case. Large developing countries such as India and Indonesia, which can significantly impact global warming, do not yet realize that unconstrained climate change will have devastating effects on their ability to resolve what they regard as the most urgent priority: namely, national economic development.

There are also opportunities. China, the EU, and the United States all recognize that ambitions for global economic leadership require considering green industries. The critical minerals initiative of the United States reflects the concerns around these emerging vital supply chains in the same way as China's push toward leadership of electric vehicle and batteries. Thus, the wholly "negative" approach of the IPCC has to be balanced with a more positive approach of the opportunities that the green transition represents for economic development (Meckling, 2018). China's growing technological capacity and financial power offer the potential for speeding through breakthroughs that will fundamentally shift the costs of green energy.

While there is much to be admired for the way that the Chinese state has been able to pivot its economy, a polycentric system has the advantages of allowing for policy innovation. The United States offers several competing models from California and New York for climate transition. This would be reflected at the global level by the need to acknowledge local energy conditions and vulnerabilities to climate change. In the larger sense of collective action, as long as there is transparency in emissions, then the path individual countries follow to meet their obligations is not important.

This brings us back to the EU governance model, which shows information alone is not enough given the urgency of the problem. Different countries are operating at different speeds. The Nordic countries have been particularly aggressive in targeting near-zero emission energy systems by 2050, reflecting their high levels of income and their long-standing collective culture (Kotilainen et al., 2019). The EU provides subsidies, inducements, and other assistance to the "losers" of climate change, namely the fossil fuel industry; parallel to climate change aid pledges on the global level. It also attempts to create an energy market across states with a gradually declining ceiling for emissions. In this sense, it offers another insight into how global governance can be established, by creating market ties across states.

Integration of energy markets has huge potential advantages. It ties states' energy sectors together, thereby creating momentum for policy coordination. It also offers the ability to reduce the disadvantages of intermittency by developing a wider array of renewable sources and shifting demand management through complementary seasonality and time profiles. It furthermore allows for the sharing of costs of new climate change infrastructure, offering the advantages of economies of scale and greater competition. The challenge, as seen in the floundering of the ETS, is whether financial inducements will overcome the resistance of incumbent forces in the fossil fuel and utility sectors. They may be considered insufficient compared to the massive bailouts granted during the 2008 great recession and the 2020–2022 COVID-19 pandemic. This leaves one last tool as demonstrated by the EU. That is, tying market access to sustainability requirements through a carbon border tax. If the EU manages to hold steadfast in such policies, as in the case of California, this could have a major effect in accelerating the green transition.

Contingencies always matter in policy evolution. The Russian invasion of Ukraine may have speeded up global sentiments to reduce dependence on fossil fuel imports. However, it has also revealed that many economic sectors are based on fossil fuels. Higher prices perversely incentivize new exploration and development. All of this suggests that progress is likely to be slow, involving multiple compromises and negotiations with vested interests, as the world moves haltingly toward more sustainable economic systems. Such paradoxes are manifest in the fact that higher oil prices incentivize transition meanwhile they create cries for economic relief, presently directed toward reducing fossil fuel costs. Thus, a large popular and institutional push is required to reach the "tipping point" of mass market introduction of fossil fuel alternatives. Social forces along with entrepreneurs can accelerate such efforts not only by voting and lobbying but also through applying pressure for transparency around risks and financial costs of climate change, which could affect the highly concentrated large pools of investment capital represented by major pension funds, for example (Hira, 2023).

Building upon the Paris Agreement, the COP27 meeting in Sharm El Sheikh (November 2022) sought to improve monitoring and address the long-standing grievance of the South at the North's reluctance to take on historical responsibility and compensate the South for the costs of mitigation and adaptation. The meeting did not make progress on monitoring but a pledge for a compensation fund was agreed upon once assurances of no legal liability were gained. However, there is general skepticism about this move: in 2009, pledges had been made for $100 billion in global funding but very little actually materialized. Details are clearly lacking. Moreover, China has resisted committing to such a fund whereas the EU has pledged more than $300 million toward a climate insurance fund.[11]

A coherent regime is required to share knowledge around emissions reduction and climate change mitigation and adaptation, given the short time frames before intense weather changes will develop. One can also hope for large shifts in existing international regimes as climate change manifests, from changes and increases in migration patterns to attempts to keep green industrial policies within existing trading rules and norms.

Perhaps the most positive sign is that there is a generational shift in Western values as awareness of climate change and sensitivity to its effects deepen (Hamilton et al., 2019). Unfortunately, this shift has yet to be reflected in U.S. policy choices. Polycentric progress using the tools outlined in this chapter can be made only if the United States and China move toward a more aggressive phase-out of fossil fuels. Until then, we can expect climate change to exacerbate economic and geopolitical risks, including price volatility in food markets and massive migration.

Notes

1 See https://commission.europa.eu/strategy-and-policy/priorities-2019-2024/european-green-deal_en.
2 See https://taxation-customs.ec.europa.eu/green-taxation-0/carbon-border-adjustment-mechanism_en and https://ec.europa.eu/commission/presscorner/detail/en/qanda_21_3661.
3 See https://www.state.gov/u-s-china-joint-glasgow-declaration-on-enhancing-climate-action-in-the-2020s.
4 See https://afdc.energy.gov/fuels/laws/ELEC?state=CA.

5 See https://ww2.arb.ca.gov/our-work/programs/cap-and-trade-program/about.
6 See https://unfccc.int/news/china-meets-2020-carbon-target-three-years-ahead-of-schedule.
7 See https://asia.nikkei.com/Spotlight/Environment/Climate-Change/COP26/Full-text-of-Xi-Jinping-s-statement-at-COP26-climate-summit.
8 See https://www.chinadaily.com.cn/world/XiattendsParisclimateconference/2015-12/01/content_22592469.htm.
9 See https://www.ndrc.gov.cn/fggz/jjyxtj/yjgl/202107/t20210728_1291935.html?code=&state=123.
10 J. Clemente, "China Is the World's Largest Oil & Gas Importer," *Forbes*, 17 October 2019, available at https://www.forbes.com/sites/judeclemente/2019/10/17/china-is-the-worlds-largest-oil--gas-importer/?sh=4a917e435441.
11 B. Plumer, L. Friedman, M. Bearak, and J. Gross, "In a First, Rich Countries Agree to Pay for Climate Damages in Poor Nations," *New York Times*, 19 November 2022, available at https://www.nytimes.com/2022/11/19/climate/un-climate-damage-cop27.html; Z. Usman, "As Financial Pledges Trickle In, Did COP27 Meet Its Goal of Implementation?," *Carnegie Endowment for International Peace*, 21 November 2022, available at https://carnegieendowment.org/2022/11/21/as-financial-pledges-trickle-in-did-cop27-meet-its-goal-of-implementation-pub-88452.

References

Abbott, K. W. (2012) "The Transnational Regime Complex for Climate Change," *Environment and Planning C: Politics and Space*, Vol. 30, No. 4, pp. 571–590.

Asian Development Bank (2015) *Addressing Climate Change Risks, Disasters, and Adaptation in the People's Republic of China*. Manila: Asian Development Bank.

Bang, G. and Schreurs, M. A. (2017) "The United States: The Challenge of Global Climate Leadership in a Politically Divided State," in Wurzel, R., Connelly, J. and Liefferink, D. (Eds) *The European Union in International Climate Change Politics: Still Taking a Lead?* London: Routledge.

Bernauer, T. (2013) "Climate Change Politics," *Annual Review of Political Science*, Vol. 16, pp. 421–448.

Biermann, F., Pattberg, P., van Asselt, H. and Zelli, F. (2009) "The Fragmentation of Global Governance Architectures: A Framework for Analysis," *Global Environmental Politics*, Vol. 9, No. 4, pp. 14–40.

Bloomfield, J. and Steward, F. (2020) "The Politics of the Green New Deal," *The Political Quarterly*, Vol. 91, No. 4, pp. 770–779.

Böhringer, C., Löschel, A., Moslener, U. and Rutherford, T. S. (2009) "EU Climate Policy up to 2020: An Economic Impact Assessment," *Energy Economics*, Vol. 31, Sup. 2, pp. S295–S305.

Bromley-Trujillo, R. and Holman, M. R. (2020) "Climate Change Policymaking in the States: A View at 2020," *Publius: The Journal of Federalism*, Vol. 50, No. 3, pp. 446–472.

Carlisle, K. and Gruby, R. L. (2019) "Polycentric Systems of Governance: A Theoretical Model for the Commons," *Policy Studies Journal*, Vol. 47, No. 4, pp. 927–952.

Chaffin, B. C., Gosnell, H. and Cosens, B. A. (2014) "A Decade of Adaptive Governance Scholarship: Synthesis and Future Directions," *Ecology and Society*, Vol. 19, No. 3, Article 56.

Coase, R. H. (1960) "The Problem of Social Cost," *Journal of Law and Economics*, Vol. 3, No. 1, pp. 1–44.

Culhane, T., Hall, G. and Roberts, J. T. (2021) "Who Delays Climate Action? Interest Groups and Coalitions in State Legislative Struggles in the United States," *Energy Research & Social Science*, Vol. 79, 102114.

Dietz, T., Ostrom, E. and Stern, P. C. (2003) "The Struggle to Govern the Commons," *Science*, Vol. 302, No. 5652, pp. 1907–1912.

Dupont, C. (2015) *Climate Policy Integration into EU Energy Policy – Progress and Prospects*. London: Routledge.

Eisenack, K., Moser, S., Hoffmann, E., Klein, R., Oberlack, C., Pechan, A., Rotter, M. and Termeer, C. (2014) "Explaining and Overcoming Barriers to Climate Change Adaptation," *Nature Climate Change*, Vol. 4, pp. 867–872.

Grant, Z. P. and Tilley, J. (2019) "Fertile Soil: Explaining Variation in the Success of Green Parties," *West European Politics*, Vol. 42, No. 3, pp. 495–516.

Hale, T. and Roger, C. (2014) "Orchestration and Transnational Climate Governance," *Review of International Organizations*, Vol. 9, No. 1, pp. 59–82.

Hamilton, L. C., Hartter, J. and Bell, E. (2019) "Generation Gaps in US Public Opinion on Renewable Energy and Climate Change," *PLoS One*, Vol. 14, No. 7, pp. 1–20.

Hardin, G. (1968) "The Tragedy of the Commons," *Science*, Vol. 162, No. 3859, pp. 1243–1248.

Hayes, J. and Knox-Hayes, J. (2014) "Security in Climate Change Discourse: Analyzing the Divergence between US and EU Approaches to Policy," *Global Environmental Politics*, Vol. 14, No. 2, pp. 82–101.

Heggelund, G., Andresen, S. and Buan, I. F. (2010) "Chinese Climate Policy: Domestic Priorities, Foreign Policy, and Emerging Implementation," in Harrison, K. and McIntosh Sundstrom, L. (Eds) *Global Commons, Domestic Decisions – The Comparative Politics of Climate Change*. Cambridge (MA): MIT Press.

Hein, J. E. and Jenkins, J. C. (2017) "Why Does the United States Lack a Global Warming Policy? The Corporate Inner Circle versus Public Interest Sector Elites," *Environmental Politics*, Vol. 26, No. 1, pp. 97–117.

Helm, D. (2014) "The European Framework for Energy and Climate Policies," *Energy Policy*, Vol. 64, January, pp. 29–35.

Hira, A. (2023) *The Smoke and Mirrors Game of Global CSR Reporting – Issues and Fixes*. London: Anthem Press.

Hodzi, O. and Yu-Wen, C. (2018) "Following the Flow: China's Approach to Global Leadership," *China Quarterly of International Strategic Studies*, Vol. 4, No. 1, pp. 1–21.

Information Office of the State Council of the People's Republic of China (2008) *China's Policies and Actions for Addressing Climate Change*. Beijing: State Council.

Information Office of the State Council of the People's Republic of China (2009) *China's Policies and Actions for Addressing Climate Change*. Beijing: State Council.

Information Office of the State Council of the People's Republic of China (2021) *China's Policies and Actions to Address Climate Change*. Beijing: State Council.

International Panel on Climate Change (2021) *Climate Change 2021: The Physical Science Basis – Summary for Policymakers*. Cambridge and New York City: Cambridge University Press.

International Renewable Energy Agency and International Labour Organization (2021) *Renewable Energy and Jobs – Annual Review 2021*. Abu Dhabi and Geneva: International Renewable Energy Agency and International Labour Organization.

Jaffe, A. B., Newell, R. G. and Stavins, R. N. (2005) "A Tale of Two Market Failures: Technology and Environmental Policy," *Ecological Economics*, Vol. 54, No. 2–3, pp. 164–174.

Jägemann, C., Fürsch, M., Hagspiel, S. and Nagl, S. (2013) "Decarbonizing Europe's Power Sector by 2050 — Analyzing the Economic Implications of Alternative Decarbonization Pathways," *Energy Economics*, Vol. 40, No. C, pp. 622–636.

Jahn, D. (2021) "Quick and Dirty: How Populist Parties in Government Affect Greenhouse Gas Emissions in EU Member States," *Journal of European Public Policy*, Vol. 28, No. 7, pp. 980–997.

Jordan, A., van Asselt, H., Berkhout, F., Huitema, D. and Rayner, T. (2012) "Understanding the Paradoxes of Multilevel Governing: Climate Change Policy in the European Union," *Global Environmental Politics*, Vol. 12, No. 2, pp. 43–66.

King, D., Schrag, D., Dadi, Z., Ye, Q. and Ghosh, A. (2015) *Climate Change: A Risk Assessment*. Cambridge: Centre for Science and Policy.

Kotilainen, K., Aalto, P., Valta, J., Rautiainen, A., Kojo, M. and Sovacool, B. K. (2019) "From Path Dependence to Policy Mixes for Nordic Electric Mobility: Lessons for Accelerating Future Transport Transitions," *Policy Sciences*, Vol. 52, pp. 573–600.

Kuhn, B. M. (2015) "Policies, Collaboration, and Partnership for Climate Protection in China," in Jing, Y. (Ed) *The Road to Collaborative Governance in China*. New York City: Palgrave Macmillan.

Kulp, S. A. and Strauss, B. H. (2019) "New Elevation Data Triple Estimates of Global Vulnerability to Sea-Level Rise and Coastal Flooding," *Nature Communications*, Vol. 10, 4844.

Kuzemko, C., Lockwood, M., Mitchell, C. and Hoggett, R. (2016) "Governing for Sustainable Energy System Change: Politics, Contexts and Contingency," *Energy Research & Social Science*, Vol. 12, February, pp. 96–105.

Lee, N. R. (2020) "When Competition Plays Clean: How Electricity Market Liberalization Facilitated State-Level Climate Policies in the United States," *Energy Policy*, Vol. 139, 111308.

Li, X. (2016) "China: From a Marginalized Follower to an Emerging Leader in Climate Politics," in Wurzel, R. K. W., Connelly, J. and Liefferink, D. (Eds) *The European Union in International Climate Change Politics – Still Taking a Lead?* New York City: Routledge.

Liu, L., Wang, P. and Wu, T. (2017) "The Role of Nongovernmental Organizations in China's Climate Change Governance," *WIREs Climate Change*, Vol. 8, No. 6, pp. 1–16.

Meckling, J. (2018) "The Developmental State in Global Regulation: Economic Change and Climate Policy," *European Journal of International Relations*, Vol. 24, No. 1, pp. 58–81.

Miao, Q. (2019) "What Affects Government Planning for Climate Change Adaptation: Evidence from the U.S. States," *Environmental Policy and Governance*, Vol. 29, No. 5, pp. 376–394.

National Climate Center (2021) *Zhongguo Qihou Bianhua Lanpishu 2021 [Blue Book on Climate Change in China 2021]*. Beijing: China Science Publishing.

Olson, M. (1965) *The Logic of Collective Action: Public Goods and the Theory of Groups*. Cambridge (MA): Harvard University Press.

Pigou, A. C. (1920) *The Economics of Welfare*. London: Macmillan.

Reinsch, W. and Benson E. (2021) *U.S. Views on the Trade and Climate Policy Nexus*. Washington, DC: Center for Strategic & International Studies.

Schreurs, M. A. and Tiberghien, Y. (2007) "Multi-Level Reinforcement: Explaining European Union Leadership in Climate Change Mitigation," *Global Environmental Politics*, Vol. 7, No 4, pp. 19–46.

Schroeder, M. (2008) "The Construction of China's Climate Politics: Transnational NGOs and the Spiral Model of International Relations," *Cambridge Review of International Affairs*, Vol 21, No. 4, pp. 505–525.

Sovacool, B. K. (2011) "An International Comparison of Four Polycentric Approaches to Climate and Energy Governance," *Energy Policy*, Vol. 39, No. 6, pp. 3832–3844.

State Council (2020) "新能源汽车产业发展规划 (2021–2035 年)" ["Plan on Development of New Energy Auto Industry (2021–2035)"], available at http://www.gov.cn/zhengce/content/2020-11/02/content_5556716.htm.

Supran, G. (2021) "Fueling their Own Climate Narrative," *Science*, Vol. 374, No. 6568, p. 702.

Tan, X., Gu, B. and Wang, Y. (2017) "Qihou Bianhua Dui Woguo Zhongchangqi Fazhan De Yingxiang Fenxi Ji Duicejianyi" ["Impact Analysis and Countermeasures for Climate Change on Long-Term Development of China"], *Bulletin of Chinese Academy of Sciences*, Vol. 32, No. 9, pp. 1029–1035.

Tan, Y. (2014) "Transparency without Democracy: The Unexpected Effects of China's Environmental Disclosure Policy," *Governance*, Vol. 27, No. 1, pp. 37–62.

Tan, Y. (2020) "Disaggregating 'China, Inc.': The Hierarchical Politics of WTO Entry," *Comparative Political Studies*, Vol. 53, No. 13, pp. 2118–2152.

Tan, Y. (2021) *Disaggregating China Inc. – State Strategies in the Liberal Economic Order*. Ithaca (NY): Cornell University Press.

Teng, F. and Wang, P. (2021) "The Evolution of Climate Governance in China: Drivers, Features, and Effectiveness," *Environmental Politics*, Vol. 30, Issue sup. 1, pp. 141–161.

U.S. Department of Defense (2021) *Climate Risk Analysis*. Report Submitted to National Security Council. Washington, DC: Department of Defense.

Unruh, G. C. (2000) "Understanding Carbon Lock-in," *Energy Policy*, Vol. 28, No. 12, pp. 817–830.

Wachman, A. M. (2001) "Does the Diplomacy of Shame Promote Human Rights in China?," *Third World Quarterly*, Vol. 22, No. 2, pp. 257–281.

Wang, P., Liu, L. and Wu, T. (2018) "A Review of China's Climate Governance: State, Market and Civil Society," *Climate Policy*, Vol. 18, No. 5, pp. 664–679.

Wang, R. (2016) *Zhongguo Likuang Ziyuan Diaocha Baogao [Report on Lithium Mineral Resources in China]*. Beijing: Chinese Academy of Geological Sciences.

Welton, S. (2021) "Rethinking Grid Governance for the Climate Change Era," *California Law Review*, Vol. 109, No. 1, pp. 209–275.

Zhang, H. (2007) "Zhongguo Yu Guoji Qihou Bianhua Tanpan" ["China and International Climate Change Negotiations"], *Guoji Zhengzhi Yanjiu [Journal of International Studies]*, Vol. 44, No. 1, pp. 21–36.

12 Blueprint for a successful post-globalization

Norbert Gaillard

The resurgence of nationalism and neo-mercantilism has undermined globalization, threatened critical mineral supply chains (CMSCs) and global value chains (GVCs), and increased the risk of a high-intensity conflict between the United States and China. This chapter argues that policy makers in advanced economies (especially in the United States) need to soothe diplomatic relations with China over Taiwan. Next, they should rethink the present international economic system and shift to a "post-globalized" world. Post-globalization entails a world economy governed by "a logic of high interdependence in economic, commercial, migratory and technological fields between States (and their companies) whose strategic and geopolitical interests are convergent, or at least compatible." Several criteria can be used to classify countries according to their reliability in CMSCs and GVCs: they include a country's respect of property rights and rule of law, its "geopolitical compatibility" with the investing or importing nation, and its resilience to climate change. These criteria must be kept updated and further refined to fit the needs and the interests of Western governments and multinational companies. In any case, the Western dependence on China over key products and commodities should be phased out.

12.1 Introduction

The international liberal economic order (ILEO) that emerged in the aftermath of WWII was based on a set of key international institutions, namely: the General Agreement on Tariffs and Trade (GATT),[1] the International Monetary Fund (IMF), and the World Bank. Although these three entities had specific duties (i.e., fostering free trade, solving balance-of-payments problems, and reducing poverty, respectively), all three also aimed at stimulating economic and financial flows, promoting international cooperation, and supporting the liberal international order (LIO). The development of "market socialism" in China starting in 1978 and the collapse of the Soviet Union in 1991 consolidated the ILEO and paved the way to globalization (see Gaillard, 2020a, pp. 54–74).

DOI: 10.4324/9781003340430-16

During the globalization years (1991–2016), international economic relations and economic policies were largely influenced by the Washington Consensus (Williamson, 1990). This "liberal roadmap" identifies ten instruments designed to ensure long-term growth: new public expenditure priorities, fiscal discipline, liberalization of interest rates, reform of the tax system, free trade, achievement of a competitive exchange rate, deregulation, privatization, liberalization of "inward" foreign direct investment (FDI), and enforcement of property rights. The implementation of these policy recommendations has relied on what Sinclair (1994) calls "mechanisms of governance without government." The most striking examples are the indicators that have flourished since the 1980s and measured the capacity of countries to follow the "liberal roadmap."

It is worth mentioning here the most prominent indicators scrutinized by policy makers and investors. *Sovereign ratings* issued by credit rating agencies, such as U.S. firms Moody's and Standard & Poor's (S&P Global), reflect the ability and willingness of governments to repay their debt in a timely manner (Gaillard, 2011). As credit ratings are strongly correlated with bond yields, any downgrade of a country's rating is likely to increase its borrowing costs and thus weaken its credit position. The *Global Competitiveness Index*, established by the World Economic Forum, assesses the competitiveness of a country, which considers the role of the state, the dynamics of the economy and financial markets, the quality of infrastructures and workforce, the industrial efficacy, the cost of production, and the sociopolitical consensus and stability. The *indices of economic freedom*, developed by the Heritage Foundation and the Fraser Institute, are neoliberal indicators focusing on economic freedom in key areas: e.g., the extent of government intervention in the economy, tax, trade, monetary, and banking policies, capital flows and foreign investment, wage and price controls, property rights, and regulations. The World Bank's *Doing Business* reports analyze regulations that encourage or constrain business activity. The most common indicators are *country risk scores*. The country risk assessments made by export credit agencies scrutinize business environment whereas those developed by specialized firms, such as International Country Risk Guide (ICRG) and Euromoney, encompass a wider array of criteria (or sub-scores) and reflect the credit position, the political stability, the attractiveness, and the business climate of a country.

Figure 12.1 presents Euromoney Country Risk (ECR) scores for the three largest industrialized and emerging economies (i.e., the United States, Japan, and Germany, on the one hand, and China, India, and Russia, on the other hand). One observes that the average score of the six countries increased until 2006 but has declined dramatically since then. The fall of industrialized countries' scores results from a deterioration of all sub-scores. Yet, there have been mounting concerns about the sustainability of Japanese and U.S. public debts. As suggested by Gaillard and Michalek in this book, the decline in the United States' score may reveal the fundamental weaknesses of U.S. finance capitalism: i.e., excessive leverage strategies among corporate firms, massive

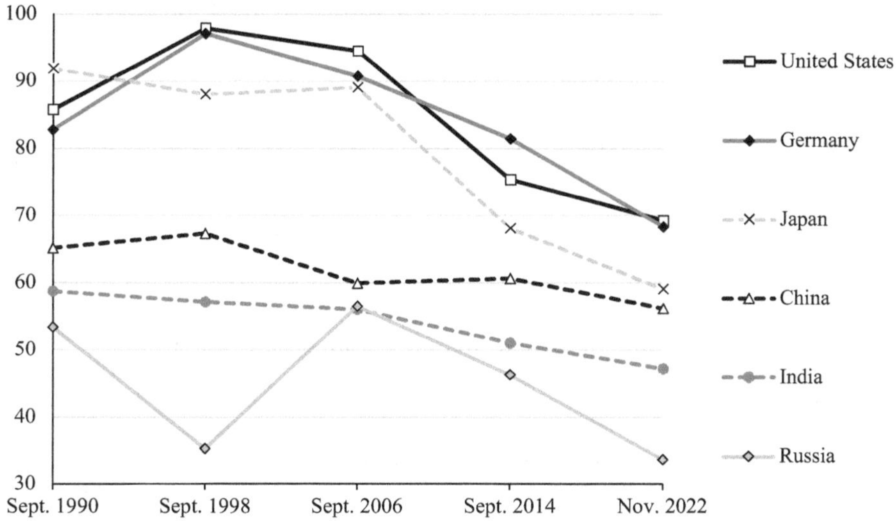

Figure 12.1 Euromoney Country Risk scores

Source: www.euromoneycountryrisk.com

Note: ECR ratings are established on a 0–100 scale, where 0 (resp. 100) corresponds to countries that are the most (resp. least) risky. ECR ratings are obtained after assigning a weighting to five categories. The four qualitative expert opinions are political risk (35% weighting), economic risk (35%), structural risk (10%) and access to international capital markets (10%). The quantitative value comes from sovereign debt indicators (10%).

bailouts during financial crises, increasing inequalities, and dangerous bipolarization of the U.S. political landscape. The picture of emerging economies is completely different. The fall of their scores was driven almost exclusively by the drop in the political score. The nationalistic stance observed in China, India, and Russia (under the auspices of Xi Jinping, Narendra Modi, and Vladimir Putin, respectively) since 2014 have worried Western investors and put into question the future of the ILEO. The invasion of Ukraine by the Russian army is the most tragic illustration.

This recent evolution validates Samuel Huntington's (1989) argument that a post-Cold War world was unlikely to be safer than the "Long Peace" experienced since 1945. Huntington warned that the record of Russia as non-Soviet great power was not reassuring for the future of Europe. It is even more interesting that he stressed that

> Chinese expansionism has yet to appear on the world scene. Britain and France, Germany and Japan, the United States and the Soviet Union, all became expansionist and imperialist powers in the course of industrialization. China is just beginning seriously to develop its industrial strength.

This "Huntingtonian" pattern is consistent with Part II of this book, which highlights the flaws of the LIO and of the ILEO.

The remainder of this chapter is organized as follows. Section 12.2 highlights the hard forms of geo-economic dynamics that have unfolded between China and the United States. Section 12.3 investigates the weaponization of commodities by several emerging nations, including China. Section 12.4 examines how the United States and the European Union (EU) have reacted to China's neo-mercantilist policy. Section 12.5 analyzes how a "post-globalized" world can be established. Section 12.6 concludes.

12.2 The geo-economic dynamics involving China and the United States

The consolidation of the ILEO in the 1990s has not prevented the recourse to antiliberal and even hostile methods aimed at defending national economic interests. These geo-economic strategies, defined by Luttwak (1990) as "the logic of war in the grammar of commerce," have been especially frequent in China and the United States.

The first and the softer of the strategies has consisted of supporting or investing massively in a key sector in order to reach a high degree of concentration, obtain economies of scale, and/or influence decisively the course of economic activities. For example, U.S. authorities have invariably promoted the finance industry (see Gaillard and Michalek's chapter in this book). Not only has financial innovation (e.g., securitization) facilitated the expansion of household and corporate credit, but it has also fostered the use of the U.S. dollar by international investors. Next, the development of asset management has constituted a powerful means to ensure the respect of property rights abroad[2] and protect the status of the United States as world's top foreign direct investor. By the same token, the quasi-duopoly structure of the credit rating industry[3] has enabled U.S. creditors to monitor and pressure foreign debtors. Turn now to China. Its FDI- and export-oriented policies have been embedded in the ILEO (see Gotoh and Li's chapter in this book). China's global ambitions have materialized since the adoption of the Belt and Road Initiative in 2013 (International Institute for Strategic Studies, 2023). A milestone was certainly the acquisition of major ports by partially state-owned enterprises. In 2018, COSCO Shipping Ports, China Merchants Port Holdings and Qingdao Port International Development held stakes in 16 ports spread across Europe and the Mediterranean Sea.[4] The exorbitant power of U.S. finance and the growing influence of Chinese shipping companies and port operators have been lamented by many European policy makers and experts.

Geo-economic tensions have long crystallized in the establishment of protectionist measures. Those are rife among the richest countries: the correlation coefficient between the total number of interventions breaching free trade rules during 2009–2021 and gross domestic products (GDP) in 2021 reached 0.93.[5] It is not surprising that the United States and China were the most protectionist economies (with 7,794 and 5,914 interventions, respectively) during 2009–2021, far ahead of Germany (2,711). The share of subsidies (excluding export subsidies) in total protectionist measures soared from 39.3% in 2009 to 63.6% in 2021.[6] China and the United States have excelled in subsidizing key sectors. Haley and Haley (2013) document how the Chinese central and local governments granted massive subsidies to the steel, glass, paper, auto-parts and solar industries while state-owned banks lent at below-market interest rates. This strategy was remarkably successful: for example, it transformed China from a net steel importer in 2005 into the world's largest exporter of steel in 2007. More recently, it propelled the country into the largest plug-in electric vehicle (PEV) market in the world and undermined the competitiveness of European and, to a lesser extent, U.S. PEV producers.[7] In terms of large-scale subsidies, the United States has followed its own way. Washington has privileged a sort of "indirect industrial policy" through the huge public procurement contracts awarded by federal executive departments of the U.S. government and federal agencies (see Cohen, 2022, pp. 72–77). In 2021, Defense contract spending totaled $408 billion.[8] The ten largest contractors included not only U.S. multinational companies (MNCs) specialized in military shipbuilding, aerospace, and information security but also U.S. health insurance and pharmaceuticals firms. The "too-big-to-fail" label granted to the largest U.S. financial institutions since 1984 is also akin to an implicit subsidy that has heightened the power of U.S. finance (see Gaillard and Michalek, 2019, p. 123 and 2022).

In addition to protectionist policies, China and the United States have developed coercive tools to thwart international competition. Beijing has established a series of red lines likely to trigger economic pressure: human rights activism in connection with Tibet, Xinjiang, and Hong Kong; support to the U.S. military presence in East Asia; dissent from Chinese views over claims in the East and South China Seas; COVID-19 origin investigation; corporate donations to "anti-China" political parties; and restrictions against Huawei. Beijing has had recourse to the following coercive measures: popular boycotts, administrative discriminations, empty threats, and tourism and immigration restrictions. The foreign firms most targeted by Chinese authorities have been those bringing few technologies, with abundant substitutes and a small investment footprint (see Adachi et al., 2022).

A key feature of the U.S. economic coercive power has been the extraterritorial application of some of its federal laws (see Loonam and Andreoli, 2022). Mention, among others, the Foreign Corrupt Practices Act (FCPA) of 1977,[9] the Sarbanes–Oxley Act of 2002 – which mandates certain practices in financial record keeping and reporting for corporations –, and the Foreign Account Tax Compliance Act of 2010. Due to their use of the U.S. financial system or the U.S. dollar for illegal purposes, several foreign firms have been prosecuted and fined by U.S. courts. The geo-economic logic has reached its climax with the adoption of international sanctions. In this area, the capacity of Washington is unsurpassable. In 2023, the Office of Foreign Assets Control of the U.S. Department of the Treasury administered and enforced 38 sanctions programs.[10] These programs may target a country, a government, an entity, or an individual; they are applicable to U.S. entities but their extraterritorial ambit constrains foreign governments and firms to comply with U.S. policy goals. The sanctions announced in 2022 against Russia after its army invaded Ukraine are comparable to an "economic war." The U.S authorities managed to cut Moscow off from the international financial system and forced it to default on its sovereign bonds owed to foreign creditors.[11]

12.3 The weaponization of commodities

Commodities have been at the core of geopolitical rivalries for centuries. During the globalization years, they have been weaponized primarily through nationalization, price manipulation, and exports restriction.

The mining, agriculture, and petroleum sectors accounted for 48% of all international expropriation acts observed during 1990–2014.[12] Two major profiles of expropriating countries emerged. On the one hand, the nationalizations implemented by Bolivia, Ecuador, and Venezuela were part of Bolivarian policies that rejected the neoliberal paradigm spread in many Latin American economies (Hira and Gaillard, 2011). On the other hand, Central Asian countries (Kazakhstan, Kyrgyzstan, Turkmenistan, and Uzbekistan) nationalized aluminum and gold mines owned by Western companies to affirm their recent independence. Disputes between host countries and aggrieved foreign investors were settled through direct negotiations or by means of arbitrational or judicial recourses.[13]

Price manipulation has been a central feature of the activity of the Organization of the Petroleum Exporting Countries (OPEC).[14] This cartel has consistently regulated the supply of oil to keep prices up, thus exerting an oligopolistic power over oil-importing countries. On several occasions (e.g., in 2021), the oil production cutbacks hampered world economic recovery and fed inflation. The most significant reaction to the OPEC policy was the No Oil Producing and Exporting Cartels Act (NOPEC) advanced in the 2000s. This U.S. Congressional bill, which has not been enacted so far, declared illegal for any foreign state to limit the production or distribution of oil or natural gas, to set their price, or to take any action consisting in restraining their trade. It denied "a foreign state engaged in such conduct sovereign immunity from the jurisdiction or judgements of U.S. courts."[15]

Export restrictions were overlooked by many policy makers for a long time. Public awareness was raised in 2009 when Mexico, the United States, and the EU filed a complaint at the WTO against China's export restrictions on nine raw materials (bauxite, coke, fluorspar, magnesium, manganese, silicon carbide, silicon metal, yellow phosphorus, and zinc).[16] In 2012, a second complaint was filed by Japan, the United States, and the EU after China imposed export duties and quotas on several forms of rare earths, tungsten, and molybdenum. Although its measures were ultimately found to be inconsistent with WTO rules,[17] China implemented a more stringent licensing system for exporters in 2015 and maintained substantial export taxes on rare earth metals (Mancheri and Marukawa, 2016, pp. 67–69).

Export restrictions on commodities have become a source of major concern because many raw materials are indispensable to produce semiconductors (commonly called "chips") and advance the clean energy transition through the development of renewable energy technologies and electric vehicles. For example, an electric car requires twice as much copper and manganese as a conventional one. The former is composed of several kilograms of lithium, nickel, cobalt, and graphite, contrary to the latter. A one-megawatt solar photovoltaic plant requires three tons of copper and four tons of silicon. Copper, nickel, manganese, chromium, molybdenum, zinc, and rare earths are key minerals for offshore and onshore wind farms (International Energy Agency, 2021, p. 6). In a sustainable development scenario (i.e., following a trajectory consistent with the Paris Agreement goals), the demand for lithium, graphite, cobalt, nickel, and rare earths should jump by a factor of 42, 25, 21, 19, and 7, respectively, between 2020 and 2040 (International Energy Agency, 2021, p. 9).

This fast-changing environment has engendered uncertainties regarding the security of critical mineral supply chains (CMSCs) and, to some extent, the stability of prices in the medium to long term. In this respect, the position of Beijing has stirred growing controversy. China is by far the largest producer of gallium, germanium, and silicon – three minerals used in semiconductor applications (U.S. Geological Survey, 2022, pp. 65, 71, and 151). It is the third largest producer of copper and lithium, owns 60% of rare earths and leads refining and processing operations for cobalt, copper, lithium, nickel, and rare earths (International Energy Agency, 2021, p. 13). In addition, Chinese direct overseas investment in mining projects increased from \$0.4 billion in 2005 to \$0.8 billion in 2012 and \$2.2 billion in 2019. Chinese companies prioritized copper, gold, cobalt, lithium, nickel, zinc, and iron ore projects (S&P Global, 2021). In 2022, they owned 15 of the 17 cobalt operations in the Democratic Republic of the Congo.[18] After the Widodo's administration banned nickel ore exports in 2020, China switched from importing nickel to establishing joint ventures with Indonesian companies to extract and refine this mineral indispensable for electric cars.[19]

12.4 Western retaliations to China's strategy

12.4.1 U.S. tough retaliations

China's neo-mercantilist policy has led to unprecedented protectionist policies by the United States, which has further put the ILEO under pressure. In 2021 and 2022, the United States was, by far, the country that implemented the highest number of protectionist measures while China was the economy most affected by all the trade restriction announcements. This contrasts with the "tit-for-tat game" observed during 2017–2020.[20] One of the most noticeable characteristics of the announcements made by U.S. authorities since the late 2010s was that they have frequently targeted China in an explicit manner.

In December 2019, the U.S. Congress mandated that the Export-Import Bank of the United States (Exim Bank) establish the "Program on China and Transformational Exports." This program has two aims: (i) "to directly neutralize export subsidies for competing goods and services financed by official export credit, tied aid, or blended financing provided by China" and (ii) "to advance the comparative leadership of the United States with respect to China, or support United States innovation, employment, and technological standards through direct exports in 10 transformational export categories," such as artificial intelligence, biotechnology, biomedical sciences, wireless communications equipment, quantum computing, renewable energy, semiconductor and semiconductor machinery manufacturing, emerging financial technologies, water treatment and sanitation, and high-performance computing (Exim Bank, 2021, p. 16). The bank must reserve no less than 20% of its total financing authority for support made pursuant to the program (Exim Bank, 2021, p. 62).[21]

Turn now to U.S. actions against Huawei, the world's largest telecommunications equipment maker. In May 2019, the Commerce Department banned the Chinese giant from purchasing components from U.S. companies without U.S. government approval. A year later, it required foreign manufacturers of semiconductors using U.S. equipment or technology to get a U.S. license before selling them to Huawei. In June 2020, the Federal Communications Commission designated Huawei as a national security threat and, in July 2021, it finalized a program subsidizing costs for U.S. telecom firms to replace Huawei equipment. In November 2022, the agency blocked the importation or sale of equipment made by Huawei, citing national security concerns. These restrictions have also hurt other Chinese companies, such as Zhongxing Telecommunication Equipment (ZTE).[22]

The CHIPS and Science Act of 2022 is an ambitious legislation aimed at restoring the U.S. dominance in chipmaking and securing supply chains of semiconductors. This act provides $52.7 billion for U.S. semiconductor research, development, manufacturing, and workforce development. This includes $39 billion in manufacturing incentives, $13.2 billion in R&D and workforce development, and $500 million for international information communications technology security and semiconductor supply chain activities (White House, 2022). The U.S. firms that obtain federal subsidies are not allowed to engage in any significant transaction "involving the material expansion of semiconductor manufacturing capacity" in China or other foreign country of concern (e.g., Iran, Russia, and North Korea). The CHIPS and Science Act is part of a re-industrialization process that convinced Taiwan Semiconductor Manufacturing Company (TSMC), the world's largest semiconductor foundry, to build two factories in Arizona. According to the National Economic Council acting deputy director for industrial policy who oversees CHIPS implementation, these two plants "could meet the entire U.S. demand for U.S. chips when they're completed."[23] It is worth noting that, two months after the CHIPS and Science Act of 2022 was signed into law, the Commerce Department issued rules imposing a wider range of new and enhanced restrictions targeting China's advanced computing and semiconductor sectors. They apply to U.S. as well as non-U.S. firms providing advanced chips or items related to supercomputers and semiconductors to or for China.[24]

U.S. authorities have also strengthened their screening of FDI to the United States. The Foreign Investment Risk Review Modernization Act of 2018 (FIRRMA) expands the jurisdiction of the Committee on Foreign Investment in the United States (CFIUS) to eliminate growing national security risks. Foreign investments from China and Russia are considered potential threats. Four new types of transactions are covered by the CFIUS: (i) any merger, acquisition, takeover, or joint venture by or with any foreign person that could result in foreign control of any U.S. business; (ii) the purchase or lease by, or concession to, a foreign entity of private or public real estate that is located in proximity to sensitive government facilities; (iii) any change in a foreign investor's rights resulting in foreign control of a U.S. business; and (iv) any transaction or other device employed for the purpose of evading FIRRMA provisions. Studying the period 2016–2021, Chorzempa (2022) finds that Chinese investors are far more likely to need to file with CFIUS than security allies like Canada, France, Germany, Japan, and the United Kingdom.

12.4.2 The EU's nuanced approach

The European Union has been more cautious than the United States regarding its policies vis-à-vis China. Four years ago, the European Commission (2019, p. 1) stated that

> China is, simultaneously, in different policy areas, a cooperation partner with whom the EU has closely aligned objectives, a negotiating partner with whom the EU needs to find a balance of interests, an economic competitor in the pursuit of technological leadership, and a systemic rival promoting alternative models of governance.

This nuanced approach has been largely driven by China's position as the European Union's largest trading partner in goods.

Regulation (EU) 2019/452 of March 2019

> establishes a framework for the screening by Member States of foreign direct investments into the Union on the grounds of security or public order and for a mechanism for cooperation between Member States, and between Member States and the Commission, with regard to foreign direct investments likely to affect security or public order.[25]

No government or country is stigmatized by this regulation.

In January 2023, EU institutions were preparing two legislative texts, in line with those already adopted in the United States. An EU "Chips Act" should address the current shortage of semiconductors in Europe. It would mobilize €43 billion in public and private investment and is designed to (i) support technological capacity building and related research and innovation, (ii) ensure security of supply and resilience by boosting investment, and (iii) monitor the semiconductor supply chain and coordinate actions in the event of crisis.[26] A complementary text would be a "European Critical Raw Materials Act," as announced by European Commission President U. von der Leyen in her 2022 State of the European Union address. This act should provide a better understanding of what critical raw materials are most strategic, create a European network of raw materials agencies to anticipate risks, build a more resilient supply chain, and ensure a robust and sustainable level playing field. In commenting on this legislative project, T. Breton, European Commissioner for Internal Market, insisted that the EU needs to be "more assertive and less naïve in defending [its] economic interests and [its] values."[27]

12.5 The road to post-globalization

The increasing restriction to free trade, the weaponization of raw materials, the threats to CMSCs and global value chains (GVCs), and the geopolitical tensions among G20 countries (especially between Russia and Western countries and between China and the United States) have meaningfully weakened the LIO and the ILEO. The establishment of a new international economic order safeguarding some key liberal features entails realism, lucidity, and pragmatism. The first priority must be the preservation of world peace. The second should be the shift to a "post-globalized" system. Post-globalization entails a world economy governed by "a logic of high interdependence in economic, commercial, migratory and technological fields between States (and their companies) whose strategic and geopolitical interests are convergent, or at least compatible" (Gaillard, 2020b). Because several major countries have free ridden on multilateralism and distorted liberal values, advanced economies need to monitor and secure CMSCs as well as GVCs.

12.5.1 Appeasing the U.S.–China geopolitical tensions

Avoiding a war involving China and the United States and implementing a military de-escalation in the Taiwan Strait must be at the top of the agenda in Beijing and Washington. These objectives may be reached provided the two sides make efforts to depart from uncompromising stances and give up confrontational rhetoric.

The dark fascination for the so-called "Thucydides Trap" (Allison, 2015) should stop. It has magnified the belief that a rising power and a ruling power will inevitably go to war against each other although this thesis is not supported by the recent evolution of international relations. Since 1945, the Soviet Union, Germany, Japan, and the European Union have not engaged in a large-scale conflict against the United States.[28]

Next, both sides must understand that the military escalation on the Taiwan issue is akin to the "dollar auction game" (Shubik, 1971). Each retaliatory measure to the opponent's latest move is rational but the ultimate outcome of such escalation is irrational as it could lead to a major conflict and a probable "lose-lose" scenario. Besides, if a war between the two superpowers occurred, it could unleash hostile forces all around the world and trigger a series of low-, medium-, and high-intensity conflicts. For example, one might fear that Russia, now a rogue state, would invade other former Soviet states or intensify its destabilizing operations in Africa or in the Balkans. The geopolitical and economic consequences of a Sino-U.S. war would be incalculable, which obliges policy makers to act quickly to save peace.

K. Rudd (2022), Australia's former Primer Minister, suggests the establishment of "strategic red lines" between China and the United States, as used during the détente of the 1970s. Concretely, Washington could return to adhering to the "one China" policy and end "provocative and unnecessary high-level visits to Taipei" while Beijing would scale back its military exercises around Taiwan (Rudd, 2022, p. 365). These prescriptions are positive, but they tend to overlook the evolution of public opinions.

In the United States, a recent poll shows that 69% of Americans support U.S. recognition of Taiwan as an independent country. Around 52% favor using U.S. troops to defend Taiwan if China were to invade the island. This latter percentage doubled compared to 2014 (Smeltz and Kafura, 2021). These growing pro-Taiwan sentiments among U.S. citizens seem to be driven by distrust of China as 61% of Americans see China as a rival or an adversary. They reflect the acceptance of a direct conflict against Beijing and are likely to fuel anti-Chinese stance among U.S. policy makers. In Taiwan, the percentage of population favoring either the "independence as soon as possible" or the "status quo with a move to independence" soared from 11% in 1994 to 30% in 2022.[29] This trend accelerated under the Trump administration, suggesting that the Taiwan Travel Act of 2018 and the massive sales of U.S. arms to Taipei (exceeding $10 billion in 2019) spurred nationalistic sentiments among Taiwanese people. This evolution should be a source of concern in Washington. In fact, a form of geopolitical moral hazard risk may be materializing in Taiwan: as U.S. leaders are increasingly eager to support the island in the event of a Chinese invasion, Taiwanese policy makers may be tempted to accelerate their move toward independence, thus triggering a conflict between the two superpowers.

To avert this scenario, U.S authorities should launch a series of initiatives designed to maintain the status quo[30] and restore Sino-U.S. relations. First, Washington should clarify its doctrine regarding Taiwan and announce explicitly that the U.S. army will not intervene in a Sino-Taiwanese war if Taipei prepared or declared its independence. Second, Washington should argue that the present status quo is the only viable option unless a peaceful settlement is reached between Beijing and Taipei, paving the way to unification. Third, the Taiwan Travel Act of 2018 should be repealed or, at least, visits of high-level officials between Taiwan and the United States should end. Fourth, Washington could create an ad hoc task force aimed at helping Chinese authorities to overcome the COVID-19 rebound observed at the date of this writing (i.e., January 2023). Fifth, the two superpowers need to develop non-traditional security cooperation everywhere possible to address long-term issues, such as global warming, natural disasters, mass migration, transnational criminality, and so on.[31]

12.5.2 Organizing a post-globalized world

The appeasement of and a revived rapprochement in Sino-U.S. diplomatic relations is a prerequisite to post-globalization. This new form of international economic order includes traditional liberal features, but also specific auto-centered development strategies intended to preserve independence, or at least, control over key products and minerals. In this post-globalized world, Western governments must build robust interdependence networks to prevent disruptions in CMSCs and GVCs. This implies efficient tools to select or replace economic partners and substitute commodities or products from unreliable countries.

12.5.2.1 Selecting partners

Gaillard (2020a) shows that several country risk rating systems (e.g., those implemented by ICRG, Euromoney, and Credendo) have performed well since the 1990s. However, investors have sometimes overlooked the decline in a country's rating. The case of Russia deserves examination. In the aftermath of Crimea's annexation in March 2014, Russia's country risk ratings fell sharply but this did not drive MNCs to divest from the country. By the same token, more than ten months after V. Putin's army invaded Ukraine on 24 February 2022, 224 foreign firms continued business as usual in Russia. More than 60% of them were headquartered in Japan, the European Union, the United Kingdom, or the United States, i.e., in jurisdictions whose governments imposed severe sanctions against Moscow.[32] These MNCs have continued operations in a sinister and recessionary environment and may face reputational damage in their home country. Their counterparts that left Russia suffered substantial losses due to expropriation acts or sell-offs.[33] In either case, investing in Russia was an awful bet reflecting the lack of geopolitical expertise among Western firms. These remainders were unable to anticipate the hardening of V. Putin's regime as well as the regime's vulnerability to Western economic sanctions. Russia's retaliatory measures have consisted of weaponizing its oil and gas exports to force the European Union to withdraw its sanctions. Combined with China's tough neo-mercantilism, this move should serve as a catalyst to select and monitor trade partners, commodity suppliers, foreign investors, and recipients of direct investments even more carefully than during the globalization years. This entails not only a thorough knowledge and a critical analysis of political, economic, and financial indicators but also the recourse to innovative screening tools.

Appendix 12.1 provides a series of indicators and data that should help Western economies reorganize their international economic relations and secure their CMSCs and GVCs. Country risk or expropriation risk scores (such as those of Credendo) remain key indicators because they assess a country's business friendliness more accurately than Moody's and S&P Global sovereign ratings (Gaillard, 2020a, p. 2). In fact, it is worth noting that economies that have been assigned high sovereign ratings but intermediate or rather low expropriation risk scores (e.g., China, Kuwait, and Saudi Arabia) have weaponized their production of energy and raw materials. I would suggest that their strong credit position and their significant trade surplus have enabled them to enhance their bargaining power over their importers.

Second, the "rule of law" indicator is helpful in the sense that two countries with high scores are less likely to confront each other militarily or through harmful protectionist measures or economic sanctions (see Oneal and Russett, 1997). This approach needs to be complemented with a focus on coalitional logics that may bring together rule-of-law and authoritarian states. For example, the Summit for Democracy, hosted by the United States in December 2021, was designed to rally the world's democracies against totalitarian and autocratic regimes. Yet, the invited participants included countries that perform poorly in terms of rule-of-law standards and respect of political and civil rights (e.g., the Democratic Republic of the Congo, the Philippines, and Serbia).[34] Their invitation to the Summit was supported by their geopolitical importance, their potential role in GVCs, or their pro-U.S. stance.

The examination of the vote regarding the Resolution of the United Nations General Assembly "Aggression against Ukraine" (dated March 2, 2022) is also instructive. Several major emerging countries (e.g., India, South Africa, and Vietnam) abstained, probably to keep their good relations with Russia. This novel form of "non-alignment" should alarm Western governments who expect to get priority access to critical resources or increase their FDI.

Two additional criteria must be considered to succeed in the post-globalization era: they involve climate risk and the threat of oligopoly, or even monopoly, over critical minerals. The Physical Vulnerability to Climate Change Index (PVCCI) is a composite indicator that helps identify the most vulnerable countries and rationalize investments abroad (Feindouno et al., 2020). Created by the Fondation pour les études et recherches sur le développement international (FERDI), the PVCCI incorporates five risks: flooding due to sea level rise or melting glaciers, increasing aridity, rainfall, aridity, and storms. The recent computation of the PVCCI at the sub-national level (Goujon et al., 2022) will improve decision-making by investing firms and countries.

Lastly, the excessive dependence on a single commodity supplier constitutes a risk that can be curbed. So, I have included a simple "concentration indicator" by listing the countries that account for more than 20% of the world production of at least one critical mineral indispensable to the present clean energy transition (namely, chromium, cobalt, copper, graphite, lithium, manganese, molybdenum, nickel, rare earths, silicon, and zinc). Among the six nations that enjoy a strong market position, China dominates the production of graphite, rare earths, and silicon, grabbing 60% of market share or more.[35]

This series of indicators and data must be kept updated and further refined to fit the needs and the interests of Western governments and MNCs. Any significant political change in a leading oil, gas, or critical mineral exporter or in a country playing a key role in GVCs will affect Western economies. As a result, geopolitical stress tests should be carried out on a semi-annual basis to anticipate shortages and disruptions in CMSCs and GVCs. In addition, the scope of these indicators could be expanded. For example, the "concentration indicator" would gain relevance if it included basic drugs (e.g., penicillin antibiotics, analgesic and antipyretic drugs), foodstuffs (e.g., mineral water, milk, and pasta), detergents (e.g., soap and bleach), and so on.

12.5.2.2 Substituting partners and products

Three types of "substitution" can be identified. The first one involves all the substitutions performed for technological or financial purposes and likely to redirect international investment and trade flows. As they are consistent with globalization as well as post-globalization dynamics, they do not need to be addressed here. In contrast, the two other types of substitution can be considered byproducts of post-globalization.

What I call "geopolitical substitution" consists of (i) "nearshoring" industrial, R&D, administrative, and/or financial activities, (ii) replacing a key supplier by another, or (iii) shifting from importing a key commodity or product to another. These three moves are primarily driven by geopolitical reasons and may generate high costs for Western MNCs and governments. Nearshoring aims at protecting CMSCs or GVCs in the medium to long term (Piatanesi and Arauzo-Carod, 2019). For example, following the Chinese government's crackdown of the 2019–2020 Hong Kong protests, foreign firms reassessed their presence in the Fragrant Harbour and relocated offices to other places, such as Singapore.[36] Replacing a key supplier is very challenging as it may disrupt economic activity in the short term. Yet, it seems inevitable when the client's interests are at complete odds with those of the supplier. The European Union's decision to eliminate its reliance on Russian gas after the invasion of Ukraine is a striking illustration (European Commission, 2022). Alternative gas suppliers exist: they include Azerbaijan, Norway, Qatar, and the United States. Substituting a key commodity or product because of the exorbitant market power held by a geopolitical rival is likely to have far-reaching consequences. China is an unavoidable case study. Dispensing with critical minerals on which China has a stranglehold (e.g., graphite, rare earths, and silicon) will entail massive investments to prospect for those minerals in reliable countries or find satisfactory substitutes.[37]

The third type of substitution goes beyond "geopolitical substitution": it is fundamentally designed to restore economic sovereignty and cut dependence on a wide array of foreign commodities and products. It may materialize through "backshoring"[38] and active industrial policies. So far, the United States has been much more prone than the European Union to implement these strategies. For H. Moser, a 50-year U.S. manufacturing industry veteran and founder of the "Reshoring Initiative" (a trade policy advocacy group), backshoring (especially from China) is feasible and desirable: it would partly offset the overvaluation of the dollar and reduce the U.S. goods trade deficit.[39] Although this analysis has shortcomings (see Gaillard and Michalek's chapter in this book), it has gained ground since the COVID-19 pandemic.[40] The reshoring trend, which shortens GVCs and is expected to increase their resilience, may accelerate in the short to medium term owing to the massive federal subsidies contained in the Inflation Reduction Act of 2022 and the CHIPS and Science Act of 2022. These two legislations pave the way to a renewed industrial policy whose objectives are to counter China, create domestic jobs, and reverse four decades of deindustrialization. These neo-protectionist strategies may look legitimate, but they could lead to de-globalization, a process that would exacerbate nationalism and predation.

12.6 Concluding remarks

A radical decoupling from China is dangerous and inopportune. On the one hand, it could aggravate geopolitical tensions and lead to a high-intensity conflict between the West and China. On the other hand, Beijing remains a major trade partner and an unavoidable supplier of critical minerals. However, the Western dependence on China over key products and commodities should be phased out. This implies a shift to a "post-globalized" world where developed countries will increase their economic and technological interdependence with States (and their companies) whose strategic and geopolitical interests are compatible.

In a recent press article,[41] S. K. O'Neil – vice president of Studies and Senior Fellow for Latin America Studies at the Council on Foreign Relations – argues that regions do matter and supports the view that the United States needs its neighbors (i.e., Canada and Mexico) to compete successfully with Asia and Europe. I am convinced that this approach is still too limited as the United States will have to expand its partnerships to secure its CMSCs and GVCs. The European Union and Japan – traditional commodity-importing economies – have already understood what is at stake. Let's hope that democracies and their allies will continue cooperating and avert any isolationist drift.

Appendix 12.1 Indicators and data to secure CMSCs and GVCs

Countries	*Credendo expropriation risk scoring*	*World Bank's rule of law indicator*	*U.S. Summit for Democracy*	*UN vote on Ukraine (March 2, 2022)*	*Physical Vulnerability to Climate Change Index*	*High concentration of critical mineral production*
Afghanistan	7	-1.87	No	Yes	59.67	No
Albania	3	-0.26	Yes	Yes	41.70	No
Algeria	5	-0.82	No	Abs	61.16	No
Andorra	NA	1.72	No	Yes	44.94	No
Angola	4	-0.95	Yes	Abs	50.24	No
Antigua & Barb.	NA	0.34	Yes	Yes	57.14	No
Argentina	5	-0.46	Yes	Yes	54.48	No
Armenia	4	-0.10	Yes	Abs	45.02	No
Aruba	NA	1.28	No	NA	NA	No
Australia	1	1.67	Yes	Yes	62.93	Yes
Austria	1	1.79	Yes	Yes	43.41	No
Azerbaijan	3	-0.58	No	NV	52.37	No
Bahamas	3	0.10	Yes	Yes	65.01	No
Bahrain	3	0.47	No	Yes	57.89	No
Bangladesh	5	-0.61	No	Abs	48.89	No
Barbados	2	0.37	Yes	Yes	50.56	No
Belarus	5	-1.10	No	No	43.29	No
Belgium	1	1.33	Yes	Yes	48.54	No
Belize	5	-0.78	Yes	Yes	56.31	No
Benin	4	-0.59	No	Yes	48.22	No
Bermuda	NA	0.70	No	NA	NA	No
Bhutan	NA	0.64	No	Yes	41.39	No
Bolivia	6	-1.16	No	Abs	48.79	No
Bosnia & H.	4	-0.28	No	Yes	41.88	No
Botswana	2	0.48	Yes	Yes	61.21	No

Brazil	3	-0.28	Yes	Yes	47.62	No
Brunei	1	0.89	No	Yes	45.71	No
Bulgaria	1	-0.04	Yes	Yes	46.87	No
Burkina Faso	5	-0.44	No	NV	61.15	No
Burundi	6	-1.29	No	Abs	50.79	No
Cabo Verde	3	0.35	Yes	Yes	52.59	No
Cambodia	4	-0.90	No	Yes	49.12	No
Cameroon	4	-1.10	No	NV	48.54	No
Canada	1	1.63	Yes	Yes	50.03	No
Cayman Isl.	NA	0.78	No	NA	NA	No
Central Afr. Rep.	7	-1.67	No	Abs	49.46	No
Chad	5	-1.33	No	Yes	64.15	No
Chile	1	0.91	Yes	Yes	52.15	Yes
China	5	0.04	No	Abs	53.12	Yes
Colombia	4	-0.45	Yes	Yes	45.43	No
Comoros	NA	-1.22	No	Yes	52.63	No
Congo, Dem. R.	6	-1.70	Yes	Yes	49.01	Yes
Congo, Rep.	5	-1.14	No	Abs	47.57	No
Costa Rica	2	0.45	Yes	Yes	51.89	No
Côte d'Ivoire	4	-0.63	No	Yes	46.01	No
Croatia	1	0.30	Yes	Yes	43.54	No
Cuba	6	-0.40	No	Abs	64.21	No
Curaçao	NA	NA	No	NA	NA	No
Cyprus	1	0.64	Yes	Yes	59.75	No
Czech Republic	1	1.13	Yes	Yes	46.51	No
Denmark	1	1.94	Yes	Yes	49.15	No
Djibouti	5	-1.01	No	Yes	63.85	No
Dominica	3	0.72	Yes	Yes	NA	No
Dominican Rep.	3	-0.10	Yes	Yes	52.44	No
Ecuador	5	-0.34	Yes	Yes	45.36	No

(Continued)

Appendix 12.1 (Continued)

Countries	*Credendo expropriation risk scoring*	*World Bank's rule of law indicator*	*U.S. Summit for Democracy*	*UN vote on Ukraine (March 2, 2022)*	*Physical Vulnerability to Climate Change Index*	*High concentration of critical mineral production*
Egypt	4	−0.24	No	Yes	61.74	No
El Salvador	4	−0.85	No	Abs	51.93	No
Eq. Guinea	6	−1.20	No	Abs	48.60	No
Eritrea	7	−1.57	No	No	63.89	No
Estonia	1	1.43	Yes	Yes	45.24	No
Eswatini	4	−0.56	No	NV	51.91	No
Ethiopia	6	−0.61	No	NV	52.92	No
Fiji	NA	0.31	Yes	Yes	60.60	No
Finland	1	2.06	Yes	Yes	41.47	No
France	1	1.29	Yes	Yes	45.67	No
Gabon	6	−0.70	No	Yes	47.56	No
Gambia	3	−0.39	No	Yes	61.88	No
Georgia	4	0.17	Yes	Yes	39.84	No
Germany	1	1.61	Yes	Yes	50.63	No
Ghana	3	−0.08	Yes	Yes	51.12	No
Greece	1	0.35	Yes	Yes	50.11	No
Grenada	NA	0.51	Yes	Yes	58.41	No
Guatemala	4	−1.09	No	Yes	48.35	No
Guinea	6	−1.13	No	NV	50.10	No
Guinea-Bissau	5	−1.44	No	NV	51.20	No
Guyana	4	−0.40	Yes	Yes	48.14	No
Haiti	6	−1.25	No	Yes	56.97	No
Honduras	4	−1.07	No	Yes	51.40	No
Hong Kong	1	1.45	No	NA	NA	No
Hungary	3	0.53	No	Yes	45.70	No

Iceland	1	1.75	Yes	Yes	45.57	No
India	3	-0.08	Yes	Abs	57.42	No
Indonesia	4	-0.22	Yes	Yes	45.68	Yes
Iran	6	-0.95	No	Abs	60.34	No
Iraq	6	-1.73	Yes	Abs	65.99	No
Ireland	1	1.53	Yes	Yes	45.83	No
Israel	1	0.94	Yes	Yes	60.54	No
Italy	1	0.27	Yes	Yes	45.35	No
Jamaica	2	-0.17	Yes	Yes	65.01	No
Japan	1	1.58	Yes	Yes	61.67	No
Jordan	3	0.21	No	Yes	60.94	No
Kazakhstan	3	-0.49	No	Abs	58.88	No
Kenya	4	-0.39	Yes	Yes	58.46	No
Kiribati	NA	0.89	Yes	Yes	65.13	No
Kosovo	4	-0.27	Yes	NA	NA	No
Kuwait	4	0.26	No	Yes	55.41	No
Kyrgyzstan	6	-1.07	No	Abs	53.93	No
Laos	4	-0.64	No	Abs	47.42	No
Latvia	1	0.98	Yes	Yes	45.72	No
Lebanon	5	-1.07	No	Yes	56.79	No
Lesotho	NA	-0.41	No	Yes	49.89	No
Liberia	5	-0.93	Yes	Yes	45.98	No
Libya	7	-1.78	No	Yes	62.63	No
Liechtenstein	NA	1.74	No	Yes	43.38	No
Lithuania	1	1.11	Yes	Yes	46.02	No
Luxembourg	1	1.79	Yes	Yes	46.53	No
Macau	NA	0.81	No	NA	NA	No
Madagascar	4	-0.87	No	Abs	61.27	No
Malawi	4	-0.24	Yes	Yes	50.30	No
Malaysia	2	0.56	Yes	Yes	42.24	No
Maldives	4	-0.17	Yes	Yes	66.52	No

(*Continued*)

Appendix 12.1 (Continued)

Countries	*Credendo expropriation risk scoring*	*World Bank's rule of law indicator*	*U.S. Summit for Democracy*	*UN vote on Ukraine (March 2, 2022)*	*Physical Vulnerability to Climate Change Index*	*High concentration of critical mineral production*
Mali	5	–0.90	No	Abs	62.83	No
Malta	1	0.86	Yes	Yes	52.43	No
Marshall Islands	NA	0.24	Yes	Yes	68.83	No
Mauritania	5	–0.67	No	Yes	64.74	No
Mauritius	1	0.87	Yes	Yes	63.77	No
Mexico	4	–0.80	Yes	Yes	58.58	No
Micronesia	NA	0.52	Yes	Yes	56.92	No
Moldova	5	–0.33	Yes	Yes	55.61	No
Monaco	NA	NA	No	Yes	NA	No
Mongolia	4	–0.23	Yes	Abs	58.41	No
Montenegro	3	–0.06	Yes	Yes	40.63	No
Morocco	3	–0.25	No	NV	58.71	No
Mozambique	5	–1.04	No	Abs	56.27	No
Myanmar	6	–1.46	No	Yes	54.02	No
Namibia	3	0.36	Yes	Abs	63.48	No
Nauru	NA	–0.78	Yes	Yes	39.91	No
Nepal	5	–0.47	Yes	Yes	51.48	No
Netherlands	1	1.74	Yes	Yes	51.83	No
New Zealand	1	1.82	Yes	Yes	40.26	No
Nicaragua	5	–1.36	No	Abs	51.52	No
Niger	5	–0.40	Yes	Yes	64.69	No
Nigeria	6	–0.86	Yes	Yes	53.88	No
North Korea	6	–1.63	No	No	42.94	No
North Macedonia	3	–0.08	Yes	Yes	NA	No
Norway	1	1.95	Yes	Yes	42.21	No

Oman	2	0.41	No	Yes	69.70	No
Pakistan	5	-0.64	Yes	Abs	61.59	No
Palau	3	-0.16	Yes	Yes	56.52	No
Panama	3	-0.25	Yes	Yes	47.29	No
Papua New G.	4	-0.74	Yes	Yes	43.94	No
Paraguay	4	-0.56	Yes	Yes	48.54	No
Peru	3	-0.52	Yes	Yes	51.17	No
Philippines	3	-0.64	Yes	Yes	55.84	No
Poland	2	0.44	Yes	Yes	47.53	No
Portugal	1	1.13	Yes	Yes	47.48	No
Qatar	3	0.93	No	Yes	55.22	No
Romania	1	0.41	Yes	Yes	44.28	No
Russia	6	-0.87	No	No	48.37	No
Rwanda	3	0.20	No	Yes	51.79	No
St. Kitts & Nevis	NA	0.50	Yes	Yes	55.50	No
St. Lucia	NA	0.63	Yes	Yes	51.80	No
St. Vincent & G.	NA	0.61	Yes	Yes	54.54	No
Samoa	NA	0.89	Yes	Yes	57.36	No
San Marino	NA	NA	No	Yes	44.45	No
Sao Tome & P.	3	-0.70	Yes	Yes	46.93	No
Saudi Arabia	4	0.23	No	Yes	63.57	No
Senegal	3	-0.36	Yes	Abs	60.88	No
Serbia	3	-0.09	Yes	Yes	43.52	No
Seychelles	1	0.34	Yes	Yes	55.26	No
Sierra Leone	5	-0.82	No	Yes	48.93	No
Singapore	1	1.86	No	Yes	46.23	No
Slovakia	1	0.71	Yes	Yes	44.88	No
Slovenia	1	1.03	Yes	Yes	43.71	No
Solomon Islands	NA	-0.35	Yes	Yes	55.37	No
Somalia	7	-2.27	No	Yes	62.99	No

(Continued)

Appendix 12.1 (Continued)

Countries	*Credendo expropriation risk scoring*	*World Bank's rule of law indicator*	*U.S. Summit for Democracy*	*UN vote on Ukraine (March 2, 2022)*	*Physical Vulnerability to Climate Change Index*	*High concentration of critical mineral production*
South Africa	4	0.13	Yes	Abs	57.86	Yes
South Korea	1	1.13	Yes	Yes	45.76	No
South Sudan	NA	-2.05	No	Abs	58.55	No
Spain	1	0.88	Yes	Yes	53.25	No
Sri Lanka	4	0.04	No	Abs	50.81	No
Sudan	6	-1.21	No	Abs	65.86	No
Suriname	5	-0.10	Yes	Yes	46.50	No
Sweden	1	1.73	Yes	Yes	41.59	No
Switzerland	1	1.81	Yes	Yes	46.79	No
Syria	7	-2.07	No	No	59.59	No
Taiwan	1	1.30	Yes	NA	NA	No
Tajikistan	5	-1.19	No	Abs	48.00	No
Tanzania	4	-0.52	No	Abs	51.48	No
Thailand	4	0.11	No	Yes	49.50	No
Timor-Leste	4	-1.00	Yes	Yes	59.53	No
Togo	5	-0.56	No	NV	51.39	No
Tonga	NA	0.45	Yes	Yes	62.48	No
Trinidad & T.	3	-0.14	Yes	Yes	52.01	No
Tunisia	3	0.10	No	Yes	61.08	No
Turkey	5	-0.42	No	Yes	51.78	No
Turkmenistan	6	-1.44	No	NV	57.56	No
Tuvalu	NA	0.72	Yes	Yes	64.88	No
Uganda	4	-0.35	No	Abs	52.50	No
Ukraine	7	-0.66	Yes	Yes	45.78	No
United Arab E.	2	0.83	No	Yes	63.67	No

United Kingdom	1	1.43	Yes	Yes	42.06	No
United States	1	1.42	Yes	Yes	57.04	No
Uruguay	1	0.73	Yes	Yes	43.12	No
Uzbekistan	5	−0.89	No	NV	57.06	No
Vanuatu	NA	0.46	Yes	Yes	59.49	No
Venezuela	7	−2.30	No	NV	48.17	No
Vietnam	3	−0.15	No	Abs	48.93	No
Yemen	7	−1.80	No	Yes	62.27	No
Zambia	5	−0.59	Yes	Yes	51.79	No
Zimbabwe	6	−1.26	No	Abs	57.98	No

Sources: www.credendo.com/country-risk, info.worldbank.org/governance/wgi, www.state.gov/participant-list-the-summit-for-democracy, www.unmultimedia.org/avlibrary/asset/2715/2715485, https://ferdi-indicators.shinyapps.io/PVCCI, and author computations based on U.S. Geological Survey (2022).

Notes: Credendo assesses expropriation risk on a scale of 1 (least risky) to 7 (most risky). The World Bank's "rule of law" indicator ranges from approximately −2.5 (weakest performance) to 2.5 (strongest performance). The fourth column indicates whether a country was invited at the Summit for Democracy held in December 2021. The fifth column indicates whether a country voted in favor of, against, abstained, or did not vote on the United Nations Resolution of March 2, 2022, demanding that Russia "immediately, completely and unconditionally withdraw all of its military forces from the territory of Ukraine within its internationally recognized borders." The Physical Vulnerability to Climate Change Index (PVCCI) ranges from 0 (least vulnerable) to 100 (most vulnerable). The last column indicates whether a country accounts for more than 20% of the world production of at least one critical mineral indispensable to the clean energy transition (namely, chromium, cobalt, copper, graphite, lithium, manganese, molybdenum, nickel, rare earths, silicon, and zinc). NA, NV, and Abs denote "Not Applicable," "No Vote," and "Abstention," respectively.

Notes

1 The World Trade Organization (WTO) succeeded the GATT in 1995.
2 In 2022, six of the seven largest asset management firms were U.S. companies (namely, BlackRock, Vanguard Group, Fidelity Investments, State Street Global Advisors, Morgan Stanley, and JPMorgan Chase); see https://www.advratings.com/top-asset-management-firms.
3 The combined market share of Moody's and S&P Global exceeded 82% in December 2020; see Securities and Exchange Commission (2022, p. 24).
4 J. Kakissis, "Chinese Firms Now Hold Stakes in Over a Dozen European Ports," *NPR*, 9 October 2018.
5 Author calculation based on IMF data and https://www.globaltradealert.org.
6 See https://www.globaltradealert.org.
7 According to Branstetter and Li (2022), the subsidies flowing into the firms involved in the "Made in China 2025" project have neither improved productivity nor increased R&D (research & development) and profitability. Although their findings need to be confirmed, they may signal the limits of Chinese interventionism.
8 See https://about.bgov.com/top-defense-contractors.
9 For example, the FCPA provisions reach "foreign persons or businesses taking acts to further certain corrupt schemes, including ones causing the payment of bribes, while present in the United States."
10 See https://home.treasury.gov/policy-issues/financial-sanctions/sanctions-programs-and-country-information.
11 This type of sovereign default seems unprecedented in financial history; see Gaillard (2014).
12 Author calculation based on Hajzler and Rosborough's (2016) database.
13 The role of the International Centre for Settlement of Investment Disputes was crucial in many cases.
14 Established in 1960, the OPEC has a total of 13 member states: Algeria, Angola, the Republic of the Congo, Equatorial Guinea, Gabon, Iran, Iraq, Kuwait, Libya, Nigeria, Saudi Arabia, the United Arab Emirates, and Venezuela.
15 See https://www.congress.gov/bill/110th-congress/house-bill/2264.
16 For a focus on how China free rides on WTO rules, see Gmeiner's chapter in this book.
17 See https://www.wto.org/english/tratop_e/dispu_e/cases_e/ds395_e.htm and https://www.wto.org/english/tratop_e/dispu_e/cases_e/ds432_e.htm.
18 See https://www.lloydsbanktrade.com/en/market-potential/democratic-republic-of-congo/investment.
19 See https://www.nbr.org/publication/indonesias-nickel-export-ban-impacts-on-supply-chains-and-the-energy-transition.
20 See https://www.globaltradealert.org.
21 After more than three decades of decline, the Exim Bank seems to regain influence and play a significant role; see Darbellay and Gaillard (2022).
22 For an overview, see https://www.reuters.com/graphics/USA-CHINA/HUAWEI-TIMELINE/zgvomxwlgvd and https://www.npr.org/2022/11/26/1139258274/us-ban-tech-china-huawei-zte.
23 E. Kinery, "TSMC to up Arizona investment to $40 billion with second semiconductor chip plant," *CNBC*, 6 December 2022.
24 For an exhaustive analysis, see https://sanctionsnews.bakermckenzie.com/bis-issues-new-export-controls-targeting-chinas-advanced-computing-and-semiconductor-sectors.
25 See https://eur-lex.europa.eu/eli/reg/2019/452/oj.

26 Council of the EU, "Chips Act: Council Adopts Position," *Press Release*, 1 December 2022.
27 European Commission, "Critical Raw Materials Act: Securing the New Gas & Oil at the Heart of Our Economy / Blog of Commissioner Thierry Breton," *Statement*, 14 September 2022.
28 Blanchette and Hass (2023) consider that, "by hyping the threat of a Chinese invasion, U.S. analysts and officials are unintentionally doing the CCP's [Chinese Communist Party] work for it by stoking fears in Taiwan."
29 Percentages based on the surveys by Election Study Center of National Chengchi University, see https://esc.nccu.edu.tw/PageDoc/Detail?fid=7801&id=6963.
30 The Taiwan Relations Act of 1979 is well balanced and should remain a pillar of U.S. foreign policy in the region.
31 Hira and Au-Yeung's chapter in this book analyzes how big powers can coordinate to fight global warming.
32 See https://www.yalerussianbusinessretreat.com.
33 For Renault Group (2022, p. 4), the discontinued operations represented a loss of EUR2.3 billion.
34 See https://www.state.gov/participant-list-the-summit-for-democracy.
35 Author's listing and computations based on U.S. Geological Survey (2022).
36 M. Farrer, "Hong Kong: International Companies Reconsider Future in Wake of Security Law," *The Guardian*, 7 September 2021.
37 For example, synthetic graphite – produced through a complex process of baking petroleum coke at very high temperatures – is a substitute for graphite and thus suitable for battery applications. See U.S. Geological Survey (2022, p. 75) and https://www.imerys.com/minerals/graphite.
38 The terms "backshoring" and "reshoring" are used interchangeably.
39 K. Rapoza, "Harry Moser: Is the U.S. Succeeding at Reshoring?," *Coalition for a Prosperous America*, 14 June 2022; available at https://prosperousamerica.org/harry-moser-is-the-u-s-succeeding-at-reshoring.
40 Di Mauro and Ancarani (2022) study the commercial and financial drivers of U.S. backshoring.
41 S. K. O'Neil, "The Globalization Myth," *The Hill*, 20 October 2022.

References

Adachi, A., Brown, A. and Zenglein, M. J. (2022) "Fasten Your Seatbelts – How to Manage China's Economic Coercion," *Mercator Institute for China Studies*, 25 August.

Allison, G. (2015) "The Thucydides Trap: Are the U.S. and China Headed for War?," *The Atlantic*, 24 September, available at https://www.theatlantic.com/international/archive/2015/09/united-states-china-war-thucydides-trap/406756.

Blanchette, J. and Hass, R. (2023) "The Taiwan Long Game," *Foreign Affairs*, Vol. 102, No. 1, pp. 102–114.

Branstetter, L. G. and Li, G. (2022) "Does "Made in China 2025" Work for China? Evidence from Chinese Listed Firms," *NBER Working Paper No. 30676*.

Chorzempa, M. (2022) "US Security Scrutiny of Foreign Investment Rises, But so Does Foreign Investment," *Peterson Institute for International Economics*, 1 September, available at https://www.piie.com/blogs/realtime-economic-issues-watch/us-security-scrutiny-foreign-investment-rises-so-does-foreign.

Cohen, E. (2022) *Souveraineté industrielle – Vers un nouveau modèle productif*. Paris: Odile Jacob.

Darbellay, A. and Gaillard, N. (2022) "Moral Hazard in the Export Credit Industry," in Flores Zendejas, J., Gaillard, N. and Michalek, R. (Eds) *Moral Hazard: A Financial, Legal, and Economic Perspective*. Abingdon and New York City: Routledge.

Di Mauro, C. and Ancarani, A. (October 2022) "A Taxonomy of Back-Shoring Initiatives in the US," *International Business Review*, Vol. 31, No. 5, 102006.

European Commission (2019) "EU-China – A Strategic Outlook," *European Commission and HR/VP Contribution to the European Council*, 12 March.

European Commission (2022) "REPowerEU: Joint European Action for More Affordable, Secure and Sustainable Energy," *Press Release*, 8 March.

Exim Bank (2021) *2020 Annual Report*. Washington, DC: Exim Bank.

Feindouno, S., Guillaumont, P. and Simonet, C. (October 2020) "The Physical Vulnerability to Climate Change Index: An Index to Be Used for International Policy," *Ecological Economics*, Vol. 176, 106752.

Gaillard, N. (2011) *A Century of Sovereign Ratings*. New York City: Springer.

Gaillard, N. (2014) *When Sovereigns Go Bankrupt – A Study on Sovereign Risk*. New York City: Springer.

Gaillard, N. (2020a) *Country Risk: The Bane of Foreign Investors*. Cham: Springer.

Gaillard, N. (2020b) "Le COVID-19, accélérateur de la post-mondialisation," *Politique étrangère*, Vol. 85, No. 3, pp. 59–70.

Gaillard, N. and Michalek, R. (2019) "How and Why Moral Hazard Has Distorted Financial Regulation," in Hira, A., Gaillard, N. and Cohn, T. H. (Eds) *The Failure of Financial Regulation – Why A Major Crisis Could Happen Again*. International Political Economy Series. Cham: Palgrave Macmillan.

Gaillard, N. and Michalek, R. (2022) "The Institutionalization of Bailouts, 1970–1984," in Flores Zendejas, J., Gaillard, N. and Michalek, R. (Eds) *Moral Hazard: A Financial, Legal, and Economic Perspective*. Abingdon and New York City: Routledge.

Goujon, M., Santoni, O. and Wagner, L. (2022) "The Physical Vulnerability to Climate Change Index Computed at the Sub-National Level," *FERDI Working Paper No. 305*.

Hajzler, C. and Rosborough, J. (2016) "Government Corruption and Foreign Direct Investment under the Threat of Expropriation," *Bank of Canada Staff Working Paper 2016-13*.

Haley, U. C. V. and Haley, G. T. (2013) *Subsidies to Chinese Industry – State Capitalism, Business Strategy, and Trade Policy*. Oxford: Oxford University Press.

Hira, A. and Gaillard, N. (2011) "The Bottom Line: The Fundamental Weaknesses of Latin American Finance," *Bulletin of Latin American Research*, Vol 30, No. 2, pp. 163–182.

Huntington, S. P. (1989) "No Exit: The Errors of Endism," *The National Interest*, No. 17, Fall, pp. 3–11.

International Energy Agency (2021) *The Role of Critical Minerals in Clean Energy Transitions*. World Energy Outlook Special Report Minerals. Paris: International Energy Agency.

International Institute for Strategic Studies (2023) *China's Belt and Road Initiative – A Geopolitical and Geo-economic Assessment*. London: Routledge.

Loonam, J. P. and Andreoli, R. J. (2022) "Extraterritoriality: The US Perspective," in Seddon, J., Davison, E., Morvillo, C. J., Bowes Q. C. M., Tolaini, L., Adams, A. A. and McGrath, T. (Eds) *The Practitioner's Guide to Global Investigations – Volume*

I: Global Investigations in the United Kingdom and the United States (6th edition). London: Law Business Research.

Luttwak, E. N. (1990) "From Geopolitics to Geo-Economics: Logic of Conflict, Grammar of Commerce," *The National Interest*, No. 20, Summer, pp. 17–23.

Mancheri, N. A. and Marukawa, T. (2016) "Rare Earth Elements – China and Japan in Industry, Trade and Value Chain," *ISS Contemporary Chinese Research Series No. 17.*

Oneal, J. R. and Russett, B. M. (1997) "The Classical Liberals Were Right: Democracy, Interdependence, and Conflict, 1950–1985," *International Studies Quarterly*, Vol. 41, No. 2, pp. 267–293.

Piatanesi, B. and Arauzo-Carod, J.-M. (2019) "Backshoring and Nearshoring: An Overview," *Growth and Change*, Vol. 50, No. 3, pp. 806–823.

Renault Group (2022) *Financial Report – First Half 2022*. Boulogne-Billancourt: Renault.

Rudd, K. (2022) *The Avoidable War: The Dangers of a Catastrophic Conflict between the U.S. and Xi Jinping's China*. New York City: PublicAffairs.

Securities and Exchange Commission (2022) "Staff Report on Nationally Recognized Statistical Rating Organizations," *Office of Credit Ratings*, January.

Shubik, M. (1971) "The Dollar Auction Game: A Paradox in Noncooperative Behavior and Escalation," *The Journal of Conflict Resolution*, Vol. 15, No. 1, pp. 109–111.

Sinclair, T. J. (1994) "Passing Judgement: Credit Rating Processes as Regulatory Mechanisms of Governance in the Emerging World Order," *Review of International Political Economy*, Vol. 1, No. 1, pp. 133–159.

Smeltz, D. and Kafura, C. (2021) "For First Time, Half of Americans Favor Defending Taiwan If China Invades," *The Chicago Council on Global Affairs and Lester Crown Center on US Foreign Policy*, August, available at https://globalaffairs.org/sites/default/files/2021-08/2021%20Taiwan%20Brief.pdf.

Standard & Poor's Global (2021) "China Outbound Mining Investment," available at https://www.spglobal.com/metals-and-mining.

U.S. Geological Survey (2022) *Mineral Commodity Summaries 2022*. Reston: U.S. Geological Survey.

White House (2022) "Fact Sheet: CHIPS and Science Act Will Lower Costs, Create Jobs, Strengthen Supply Chains, and Counter China," 9 August, available at https://www.whitehouse.gov/briefing-room/statements-releases/2022/08/09/fact-sheet-chips-and-science-act-will-lower-costs-create-jobs-strengthen-supply-chains-and-counter-china.

Williamson, J. (1990) "What Washington Means by Policy Reform," in Williamson, J. (Ed) *Latin American Adjustment: How Much Has Happened?* Washington, DC: Institute for International Economics.

Index

Pages in *italics* refer to figures and pages in **bold** refer to tables.

FSC
www.fsc.org
MIX
Papier | Fördert
gute Waldnutzung
FSC® C083411

Kolibri 360 GmbH
Ferdinand-Jühlke-Straße 7
99095 Erfurt, Deutschland
produktsicherheit@kolibri360.de